The Invention of

Brownstone Brook

D1204864

THE
Invention OF
Brownstone
Brooklyn

Gentrification and the
Search for Authenticity
in Postwar New York

Suleiman Osman

OXFORD
UNIVERSITY PRESS

OXFORD
UNIVERSITY PRESS

Oxford University Press is a department of the University of Oxford.
It furthers the University's objective of excellence in research, scholarship,
and education by publishing worldwide.

Oxford   New York
Auckland   Cape Town   Dar es Salaam   Hong Kong   Karachi
Kuala Lumpur   Madrid   Melbourne   Mexico City   Nairobi
New Delhi   Shanghai   Taipei   Toronto

With offices in
Argentina   Austria   Brazil   Chile   Czech Republic   France   Greece
Guatemala   Hungary   Italy   Japan   Poland   Portugal   Singapore
South Korea   Switzerland   Thailand   Turkey   Ukraine   Vietnam

Oxford is a registered trade mark of Oxford University Press
in the UK and certain other countries.

Published in the United States of America by
Oxford University Press
198 Madison Avenue, New York, NY 10016

Library of Congress Cataloging-in-Publication Data
Osman, Suleiman.
The invention of brownstone Brooklyn: gentrification and
the search for authenticity in postwar New York/Suleiman Osman.
p.   cm.
Includes bibliographical references and index.
ISBN 978-0-19-538731-5 (hardcover); 978-0-19-993034-0 (paperback)
1. Brooklyn (New York, N.Y.)—History—20th century.
2. Gentrification—New York (State)—Brooklyn—History—20th century.
3. City planning—New York (State)—Brooklyn—History—20th century.
4. Community development—New York (State)—Brooklyn—History—
20th century. I. Title.
F129.B7O79 2011
307.3'4160974723—dc22
2010023195

Printed in the United States of America
on acid-free paper

For my parents

Contents

Acknowledgments

I would not have been able to complete this book without the generous help of many people. The manuscript began many years ago as a dissertation at Harvard, where I was blessed with wonderful mentors. My primary advisor, Lizabeth Cohen, read countless drafts, wrote pages of astute comments, and spent hours talking with me about the project. She continually encouraged, inspired, and challenged me. Lawrence Buell transformed the way I think about cities, introducing me to a new world of ideas about space and place, geography, and environmental criticism. His wisdom about both scholarly matters and life in general has been invaluable. I could not have completed graduate school, survived my first years of university teaching, and written this book without Bruce Schulman. A brilliant scholar, masterly lecturer, insightful editor, and generous mentor, Bruce Schulman embodies the ideal of the teacher-scholar. I cannot thank him enough for all his help.

One of the most important things I received in graduate school was a core of brilliant friends on whom I still rely on for guidance: Salamishah Tillet, Dagmawi Woubshet, Hua Hsu, and David Mulrooney. I would additionally like to thank Sonia Lee, Matthew Briones, Michael Kimmage, Kimberly Sims, Heather Lewis, Robert Breugmann, Matthew Lasner, Kevin Burke, Evelyn Higginbotham, Margaret Crawford, Julian Zelizer, Martha Nadell, Sharon Zukin, Becky Nicolaides, and others for reading and commenting on the project at different stages. From the days of being my mentor at the Miller Center at the University of Virginia, Tom Sugrue has generously read and commented on different versions of the project. His insight has been invaluable.

My colleagues at the American Studies Department at George Washington University have been wonderfully supportive these past several years: Terry Murphy, James Miller, Kip Kosek, Libby Anker, Phyllis Palmer, Melani McAlister, Chad Heap, and John Vlach. Richard Longstreth, Tom Guglielmo, and Elaine Peña generously read and commented on parts of the manuscript. I could not have completed the project without them. The History Department's Tyler Anbinder, Richard Stout, and Chris Klemek and the Geography Department's Elizabeth Chacko and David Rain have provided important feedback about the project as well. Cartographer Nuala Cowan helped design the book's many maps.

I have also received support from many institutions. The University of Virginia's Miller Center for Public Affairs offered me more than financial support. Directors Sidney Milkis and Brian Balogh put together a terrific program that introduced me to a new community of historians and political scientists. Brian Balogh continues to be an important mentor, editor, and friend. The Graham Foundation for Advanced Studies in the Fine Arts provided me with a grant to help me complete the book. The librarians and archivists at the Brooklyn and New York Public Libraries, Chela Scott Weber at the Brooklyn Historical Society, and Kenneth Cobb at the New York Municipal Library were enormously helpful. Thomas Miskel and Ann Kalkhoff of the Park Slope Civic Council deserve special thanks. Along with allowing me to comb through the PSCC archives, they happily shared with me their encyclopedic knowledge of Park Slope history. I would like to thank Charles and Jennifer Monaghan, Salvatore Scotto and Joseph Ferris for generously allowing me into their homes and granting me interviews. I also want to thank those who did not appear in the book as well: Rose Ann Scamardella, James Goetz, MacDonald Phipps, Bill Jesinkey, the Maloneys, and others.

Susan Ferber at Oxford University Press has been a wonderfully attentive editor who closely read several drafts of the manuscript. I would also like to give a special thank-you to the two anonymous reviewers who meticulously read the manuscript and provided extensive comments. Their tough yet supportive feedback helped me reshape large portions of the book. The book is much stronger because of their dedication to the review process.

I could not have finished this book without the support of friends and family. My sister Nura, Mark, Reuben, and Alessandra were always loving and helpful. Rob Deegan, Eoin West, Sam Rubin, and Steve Ford spent many an hour on the phone listening to me talk about the project. An assortment of other friends and family provided helpful assurance as I pushed to complete the manuscript.

But I am most grateful to my parents, Yusuf and Marjorie Osman. More than a decade of graduate school and university teaching has been a long path along which I've often stumbled. During the many solitary hours of research and writing, I often experienced deep self-doubt. But during those moments, I've always been buoyed by the unconditional love and support of my parents. They have inspired me intellectually and spiritually. I owe my parents everything.

The Invention of
Brownstone Brooklyn

Introduction

On November 22, 1966, a small group of city construction workers arrived at the corner of State and Nevins streets in Brooklyn with orders to raze an abandoned brownstone. Having recently gained possession of the dilapidated four-story building through nonpayment of taxes, the city had become concerned that the empty townhouse was a gathering place for homeless men and drug users and decided to demolish it. For local residents, the sight of helmeted workers and bulldozers was a common one. Although only a few blocks away from the borough's downtown, North Gowanus, as some locals called it, was a struggling inner-city district hit hard by the same trends affecting most American cities in the 1960s. A once thriving industrial economy centered around the Gowanus Canal and waterfront was fading as firms left for the suburbs or the South. Working-class white residents anxious about the changing racial composition of the area and declining work opportunities fled for Staten Island, New Jersey, or Long Island. African American and Puerto Rican migrants arrived on the heels of departing white ethnics in search for work, but soon found themselves trapped in decaying tenements surrounded by abandoned townhouses. To stem the spread of blight and urban decay, ambitious city planners hoped to raze and rebuild, replacing outdated Victorian housing with modern high-rises, open space, and green parks. A few blocks away, the city had recently blasted several square blocks of brownstones and would soon complete the enormous Wyckoff Gardens low-income housing project.[1]

On this morning, however, workers were confronted with the unexpected: a group of thirty members of the Boerum Hill Association stood in front of the building protesting with placards, bullhorns, and pamphlets. An organization of young homeowners who recently moved to the area, the BHA demanded that the city halt demolition of the building. An abandoned lot would scar the

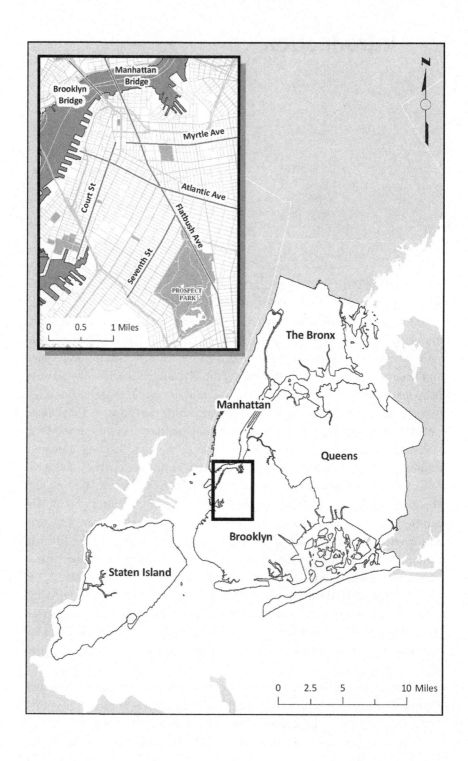

townhouse-lined block. Some sat in front of the equipment. Others held signs saying "Don't Destroy Our Neighborhood" and "People Need Homes—Not Parking Lots." Two housewives sat at the entrance holding infants. Another group of mothers lined up five strollers bumper to bumper in front of the stoop, forming a "baby-carriage brigade" of protest. Hanging on another stroller, a sign invited spectators to attend a house tour organized by the new group. "Care, don't clear!" cried one of the protesters.

As the construction workers watched the protesters, they were likely taken aback. Most surely had not heard of Boerum Hill. While some referred to the area as North Gowanus, for most Brooklynites in the 1960s the block was an indistinguishable part of South Brooklyn, a vaguely defined zone consisting of two congressional districts that extended about two miles from the docks and factories by the East River inland to majestic Prospect Park. Perhaps, too, the workers were struck by the accents and dress of the protesters. While South Brooklyn was primarily a white, working-class district with a growing number of African Americans and Puerto Ricans, the members of the BHA were young white-collar professionals. Robert T. Snyder, the president, was a Columbia-educated labor lawyer. David Preiss, the spokesman at the protest, was an editor of the magazine *American Artist*. The protesters spoke confidently and articulately. Their speech, with all the shibboleths of Manhattan's educated class and no trace of Brooklyn brogue, seemed incongruous with their surroundings.[2]

They called themselves "the brownstoners." They had first begun to appear in Brooklyn Heights in the late 1940s. Artists, lawyers, bankers, and other white-collar workers migrated to the aging Gold Coast district, restoring old townhouses and moving into run-down tenements. By the 1960s, white-collar professionals priced out of Manhattan flooded into surrounding areas in search of cheap housing. "More and more people now are packing up, moving out of their aseptic uptown apartments," explained *New York* about "brownstone fever" in 1969, "making new homes out of old, forlorn but solid and roomy brownstones, restoring them to pristine glory." As brownstoners spilled past the boundaries of Brooklyn Heights, they created new names for revitalizing blocks. Cobble Hill was named in the late 1950s. Boerum Hill and Carroll Gardens soon followed. By the mid-1970s, few people remembered the name South Brooklyn. In brochures, newspapers, and real estate guides, the area had become "Brownstone Brooklyn"—a constellation of revitalized townhouse districts including Clinton Hill, Park Slope, and Prospect Heights.[3]

Brownstoners, however, believed they were involved in something more than a renovation fad. Brownstoning was a cultural revolt against sameness, conformity, and bureaucracy. In a city that was increasingly technocratic, Boerum Hill was a "real neighborhood," a vestige of an "authentic community" lost in a modernizing society. "Many enthusiastic brownstoners, particularly those recent escapees from 'the boring sameness of suburbia,' emphasize the social value of their decision to live in the city," explained the *Brownstoner*, a local newsletter, in 1969. Where midtown Manhattan and the suburbs were atomizing and mass-produced, Boerum Hill appeared "historic" and "diverse." "On Wyckoff Street, an eccentric block of three-story workmen's cottages have been rescued by young homemakers and turned into a happy, house-proud community," described the *Boerum Hill Times* in 1974. "Indeed it's quite possible to feel, while walking tree-lined streets, that one has broken through the time barrier and landed smack in the middle of the 19th century. Gentle ghosts of ladies in hoops skirts and gentlemen in frock coats can almost be seen among the leafy shadows." "My children can grow in a stimulating atmosphere and be exposed to many new experiences," explained a brownstoner about his move to Boerum Hill. "They will know and understand people of all economic backgrounds, and they will have the cultural, educational, and institutional facilities of New York City at their doorstep."[4]

Brooklyn's young white-collar émigrés moved there with a sense of zeal. They started block associations, organized street festivals, and opened food cooperatives to foster a sense of community, place, and history. As they planted trees and dug community gardens in abandoned lots, they described themselves as "greening" the city and echoed the themes of a nascent environmental movement. They avidly renovated houses, stripping away paint and aluminum siding, as well as symbolically ripping off the trappings of mass consumer society to return to an older, more authentic form of life. But as their poorer neighbors warily eyed them hammering and planting, some brownstoners had a gnawing sense of doubt about their project. "I wonder . . . are my own home improvements and those of my neighbors . . . are the friends that are brought in to buy that decrepit rooming house down the street . . . are our civic activities . . . and our walking tours," wondered one brownstoner in 1969, "all part of a trend that is turning our own neighborhoods into suburban-like middle-class ghettoes?"[5]

By 1980, Boerum Hill had dramatically changed. Fifteen years after they demonstrated on State Street to protect the fledgling enclave, the members of the BHA found themselves the targets of a new wave of protests. In August, *The Displacement Report*, a pamphlet produced by Acción Latina and the Tenants Action Committee, began to circulate around the neighborhood. Revitalization, the group complained, was resulting in the displacement of low-income renters from the area. Greedy speculation by real estate agents and middle-class homeowners was leading to the eviction and harassment of longtime residents of color. Local bodegas and storefront churches were pressured to close.

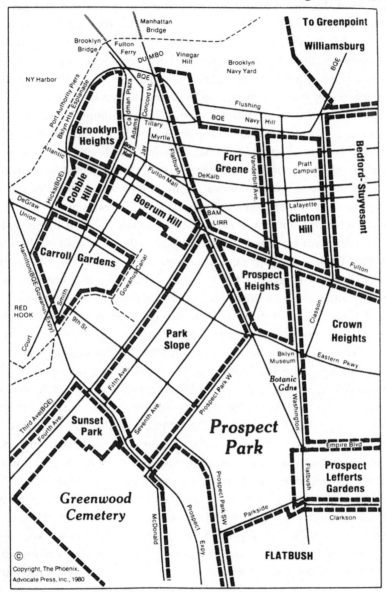

A 1980 map of "brownstone neighborhoods" from the *Brooklyn Phoenix Brownstone Guide*. Many of these neighborhood names were coined by brownstoners in the 1960s and 1970s. (Courtesy of the Brooklyn *Phoenix*)

Most striking, though, was a new word that the pamphlet had adopted from headlines in the media: "gentrification." The members of the BHA perhaps read the pamphlet with a sense of defensiveness. Had they not arrived in Boerum Hill with the fresh idealism of the 1960s? How had they become villains? Some perhaps read the pamphlet more wistfully. Decades ago, they had arrived in search of an authentic community not available in Manhattan and suburbia. But had they ironically destroyed the authenticity they once craved?[6]

Whether referred to as "gentrification," "brownstoning," "neighborhood revitalization," or the "back-to-the-city movement," the influx of white-collar professionals into low-income central city areas has been one of the most striking developments in postwar urban history. Once redlined by banks and slated for large-scale urban renewal in the 1950s, Brownstone Brooklyn's enclaves by the 1980s had some of the most expensive real estate in the nation. A Brooklyn brownstone, once considered a symbol of blight in the 1940s, today is de rigueur for New York's wealthy and educated. With hip bars and cafés, used-book stores, yoga studios, and renovated townhouses, Brownstone Brooklyn is no longer regarded by the public as blighted, but instead is both celebrated and reviled as a site of cultural consumption for a new middle class. Once dismissed by sophisticated Manhattanites, Brownstone Brooklyn since the 1990s has even begun to eclipse its neighbor as an intellectual and cultural center. "Manhattan: The New Brooklyn?" asked a local magazine in 2002, playfully inverting the relationship between province and metropole.[7]

Brooklyn's brownstone belt was not alone. An early version of brownstoning was already occurring in Chicago's Towertown and New York's Greenwich Village as early as the 1910s and 1920s. While gentrification tapered off in most cities during the Depression, Washington, D.C.'s, Georgetown experienced an influx of white-collar government employees working for a newly expanded federal government during the New Deal. After World War II, the trend resumed on the periphery of aging Gold Coasts and silk-stocking districts such as Boston's Beacon Hill. In New York City from the 1950s to the 1970s, a new middle class expanded from older gentrified Gold Coasts into SoHo, the Upper West Side, and other newly named enclaves surrounding Manhattan's midtown and downtown central business districts. Washington, D.C.'s Dupont Circle, Capitol Hill, and Adams Morgan, New Orleans' French Quarter, Boston's South End, Atlanta's Inman Park, Chicago's Lincoln Park, and San Francisco's Castro and Haight-Ashbury are all famous examples of areas gentrified in a pattern similar to Brownstone Brooklyn. In 1972–73 alone, the National Urban Coalition reported the beginnings of gentrification in Houston's Montrose, Cleveland's Ohio City, Seattle's Capitol Hill, New Orleans' City Park, San Antonio's King William, and dozens of other inner-city districts.

Even smaller cities experienced the phenomenon: Bridgeport's South End, South Bend's Park Avenue, and Albuquerque's South Martineztown, for example. By 1976, an Urban Land Institute study found versions of brownstoning in a majority of the nation's 260 cities with populations exceeding 50,000. In cities with populations of 500,000 or more, three-quarters were experiencing gentrification.[8]

American urban historians have largely overlooked gentrification.[9] Focusing on the postwar urban crisis in cities such as Detroit and St. Louis, historians for good reason have focused on examining the political and social consequences of urban industrial decline. The declension narrative they told is important and powerful. As industry migrated to the suburbs, southward, and overseas, white residents after World War II fled landscapes such as Brownstone Brooklyn for the suburbs, leaving depopulated and decaying neighborhoods in their wake. African American migrants moving north for work and to escape Jim Crow found themselves closed off from the suburbs by discrimination, relegated to deteriorating and segregated housing, and unable to find unskilled work in factories, which were being shuttered. Misguided city leaders eager to revive the center city bulldozed fragile neighborhoods and built massive highways, alienating public housing projects, and sterile civic centers. By the late 1960s, cities from Boston to Oakland had become terminally ill. The racial uprisings of that decade provided an incendiary conclusion to the city's slow economic death, the fires lit by rioters only cremating an already withering urban corpse.

More than just telling a tale of economic collapse, historians of postwar cities describe a political death. The decline of the industrial city also marked the demise of postwar liberalism. Once the bedrock of New Deal Democratic politics, Detroit, Chicago, and other fading cities were torn apart by racial clashes over housing and competition for increasingly scarce manufacturing jobs. Destructive urban renewal programs led to growing disenchantment with government planners. As young African Americans increasingly disillusioned by the meager gains of racial liberalism turned to black power politics and a hostile white ethnic working class turned to conservative backlash politics, a once cohesive Democratic coalition crumbled. The ghetto of the 1970s with its boarded-up homes, empty stores, and impoverished schools surrounded by conservative suburbs marked the denouement not just of industrial urban America but of a once powerful liberal coalition.[10]

Brooklyn experienced many of the same shocks after World War II.[11] But economic crisis and political backlash were only part of the story. While white working-class residents from most of the borough moved to the suburbs, brownstoners enthusiastically moved into old townhouse districts

surrounding the central business area. Rather than laborers in declining industries along the waterfront and Gowanus Canal, Brooklyn's new residents
worked in finance, law, publishing, education, and the arts. Instead of celebrating the suburban ideal of a single-family tract home and private lawn,
Brooklyn's new residents championed a new urban ideal of close-knit housing,
street life, and face-to-face contact. Rather than seeking race and class homogeneity, middle-class beatniks, radicals, settlement workers, and gay men pushed
into poor districts in search of "diversity." Rather than rejecting the aging
dilapidated housing stock of the inner city, brownstoners sought to purchase,
restore, and preserve the "historic" architecture of the urban core.

Rather than simply declining, Brownstone Brooklyn made a transition to a
landscape that has been labeled with a cornucopia of "posts": postindustrial,
post-Fordist, post-reform, post-Keynesian, postmaterial, and postmodern.[12]
While New York City's industrial employment dropped by 49 percent between
1950 and 1975, the city's employment in finance, insurance, and real estate
increased by 25 percent, in services by 52 percent, and in government by 53
percent. Even during the economically depressed 1970s, when the city was
losing 50,000 manufacturing jobs a year, it saw continued growth in banking,
media, and services. Some dismayed commentators at the time pointed to the
drop in the number of Fortune 500 headquarters from 128 to 90 between 1966
and 1976 as evidence that New York's days as an office center were limited as
well. But as old industrial headquarters left, the city gained more dynamic
firms with an increasingly international orientation. During the 1970s, six
new Fortune 500 firms relocated to the city and twenty smaller ones expanded
onto the list. These, along with the other Fortune 500 companies that stayed
in the city, on average made over 50 percent of their sales overseas. Foreign
banks with offices in the city nearly doubled, from forty-six to eighty-four,
between 1970 and 1976. New York was no longer an industrial headquarters
town. Instead it was becoming a command-and-control center for a global
economy.[13]

The intention here is not to question the history of urban crisis, to exag-
gerate the limited extent of gentrification before 1980, or to downplay the
broader troubles faced by industrial cities after World War II. But by examining
the postindustrialization rather than the deindustrialization of Brooklyn, this
book hopes to contribute to a growing body of scholarship that has begun
to complicate the narrative of urban decline in order to examine the roots of
the subsequent post-1980 revival of cities such as New York, Boston, and San
Francisco. Rather than a unidirectional narrative of decline, the book describes
a landscape shaped by multidirectional trends as manufacturing contracted
and corporate and financial services expanded. Brownstone Brooklyn was

simultaneously reviving and declining in the period under study. Rather than the site of a bipolar conflict between black and white, Brownstone Brooklyn was a multiethnic, multiclass, and polyglot landscape with multiple and shifting conflicts and coalitions. Rather than simply dissolving, liberalism in Brownstone Brooklyn, San Francisco, and other similar cities transformed from an older industrial type to a newer postindustrial version. Rather than a flat space, Brownstone Brooklyn's deindustrialized landscape was a layered landscape that retained the imprints of previous eras of economic structuring. This palimpsest of empty factories, waterfront piers, and Victorian townhouses was a repository of symbolic value for white-collar enthusiasts, black power activists, white ethnic homeowners, and a variety of neighborhood groups. Brownstone Brooklyn's symbolic landscape was crucial in shaping its political and economic landscape. Finally, the book offers a slightly different periodization than the narrative of urban decline. Rather than the denouement of the industrial city, the 1970s were a dynamic decade of transition that formed a crucial bridge between the participatory movements of the 1960s and gentrification and urban revival in the 1980s.[14]

A comprehensive history of the "post-" city is certainly beyond the scope of this book.[15] The impact of post-1965 immigration, the rise of Sunbelt cities, sprawl, and the formation of edge cities, for example, are also part of this larger national urban story. Brownstone Brooklyn from 1945 to 1980, though, is an instructive case study for several reasons.

The history of brownstoning is the story of the formation of a new postindustrial middle class. Brownstoners represented a new labor force working in expanded administrative services in the central business district, and they dramatically reshaped the cultural and political landscape of American cities. A 1976 survey of the Brownstone Revival Committee, for example, found that the eight professions most represented in their membership were law, writing, teaching, editing, architecture, banking, psychology, and psychiatry. Close behind were accounting, computer technology, construction, interior design, art, medicine, engineering, finance, acting, insurance, photography, and library work. Brooklyn's new middle class was not alone. Another poll that year revealed that 60 percent of Harvard's class of 1968 was engaged in home restoration.

In 1971, a local civic group conducted a survey of 326 new brownstone owners in Brooklyn and Manhattan. The respondents were overwhelmingly whiter, wealthier, and more educated than the average New York resident. Whereas 30 percent of New Yorkers were nonwhite, brownstone renovators were 99 percent white. While only 17 percent of New Yorkers earned more than $10,000, 98.3 percent of respondents had higher incomes. But more than financial capital, what distinguished Brooklyn's new brownstone middle class was its cultural and social capital. In a city where just over 50 percent of people twenty-five or older were high school graduates, 99.9 percent of respondents had high school diplomas, and a striking 60 percent had attended graduate school. Surprisingly, historians have not paid much attention to this powerful urban constituency.[16]

Because brownstoners do not fit easily into a binary of rich and poor, or bourgeoisie and proletariat, scholars and journalists since World War II have struggled to come up with a label for them. Names have ranged from "new class," "new middle class," and "professional-managerial class" to "white-collar proletariat," "knowledge workers," and "intelligentsia." Some names, such as "creative class," emphasize new forms of production. Others, such as "bohemian bourgeoisie," refer to taste and consumption. For some New Left theorists in the 1960s, the "new class" represented a possible revolutionary vanguard in a country in which the industrial working class had become increasingly conservative. Disillusioned old left and neoconservative intellectuals in the 1970s used the term with unveiled contempt for a new elite. The most recognizable term today, however, was coined by *Newsweek* in 1984: "yuppie," or young urban professional. This book will use the term "brownstoners" interchangeably with geographer David Ley's "new middle class."[17]

Although theorists debated how to define them, brownstoners themselves had a strong sense of identity as a new and distinctly urban bourgeoisie with shared forms of consumption and lifestyle patterns that distinguished them from their suburban counterparts. Moving to Brooklyn was an integral step in developing this class consciousness. A local newspaper found that brownstoners used an alphabet of adjectives to describe their move: "adventurous, avid, bargain-minded, brave, city-loving, courageous, dedicated, determined, enthusiastic, fervent, gutsy—all the way down to young-at-heart, zealous, and even zany." "[We are] an almost superhuman group known as Brownstoners," explained a young renovator in 1969 with the self-assuredness of the emerging young urban professional class.

> There is something unique coursing through his veins which makes him unique among homeowners. . . . He is a man dedicated to escaping the stagnation and boredom of suburban living, and while he is apt to spend just as much time on his small 20×30-foot garden as the suburbanite on his "grounds," he has given up the vast glories of nature in order to surround himself with the vast glories of humanity. The Brownstoner becomes accustomed to living in peaceful coexistence with all manner of men. . . . The Brownstoner is often a man who wants his children to grow in a mentally

stimulating atmosphere, exposed to many cultural, educational, institutional outlets, and most importantly, to people of all heritages and economic backgrounds.[18]

As a new middle-class landscape, Brownstone Brooklyn provides a new spatial context to the social and cultural revolts of the 1960s and 1970s. Just as brownstoners refashioned and renovated new enclaves, Brooklyn's brownstones and tenements helped spark the political awakening of postindustrial workers. A new middle class, this book argues, moved to aging Victorian districts as part of a search for the authenticity they felt was lacking in the new university campuses, government complexes, and corporate skyscrapers they worked and studied in. As brownstoners absorbed ideas from the grassroots movements of the urban poor and struggled with city bureaucracy, they joined calls for community planning boards, reform politics, participatory democracy, and democracy in the streets. The new social movements of the 1960s and 1970s—the New Left, the counterculture, the environmental movement, and the student movement—all emerged on an imagined urban frontier along a belt of Victorian housing surrounding the expanding central business districts and university campuses of cities such as New York and San Francisco.[19]

The story of gentrification thus is also a political history that can contribute to the work historians have done to explain the collapse of New Deal liberalism. While historians have detailed well the tensions between white ethnics and African Americans in declining working-class residential districts, few have examined the "silk-stocking rebellion" of white-collar professionals, artists, and students in neighborhoods such as Park Slope and Brooklyn Heights. Brownstoners forged a "new politics" and formed a new reform wing of the Democratic party that imagined itself in a battle against the two machines that made up the older New Deal liberal coalition. First, young reformers engaged in acrimonious battle against an old machine of aging ward bosses in neighborhood clubhouses. At the same time, brownstoners described an existential battle against a new machine—the New Deal progrowth coalition of real estate agents, planners, business leaders, politicians, civic groups, and directors of nonprofit institutions, who since World War II spearheaded a program of urban redevelopment in cities around the country. Brownstoners fought against urban renewal and expressways, using their financial and political clout to promote neighborhood conservation. Whereas earlier middle-class reformers fought to centralize city government in the hands of a scientific, impartial city manager, they championed the decentralization of municipal power, replacing the ideal of a regional, integrated city system with a diverse mosaic of local participatory democracies.

Rather than the death of liberalism, this book analyzes the emergence of a new postindustrial version spearheaded by white-collar professionals. By the 1970s, Brownstone Brooklyn formed a powerful wing of a national, interracial "neighborhood movement" that expressed a deep distrust of large institutions, expertise, universal social programs, and private-public consensus. Suspicious of the metanarratives of highways and urban renewal master plans, brownstoners and their allies championed voluntary service, homeownership, privatism, ethnic heritage, history, self-determination, and do-it-yourself bootstrap neighborhood rehabilitation. Rather than an example of right-wing politics, the new localism of the 1970s contained both progressive and conservative strains as white-collar reformers formed complex coalitions with angry white ethnics, black power activists, small business owners, and other members of a new slow-growth coalition. By the late 1970s, this new localist version of liberalism unintentionally dovetailed with a national conservative movement that was similarly hostile to government regulation and regional planning. The result was a new type of anti-statist politics with origins in both the right and the left. To say that the origins of neoliberalism were in Park Slope and Haight-Ashbury rather than Orange County and the suburban South might be overstating the case. But as many recent works by historians have shown, conservative thought emerged in unexpected places.[20]

More than a political and social history of a postindustrial middle class, the history of gentrification in Brooklyn also charts the evolution of a new type of postmodern urbanism. Rather than a scheme by developers and real estate agents (who were uniformly hostile to brownstoning in the early stages), Cobble Hill, Carroll Gardens, and other gentrified enclaves were the spatial expression of a broader cultural revolt against urban modernism. Gentrification in its early years was a form of white-collar urban romanticism with links to the counterculture and New Left. Describing themselves as "urban Thoreaus," Brooklyn's new middle class recast brownstones and industrial lofts as an organic and authentic "middle cityscape" lodged between overmodernized skyscrapers, suburban tract homes, and the "wild" ghetto.[21]

Brownstone Brooklyn represented a radical postindustrial reimagining of a declining industrial landscape. Where modernist city planners and union leaders hope to rebuild the borough's decaying infrastructure of industrial lofts and townhouses, Brooklyn's new white-collar residents commemorated its historical value. While a growth coalition of city planners and businessmen looked hopefully to new highways, airports, and automobiles to create a kinetic, open city, brownstoners celebrated Brooklyn's aging Victorian street grid as a site for walking, face-to-face contact, and intimacy. Modernists hoped with science and top-down planning to integrate spatially and racially a disparate megalopolis. Brooklyn's new middle class instead championed unplanned mixed uses and diversity. Rather than renewal, neighborhood groups talked of preservation: preserving old buildings, preserving ethnic identity, and preserving authentic communities. By the 1970s, Brownstone Brooklyn had become the template for a new postmodern school of planning that rejected large-scale development plans and instead called for "mini-planning," festival marketplaces, and neotraditional architecture. When developers began to build large-scale, neotraditional luxury developments in the 1980s, brownstoners debated whether the postmodern landscape was a sign of the movement's success or failure.

Finally, the history of brownstoning analyzes the formation of a stratified postindustrial racial landscape in which white-collar professionals lived in uneasy proximity to the nonwhite poor. The trajectory of gentrification in many ways ran counter to broader pattern of white flight described by historians. White brownstoners moved into older districts alongside African Americans and Latinos. In some cases, white-collar professionals offset their anxiety about racial mixing with their desire for attractive, affordable central city housing. In other cases, white liberal activists and countercultural artists actively sought to live in neighborhoods with African Americans and Latinos. Brownstoners, African Americans, Latinos, and white ethnics also formed political alliances to battle urban renewal and redlining (the practice of banks, insurance companies, and other lenders refusing to provide mortgages or other financing for homes within a poor, and often largely nonwhite, area). But the book does not present a Pollyannaish view of race in the city. Brownstoning was from the onset a movement rife with racial and class conflict. While some new arrivals sought to progressively engage locals in political and community organizations, the relationship with existing residents was tense. Some brownstoners described themselves as urban pioneers building settlements in the wilderness and drew comparisons between poorer residents and hostile natives. Others sought to rid neighborhoods of "inauthentic" rooming houses and blocked modern public housing and affordable supermarkets. Brownstones clashed with politically conservative white ethnics already established in the neighborhoods and shared an uneasy coexistence with poorer blacks and Puerto Ricans who had migrated in. Revitalization led to high rents and at times the eviction of poorer residents.[22]

Was the migration of white-collar professionals to Brooklyn something to be condemned or celebrated? This book has tried to avoid the Scylla of lionizing a creative class and the Charybdis of yuppie bashing. But in exploring the complexities of the question, this history of gentrification may appear to be a frustrating example of fence-sitting. Brownstoning, however, was a bundle of contradictions. Rather than modeling themselves after pernicious developers or city bureaucrats, gentrifiers drew from the language of Jane Jacobs, C. Wright Mills, Herbert Marcuse, Saul Alinsky, the student revolts of 1968, the civil rights and environmental movements, and the counterculture. The early history of gentrification is less a story of rapacious real estate specu- lation and more a tale of dashed idealism, contradictory goals, unintended consequences, and at times outright hypocrisy. But if gentrification is a saga of mixed intentions, sincere racial idealism mixed with disdain toward the non- white poor, and class populism blended with class snobbery, that is what makes it so rich a way to describe the cultural and social complexities of the nation's new postwar middle class.

1   Urban Wilderness

I went to the woods because I wished to live deliberately.
　　　　　　　　　　　　　—Henry David Thoreau

In 1958, a decade before new middle-class residents would invent the name, Harrison Salisbury entered the wilderness of Brownstone Brooklyn. Investigating the city's rising gang problem, the young *New York Times* reporter crossed the East River to explore an impoverished waterfront district with one of the highest juvenile delinquency rates in New York. As the subway rumbled through the subterranean darkness, Salisbury apprehensively contrasted the familiar bustle of midtown Manhattan with the untamed dangers of the periphery. The distance was short but the gulf between the two regions enormous. "The subway ride from Times Square to Brooklyn costs fifteen cents. It is a quick trip, just eighteen minutes from Forty-second Street to Smith-Ninth station in Brooklyn. No visa and no passport are required."

The train soon emerged from the dark tunnel onto a sunlit elevated track. As "the train climbed the steel trestle high over the forest of red and brown buildings that tumbled across the landscape," Salisbury was presented with a panoramic view of Brownstone Brooklyn. The area appeared an incoherent jumble of old buildings, tenements, and factories, and the reporter tried to make sense of the area by drawing boundaries and referring to place markers. "Close at hand loomed two great black gas tanks. A block away the tubular monstrosity of Gowanus Super-Highway bestrode the city like a giant's trampoline. . . . Here and there among the row houses and tenements rose eight- or ten-story plants and warehouses of reinforced concrete, once painted white but long since chipped and fading." Gazing at the horizon from the elevated Smith/Ninth Street station, Salisbury compared the elegant harmony of the Manhattan skyline to the sorry scene below him. "From the platform I looked back—dim in the foggy distance was the gleam of Wall Street's spires and the lacy East River bridges. I looked down in the tenement back yards, the rubbish piles and paper tatters brightened by wash lines of blue and pink, purple and yellow. Here and there I saw the scraggly green of Brooklyn back-yard trees, dwarfed by soot and sickened by cinders."[1]

Perched atop the elevated platform with a bird's-eye view of Brooklyn, Salisbury initially felt overwhelmed by the slum's amorphous vastness. But as he descended to the street, he saw that the wilderness in fact had form. No more than incoherent markings from afar, a rich graffiti text covered the walls. "The platform and stair wells of the Smith-Ninth station are covered with what first appears to be an embroidery of white chalk, red paint and black crayon. The tracery of lines is everywhere but it is not embroidery. It is a living newspaper of the streets." Brooklyn was not a no-man's land but a violently contested local place. "Here are the threats and taunts of rival gangs, the challenges and defiances. Here is word of neighborhood romance, old flames and new loves. Here bids are staked for leadership. Here bulletins are posted on rumbles."[2]

"Brooklyn wilderness." View from the Smith–Ninth Street Station looking northeast. Photograph taken December 15, 1958. (Courtesy of the Brooklyn Historical Society)

Where is Brownstone Brooklyn? Middle-class townhouse renovators invented the term in the early 1970s to describe an amorphous belt of nineteenth- and early twentieth-century housing and industrial buildings surrounding the borough's central business district. Brooklyn's new residents used the name interchangeably with other place labels. Some referred to the district as "Old Brooklyn." Others simply described themselves as moving to Brooklyn, a synecdoche for a small collection of gentrified districts across the river. Many of the individual names of Brownstone Brooklyn's enclaves were similarly created by middle-class migrants in the 1960s and 1970s: Boerum Hill, Carroll Gardens, and Cobble Hill. Much of the area did not have brownstones. Other impoverished blocks with townhouses did not appear on middle-class neighborhood maps. Brownstone Brooklyn had no distinct characteristics that distinguished it from the surrounding cityscape, as it sat on a broad ring of Victorian tenements and townhouses that ran from Brooklyn across to Manhattan's Greenwich Village, midtown, the East and West Sides, and lower Harlem. Brownstone Brooklyn remained a powerful repository of symbolic value, however, and the new middle-class enthusiasts in the 1970s who coined the name passionately described a distinct sense of local place.

If Brownstone Brooklyn was an invented landscape, what was really there? What landscape existed before a new middle class began to migrate to the area in the 1950s and renovate brownstones and tenements? What place names existed before middle-class professionals invented names such as Cobble Hill and Boerum Hill in the 1960s? How well did the label "Brownstone Brooklyn" correlate to the existing people and built environment of Brooklyn's declining industrial landscape? How much was a product of middle-class imagination? The new middle-class migrants of the 1960s and 1970s who coined the name were similarly preoccupied with what constituted the real and invented Brownstone Brooklyn.[3]

Brownstone Brooklyn had no real neighborhoods. When new enthusiasts created the name in the early 1970s, they were not using a preexisting place name. Some residents in the 1940s and 1950s referred to the area generally as "South Brooklyn" or "downtown." Others oriented themselves by using city district lines or Catholic parish boundaries. Those who did use enclave names could rarely distinguish where the area began or ended. Early attempts to locate Brooklyn's authentic neighborhoods were not by local residents but by two groups of outsiders with very different motives: community organizers and real estate agents. In 1941, Herbert J. Ballon of the Brooklyn Council for Social Planning drew one of the first maps of Brooklyn's enclaves. Dismissing political, school, health, and police district maps as too abstract, Ballon hoped to locate a more organic and historic sense of place. Upon interviewing residents, however, he found a mishmash of approximately one hundred overlapping neighborhood names with inconsistent borders, ages, and sizes. Further dismaying Ballon, a large number of names had been cynically invented by real estate agents. Ballon picked twenty-two names, many of which are still used today.[4]

Institutional maps from the 1940s and 1950s were just as inconsistent. Consolidated Edison in the 1940s used the name Old Brooklyn for the entire meter area between the East River and Prospect Park. A 1955 study by the Protestant Council of the City of New York referred to "downtown Brooklyn" as consisting of Fort Greene, Old South Brooklyn, and Park Slope. A census study from 1959 subdivided the area into smaller regions: Park Slope, Brooklyn Heights–Fort Greene, and South Brooklyn–Red Hook. In his 1958 youth gang study, Harrison Salisbury offered a sprawling definition of South Brooklyn: "a crowded territory, jammed between the white limestone towers of Borough Hall, the jagged steel fretwork of Navy Yard and the sawtooth of Red Hook, Erie Basin and Greenpoint." The New York City Youth Board offered expansive boundaries for the "high-delinquency" area of South Brooklyn with borders stretching from Prospect Park to Red Hook and the Navy Yard. "Park Slope, Gowanus or South Brooklyn. All three of these names are used to describe the area between Red Hook, Atlantic Avenue, Prospect Park and Green-Wood Cemetery," explained a social worker in 1944. No map had an area marked "Brownstone Brooklyn."[5]

Middle-class pioneers who combed maps in the archives were similarly hard pressed to find any historic neighborhoods in Brownstone Brooklyn. "While official records contain verbal descriptions of many of the [original] village boundaries, the landmarks by which the boundaries are identified have long since disappeared," lamented Herbert Ballon in 1941. "Not even official Borough cartographers have made the extensive research necessary to trace these boundaries on a map." Clear neighborhood borders in Brooklyn never existed. From the moment developers laid down the nineteenth-century street grid, labels were always elastic and contested. "South Brooklyn is a term which has grown to be somewhat vague," explained the *Brooklyn Eagle* in 1886, "owing to the extraordinary rapidity with which this city has grown. . . . [It] ought to be termed West Brooklyn, if indeed any special name is needed. . . . The name South Brooklyn has not had a good favor with some Brooklyn people, especially those who were so fortunate as to have houses on the Heights or Hill." "It is amusing to see the attempts made to fix upon a name for the rapidly growing part of Brooklyn near Prospect Park," complained residents in 1889. "Some call it Park Slope, some Park Hill Side, some Prospect Heights and others Prospect Hill. . . . Yet some people are trying to fasten upon it the name of Prospect Heights, a name which is never used in common conversation, and which smacks a little of affectation."[6]

Brownstone Brooklyn cannot simply be dismissed as an "invented" landscape, though. In fact, what makes Harrison Salisbury's 1958 description of Brownstone Brooklyn so vivid is that it belies the most common images of Brooklyn before gentrification. First, the area was not the non-place often described by both proponents and critics of gentrification. Although initially incoherent from a bird's-eye view, Salisbury's Brooklyn was not a terra incognita or a formless ghetto inhabited by racial Others into which brave middle-class pioneers would later heroically venture to cultivate new neighborhoods. At the same time, however, the area was not a blank backdrop against which yuppies and developers perniciously "imagineered" a simulacrum of a historic place. When a new middle class coined the label "Brownstone Brooklyn," they were describing something that was really there. But Salisbury's description of Brooklyn also did not resemble the urban place just as often commemorated by both proponents and critics of gentrification. Brownstone Brooklyn before gentrification was not a premodern gemeinschaft with aging Brahmins and Old World ethnics shielded from mass consumer culture. No authentic communities or traditional neighborhoods sat ready to be discovered—or, alternatively, destroyed—by young urban professionals. Brownstone Brooklyn offered a rich sense of place and history. But it was a landscape that was perpetually changing, fluid, polycentric, and hybrid.[7]

Brownstone Brooklyn was neither completely real nor invented. Rather like the graffiti-covered walls of Smith/Ninth Street station, Brooklyn was a text that Salisbury and other middle-class migrants creatively read and rewrote. Some middle-class arrivals commemorated the area's narrow streets, brownstones, aged surfaces, and wooden piers. Others relished the ethnic restaurants, foreign-language signage, street festivals, and elderly stoop dwellers of the area's second- and third-generation immigrant enclaves. Some scoured old maps for neighborhood names to revive historic places real and imagined. Others established farmers' markets and planted gardens to hark back to a lost agrarian landscape. Some, dissatisfied with their upbringing in assimilated suburbia, imagined a site of ethnogenesis where they could return to "find their roots" in the shtetls and barrios of their grandfathers and great-grandfathers.[8]

What made this text particularly legible for new middle-class migrants? From a bird's-eye view, Brownstone Brooklyn prior to gentrification seemed a rather uniform inner-city district, typical of older American cities. Brownstone Brooklyn in the 1940s and 1950s was home to about 300,000 largely poor and working-class white immigrants and their descendants, living in ramshackle nineteenth-century tenements and townhouses surrounding the borough's downtown. According to the 1948 Con Edison study, Old Brooklyn had the oldest housing in New York City, with more than 65 percent built before 1899 and almost 90 percent before 1920. It was also the most dilapidated, with about one in three buildings needing major repairs or lacking a private bath. Furthermore, like many inner-city districts after World War II, Brownstone Brooklyn was undergoing a rapid racial transition as in-migrating African Americans and Puerto Ricans replaced whites departing for the suburbs.[9]

Upon a closer look, Brownstone Brooklyn, like most inner-city districts of older American cities, did have distinctive zones in the 1940s and 1950s around which new middle-class arrivals could draw boundaries and place neighborhood labels. Several Gold Coasts gave the area a sense of aristocratic heritage. South of Brooklyn Bridge sat the borough's oldest district, Brooklyn Heights, which after years of decline still had a core of high-rent housing surrounding Montague Street. In the northeastern section of Park Slope, magnificent luxury apartment buildings and large brownstone mansions overlooked Prospect Park. West of Fort Greene Park, a small cluster of high-rent townhouses and apartments sat between Willoughby and Lafayette avenues. Surrounding the Gold Coasts sat a sprawling landscape of subdivided brownstones and railroad flats home to largely Italian and Irish Catholic immigrants and their descendants, as well as increasing numbers of Puerto Ricans and African Americans. Brooklyn's rapidly growing African American population lived in an expanding black belt that ran along Fulton Street into the growing district of Bedford-Stuyvesant. The city's oldest Puerto Rican community clustered along the waterfront and Atlantic Avenue. A waterfront belt of piers, light industry, shipyards, and warehouses formed Brooklyn's thriving industrial district. Warehouses and light industry also clustered around the Gowanus Canal. Along trolley, bus, and elevated train lines, strips of small stores and small apartments formed the area's commercial thoroughfares: Montague, Smith, and Court streets, Atlantic, Myrtle, Seventh, and Fifth avenues. Surrounding city hall at the foot of the Brooklyn Bridge sat Brooklyn's central business district, with government office buildings, hotels, and major department stores.[10]

But Brownstone Brooklyn was too messy to be split neatly into flat, horizontal zones. What made the area such a legible and rewritable urban text were its multiple layers. With the borough's oldest street grid and an assortment of buildings dating back to the colonial era, Brownstone Brooklyn was a tectonic cityscape with the architectural and social imprints of multiple economic stages: a Dutch agricultural economy, a mercantile port city, an immigrant industrial city, and an administrative office city. Remnants of past and present lay atop one another, the sediment from each historic cityscape seeping into the others. The city "is changing," explained sociologist Daniel Bell in 1961, "but enough survives, as does something of the city's early history . . . [its] faces exist as on a palimpsest. To understand New York, one must know all the faces."[11]

Brownstone Brooklyn was also a palimpsest of memories, symbols, and imagined places. In response to previous waves of development, earlier generations penned nostalgic accounts of Brooklyn's Dutch, Native American, and Brahmin past, protected individual buildings, invented historic place names, developed legends about fecund natural landscapes, and established romantic-style parks to re-create a green past. Along with excavating remnants of farms, industrial piers, Victorian brownstones, and turn-of-the-century apartment buildings, Brooklyn's new middle class drew from rich layers of imaginary places created by writers such as Washington Irving, Edith Wharton, Walt Whitman, Thomas Wolfe, and Beat writers. An invented neighborhood such as Cobble Hill was a landscape collage, with the scars of modern development intertwined with sites of nostalgia.[12]

Brooklyn's people and institutions formed just as multilayered a landscape. If one asked a Brownstone Brooklyn resident in 1950 where he lived, he or she would most likely not refer to a neighborhood name like Park Slope. Instead he would refer to a variety of places, each overlapping, partially intersecting, and in some cases contradictory. Based on the context of the question, he would likely have selected from a series of local affiliations. He could describe himself as part of a union local, refer to a social club, or delineate the turf boundaries of the gang he belonged to. He might point to a playground where friends gather to watch their children play. He might describe the area as being Italian or Irish or Arab, or simply as white. He might cite a neighborhood name—South Brooklyn, Park Slope—but the sense of place would likely be much more focused, concentrated on a block or even a single household. Part of the "borough of churches," Brownstone Brooklyn was largely Catholic, and a resident might locate himself by referring to the parish boundaries that divided the landscape. He might name the local bar that acted as a center for political organizing and socializing. Candy stores, bars, and other storefronts were important place markers and centers. Race and class too provided a sense of place. He might live in the "nice section," the projects, or the slum.

To invent Brownstone Brooklyn, the new middle class literally and figuratively excavated the landscape. As they sandblasted paint and pulled off cheap siding from townhouses, brownstone renovators symbolically stripped layers off the built environment to restore a seemingly authentic past. As they dug through the earth to plant trees and urban gardens, green activists imagined themselves clearing away industrial debris and other traces of modernity to expose a pastoral landscape. As they started block associations and food cooperatives, community organizers sought to recapture the intimacy of older village life. As others converted rooming houses to single-family buildings, at times evicting the residents, they imagined themselves restoring the buildings to their former aristocratic grandeur. Particular layers were commemorated and exaggerated; others were ignored. Like an archivist using an X-ray to recover text from a parchment, Brooklyn revivalists peered through "inauthentic" rooming houses, gang graffiti, and public housing. Postwar buildings, particularly modernist and institutional ones, were universally reviled. Highways were seen as artificial impositions on a natural cityscape, something to be stripped away. Black and Puerto Rican residents were at times celebrated as sources of anti-bureaucratic authenticity and at other times studiously avoided.[13]

Brownstone Brooklyn thus was a bricolage of images. And to describe the invention of this landscape, one must, to paraphrase Daniel Bell, first know all of Brooklyn's layers—layers that were both "hard" and "soft."[14]

When middle-class migrants described a "sense of place" in the 1960s and 1970s, they first looked to the area's hard landscape of buildings, streets, and waterways. With almost 80 percent of its housing built before 1920, Brownstone Brooklyn was for new arrivals a vestige of old Brooklyn. The area's antiquated architecture and street grid gave it a historic gestalt that distinguished it from its surroundings. What layers of Brownstone Brooklyn's hard landscape did middle-class brownstone renovators regard as authentic?

Some dug symbolically underneath the city to uncover a green landscape. When coining neighborhood names, middle-class enthusiasts assigned labels such as "Gardens," "Hill," and "Heights" that harked back to Brooklyn's pre-urban topography of hills, valleys, and brooks. Others planted sidewalk trees and started gardens in abandoned lots. Some described themselves as heading into Brooklyn's wilderness like pioneers in covered Conestoga wagons. Other community activists fighting development projects borrowed the imagery of Native American tribes in a defense of indigenous soil.[15]

Brownstone Brooklyn did have a distinct topography, with several slopes that rose to as high as 100 feet. Brooklyn Heights, Fort Greene Park, and Carroll Park were peaks that ranged from 65 to 100 feet above sea level. Park Slope rose from Atlantic Avenue to about 150 feet near the park. But much of this primordial landscape described by brownstoners in the 1960s and 1970s was also richly symbolic. The handful of early American maps in city archives had limited detail about Brooklyn's historic Indian trails, Dutch trading posts, and natural wetlands. Jaspar Dankers and Peter Sluyter's *Journal of a Voyage to New York and a Tour in Several of the American Colonies, 1679–1680* had only a few sentences about Brooklyn's topography. Some place names referred to a completely imaginary natural terrain. Boerum Hill, for example, was a name invented in the 1960s and 1970s to describe an area that had always been flat.[16]

Brownstone Brooklyn's pre-European landscape was not the only layer that middle-class pioneers excavated. As they started farmers' markets and food cooperatives, neighborhood revivalists also looked longingly to the borough's former agricultural landscape. At the end of the eighteenth century, Kings County was still mostly rural and divided into plantations owned by farmers most frequently of English and Dutch descent. With large numbers of African Americans working the land, Kings County in the early nineteenth century had the highest ratio of slaves to slave holders in the North. While few farm buildings existed by the 1940s, the memory of the old landowners could be found in street names such as Bergen, Schermerhorn, Remsen, and Boerum. To situate renovation efforts in an imagined tradition of land settlement and homeownership, new maps of Boerum Hill made for house-and-garden-tour brochures in the 1960s included outlines of these old farm boundaries.[17]

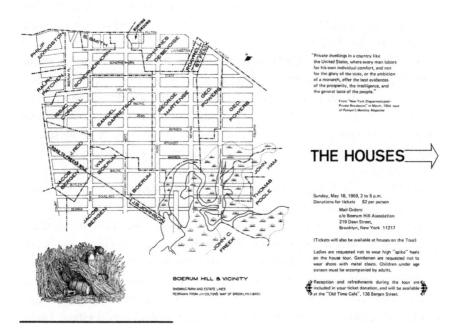

"Brooklyn as palimpsest." A 1969 Boerum Hill Association house tour brochure contains an 1849 map with overlaying maps of eighteenth-century farm boundaries and the nineteenth-century street grid. (Courtesy of the Boerum Hill Asssociation)

Brownstone Brooklyn, however, was for new arrivals a distinctly urban landscape. Rather than the memory of farms and creeks, neighborhood revivalists spoke most passionately about the compact nineteenth-century urban fabric. In contrast to the superblocks, suburban developments, and expressways designed by modernist developers and planners in the 1950s and 1960s, Brownstone Brooklyn's street grid of short street blocks, townhouses, waterfront piers, and lofts appeared organic, human-scale, and traditional.

While over time it would become a repository of historical memory, Brooklyn's historic street grid was initially as much a product of ruthless urban real estate development and technological disruption as were the expressways that later cut through it. Just as the car transfigured the borough in the twentieth century, new forms of transportation transformed Brooklyn from a muddy farming village to a sprawling metropolis. With the opening of the first steam ferry to Manhattan's financial and industrial district in 1814, Brooklyn exploded in size. In 1820, only 7,175 residents lived in the village. By 1835, Brooklyn boasted 24,592 residents and a new city charter, and it was the seventh-largest city in the country. By 1850, the population had grown to 96,838. After annexing the neighboring villages of Williamsburg, Bushwick, and Greenpoint, the consolidated city of Brooklyn in 1855 was the third-largest city in America, with 205,250 residents. By 1860, the city grew to 266,661 residents, and by 1870, to 396,099. By 1876, it had surpassed Boston, Chicago, St. Louis, and San Francisco in size.[18]

Brooklyn's nineteenth-century streetscape was modern and abstract. While postwar expressway designers studied existing traffic flows and built urban highways mostly atop older roadways, Brownstone Brooklyn's short street blocks were geometrically designed by speculators primarily to transform land into a financial commodity. In a nineteenth-century version of urban sprawl, New York's first suburb developed at a breakneck pace. Brooklyn developers erected large tracts of housing at an unrelenting speed with little civic vision beyond the search for quick profit. In Clover Hill, soon to become known as Brooklyn Heights, Henry Pierrepont envisioned an exclusive suburb with upscale mansions surrounded by spacious lawns. But as more tenants demanded housing in the area, speculators snapped up farm plots and developers slapped together buildings at a feverish pace. Horsecar lines, soon replaced by trolley lines, ripped across green agricultural land. As real estate prices soared, developers began to build cramped multifamily homes and apartments to maximize profits on increasingly expensive real estate. Small, cheaply made row houses were rented as fast they could be erected. Brooklyn's retail landscape was similarly slapdash. Along trolley lines, developers erected cheap three-story buildings with a storefront and two floors of apartments, temporary placeholders meant to collect rent until land could be developed for more intensive use. Other speculators purchased farmland in anticipation of urban expansion and temporarily rented plots to squatters. These tenant farmers built ramshackle wood shanties and small gardens that sat amidst rows of townhouses. Entire districts seem to rise overnight.[19]

The most influential legacy of the nineteenth-century building boom was the brownstone. Ornate churches, Federalist wooden homes, and cobblestone streets dotted the city's historic architectural landscape. But the tall sandstone-fronted row house gave the area a particular sense of place. Rather than high-rises or single-tract homes found in the rest of the borough, Brooklyn's Victorian brownstone cityscape with its rows of trees, stoops, and small street blocks became the template for a new romantic urban ideal. The brownstone was not just another city building to a new middle class in the 1960s and 1970s. The brownstone was cityness.

The word "brownstone" denoted a distinct type of row house. Originally referred to as "brownstone fronts" in the nineteenth century, the brick buildings acquired their name from the four-to-six-inch-thick stone veneer that covered the front side. This striking facing was normally made of soft Triassic sandstone cut from a belt of local quarries that ran from Portland, Connecticut, to Paterson, New Jersey. Although pink when first cut, over time the stone turned to a chocolate brown when exposed to the elements. Brownstones were the most numerous and influential of row houses, and by the 1950s the name was often used to describe any kind of row house regardless of its facing.[20]

While over time they would weather and develop richly unique surfaces, brownstones were in original design and intention no more or less authentic than a Levittown Cape Cod. Brownstones were an architectural trompe l'oeil designed to give a faux sense of historic grandeur. In an era when stone was seen as more monumental than brick or wood, builders used sandstone as a cheap substitute for marble. The facing was carefully designed to give the illusion that the entire building was constructed of stone. Builders cut large slabs of stone to minimize any visible seams, giving the townhouse a solid brown and austere look. Elaborately adorned stone doorways and windows added to the buildings' impression of luxury.[21]

Despite their aristocratic look, rowhouses were built to house a variety of social classes. Some brownstones were imposing mansions constructed for wealthy businessmen and merchants. In the Gold Coast areas, Brooklyn Heights and Park Slope, Brooklyn's elite lived in expansive townhouses with servants' quarters and large parlors. But as steam-cutting technology made sandstone affordable, the buildings soon became popular as single-family

The northeast section of Park Slope near Grand Army Plaza was one of Brownstone Brooklyn's "Gold Coasts." Corner of Eighth Avenue and Lincoln Place. Photograph taken February 28, 1960. (Courtesy of the Brooklyn Historical Society)

housing for the middle class. Built in repetitive bulk by speculators, brownstones were the suburban tract homes of the nineteenth century. After buying a parcel of land, developers often erected the buildings in groups of three or four. Some quickly threw up entire city blocks. As demand grew and land prices rose, the size of brownstones continued to shrink. While brownstones in the early part of the century could be 27 to 29 feet wide, by the 1860s middle-class families squeezed into brownstones only 16 feet wide. Some New York City townhouses were as narrow as 12 feet.[22]

No grand architectural vision underlay the design of Brownstone Brooklyn. Buildings variously followed a range of architectural style, from Federalist, Greek Revival, and Neo-Gothic to Italianate and Queen Anne. Like homebuilders across nineteenth-century America, developers designed the townhouses with little stylistic consistency. In some years they favored simple lines and stark simplicity; in other years they covered facades with elaborate ornamentation. In search of maximum profit, few developers hired architects. Brownstones were thrown together in a quick and haphazard manner. Some builders copied the ornamentation of other buildings or relied on a few informal manuals that circulated in the city. Others depended on the particular skills of the stonemasons they contracted. Rather than keeping up to date with the latest architectural fashion, masons often learned a few simple designs that they used for every project. Some even changed styles abruptly in the middle of construction; the result was an inconsistent and colorful mishmash.[23]

Brownstones were products of the mechanical age. The florid embellishments that covered brownstones were rarely produced by individual artists. Most of the intricate ornamentation was machine-cut and mass-produced. Some developers salvaged secondhand ornaments and fixtures from demolished homes to sell or reuse on new structures. Despite their monumental appearance, the stone exteriors were poorly built and subject to quick decay. When properly cut against the grain, sandstone could last for decades. But in the speculative building frenzy, few developers bothered to cut the stone correctly, and the exteriors were notorious for crumbling easily. When middle-class renovators in the 1970s complained that working-class residents had added paint and siding to brownstones, they mistakenly accused them of destroying the integrity of the building. Brownstones had from their inception been a bricolage.[24]

While they would later be viewed as authentic, contemporaries dismissed brownstones as modern and artificial. Foreshadowing post–World War II broadsides against urban renewal and suburban architecture, critics in the nineteenth century decried the mechanical, dehumanizing monotony of brownstone rows. "When one has seen one house he has seen them all," wrote one writer, "the same everlasting high stoops and gloomy brown-stone fronts, the same number of holes punched in precisely same places." "The architecture is not only impressive, it is oppressive," complained another critic. "Its great defect is its monotony, which soon grows tiresome." Still others, prefiguring 1990s dismissals of McMansions, lambasted the gaudy, overadorned stone fronts preferred by New York's brownstone nouveau riche: "What we lack in invention, we can cover by 'ornamentation' and hence we have miles of reiterated and unmeaning rope mouldings, filigreed jambs, and window-heads twisted into all sorts of conceivable contortions."[25] Some regarded Brooklyn brownstones as particularly fake. "The majority are deceptive, fraudulent, pretentious—mere shells," complained a *Washington Post* writer in 1886 of the rows of small, boxy townhouses. "[They are] plated, so to speak, with a coating of brownstone in front and trimmed inside with cheap pine so that a poor man may boast a brown-stone house. And they have alcove bed-rooms and marble buffet niches and factory-made stained glass door panes, so that the clerk may live like the shadow of a millionaire."[26]

These critiques extended to Brooklyn's nineteenth-century transportation grid. Contemporaries regarded the new trolleys and streetcars—horse-drawn and then electric—that formed the skeleton for Brooklyn's brownstone sprawl as modern and dehumanizing. Although in the 1970s enthusiasts would look to revive trolleys as a possible antidote to automobile expressways, residents in the 1890s described the wires and tracks as noisy, polluting, and dangerous. A "monster gridiron" threatened to swallow the area, complained protesters at Borough Hall in 1895 after the city granted development rights to a local trolley company. The "City of Churches," they cried, was in danger of becoming the "City of Trolleys." "Wires of death" covered the sky. "Glissing, hissing cars" raced through narrow streets at perilous speeds, killing eleven Brooklynites in 1892 and seriously injuring more than eighty.[27]

Just as postwar superblock developments later sparked an appreciation for the Victorian cityscape, the new brownstone and trolley grid inspired nineteenth-century eulogies for a real and imagined agricultural landscape. Brooklyn's wealthy fondly remembered the county's lost farms, creeks, winding dirt roads, wooden homes, and plantation mansions. By the turn of the century, a virtual topography of lost Indian trails, trading villages, and virgin forest became part of the city's collective memory. Authors published nostalgic accounts of Dutch New York that blurred fiction and history. Peering at filthy industrial waterfronts, residents reminisced about fishermen catching oysters along the Gowanus. Legends grew about herders and cattle once wading from Brooklyn to Governor's Island across Buttermilk Channel. In an effort to re-create pre-urban pastoral landscapes, Victorian bourgeois reformers moved thousands of tons of dirt to manufacture beautiful yet artificial green spaces such as Prospect Park and Fort Greene Park. The result was a richly layered romantic-style landscape that Brownstone Brooklyn's new middle class would later avidly excavate.[28]

Obscured in this early wave of Victorian nostalgia were the less romantic aspects of the obsolete agricultural economy: slavery, tenant labor, and the stench of horse manure. While uneasy with the city's destructive modernity, nostalgic Brooklynites were equally disturbed by the remnants of its rural past that coexisted with the newer layer of urban development. In notorious shantytown districts such as Darby's Patch and Jackson's Hollow, developers fought acrimonious court battles to evict squatters from the wood shacks, small gardens, and farms that sat abreast of Brooklyn's new brownstones. Civic groups fretted that former tenant farmers turned urban dwellers kept livestock in and around muddy city buildings. Goats and chickens ran wild in the streets. Workers adjusted poorly to the strict time regimens of industrial labor. Alcoholism was rampant.[29]

But brownstones were not the last layer of the housing that new middle-class residents looked to as a source of authenticity in the 1960s and 1970s. Brownstone Brooklyn's array of elegant turn-of-the-century apartment buildings formed another layer of legible text that was later creatively interpreted. For some brownstone renovators, Brooklyn's older high-rises marked the first intrusion of modernity and the encroachment of abstract space across the "borough of homes." But most pioneers looked to the older majestic luxury apartment towers of the late nineteenth and early twentieth centuries as an authentic contrast to the seemingly boxy towers of postwar public housing projects and midtown Manhattan apartments. Tenements similarly evoked memories of ethnic heritage, communal street life, and open-air markets.

In many ways, brownstoners who dismissed Brooklyn's high-rise apartments as a bureaucratic addition to an organic landscape were correct. Just as the steam ferry had sparked the nineteenth-century building boom, Brooklyn's apartment-scape grew partly as a result of a modern transportation grid. The opening of the Brooklyn and Manhattan bridges in 1883 and 1909, respectively, made Brooklyn easily accessible for Manhattan's immigrant working class. As the city laid down electric trolley and elevated train lines, thousands of Irish, Italian, and Jewish families moved to Brownstone Brooklyn to avoid the slums of lower Manhattan. White-collar workers displaced by industrial expansion along the waterfront and eager for housing in commuting distance to Manhattan's growing skyscraper district also poured into the area. When the first subway lines reached Brownstone Brooklyn in the early twentieth century, the area rapidly became a landscape of working-class and white-collar renters. In a process that could be described as the proletarianization of the landscape, Brooklyn's new immigrant and white-collar migrants transformed the area physically and socially from an area of small homes to multifamily rental apartment buildings.[30]

Yet Brooklyn's new high-rise rental apartments were as vernacular as single-family brownstones in many respects. Brooklyn had never been a "borough of homes." Middle-class clerks and businessmen had always rented their small townhouses from developers. Only wealthy families in Park Slope and Brooklyn Heights ever owned their brownstones. As land costs and rents skyrocketed throughout the nineteenth century, Brooklynites increasingly experimented with ways to create smaller rental units within existing structures. The earliest apartments were ad hoc dwellings for the poor, as laborers slept in warehouses and lofts along the waterfront. On Baltic Street and other blocks by the water-front, poor midcentury dockworkers crammed into subdivided and crowded row houses. Struggling middle-class families also began to take in boarders to cover skyrocketing rents. A shifting and imprecise terminology emerged to describe these new dwellings: "tenements," "apartments," "rookeries," "board-inghouses," and "hotels." With no legal distinction between tenements and apartments until the Tenement Act of 1901, the line between rich and poor multiple-dwelling units was blurred.[31]

The shift to purpose-built high-rises was similarly organic. In the 1880s, developers in southern Park Slope and around the Long Island Rail Road depot built larger versions of brownstones with separate rental units on three or four stories. By the early twentieth century, developers had erected high-rise apart-ments throughout Brownstone Brooklyn. In Brooklyn Heights, larger luxury towers modeled after Manhattan's majestic Beaux Arts apartment buildings such as the Ansonia rose along Montague Street. In response to the squalid conditions of tenements along the waterfront, local reformers looked optimis-tically toward the apartment as a model for affordable, modern housing for the poor and working class. South of Brooklyn Heights, wealthy businessman and philanthropist Alfred T. White built Brooklyn's first social housing. The Tower and Home projects, on Hicks Street, were Romanesque Revival apart-ment complexes built for low-income tenants. Riverside Houses, built in 1890 on Columbia Place, housed nineteen stores and 280 two- to four-room apart-ments. Blocks away, White's Warren Place mews consisted of thirty-four modest rowhouses between Baltic and Warren streets with rents targeted for craftsmen and foremen of modest means. Relying on the private sector to build and run all his projects, White hoped to provide philanthropic housing that still adhered to capitalist principles and offered profits to investors. The first elevator apartments rose in Brooklyn Heights and along Prospect Park in the early 1900s. By the 1920s, cheaper elevator technology and high demand soon resulted in scores of Art Deco apartment buildings with moderately priced, modern apartments and grandiose names such as Roosevelt Arms.[32]

As part of the organic process of "apartmentization," the 1910s and 1920s also saw the beginnings of an early form of gentrification. In the midst of a housing shortage in 1919, the city passed an amended tenement law allowing the subdivision of single-family rowhouses into multiple-unit apartment buildings. Property owners soon began a wave of brownstone conversions. On most blocks landlords chopped up brownstones into rooming houses and low-rent apartments, causing residents to lament that the area was going into decline. On other blocks, groups such as the Heights Company avidly refurbished dilapidated townhouses into modern luxury apartments for a new white-collar clientele, sparking some of the earliest complaints about displacement. After a 1916 zoning ordinance, developers also began to convert brownstones along trolley lines on Seventh Avenue and other thoroughfares to retail and apartment space. New first-floor stores with windows were topped by two or three levels of apartments. By the 1920s, Brownstone Brooklyn was a diverse landscape of wealthy and impoverished renters, a new constituency that became a strong force in New York City politics.[33]

Although apartments were widely popular among New Yorkers, this latest modernization of the landscape did not escape criticism. Towering over formerly single-family rowhouses, apartment buildings sparked widespread anxiety in the early twentieth century about the "Manhattanization" of Brooklyn. Brownstones, once themselves cause for consternation, became the subjects for a new strain of nostalgia. Brooklyn Heights, wrote the *New York Times* in 1902, was rapidly changing from a neighborhood "given over entirely to the mansions of the richest, the proudest, the most aristocratic of Brooklyn folk to a district of boarding and furnished-room establishments, of towering apartment houses and hotels, of artists' studios, and even of noisy, bustling commerce."[34] In 1910 the Brooklyn Heights Association (BHA) formed partly in response to the encroachment of apartment towers and skyscrapers from the neighboring downtown business district. "Brooklyn Heights, as we all know, from days prior to the Revolution has always had the reputation of being the seat of the aristocracy of the Metropolis," explained the BHA in a 1920 announcement for a new tree planting campaign. "It is true that a large number of our old families have disappeared from our neighborhood, but the traditions and the forethought of these founders of the Heights will remain with it for many a day." Apartments, however, threatened the area's aristocratic ambience. "Before the incoming of the subway, an Association of our kind was not required. Everybody in those days knew the Heights and knew what it stood for. Subways brought new people, old homes disappeared and apartments were built and the unheeding ones threatened to encroach on this sanctum of the home lover."[35]

But Brownstone Brooklyn was not just a place where people slept. It was placed where they worked. When a new postindustrial middle class celebrated Brooklyn's sense of place, they looked not just to its brownstones and apartments but also to its aging industrial landscape. Downtown Brooklyn formed the manufacturing and commercial nucleus of the borough. A belt of industry hugged the coastline, and scores of small factories, warehouses, garages, and repair shops sat next to brownstones and apartment buildings. The long and deep waterfront was one of the most active ports in the United States. A small central business district contained Brooklyn's Borough Hall, and aging skyscrapers were home to financial and municipal headquarters. Along Fulton Street, shoppers patronized Brooklyn's department stores. All these economic functions created a legible city text that middle-class pioneers in the 1960s and 1970s avidly read and reimagined.

Brownstone Brooklyn's mixed and diverse industrial and commercial landscape made it fertile soil for gentrification. First its collection of small manufacturing firms tempered the cataclysmic shocks of deindustrialization after the war. While Brooklyn would see much of its manufacturing disappear after World War II, and would suffer many of the economic problems of other older urban areas, the process would be gradual and piecemeal. The messy coexistence of the two sectors also blurred the line between industrial and residential space. Factories long sat near the homes of Brooklynites; it was only natural that some Brooklynites in a postindustrial city relished residing near or even within lofts and warehouses. But mostly Brownstone Brooklyn's historic architecture, its diverse antiquated manufacturing sector, its colorful international waterfront culture, and its non-bureaucratic gestalt would in the postwar period capture the imagination of New York's new bureaucratic white-collar labor force. Along with the brownstones and mom-and-pop shops of its residential area, Brooklyn's non-Fordist industrial and commercial landscape formed the template for a new post-Fordist middle-class romantic urbanism.

Brownstone Brooklyn's industrial and commercial functions always coexisted with its role as a residential retreat for Manhattan's labor force. While the first developers were erecting homes for lower Manhattan businessmen in the early nineteenth century, another group of builders eyed Brooklyn's long waterfront and open land as a potential site for industrial expansion. With the opening of steam ferry service in 1814, Manhattan firms began to build warehouses directly across the river. As the United States made the transition to an industrial and urban nation, Brooklyn experienced rapid economic growth. From 1860 to 1870 alone, the value of goods manufactured in Brooklyn grew from $34 million to $61 million. By 1890, Brownstone Brooklyn formed a segment of one of the country's largest industrial centers. Brooklyn by century's end enjoyed the fourth-largest industrial output in the nation, producing $269 million worth of goods and employing 110,000 workers.[36]

By the early 1950s, Brownstone Brooklyn lay at the center of the borough's industrial belt that ran along the ten-mile waterfront from Red Hook to neighboring Williamsburg and was home to much of the borough's approximately eight thousand manufacturing firms. While partly a secluded residential

Poorer areas of Park Slope like Thirteenth Street had a mix of houses and industry. Dilapidated tenements and townhouses share a block with the Ansonia Clock Factory. View of north side of Thirteenth Street between Seventh and Eighth Avenues. Photograph taken June 11, 1961. (Courtesy of the Brooklyn Historical Association)

escape from its high-rise neighbor, Brownstone Brooklyn was also an urban extension of lower Manhattan's highly concentrated industrial and commercial landscape. From a point on the East River near Manhattan's Houston Street, a three-mile-radius circle contained the place of employment of three-fourths of the entire city's workforce in 1950, nearly 2,632,000 workers.[37]

Brownstone Brooklyn's industrial and commercial activity was linked to its waterfront. With about two hundred piers, the Port of Brooklyn handled around 45 percent of the city's waterfront commerce. In an average month in 1957, fifty-two steamship lines sent out 180 vessels a month to about 250 ports around the world. An equal number arrived from overseas. Thousands of longshoremen unloaded cargo to be sent by freight train around the country. Other privately owned docks and wharves handled fuel, oil, chemicals, sand, and gravel for manufacturing and processing plants that operated in the area. On other piers, private shipyards built and repaired ships.[38]

At the heart of Brownstone Brooklyn's waterfront economy was the enormous Brooklyn Navy Yard. The largest in the country since its opening in 1801, the historic Navy Yard built and repaired some the nation's most famous warships: the *Fulton*, the *Monitor*, the *Maine*, the U.S.S. *Missouri*. With an area of 291 acres, 6 dry docks, 9 piers, 17,000 linear feet of berthing space, and 270 major buildings with over 6 million square feet of floor space, the yard in 1959 employed around 15,000 people. A few miles south of the Navy Yard lay the Bush Terminal, another large industrial complex with 36 acres, 16 buildings, piers, railways, and more than 100 tenants employing 20,000 workers.[39]

Brownstone Brooklyn's industrial landscape boasted an incredibly diverse collection of small firms. Along the waterfront, hundreds of manufacturers made paint, apparel, bakery products, special machinery, electronic parts, and textiles. Brownstone Brooklyn benefited greatly from government spending during and after World War II. While the Navy Yard built and repaired ships, a host of smaller manufacturers provided bolts, castings, and tools, as well as miscellaneous goods such as spaghetti, sandbags, portable operating tables, bakers' and cooks' caps, and canvas leggings. The Gowanus Canal area was home to confectionaries, paint factories, metal shops, and a host of other light manufacturing.[40]

Brownstone Brooklyn's collage of small firms, along with that of lower Manhattan and North Brooklyn, formed an eclectically non-Fordist industrial cityscape. Rather than being dominated by one or two large industries, Brooklyn hosted an assortment of small businesses with a mix of unskilled and skilled workers often working side by side. Out of 7,851 manufacturing establishments in the borough in 1953, only 462 hired more than a hundred people. More than 5,000 hired fewer than twenty. Rather than large industrial plants with mass assembly lines and heavy machinery, Brooklyn's crowded and aging lofts and warehouses housed an interactive web of small players that relied heavily on subcontractors, seasonal outputs, piecework, face-to-face relations, and a rapid exchange of ideas.[41]

While in Fordist cityscapes such as Detroit, laborers lived in mass-produced homes distinctly segregated from production plants, Brownstone Brooklyn was a jumbled mix of industry and residences. While the Bush Terminal and the Navy Yard were distinct industrial areas, much of Brooklyn's workspace uncleanly merged with its living space. Myriad auto repair shops, garages, warehouses, and light manufacturing facilities sat in close proximity to brownstones and apartment houses. As in many older cities, Brooklyn's housing stock became less luxurious as it neared active industry. Brownstones were built in tiers, each row of townhouses shrinking in size and quality as they rippled toward industrial areas. In Park Slope, brownstone mansions for the wealthy sat closer to Prospect Park. As one moved down the slope toward the Gowanus industrial district, the housing gradually turned to dilapidated tenements and smaller townhouses. Red Hook, Gowanus, and the area near the Navy Yard were among the most notorious slums in the city. But small workshops and garages could be found near the homes of the wealthy as well. Brooklyn Heights after World War II was home to some of the area's priciest real estate as well as 13,800 manufacturing jobs. With factories, warehouses and lofts making up about 20 percent of its nonresidential building stock, Park Slope in the 1940s had 4,500 manufacturing jobs near its brownstones. The waterfront further added to Brooklyn's mix of industrial and residential areas. Built by nineteenth-century merchants during the borough's commercial era, many of the oldest and most prestigious mansions sat close to warehouses and piers of the waterfront. The most expensive brownstones of Brooklyn Heights sat on a bluff overlooking the port. While the view of Manhattan was magnificent, the buildings were also steps away from the rough-and-tumble docks and warehouses of Furman Street.[42]

Blue-collar laborers were not the only workers in Brownstone Brooklyn on the eve of World War II. Brownstone Brooklyn was the borough's downtown, the central business district where about fifty thousand white-collar and retail workers worked in banks, government offices, and department stores. Running along Fulton Street, the borough's oldest thoroughfare, were Brooklyn's Borough Hall, several hotels, banks, department stores, and theaters. Along Adams Street, construction workers worked on Brooklyn's gleaming Civic Center, the showcase public works project of the postwar period. Having demolished forty-five acres encompassing more than three hundred buildings, the city planned to create a large boulevard flanked by open plazas, superblocks, and gleaming modernist municipal buildings.[43]

Brooklyn's white-collar skyscrapers, bank buildings, and government offices formed a richly layered palimpsest shaped by several eras of economic restructuring. Brooklyn's nineteenth-century downtown consisted of newspaper headquarters, insurance companies, and banks centered around the Fulton Ferry port by the East River. After construction of the Brooklyn Bridge demolished much of the area and the bridge itself replaced ferry service, a new financial district grew around Borough Hall with a neighboring retail district of department stores along Fulton Street. As part of a new Civic Center project starting in the 1940s, the city targeted many of these early twentieth-century hotels, office buildings, and warehouses for demolition. As new modernist structures rose in their stead, the remnants of the older central business districts caught the attention of the Brooklyn's new middle class. In the 1970s, rehabilitation projects such as Brooklyn's Fulton Ferry recast older office and warehouse districts as sites of authenticity. Even early twentieth-century national corporate headquarters for banks and insurance companies also offered a rich sense of place. Starting in the late 1970s, developers began to convert former white-collar workspace such as Brooklyn Heights's 130 Clinton Street and lower Manhattan's Liberty Tower into luxury cooperatives and condominiums.[44]

But Brownstone Brooklyn's hardscape alone did not provide a sense of place for the new middle class. When new arrivals described the area's authenticity, they referred not just to its array of brownstones and apartments or assortment of lofts and piers, but also to its people. Three hundred thousand residents formed a soft cityscape equally as layered and complex a text. More than a piece of land or a collection of buildings, Brownstone Brooklyn was a social web of personal relationships, political and cultural organizations, ethnic divisions, and religious lines. Each of these turfs overlapped and at times conflicted with one another to form a dynamic and layered place that the new middle class avidly excavated.

"Neighborhood" was the most common label used by the new middle class to describe Brownstone Brooklyn's landscape. Searching for an alternative to the apartment towers of Manhattan and tract homes of suburbia that they described as alienating and atomizing, new arrivals in the 1960s and 1970s used phrases such as "neighborhoody," "neighborly," "traditional neighborhood," or "real neighborhood" to describe the area. While it would be easy to dismiss this as simple romantic nostalgia, new arrivals were detecting a salient sense of place that existed among residents. A cohesive, safe, and homogeneous enclosed space, the neighborhood is often recalled by former residents as the principal institution that oriented their lives. In his memoir of growing up in Park Slope during the 1940s, Pete Hamill describes this powerful feeling of place: "On the streets I learned the limits of the Neighborhood. This was our hamlet, marked by clear boundaries. Sometimes were moved beyond those boundaries: to visit aunts and uncles out in Bay Ridge . . . but it was to the Neighborhood that we always returned. Other neighborhoods were not simply strange; they were probably unknowable. I was like everybody else. In the Neighborhood I always knew where I was; it provided my center of gravity. And on its streets I learned certain secrets that were shared by the others."[45]

Yet one must be careful not to overstate the importance of the Brooklyn neighborhood. The accounts of the neighborhood found in memoirs and oral histories of the 1970s and 1980s were often tainted by nostalgia. Juxtaposed to the present modern, dehumanizing urban landscape, or eulogized as a place that existed before a major racial or infrastructural change, the neighborhood functioned in these accounts as a pastoral haven free of ethnic conflict, class divides, shifting locations of capital, and demographic change. Too, the rhetoric of black power and the white ethnic revival of the 1970s, with its celebration of neighborhood cohesion and political clout, was often prescriptive rather than descriptive. For some new middle-class residents, the neighborhood could also be a negative concept. Middle-class pioneers migrating to poor (particularly nonwhite) ethnic areas often felt displaced and alienated. Isolated in a foreign crowd, they interpreted icy stares and hostile interchanges to be evidence of a homogenous, threatening, unified community.[46]

At its best, the "neighborhood" was an important concept around which Brooklynites built political ties, defended against the wanton destructiveness of capital, and formed integrative bonds between disparate social groups. At its worst, the history of the neighborhood deteriorated into shameless Brooklyniana: a nostalgic collage of Dodgers pennants, pushcarts, stickball, Old World cooking, cries of *fuggedaboutit*, and other ethnic kitsch. Whether in New Left celebrations of working-class community, the nostalgic reveries of 1970s ethnic revivalists, or conservative eulogies of city life before the arrival of African Americans, this seductive commemoration of urban ethnic folk culture, working-class comity, and pastoral innocence remains a common and powerful trope.[47]

Brownstone Brooklyn in reality was a more complex array of places. Contemporary social scientists studying areas such as Brownstone Brooklyn found that in fact few residents had any concept of a large neighborhood. Most simply used general names like "this part of town" or "the West Side." Few had an attachment to the area at large, and the largest number spoke most often of a small group of friends, their homes, or a few stores. Rather than referring to neighborhoods, residents instead divided the landscape into distinct subareas. These subareas were not mini-neighborhoods but streams of social affiliations: a playground where a group of mothers met with their children, a collection of apartments that housed an extended family, a line of local bars and clubs along an avenue, a group of ethnic and religious institutions. Neighborhood identity temporarily coalesced in response to external threats: urban renewal, the arrival of a new ethnic group, or gentrification. But rather than a neighborhood, Brownstone Brooklyn was a spectrum of places.[48]

Even Brooklyn's short street blocks did not provide residents with a strong block identity. Brownstone Brooklyn's population, like in most of New York City, was transient. Rarely did a family stay in the same building for more than a few years. A 1938 study of a middle-class brownstone block in Park Slope found that few residents had engaged in conversation with their neighbors. Home visits were rare. The two rooming houses at the end of the block were regarded as completely alien space and avoided. The block association rarely met. Instead, block residents socialized through crossing streams of affiliations. Families on opposite ends of the block gathered in churches, dinner clubs, and extended-family gatherings, often in a different section of Brooklyn. Through the rigid street grid ran a web of crossing and flowing places.[49]

While clear neighborhood boundaries did not exist, other spatial categories provided the area with a sense of place. Perhaps the feature that made Brooklyn seem most authentic to Brooklyn's new enthusiasts was its seemingly strong sense of ethnic identity. For some middle-class migrants seeking a contrast to modern apartment towers and suburban developments, Brownstone Brooklyn was a diverse landscape of Old World immigrants, Middle Eastern spice shops, foreign-language newspapers, Irish bars, and Italian restaurants. For others, white ethnic, Arab, and Caribbean enclaves formed a colorful third space that they contrasted to completely black districts in central Brooklyn or upper Manhattan. Most important, though, Brownstone Brooklyn's numerous ethnic enclaves allowed multiple groups to seek historic and ethnic authenticity in the same urban space. Suburban-raised white ethnics, second-generation Latinos, and middle-class African Americans could all look toward the same Brownstone Brooklyn brownstones as an imagined site of ethnogenesis.

Ethnicity was certainly a crucial category used by Brownstone Brooklyn's residents prior to gentrification to describe where they lived. With areas ranging from 85 percent (Brooklyn Heights–Fort Greene) to 95 percent white (Park Slope) in 1957, Brownstone Brooklyn was divided into smaller enclaves of primarily Italian and Irish Catholic immigrants and their descendants. In 1950, according to one study, 16 percent of Fort Greene, 22 percent of Old South Brooklyn, and 20 percent of Park Slope was foreign-born. Over half the foreign-born in 1950 were Italian. In South Brooklyn and Red Hook, the percentage of Italians among the foreign-born rose to three-fifths. Park Slope had a significant Irish population, making up almost 20 percent of the foreign-born. A smaller population of Middle Easterners, Scandinavians, Poles, and Russian Jews lived in the area as well. Each group contributed a rich array of shops, social and political clubhouses, and religious institutions that gave the area a sense of place. Even as late as 1968, according to one study of a Polish parish in South Brooklyn, second- and third-generation Polish Americans retained a strong sense of ethnic identity.[50]

Brownstone Brooklyn's ethnic landscape, however, was never a collection of bounded Old World villages. In some areas there was a high degree of ethnic clustering. In one tract of what in the 1960s would become Carroll Gardens, 1,588 out of the 1,858 foreign-born residents were Italian. But labels such as "Little Italy" or "Irishtown" failed to describe accurately a broader and more hybrid landscape with higher mobility rates and fewer foreign-born residents than other areas of the city. In Brooklyn in 1950 as a whole, the population was about 25 percent foreign-born. While 14 percent of Old South Brooklyn was Italian-born in 1950, according to one study, no other group consisted of more than 2 percent anywhere in the area. In Park Slope, the Irish-born population was only 3 percent of the total population.[51]

Even in more densely concentrated Italian American areas, ethnic identity was concentrated more around the home, the extended family, or a single block than around a neighborhood. Arriving from a country with strong internal regional differences in dialects, culture, and religious rituals, older residents were more likely to affiliate with other immigrants from the same area of Italy. While younger American-born Italians adhered less to the spirit of *campanilismo*, or regionalism, the social divisions in clubs and fraternal societies between different subsections of Italians still remained salient in the 1940s and 1950s.[52] The continual arrival of new immigrants both legal and illegal further divided ethnic enclaves into those who were "fresh off the boat" and those who were more assimilated. In Brownstone Brooklyn, American-born Italian teenagers spoke with disdain of the "geeps" in the area, a derogatory term for Italian immigrants. Rather than a flat landscape divided into ethnic villages, Brownstone Brooklyn was a layered ethnic landscape shaped by demographic waves. Each immigrant group left an imprint of people, buildings, institutions, and memories that later generations could selectively excavate to revive a sense of place. Rather than a landscape of ethnic roots, Brownstone Brooklyn was a complex network of routes.[53]

The arrival of African Americans and Puerto Ricans further added to the layered complexity of the area. Brownstone Brooklyn was home to one of New York's oldest Puerto Rican settlements. From roughly 1910 until the late 1930s, the three major steamship companies with passenger and cargo lines running between New York City and Puerto Rico had their piers in the Erie Basin section of Brooklyn. By 1926, an estimated twenty-six thousand Puerto Ricans had settled along Brownstone Brooklyn's waterfront and the borough's downtown, with those two areas joining Harlem as the major Puerto Rican enclaves in New York City. While Puerto Rican migration dramatically rose after World War II and spread throughout the borough, in 1959 the Community Council of New York estimated that 35 percent of the borough's Puerto

Rican population still lived in Brooklyn Heights, Fort Greene, South Brooklyn, and Red Hook.[54]

Because of its ramshackle waterfront housing and industrial location, Brownstone Brooklyn remained a provincial and poorer cousin to the more dynamic cultural center in upper Manhattan. Doctors, small business owners, lawyers, and other upwardly mobile Puerto Ricans who arrived by ship in Brownstone Brooklyn moved to the apartment buildings and brownstones of East Harlem. Puerto Ricans who lived in Brownstone Brooklyn traveled uptown to Harlem at great cost to shop, visit the doctor, and obtain legal services. The differences between the two centers also reflected Puerto Rico's class and racial stratification. Whereas East Harlem was home to the *blanquitos*, or "whiteys," as one activist described it, Brownstone Brooklyn's Puerto Ricans were dark-skinned.[55]

For African Americans, the early trajectory between Harlem and Brooklyn ran precisely in the opposite direction. For black New Yorkers, the brownstones of Bedford-Stuyvesant were initially regarded as superior to Harlem's overcrowded slums. African Americans had been a continual presence in Brooklyn since the colonial era. But rather than a permanent community, historic black Brooklyn retained the imprints of several waves of migrants over three centuries who settled and left the area, often having had no relationship with one another. During the nineteenth century, free African Americans were scattered throughout Brownstone Brooklyn, working as coachmen, waiters, barbers, masons, and menial laborers. Many migrated elsewhere as the city industrialized. In southern Brooklyn Heights, a small community of black workers imported by a tile factory from South Carolina ran a baseball team called the Colored Niantics. When the factory left before World War I, the laborers left with it. During and after World War I, the first Great Migration from the South and the Caribbean led to the growth of a significant black community along Fulton Street, spurring a group of white residents to organize the anti-black Gates Avenue Association in 1922.[56]

During and after World War II, southern black workers fleeing Jim Crow and seeking industrial jobs rapidly migrated into New York City, part of a nationwide Second Great Migration of African Americans from the South to the North. With the opening of an A-train link from Harlem to Bedford-Stuyvesant in 1936 and high demand for wartime labor in the Navy Yard, Brownstone Brooklyn's black population rose dramatically. Many of the first arrivals were upwardly mobile African Americans who looked to Bedford-Stuyvesant's brownstones as a step up from Manhattan's overcrowded slum conditions. As poorer migrants followed, Bedford-Stuyvesant's black population rose from 24 percent in 1940 to 66 percent in 1957. Limited by discrimination from freely moving to other districts or the suburbs, African Americans found themselves crowded into dilapidated tenements and brownstones subdivided into small apartments and rooming houses.[57]

As more African Americans and Puerto Ricans migrated to the city during and after World War II, race began to replace ethnicity as a spatial category by which Brooklynites oriented themselves. While scholars debate about whether they learned to be white over time or were "white on arrival," working-class European immigrants and their descendants in Brooklyn by the 1940s had developed a strong collective racial identity. Brooklyn's downtown manufacturing and waterfront had long been segregated workspaces in which African Americans were relegated by both employers and unions to unskilled and menial tasks. Yet at the same time, in the 1920s and early 1930s, African Americans were relatively dispersed and lived in more integrated areas than new immigrants. But as more African Americans and Puerto Ricans migrated to the borough after World War II, a racialized and highly segregated ghetto took form. White and black areas cut across class and ethnic lines. Bedford-Stuyvesant after 1950 became an elastic label to describe an expanding, highly segregated, and impoverished black and brown area spreading northward toward Bushwick, southward into Crown Heights, eastward into East New York, and westward into Park Slope, Fort Greene, and other areas of Brownstone Brooklyn. The ghetto blended together Brooklyn's black middle class and poor, landlord and renter, Caribbean and native-born, as well as Spanish- and English-speakers. Segregated enclaves were not simply symbolic. The racial map of the Brooklyn ghetto was codified in official maps and shaped by public policy. Starting in the 1930s, New Deal programs such as the Home Owners' Loan Corporation, as well as the borough's banks and insurance companies, drew up maps distinguishing between white areas and high-risk black areas, formalizing racial boundaries. By the 1960s, the ghetto was a lived experience, an abstract category on a map, and a symbolic category used by local residents to orient themselves.[58]

To determine the boundaries of new brownstone neighborhoods such as Boerum Hill, brownstoners drew from this map of shrinking white and expanding black cityscapes. For some pioneers, Brooklyn's remaining white ethnic urban villages represented a fragile middle space between the central business district and the spreading black ghetto. Others favorably contrasted Brooklyn's white immigrant "old" slums to the "new" modernist public housing complexes home to nonwhites. Racial categories allowed for a sense of connection to the area's past. Although new white-collar brownstone renovators had little in common with departed immigrant blue-collar renters, the back-to-the-city rhetoric of renovators also drew on the memory, real and imagined, that brownstones with African American and Puerto Ricans roomers once had been home to white families. These categories became all the more salient as areas such as Park Slope and Boerum Hill became increasingly non-white in the 1960s and 1970s.

Along with race and ethnicity, social class also provided Brownstone Brooklyn with a sense of local place. When they described the area's authenticity, Brooklyn's new middle class described sections that were "nice" and ones that were "seedy," as well as places that were "on the upswing" and those that were "on the decline." Some of this language was borrowed from previous residents. Brownstone Brooklyn was an uneven landscape with pockets of extreme poverty next to wealth. Large brownstones and luxury apartments in the Gold Coasts of Brooklyn Heights, Park Slope, and "the Hill" sat surrounded by rooming houses and tenements. In a city with a multitiered economy of finance, media, manufacturing, and waterfront commerce, white-collar managers, bankers, and lawyers lived adjacent to blue-collar longshoremen and factory workers. "Danno's blocks were not part of the Neighborhood," Pete Hamill describes as he left the working-class section of southern Park Slope to deliver papers in the northern Gold Coast area near Prospect Park, "the comfortable people lived here. . . .There were no fire escapes on these blocks, no stores or bars, and every houses had a backyard . . . polished tables, muted lamps, elaborate wallpapers, rugs on wood floors."[59]

But what made Brooklyn's class identity so open to multiple readings was its messy incoherence. The geography of social class in Brownstone Brooklyn was not a simple dichotomy of rich areas and poor areas. Between the slum of the Red Hook industrial area and the Gold Coast of Brooklyn Heights and Park Slope was a layered landscape of brownstone blocks housing clusters of different income groups. Ethnic areas had internal class hierarchies. A petit bourgeoisie of funeral home owners, bartenders, butchers, and grocers—later reimagined as "mom and pop"—held positions of power and privilege. Residents made subtle distinctions between levels of poverty, differentiating between those who were extremely poor and those who were "respectable." The Gold Coasts housed a mix of wealthy white-collar professionals and their less wealthy middle-class counterparts who worked in public service, academia, and the arts.[60]

In working-class districts largely of tenements and subdivided rowhouses, the divide between landlords and renters was another important spatio-class category. Brooklyn's landlords had a strong class identity and envisioned themselves in a constant power struggle with tenants. Renters feared, envied, and resented landlords for their unique independence and control over the environment. At the same time, the relationship between the two groups in

Brownstone Brooklyn was fluid. Rather than wealthy slumlords battling the poor, Brownstone Brooklyn's housing market consisted mostly of small-time ethnic landlords and renters ranging from the destitute to the wealthy. According to a 1940 study of rooming houses in Manhattan, many of the owners were elderly women or young couples. And not infrequently, rooming house operators were tenants themselves who leased a brownstone or large apartment from a property owner in order to rent out individual rooms. The buildings were not meant to be highly profitable, but were a way for people of moderate means to supplement income or subsidize a unit in a brownstone beyond what they would otherwise be able to afford. While in the early twentieth century they were largely single white-collar and skilled blue-collar workers, by the 1940s roomers consisted of largely low-income singles and growing numbers of poor families. When the *Brooklyn Eagle* in 1952 ran a series of articles exposing the problem of slum housing in the borough, the newspaper was surprised to find local landlords barely one step above poor renter status themselves. When reporters following a tip crashed a dilapidated brownstone in Park Slope, they disappointingly confronted a young landlady in her twenties married to a GI. Having spent all their savings on the brownstone as an investment, the two found themselves financially in over their heads, overwhelmed by tenants, and unable to afford upkeep. "It is a firetrap," admitted the landlady, sobbing. "Come over here to the window and I'll show you more." Brownstone Brooklyn was not alone. Studies showed that small-time amateur landlords and local homeowners owned the majority of slum housing in Newark, New Jersey, and other older cities as well.[61]

In enclaves such as Boerum Hill and Carroll Gardens, this fluid relationship between class and tenure would later make for complex conflicts and coalitions in battles over gentrification. Brownstone renovators did not simply upgrade townhouses from poor to wealthy abodes. They often converted (or "restored," in their words) rented space to owned space. Other young, college-educated artists or bohemians who moved into a poorer district in search of cheap rents were of a higher social class than their ethnic landlords. The result was a confusing landscape in which white college-educated renters battled working-class landlords and poorer tenants fought eviction by guilt-ridden new middle-class brownstone owners. In the 1970s, a multiclass and interracial coalition of homeowners and landlords battled redlining in the area. A similarly diverse array of wealthy and poor renters battled to stop development projects in the area and to save rent control laws designed to prevent landlords from gouging tenants. The rise of the antigentrification movement in the late 1970s also led to unexpected clashes between ethnic working-class landlords enthusiastic about rising home prices and college-educated countercultural renters concerned about displacement of both themselves and the poor.

Along with celebrating its ethnic flavor and mixed class landscape, some new middle-class residents also looked to Brownstone Brooklyn's neighborhoods as spiritual, mystical, or sacred spaces that they contrasted to the institutional and rational spaces of modern downtown. Religion certainly was one of the most important spatial categories for Brooklynites prior to gentrification. In the "borough of churches," Brownstone Brooklyn in the 1950s was home to dozens of synagogues, churches, and chapels, dividing the area along religious lines. Park Slope alone had twenty-eight Protestant churches—Baptist, Lutheran, Methodist, Seventh-Day Adventist, a Spanish-language church, a Pentecostal church, and a Christian Science reading room—along with eight Catholic parishes, four synagogues, and a meeting place of the Brooklyn Society for Ethical Culture.[62] In an area populated largely by Catholics of Irish and Italian descent, the Catholic Church was central to the lives of Brownstone Brooklynites. Parochial schools were heavily attended. In Park Slope, 49.3 percent of children in 1959 attended the seven parochial schools in the district. Thirty percent of schoolchildren in Brooklyn Heights and Red Hook attended Catholic school.[63]

But if Brooklyn was a "sacred space," that religious sense of place was as abstract and institutional as it was romantically spiritual. With its centralized bureaucracy and clearly marked parish boundaries, the Catholic Church offered residents a clearly outlined religious map of Brownstone Brooklyn. Parishes were tightly defined administrative areas, each with a church and parochial school at its core. Moving from one parish to another—even within Brownstone Brooklyn—was a major ordeal that required children to change schools and parents to join a new church community. Catholic Brownstone Brooklynites in fact relied more often on parish boundaries than neighborhood names to orient themselves. In 1950, Catholic residents were as likely to identify themselves as living in "St. Saviour" or "St. Francis Xavier" as in Park Slope or Red Hook.[64]

While the area was largely Catholic, other significant groups maintained distinct religious spaces in Brownstone Brooklyn. Originally clustered downtown on Fulton Street, a diverse array of black churches followed migrants to Bedford-Stuyvesant. Elsewhere, Jewish, Maronite, Protestant, and Greek Orthodox residents lived scattered among Catholics of the same social class. Brooklyn Heights was home to some of the oldest churches in the country, such as Grace Church, founded in 1847, and Plymouth Church of the Pilgrims, founded in 1844. Next to the Brooklyn Bridge sat the massive national headquarters of the Jehovah's Witnesses. As the Witnesses expanded this massive institutional/sacred space during the 1950s and 1960s, they fought heated battles with Brooklyn Heights brownstone renovators and acted as one of the catalysts for the Heights anti-urban-renewal movement.[65]

When inventing Brownstone Brooklyn, thus, new middle-class pioneers drew from a richly legible landscape of preexisting places. But in drawing borders around enclaves such as Boerum Hill, new middle-class residents also transgressed other indigenous places. In an industrial cityscape with a large working class, an assortment of machine politicians, unions, organized crime syndicates, and street gangs divided the area into fiercely defended "turfs" and "corners." Many of the later conflicts between the new middle-class and poorer residents over gentrification were rooted in these conflicting conceptions of urban place.

Perhaps the most acrimonious battles in Brownstone Brooklyn over turf would be between new middle-class reformers and older machine politicians. In the 1940s and 1950s, one of the nation's largest and most powerful Democratic political machines in the country controlled the borough of Brooklyn, rivaled only by Tammany Hall in Manhattan and the machine of Cook County, Chicago. In Brownstone Brooklyn, the "regulars" handpicked the winners of nearly every local election. But rather than a top-down bureaucracy, the political machine was intimately linked to local place. Once a strictly centralized boroughwide organization ruled by a single boss, the Brooklyn machine began to loosen after 1930. With immigration restriction in 1924 cutting off the flow of its major constituency, New Deal programs limiting opportunities for patronage, civil service reform, and the advent of direct primaries, Brooklyn's political machine reshaped itself. By the 1950s, the machine was an elaborate feudal system of competing local clubs. A county boss sat uneasily atop a pyramid of assembly district leaders who formed the county executive committee. New rules in 1952 gave the committee the right to remove and replace the leader with a simple majority vote. Under Kings County Democratic party rules, district leaders were elected by voters during primaries. (The position was officially called "state committeeman.") In Brooklyn's large assembly districts, this meant that victorious leaders emerged from the most powerful of a coalition of smaller neighborhood clubs. Powerful clubs that gained control of district leadership rewarded supportive smaller clubs with patronage posts.

What gave a clubhouse its strength relative to other clubs was its ability to mobilize voters within its turf. In each turf, a local boss controlled a network of election district captains responsible for a cultivating a core group of loyal voters in an area of a few blocks with favors, job placements, personal relationships, and sometimes bribes. The Kings County machine was quite disciplined, but ferocious battles between clubs jockeying for power often disrupted the delicate feudal arrangement. In Brownstone Brooklyn, a network of Irish and Italian political clubhouses shared political power. While Frank Cunningham and other Irish politicians held most of the elected posts, they relied heavily on the support of Italian social and political clubs throughout the area. The Mazzini Democratic Club, headed by local boss James Mangano, was one of the area's most powerful.

Local clubs were highly personal and grassroots institutions. Effective clubhouses developed a sense of loyalty and social connection with voters. Politicians belonged to the local parish and fraternal organizations, such as the Knights of Columbus. They attended weddings, funerals, and bar mitzvahs. Precinct captains were raised in the neighborhood and knew their constituents as childhood friends. Machines were organized not around "issues" but around the immediate needs of local residents. Rather than debates about national issues or foreign policy forums, clubhouse politics consisted of local residents waiting to meet with a precinct captain to arrange for favors: a job on the waterfront or in city government, a liquor license for a bar, a visa for a relative, help dealing with a difficult landlord, or a call to a judge dealing with a mother's wayward teen in juvenile court.[66]

In a largely working-class area, unions were also important institutions that gave Brooklyn a sense of place. With over a million dues-paying members in New York City, according to some estimates, Brownstone Brooklyn in the 1940s and 1950s was home to a rich array of craft and industrial unions. While in some cities the divide between the two types of unions was strong, in New York City most blended the organizational structure of both. While their homes may have been in Red Hook or Park Slope, union members also described themselves as being members of Local 968 or Local 475, for example. The name not only was a bureaucratic category but also represented a spatial identity that unified neighborhood workers around a common occupational identity, a section of the waterfront or another landscape of production, a shared craft, an ethnic identity, family and kin, a union hall, or local bars and other hangouts.[67]

To describe Brownstone Brooklyn's unions and political machines as place-centric is not to romanticize an older working-class gemeinschaft. In fact, no union in the area was more powerful than the infamous International Longshoremen's Association (ILA). With almost twenty-two thousand members citywide, the ILA negotiated with shipping companies for wage increases and dispensed coveted unloading and loading jobs among the thousands of longshoremen daily along the waterfront. After a series of mergers of smaller locals in the early 1950s, Brooklyn's Local 1814, controlled by Anthony "Tough

Tony" Anastasia and later by his son-in-law Anthony Scotto, was the largest, with almost ten thousand members. One of the more corrupt organizations in 1940s and 1950s New York City, the local was widely feared by residents and linked to Brownstone Brooklyn's powerful organized crime network.[68]

Organized crime syndicates also ordered Brooklyn spatially and provided a sense of place. Although tempered in later decades by the formation of a waterfront commission and the shift to containerization, the Brooklyn waterfront in the 1940s and 1950s was a notorious nest of racketeering, pilfering, narcotics smuggling, and extortion. Until his assassination in a barber's chair, Albert Anastasia, Tough Tony's brother, and other mobsters controlled a powerful crime organization with ties to both the ILA and the local political machine. The relationship between the syndicate and the Brownstone Brooklyn was intimate and place-centric. Many mobsters belonged to local institutions such as the Longshoremen's Clerks and Checkers Social Club or the infamous City Democratic Club and knew residents personally. Many were also cruel thugs, maintaining power over the waterfront through fear and horrific violence. By the late 1960s, the links between organized crime and the waterfront became more complex. Anthony Scotto, linked to the Anastasia family by marriage, was a college-educated supporter of Mayor John Lindsay who, after inheriting the union from his late father-in-law, genuinely hoped to modernize the ILA and shed its Mafia image. Yet he remained inextricably tied to organized crime.[69]

Teenage street gangs also offered their own map of Brownstone Brooklyn. With one of the highest rates of gang membership in the city, Brownstone Brooklyn was the epicenter of a nationwide postwar epidemic of juvenile delinquency. A host of factors—rising unemployment, racial transition and battles over turf, the absence of male role models as young adult men left to fight in World War II and Korea, alcohol, and eventually devastating heroin use—contributed to the rise of about a thousand youth gangs in New York during the decade after the war. With colorful names, including the Chaplains, the Apaches, the Mau-maus, the South Brooklyns, and the Gowanus Boys, the gangs of postwar Brownstone Brooklyn engaged in ferocious battles throughout the area. Gangs were intimately connected to local place. Small groups of teenagers laid claim to a block or corner, opened a clubhouse, marked territory with graffiti and other signs, and often rumbled with other groups who invaded their space.[70]

These multiple turfs interconnected at nodes in Brownstone Brooklyn's landscape. On street corners and in bars, candy stores, local restaurants, social clubs, and storefront meeting halls, union activity, political machines, and gang life came together.[71] In his memoir, Pete Hamill describes one of these focal points in working-class Park Slope:

In the center, of course, was Rattigan's, directly across the street, packed and smoky. . . . [Inside] were bar tabs or messages, tickets for racetracks or ballparks left by local politicians.

They give you a racetrack ticket, my father explained, and you give them a vote. It's a good deal. . . .

Presiding over the place was a huge man named Patty Rattigan, round-faced and balding, like a pink version of the Jolly Green Giant. He had a generous heart, a thick brogue, a job in the borough president's office, and proud membership in the Democratic party. Patty wasn't simply a saloon-keeper. He helped find jobs for customers or their sons. He loaned them money. He threw out crazy people. He loved singing and food and men drinking on summer afternoons.[72]

In the wealthier enclaves of Brooklyn Heights and northern Park Slope, few adhered to the working-class turfs delineated by political machines, unions, and street gangs. With quieter streets and an indoor social life, most wealthier residents looked askance at the "hanging-out" street culture of the poorer areas nearby. But the line between wealthy and poor was blurred. Turfs over-lapped, leading to class and spatial tensions. Brooklyn Heights was home to many hotels and bars where late-night revelers sparked the ire of residents. "Many 'wolves' roam Brooklyn Heights annoying Little Red Riding Hoods," complained the *Brooklyn Heights Press* in 1944 of the sailors hanging out in the area and making advances on Heights women. "Some of these 2-legged ani-mals stalk their prey on quiet street corners, others prefer to 'put on the dog' and attempt enticing 'sweet young things' in hotel lobbies." In their quest to shut down noisy establishments, white-collar professionals clashed with local police and judges. Defending the right of party-goers to "have some fun once in a while," for example, one Italian American magistrate blasted a petition from the Brooklyn Heights Association to punish nine men who noisily marched through the neighborhood drunk after a employee mutual aid asso-ciation dinner. Perhaps the "most sensitive," sneered the judge, should "move up to Westchester or out to Montauk Point."[73]

What was Brownstone Brooklyn? In analyzing its multiple layers of people and buildings, one gets a three-dimensional picture of the area before gentri-fication. From a bird's-eye view, the area appeared to be spilt into zones. Brownstone Brooklyn was a place where people came to work. Around its edge, the waterfront bustled with longshoremen unloading goods and workmen fixing ships at the Navy Yard. Along the coast and the Gowanus Canal, an industrial district housed an assortment of light manufacturing firms. Near the Brooklyn Bridge, the central business district held government buildings, corporate headquarters, banks, and factories. Brownstone Brooklyn was a place where people lived. White-collar professionals lived in the Gold Coasts of Brooklyn Heights, Park Slope, and west of Fort Greene. Tall luxury apartment buildings hugged Prospect Park and Montague Street, providing the wealthy with magnificent views. Next to the Gold Coasts lay an impoverished belt of brownstones and tenements in which the descendants of Italian, Irish, and other immigrants lived among a growing African American and Puerto Rican population in apartments and rooming houses. Running along Fulton Street to Bedford-Stuyvesant was the borough's black belt, which was increasingly impoverished but also beginning to rival Manhattan's Harlem as New York's center for African American culture. But rather than flat zones, Brownstone Brooklyn was a layered palimpsest. Industry meshed with residential areas. The poor often lived mere blocks away or even on the same block as the wealthy. Enclaves retained the historic buildings, ethnic institutions, elderly residents, legends, and memories from previous waves of migration and economic restructuring.

As a polycultural, polycentric, and polyhistorical cityscape, Brownstone Brooklyn certainly appeared to be an urban wilderness. It is precisely these "wild" characteristics that made the area a rich text for new middle-class pioneers to selectively read as a source of authenticity. A new middle class seeking affordable housing and a cultural alternative to the postwar modern landscape would reimagine this landscape as "authentic." These buildings and institutions—the brownstone, the industrial loft, the machine politician, the street gang, and the waterfront bar—would be the props for a new urban middle-class drama of local place. Brooklyn's landscape would also shape the self-conception of new arrivals. As they came into contact with urban political machines, African American migrants, street gangs, and historic buildings, they formed a new urban middle-class identity on the urban frontier.

2 Concord Village

On April 1, 1951, Concord Village officially opened its doors to the public. Steps away from the entrance to Brooklyn Bridge, the new apartment complex presented a striking contrast to Brownstone Brooklyn's aging landscape. A clearing in a thicket of crowded tenements and aging townhouses, three gleaming fifteen-story rectangular towers with 478 light-filled apartments and ten professional suites stood amid manicured lawns, parking facilities, and a modern shopping complex. While the rest of Brownstone Brooklyn suffered from oppressive traffic and constant noise, Concord Village offered a new streetscape that sheltered residents from the bustle of city life. An enclosed park with green grass and paved walkways surrounded the three towers. In contrast to Brownstone Brooklyn's small, congested city blocks, multilane streets bordered the development's superblocks, allowing traffic to flow smoothly around the complex without violating the tranquility of the interior. Adjacent to downtown Brooklyn and a one-stop train ride to lower Manhattan, Concord Village targeted white-collar professionals seeking attractive housing close to work. The public responded enthusiastically, and by 1957 the complex expanded to seven buildings with almost a thousand families.[1]

Concord Village's advertisements boasted of more than simply new apartments. In a blighted and chaotic urban jungle, the scientifically planned complex offered residents the liberating potential of modernity. Soaring away from the earth into the sky, the three towers covered only 18 percent of the grounds, bathing the apartments in light and air. Roof terraces offered unbroken views in every direction. Banks of "most modern" elevators gave residents the power to move quickly and effortlessly though space. "Streamlined" steel kitchens with Frigidaires, tile floors, and Micarta countertops were impervious to rust or decay. Twenty-four-hour doorman service and laundries kept the building fully functional no matter the time of day.

Mechanically ventilated air made interiors impermeable to changes in weather. Professional landscapers kept the immaculate grounds immune to changes in season. Elegant music by Muzak played twenty-four hours a day in the lobbies and laundry room offered lab-tested relief from cacophonic street noise. If Brooklyn's surrounding landscape was mired in obsolescence,

Concord Village in May 2010. (Photograph taken by author)

Concord Village's towers symbolically broke free from the constraints of space and time.[2]

On the periphery of Concord Village, the residents of Brooklyn Heights watched the expanding apartment development with apprehension. While a host of business-oriented civic groups supported the modernization of downtown, most residents of the aging Gold Coast saw in the complex only the frightening specter of Manhattanization. Although demolition had been quick, construction was slow, held up by red tape and poor planning. For years, a scar of empty, treeless space cut across the landscape. Piles of rubbish sat in dust-strewn empty lots. Riveting guns noisily thundered during the day. "Big Red," an eight-story crane, towered over commuters as they left the Jay Street train station and scurried home in the evenings. Heights residents watched sadly as 250 low-income renters marched futilely to the First District Municipal Court to protest their eviction. While advertisements boasted of modern amenities and light-filled apartments, the rectangular towers looked sterile and boxy. As developers talked of renewal projects, a newly formed preservation group looked protectively at the smattering of old brownstones and tenements sitting in the shadows of the expanding apartment complex. In one of those buildings, members lamented, Walt Whitman had printed *Leaves of Grass*. Would a Transcendentalist sanctuary be swallowed by an expanding Concord Village?[3]

Manhattanization as both fact and symbol is crucial to the history of gentrification. If the previous chapter described what Brownstone Brooklyn was, Concord Village represented what Brownstone Brooklyn was not. The neoromantic impulse that inspired new middle-class gentrifiers formed as a reaction to an imagined modern city of office towers, highways, and public housing emerging after World War II. While postwar developers championed the rational technological future, the new middle class celebrated Brownstone Brooklyn's "diverse" present and "historic" past.[4]

Yet Brownstone Brooklyn was more than symbolically linked to the modern city. The glass-sheathed towers and institutional buildings of the central business district embodied a new postindustrial landscape to which Brooklyn's new middle class was inextricably tied both economically and socially. The white-collar professionals, artists, writers, and academics cultivating the "historic" neighborhoods of Brownstone Brooklyn worked in the corporate headquarters, research universities, medical centers, and media conglomerates of high-rise Manhattan and downtown Brooklyn. Concord Village and Brownstone Brooklyn were twin products of the same economic restructuring. Rather than threatening to destroy Brownstone Brooklyn's authenticity, Manhattanization gave birth to it.

Manhattanization referred to more than a few isolated construction projects. The threat of "Manhattan" for Brownstone Brooklyn residents in the 1950s specifically referred to a massive program of modernist urban redevelopment that transformed New York City after World War II. Led by a progrowth coalition of city planners, banks, insurance companies, universities, unions, municipal agencies, civic groups, and hospital boards, developers aided by millions of federal urban renewal dollars demolished large swaths of the cityscape to build modern apartments, offices, convention centers, and roadways. Small commuter schools expanded into major universities with new lab facilities and dormitories. Hospitals grew from small health care facilities into massive urban research centers. The city ambitiously bulldozed new expressways through cramped neighborhoods, opened a new airport, and modernized dozens of bridges and tunnels. New public housing towers replaced tenements and townhouses. Corporations built new skyscraper headquarters surrounded by open plazas. Unions built high-rise middle-income cooperatives. By 1970, the city's landscape had been dramatically transformed. A modern city with windswept plazas, glass-encased office buildings, superblocks, concrete apartment towers, and massive research centers expanded across an older industrial landscape of small blocks, townhouses, small factories, and lofts.[5]

No section of the city was Manhattanized more than Brownstone Brooklyn. Concord Village was only the first completed section of a colossal development project in the borough's downtown. In 1945, the New York City Planning Commission released its plan for Brooklyn's Civic Center: an enormous complex of government buildings, apartment towers, and research facilities stretching from the Brooklyn Bridge to Borough Hall. Blueprints proposed bold changes to the area's rusty landscape. Having recently torn down the Fulton elevated train, the city would condemn and demolish fifty-eight acres of factories, lofts, hotels, and townhouses. Replacing the area's tangled mess of decaying buildings and congested streets, Brooklyn's Civic Center was to be open, clean, and geometric. Like a Parisian boulevard, a widened Adams Street would cut through the obsolete street grid, allowing traffic to flow smoothly from the interior of the borough to the Brooklyn Bridge and the new and majestic Brooklyn-Queens Expressway. Small parks would provide residents with oases of clean air and green grass. A complex of modern government facilities surrounded by open plazas would bring order and efficiency to the messy smattering of lofts, warehouses, and cheap hotels that clogged the central business district.[6] "This Civic Center is to Brooklyn what the great cathedral and opera plazas are to European cities," boasted city construction coordinator Robert Moses in 1955. "When the great Court House doors are thrown open, when the Heights frontage is cleared, when the bottleneck to Borough Hall is widened, when small patches of intervening park are green, when the avenues to the expressways and boulevards are traveled, the Civic Center will be as much the pride of Brooklyn as the Piazza San Marco is the pride of Venice and the Place de la Concorde the cynosure of Paris." For the next twenty years, the city slowly built the Civic Center, demolishing more than three hundred buildings over 130 acres at a cost of over $125 million in public and private funds.[7]

City leaders hoped that the new Civic Center would be the cornerstone for a broader renewal of the central business district. "Today, the noises of building mix with those of demolition to create a polyphonic hymn to progress," exclaimed a *New York Times* editorial in 1955. "The Civic Center will be a piece of a modern city, a concentration of public works designed to attract private works to its periphery." Steps away from Concord Village, the New York City Housing Authority opened the 3,500-unit Fort Greene and 1,390-unit Farragut public housing complexes in 1944 and 1952 with the goal of providing modern and affordable flats to low-income residents. Across Flatbush Avenue from the Civic Center, Robert Moses' Slum Clearance Committee in 1952 bulldozed twenty acres of "unsanitary cold water tenements, factories, vacant lots, junk yards and automotive services" as part of a Fort Greene Title I urban renewal plan. Creating three new superblocks, Moses hoped to subsidize the expansion of Long Island University and Brooklyn Hospital, the opening of a new shopping center, and the erection of two middle-income housing apartment developments. Nearby in another urban renewal site, the city razed forty acres around Pratt Institute for the development of new dormitories, three high-rise limited-equity co-ops, and a rental apartment tower. In 1962 the City Planning Commission began preliminary discussions for a $150 million Atlantic Terminal urban renewal plan that would relocate the Fort Greene Meat Market and demolish dilapidated buildings for modern low- and middle-income housing. By 1968, the city had constructed or assisted in constructing more than 130 apartment buildings, totaling more than thirteen thousand units, for low- and middle-income tenants in Brownstone Brooklyn.[8]

Concord Village and the Civic Center formed a striking addition to Brooklyn's palimpsest. "Downtown glistens," gushed the *New York Times* in 1955. "The recent history of downtown Brooklyn has been written by steam shovels and riveting guns." Like the farmhouses, brownstones, and early-century apartment towers that preceded it, Manhattanization created a new and legible layer of text that Brownstone Brooklyn's new middle class creatively interpreted. Incoming residents of brownstone enclaves such as Brooklyn Heights and Cobble Hill would describe a modern city that was "impersonal," "abstract," "alienating," or "inauthentic." Others referred to an "organizational bureau-cracy," "technocracy," "papa institution," "the system," or simply "the city." In contrast, they would describe Brownstone Brooklyn as "local," "decentralized," "grassroots," and "historically diverse." If Brownstone Brooklyn offered a sense of place, Concord Village, the Civic Center, and urban renewal superblocks represented a landscape of sameness, or simply a non-place.[9]

One must be wary in using the term "modern city." Concord Village and surrounding buildings did not form a landscape of sameness. Although the austere geometric buildings and open plazas looked uniform, no monolithic ideology underlay this design. The groups who spearheaded urban redevelop-ment in Brooklyn were an eclectic pro-growth coalition of idealistic housing reformers, tax-hungry city officials, rapacious luxury apartment developers, nonprofit hospital and university directors, union activists, and civil rights leaders. With leaders as varied as *Brooklyn Eagle* editor Cleveland Rodgers, labor leader and cooperative housing advocate Abraham Kazan, real estate devel-oper Robert Zeckendorf, and city construction czar Robert Moses, Brooklyn's redevelopment drew support from groups such as the American Labor party, Long Island University, the United Housing Foundation, the Republican party, and the National Urban League. Contradictory goals motivated this hodge-podge of private and public developers. Public housing advocates hoped to replace Brooklyn's slum housing with modern, affordable apartments for low-income families. Business leaders hoped to revive economic activity down-town with new offices and modern transportation arteries. Retail establishments hoped to attract suburbanites increasingly dependent on cars. Universities and hospitals hoped to modernize and expand their facilities. Union leaders hoped to build subsidized high-rise co-ops that would provide affordable housing and a possible alternative to the rapacious real estate market. City bursars hoped to boost property values and increase tax revenues. All were inspired by a mix of philanthropic zeal, civic duty, self-preservation, a desire to revive the economic vitality of the city core, and a search for raw profit in a tight housing market. Some neighborhood groups supported redevelopment as well. In the early 1960s, local churches, tenants' groups, and business leaders anxious about decline formed grassroots groups such as the University-Clinton Area Renewal Effort (U-CARE) and the Downtown Area Renewal Effort (DARE) to support redevelopment and rehabilitation efforts as well.[10]

Despite its bureaucratic and institutional ambiance, the Civic Center and surrounding residential towers were in fact a diverse patchwork of small pro-jects realized incrementally over many years. A consortium of sixteen local saving banks funded Concord Village. Developer and trustee Robert Zeckend-orf donated funds for Long Island University's expansion. The nonprofit

United Housing Foundation, led by labor union leaders, subsidized a complex of middle-income co-ops. The New York City Housing Authority built and administered the low-income housing projects. The federal and state governments appropriated funds for the new courthouses and prisons. Robert Moses stood at the nexus, recruiting each of the developers and masterfully coordinating their projects to fit into an integrated whole.[11]

While Le Corbusier and the Congrès International d'Architecture Moderne (CIAM) influenced many individual designers, the modern city had no single architectural vision. The Civic Center had its antecedents in the National Mall in Washington, D.C., and other civic spaces of the City Beautiful movement. Benjamin Braunstein, the architect of Concord Village, built his career designing modest red brick garden apartments in outer Queens. While turning to Modernist architects, the business leaders, union officials, and city planners who spearheaded Brooklyn's pro-growth coalition were self-acclaimed realists who were pointedly anti-intellectual and openly hostile to abstraction. "Dreamers' plans [are] too far removed from the mainstream of urban political life," charged future New York State Urban Development Corporation director Edward Logue, "too many theoretical planners prefer the applause of elegant critics to the earthier appreciation of politicians who ha[ve] to try to carry out the plans and get re-elected too." Robert Moses spent his career blasting "long-haired planners," "eunuchs" who sit in ivory towers, and "subsidized lamas in their remote mountain temples [sheltered from] those who must work in the marketplace." "[I've] developed a healthy contempt for the kind of water-color planning which consists of splashing green paint on a map and labeling the resulting blobs as 'open areas,' 'greenbelts,' 'breathing-spaces,'" Moses angrily shouted at the City Planning Commission. "Actual accomplishments in New York City since 1934 . . . were bought about by people who labored day and night for limited objectives in the face of great difficulties . . . not by itinerant carpet-bag experts splashing at a ten-league canvas with brushes of comet's hair."[12]

"The Plan for the Brooklyn Civic Center and Downtown Area is not a visionary picture of the glorified 'City Beautiful' type," insisted borough president John Cashmore. "It is a practical, realistic program to provide adequately for the movements of existing and future traffic, to make available desirable sites for necessary public buildings and to clear away blight and restore property values, on which the city depends for revenue, by encouraging private enterprise to participate in the redevelopment of the section in conformity to a comprehensive, integrated plan."[13]

While much of the architecture was influenced by high modernism, the subsidized apartments and civic buildings of the Civic Center were also the spatial expression of New Deal liberalism. As they bulldozed brownstones and lofts, leaders of urban redevelopment such as city planning czar Robert Moses and later Edward Logue brought a faith in government regulation, pragmatic experimentation, and human ingenuity. They saw themselves as hard-nosed public servants able to cut through red tape to "get things done." They championed the power of human rationality and expertise to devise immediate, measurable solutions to existing problems. Like the Modernist architects they hired, New Deal liberals harbored a mistrust of the speculative housing market, which they blamed for run-down, dense neighborhoods with exorbitant rents. But they viewed planning as a process of experimentation rather than an imposition of an abstract master plan on the city. "Every approach to the task of preparing a master plan . . . must be made in a spirit of experimentation," explained *Brooklyn Eagle* editor and City Planning Commission member Cleveland Rodgers. "The evolving plan should be based on reasonable expectations of a continuance of discernible trends, untinged by fantasy. Utopias remained unrealized because they are creations of dreamers and idealists undisturbed by hard reality." "It is easy enough for starry-eyed planners to make pretty pictures of wholesale slum clearance," exploded Moses at a critic. "The real job is to find responsible public officials who will do something concrete, if necessary on a small scale, which will actually tear down the tenements, widen the streets, and provide not only better living conditions for those lucky enough to get into the new houses, but facilities and improvements for an entire neighborhood."[14]

The modern city, however, remained a salient political and cultural landscape for both proponents and critics. While their motives may have been diverse, the developers of Concord Village and the Civic Center shared a unified faith in modernity as the solution to the city's ills. The new landscape embodied a modern urban ideal that sought newness, mobility, impermeability, disposability, and openness; a modern political ideal, rooted in the Progressive movement and New Deal liberalism, that was both pan–New York City and Manhattan-centric, seeking both to centralize authority in the executive branch and to integrate local governments into a rational metropolitan system; and a modern architecture that favored functional design, geometric form, smooth surfaces, new technology, open space, light, and bigness. But most important, the modern city was *becoming* rather than *being*, with new constantly replacing old, difference integrating into a universal whole, and human agency facilitating the inevitable march of progress.[15]

If Concord Village and the modern city it represented appeared a contrast to its older surroundings, it was intentionally so. Postwar redevelopers offered their own skewed textual reading of the postwar cityscape. As they devised clearance plans for Brooklyn, they set up a series of binaries that new middle-class activists would later invert. Rather than offering a sense of place, Brownstone Brooklyn was for postwar redevelopers a non-place. Instead of a collection of traditional neighborhoods, the Victorian townhouses, tenements, and lofts surrounding the Civic Center were slums. The idea that slums were a problem to be solved was not a new one. Brooklyn's redevelopers belonged to a long tradition of urban reformers dating to the Progressive era who sought to build model housing for the poor, control industrial pollution, preserve light and space between buildings, and alleviate traffic congestion. The modern city, however, was built to tackle a fundamentally different problem than city planners of the past.

While Progressive reformers had fretted about an inner city overcrowded with industry and immigrants, postwar city planners worried about the effects of decentralization on Brooklyn. In meetings, master plans, and reports, city leaders worried about a city losing its lifeblood to the suburbs. While some reformers in the 1920s had championed suburbanization as an antidote to urban congestion, postwar city leaders agonized that out-migration was destroying downtown. Factories abandoned the crowded lofts of the central city for spacious new plants on the city's periphery. Young World War II veterans and their families left the city in droves, buying single-family tract homes in newer, cheaper, and more modern suburban developments. New peripheral shopping centers threatened the vitality of downtown department stores. Once the nucleus of a unified city, downtown was rapidly hemorrhaging, with fatal ramifications for urban America. "The physical decline of the older sections of our cities and the dispersion of their populations, taking industries and retail businesses with them to the suburbs and countryside, are too plain even to [the] casual observer to need statistical proof," explained a prominent real estate fund director. "[The] result [is] in shattered realty values, threatened mortgage investment, inefficiently utilized schools and utilities, tax delinquency, and a host of other difficulties." Postwar cities were like sickly "trees," complained *Fortune* magazine, "decaying at the core while growing wider and wider."[16]

Across a landscape that a new middle class would later commemorate as historic, liberal planners and Modernist architects saw only the specter of obsolescence. While a changing economy demanded new forms of transportation and facilities, Brooklyn remained saddled with a heavy and aging infrastructure from an earlier era. "Obsolete" soon became a city planning buzzword. "The street system is obsolete," complained planner Clarence Stein about New York City in 1943, "[with] insufficient space for parking and loading, or for workers' autos. . . . A large number of the factories are obsolete and wastefully planned, as well as dark and ill ventilated. Antiquated methods, obsolete machinery, and non-progressive management are other handicaps."[17]

If obsolescence was a terminal illness, Brooklyn's physical symptoms were characterized as "blight." While reformers had used the plant disease metaphor to loosely describe general urban ills since the 1910s, postwar planners employed the term to describe a specific locale: the wilting industrial landscape of nineteenth-century tenements, brownstones, lofts, and warehouses that in the 1940s still formed the core of American central business districts. It was a striking rereading of the Victorian cityscape. For turn-of-the-century reformers, teeming and volatile slums represented the frightening face of modernity and the unbridled expansion of industrial America. But to postwar planners, the blighted cityscape was fatally anachronistic. It retained the skeleton of a once vibrant economy, but with that economy now defunct, it slowly wasted away. "Blight has crept through Downtown, turning parts of it into a ghost town," complained the *New York Times*. "Where majestic clippers once were moored, piers are decaying. Narrow and filthy streets, east side and west side, are lined with decrepit structures, acre after acre of three, four or five-story buildings, often with seedy stores or offices in the ground floor and nothing but blind windows above. Some of them are good for dead storage; many are good for nothing at all."[18] Complacent city leaders should take "walks through the slums, up the stinking stairways into the overcrowded, shabby rooms," warned Edward Logue, "walks through the run-down commercial areas, taking care to glance above the first-floor store fronts at the dusty windows of the deserted upper floors; walks though the oil-soaked, dreary factory lofts built before the assembly line was even heard of. The filth, the misery and the danger are all there—easy to see and, once seen, impossible to forget."[19]

No inner-city area appeared more blighted than Brownstone Brooklyn. The residential areas had obsolete housing that was a breeding ground for disease, crime, and juvenile delinquency. In the three census health areas that made up the area north of the Civic Center, more than 20 percent of the buildings had inadequate plumbing facilities. If one excluded new city public housing, the percentages were even higher. The juvenile delinquency rates in Brooklyn Heights, Park Slope, Red Hook, and Fort Greene were 50 to 150 percent higher than the borough average; tuberculosis rates and infant mortality rates were the highest in the borough. A 1943 study of Fort Greene by the Welfare Council of New York City found that 5,499 apartments in a single seven-block area had no bath or toilet facilities and fifty-seven had no running water. After a horrific fire in 1952 killed seven Puerto Rican women and children living illegally in an 1890 Bedford-Stuyvesant tenement, a special committee led by Robert Moses complained that the borough's aging buildings were dangerous firetraps and needed to be razed. "Unless something is done, Park Slope is doomed to be stricken by the deadly 'blight disease,'" concluded the *Brooklyn Eagle* in 1949 in a series about the borough's housing crisis.[20]

Of all of the miserable housing stock surrounding the central business district, no building type appeared more dilapidated than the ubiquitous brownstone. Subdivided into rooming houses and railroad flats, the antiquated townhouses were dark, crowded, and equipped with faulty plumbing and wires. "The [brownstone] was once a proud possession of one family," explained a 1959 report by the Pratt Institute Planning Department studying 120 blocks in what would later be called Boerum Hill. "Today the converted brownstone has become a rooming house, whole families occupy each one of its 8 or 9 rooms for which they pay a Park Avenue rental and provide an exorbitant income to an absentee landlord." Planners pointed to brownstones as a citywide problem. "Standing in solid rows, using every foot of frontage, even the best brownstone house districts are today potential slums," warned Cleveland Rodgers. "[Tenements] were at least designed for multiple-family use; brownstone houses were not, and the absence of courts and yards leaves no open space for children or grownups."[21]

Business leaders, union officials, and city planners lamented that Brownstone Brooklyn was economically defunct as well. Manufacturing firms complained of antiquated machinery, insufficient parking facilities, and clogged roadways. With households and industry increasingly dependent on cars and freight, horrendous traffic overwhelmed a street grid designed for horse and buggy. As cars became mass consumer items, thousands of first-time motorists raced down city blocks with poor signage and no streetlights, making the simple act of crossing the street increasingly deadly for Brooklyn's "dodgers." According to one 1940 study, one-fifth of New York State's auto accidents occurred in the borough. With mounting casualties on Brownstone Brooklyn's narrow blocks, a local newspaper habitually begged in bold print for new car owners to drive carefully: "WHETHER YOU WALK OR WHETHER YOU DRIVE—THE IMPORTANT THING IS TO STAY ALIVE"; "EVEN WHEN THE LIGHT IS GREEN, LOOK OUT FOR THE RECKLESS DRIVER COMING FROM THE LEFT OR RIGHT WHO IS IGNORING THE RED LIGHT AGAINST HIM"; "THE REAL PUBLIC ENEMY NO. 1 IS A FOUR WHEELED GANGSTER—THE AUTOMOBILE. KEEP IT UNDER CONTROL." With few regulations and fewer garages, a glut of parked cars clogged alleyways, sidewalks, and narrow streets. One 1940 study showed that on average 42 percent of cars in downtown Brooklyn were parked illegally. Traffic, warned the Institute of Traffic Engineers in 1949, was disintegrating the city as thoroughly as an atom bomb. "Both of these powerful forces have the same effect in scattering the population, only the explosive qualities of the bomb operate more quickly."[22]

In addition to declaring it physically and economically defunct, good government reformers complained that the "blighted" district was politically obsolete. The scattered industries still operating in Brownstone Brooklyn's lofts and warehouses used outdated managerial techniques. In 1953, the interstate Waterfront Crime Commission described a Brownstone Brooklyn waterfront of rotting piers where violent organized crime syndicates controlled a network of bribery, racketeering, and pilfering. Manufacturing firms complained that equipment needed updating and union regulations limited corporate flexibility and kept wages artificially high. Others blamed an archaic government structure too cumbersome and inflexible to adjust to the changing times. Political machines were parochial and unimaginative. Local bosses had neither the desire nor the capacity to think broadly about the city's future, instead concentrating on handing out kickbacks to loyal constituents.[23]

The concept of "blight" had a pernicious racial connotation as well. Since the turn of the century, African Americans had been migrating from the rural South and Caribbean to New York in search of work and to escape discrimination. With increased wartime demand for labor in the city and the mechanization of southern agriculture, black migration to the urban North rose dramatically after World War II. As Puerto Rico industrialized in the 1940s and '50s, rural Puerto Ricans migrated in great numbers to New York City as well. The rapid influx of African Americans and Puerto Ricans dramatically changed the ethnic makeup of New York and other major cities. While the white population dropped by half a million, between 1940 and 1960 New York's black population rose from 458,000 to 1 million. In the same period, the number of Puerto Ricans rose from 70,000 to 720,000. In other cities, the numbers were even more dramatic.[24] As both African Americans and Puerto Ricans arrived in the borough, many settled in the ring of tenements and townhouses that surrounded downtown Brooklyn. In the name of clearing blight, planners often deliberately targeted the homes of the nonwhite poor. Without a vigorous redevelopment and public housing program, Brooklyn was in danger of becoming a "slum colony," warned the president of the Downtown Brooklyn Association in 1958. "We have talked endlessly about the Puerto Rican problem. It would seem to me the time has arrived to stop talking and to do something about the problem."[25]

Concord Village and the Civic Center thus represented an intentional contrast to a Brownstone Brooklyn that developers saw as terminally ill. But the modern city was not only born out of pessimism. If they built the complex in deliberate contrast to Victorian brownstones and narrow streets, the developers of Concord Village hoped to replicate a gleaming landscape emerging across the river: midtown Manhattan.

There was much for city reformers to be excited about. Out of the ashes of the old industrial city, a new and vibrant midtown Manhattan central business district was rising. Almost two hundred office buildings rose in Manhattan from 1946 to 1966, dramatically changing the landscape. Private developers added 604 mostly luxury apartment buildings with over 82,000 units. By 1970, mile-long phalanxes of imposing towers ran down Third, Fifth, and Park avenues. When in 1955 Chase Manhattan Bank announced plans for a new skyscraper headquarters in the aging financial district, construction took off in lower Manhattan as well. A few pioneering developers even erected several new apartments in Brownstone Brooklyn along Prospect Park and in Brooklyn Heights. New York City was not alone. After a decade of stasis during the Depression, downtown districts from Los Angeles to Baltimore similarly experienced a dramatic postwar real estate boom.[26]

Critics called it Manhattanization. But the city leaders who built Concord Village and Civic Center only saw the signs of rebirth. The new obliterated the old. Developers demolished run-down brownstones and tenements to build new high-rise buildings and skyscrapers. Wrecking balls smashed the luxury apartment buildings of Park Avenue to make room for scores of office towers. In other places, the modern city swallowed the older landscape. Contractors stripped older high-rises of their brick and stucco surfaces, leaving only the steel skeleton. They then enveloped the naked structure with new glass and metal skin.[27]

The rise of Manhattan's midtown business district depended heavily on high public demand. Despite the trend of suburbanization, the inner city remained a hot commodity. For many businessmen, a gleaming glass-encased office tower in the center city was a symbol of prestige and power. New buildings had cutting-edge technology such as air-conditioning, fluorescent lighting, and acoustical tile ceilings. A central location offered quick face-to-face communication with lawyers, architects, designers, and competing firms. Employees enjoyed convenient access to stores, clubs, and theaters. As companies clamored for office space, developers could not erect buildings fast enough to meet the demand. In 1956, the national office building occupancy rate was 97 percent. In New York, the vacancy rate was a tiny 1.24 percent. Luxury apartment buildings too were wildly popular. Renters paid premium prices for prestigious central city units with light and magnificent views.[28]

But midtown represented something more to planners than just new skyscrapers. The emerging central business district marked the birth of a new postindustrial economy. Commentators at the time called it a "white-collar revolution," others a "research revolution." In gleaming skyscrapers, government buildings, and research complexes, an expanding labor force of clerks, lawyers, accountants, students, writers, and publicity agents worked in a vast network of financial, legal, media, and academic institutions. The numbers were astonishing. While manufacturing employment dropped by 25 percent, between 1955 and 1970 New York City's service industry employment rose by 46 percent, finance, insurance, and real estate employment by 36 percent, and government by 44 percent. New York was not exceptional. As early as 1950, white-collar workers made up about 50 percent of the total employment in Boston, Washington, D.C., and Hartford. San Francisco most closely mirrored New York's transformation, with its banking employment doubling in the 1950s. By 1960, the nation's white-collar workers outnumbered blue-collar ones, and the white-collar workforce continued to grow.[29]

The white-collar revolution was not a countertrend to decentralization, planners argued, but part of the same economic restructuring. The same factors that depleted the center city of manufacturing spurred the centralization of administration and corporate services. As new technology made possible the geographic dispersal of production facilities, corporations increasingly found it necessary to centralize and expand administrative functions to coordinate regional, national, and international operations. Shrinking as a site of production, midtown was expanding as a command-and-control center for a scattered network of bank branches, retail outlets, production plants, and distributors.[30]

While the old industrial economy was increasingly mobile, midtown's new abstract economy in skyscrapers and labs was linked intimately to local place. As new transportation and communication technology allowed goods-based factories to move to cheap land on the periphery, idea-based offices with increasingly large and more complex administrative departments found it increasingly necessary to locate their offices downtown. White-collar firms, unlike factories, did not earn profit from efficient physical plants; rather, they depended on immediate access to information and a pool of skilled labor. While an industrial plant was self-sufficient, an office required a corollary network of lawyers, researchers, and bankers. Downtown provided instant financial news, exposure to national media outlets, and quick air and rail travel. Drawn to its museums, fashionable department stores, theaters, and bars, an unlimited pool of young talent, particularly young single women, provided an abundant labor force. Even though a suburban office park might have been cheaper, the advantages of locating downtown offset the high costs of inner-city real estate.[31]

Deindustrialization sparked not only the centralization of management but also its expansion. As factories scattered throughout the region, management became increasingly elaborate, requiring more negotiations, contracting and subcontracting, up-to-date information, paperwork, and calculations. Regional, national, and international corporations required a massive white-collar army of managers, lawyers, accountants, and advertisers to coordinate and integrate their multiple operations. Corporate headquarters demanded services from a corollary network of finance, real estate, insurance, and legal firms. Since the advent of the New Deal, a growing public sector regulated national and transnational corporations, administered an expansive and increasingly complex tax code, and directed entitlement programs. Government offices became one of the city's major employers of white-collar labor. New federal, state, and city agencies, the United Nations, and the Federal Reserve opened headquarters in the city, requiring huge numbers of accountants, clerks, lawyers, and secretaries. Expanding offices relied on an emerging mass-media market of publishers, news outlets, television stations, and advertising agencies increasingly clustered in the central business district. Foundations, universities, and research hospitals received generous grants from both corporations and government to conduct research and development projects, as well as train young graduates for the white-collar army.[32]

Of the 500 largest corporations in 1958, 139 had headquarters in New York City. The city was the nation's premier financial center, with billions passing yearly between securities exchanges, national banks, and insurance companies. Home to 110 literary agencies, the country's two largest book wholesalers, 306 publishing houses, 177 national magazine editorial offices, the three major television networks, 180 art galleries, and Broadway, New York was the nation's center for mass media. With 27 percent of the nation's foundations, collectively holding 56 percent of all foundation assets, New York was the capital of charity and social science research as well.[33]

Elated by soaring buildings and profits, the pro-growth coalition who spearheaded the redevelopment of Brooklyn spoke optimistically of the city's future. Even if industry moved to the suburbs, downtown remained the administrative core that held together the disparate parts. They used a series of geographic and political metaphors to emphasize the city's central importance in a rapidly diffusing world. New York City was a "capital," a "mecca," a "center." "New York has become the undisputed theater, opera and music and sports center of the nation," boasted Robert Moses in 1955, "the greatest urban educational center in the country . . . Great companies have made New York a management center." "This is the largest commercial construction program in all human history," proclaimed Real Estate Board of New York president Edmund Thomas, "and in effort it surpasses that of the Egyptian Pharaohs of ancient history with their colossal pyramids and temples . . . the real estate industry is keeping New York City 'The Front Office of the Nation.'"[34]

The developers of Concord Village and the Civic Center saw something more in postindustrial midtown than simply new buildings and workers. Built of glass, steel, and plastic, midtown Manhattan offered what the minions who flowed to suburbia similarly craved: the allure of modernity. "The people who populate our central areas every day," observed the leader of a downtown business association, "enjoy the basic human emotions that respond happily to the new, the clean, the bright and fresh, the convenient. They are repelled by the other side of the coin, the dark, dirty, old and inconvenient." Or as one real estate agent succinctly put it: "Newness attracts."[35]

To replicate Manhattan's modern landscape, downtown Brooklyn's new buildings and institutions rose high above the ground both literally and symbolically, obliterating the constraints of time and space and transcending the limits of geography. Manhattanization promised to free the borough from the cycle of obsolescence and demolition endemic to capitalism. "Almost from the moment the first house was erected, the first street laid, and the first drainage ditch dug in any of these embryo cities," explained Raymond Vernon, author of an influential postwar study of metropolitan New York, "a process of obsolescence took hold. . . . The first dwelling became inadequate by the standards of the people who lived in the city. . . . The street layouts, the sewage systems, and the water supply systems also became obsolescent. Almost from the first, then, there was rebuilding as well as building; a tearing down and reordering of structures and public facilities."[36] Brooklyn's new downtown marked an end to this perpetual rebuilding process. More than just blight-free, the new landscape strived to be blight-proof. By attempting to achieve four modern ideals—impermeability, disposability, openness, and mobility—the postindustrial landscape hoped to render obsolete urban obsolescence itself.[37]

The modern city sought to be impermeable to effects of weather or age. Developers designed glistening new towers to be resistant to dirt or decay. Office buildings built in the Internationalist style boasted slick glass curtain walls. Apartment towers were faced with glazed white "self-washing" bricks and surfaces that easily shed grime and dust in the rain. Inside, vinyl asbestos floors resisted fading or scratching. New air conditioners and purifiers cleaned and cooled the air. Fluorescent lighting replaced the need for natural sunlight. Acoustic technology controlled the entry of noise from outside and silenced the hum of typing and chatter from within. Whether on a blazing midsummer afternoon or a blustery winter night, the building's environment remained fixed. Impervious to the elements or passage of time, the modern city was emancipated from the constraints of Mother Nature. Immune to decay, it was inoculated from "blight."[38]

The modern city's smooth surfaces and geometric shapes aimed to be impervious to fashion trends, demographic shifts, ethnic rifts, political factions, and class divisions. The boxy buildings made no reference to local place, history, or aristocratic heritage. "From the outside, these new buildings all look as if they had all been designed by one mind, carried out by one organization, intended for one class of people, bred like bees to fit into these honeycombs," complained Lewis Mumford of the boxy low- and middle-income apartment complexes emerging around the city with surfaces of Hudson Valley red brick. The Civic Center's government buildings were also purposely austere. "There will be little to gladden admirers of the baroque ornamentation of the Victorian era," explained the *New York Times*. "The lines are taut and disciplined." Most developers turned to unadorned boxy architecture largely for pecuniary reasons. Simple and easily reproducible designs allowed housing reformers to build affordable housing on a mass scale. But the reasons were idealistic as well. Union leaders such as Abraham Kazan looked to buildings free of pretentious ornamentation as democratic and egalitarian. From afar the luxury towers of Concord Village looked virtually indistinguishable from the neighboring Farragut low-income public housing and middle-income Kingsview cooperatives.[39]

The modern city also withstood the onset of obsolescence through its disposability. In older cities, explained Vernon, planners had tried to fight decay by making cities more durable, with heavier brick and stronger concrete. "The general tendency was to add to the ossification of the structure: to surface the public streets more permanently and to cram their sub-surface with more and more cables, mains and transit conveyances; to replace wood dwellings with stone, and one-story structures with three- and four-story dwellings and factories. Each rebuilding, therefore, tended to make the next one a little more difficult than the last." As a result, the blighted city remained saddled with heavy layers of outdated infrastructure.

The modern city, in contrast, was flexible and malleable. In place of cumbersome and monumental structures, modern office buildings consisted of interchangeable parts, flexible layouts, and disposable materials. Modular walls made of prefabricated material allowed companies to tinker with layouts as they upgraded technology and developed new management techniques to increase traffic flow between departments. In one Mutual of New York skyscraper, the company shifted 30 percent of its walls over seven years. Apartment buildings also boasted moveable walls that allowed owners to adjust the size of units to meet changing demands. Because of its disposability, the modern city aimed to be immune to decay. Obsolete parts simply were replaced. Buildings flexibly adapted to changing needs. Offices were mere "shells over a mechanical process." "The test of any office buildings should not be merely whether it has a sleek façade, a gleaming lobby," explained Norman Tishman, developer of Concord Village. "Is it flexible enough to permit orderly growth or change over a long period of time?" A skyscraper is a "machine for business," he concluded.[40]

The modern city was also kinetic. In contrast to calcified and blighted Brownstone Brooklyn, the new landscape was an "open city" in which constant motion allowed residents to transcend geography, ethnicity, and class. It boasted new dynamic forms of communication and transportation that rendered irrelevant the constraints of earth and flesh. Concord Village's advertisements highlighted the complex's twenty-four-hour telephone service (apartments still relied on in-house switchboards) and high-speed elevators. Cars and trucks moved unimpeded along widened roadways. The new Brooklyn-Queens Expressway extension connected downtown Brooklyn to the periphery. Civic Center boosters called for heliports to create smooth traffic in the air. Interconnected by pneumatic tubes, helicopters, jet planes, telephones, bike messengers, highways, subways, and the automobile, the modern city was a dynamic system rather than a fixed object. Speed conquered provincialism. Urban flux turned race, age, and class differences into an indistinguishable blur. "There is nothing static or negative," exclaimed Cleveland Rodgers. "All is positive, dynamic—ever-changing, a different feel to every block, at every hour . . . Action and reaction, product and climax, provide the city's rhythm."[41]

More than a new built environment, the tall towers of the modern city represented a modern political perspective. The leaders of redevelopment in Brooklyn were liberal reformers with roots in the Progressive era and the New Deal who hoped to bring the principles of science and efficiency to city administration. Residing and working on the top floors of new apartment towers and skyscrapers, they hoped to see past Brownstone Brooklyn to a vastly expanding and interdependent metropolis that transcended local place. While not yet politically unified, the central business district and the sprawl of tract homes, shopping centers, and industrial parks that surrounded it were all parts of a collective metro area. Metro areas linked together to form even larger metro regions, surpassing many nations in size. In 1961, an influential book announced the existence of a "megalopolis," an uninterrupted urban and suburban development running down the East Coast from Boston to Washington. Some scholars predicted the eventual dissolution of the fifty states and replacement by fifteen or so giant urban governments. By the end of the twenty-first century, predicted prominent Greek architect and city planner Constantine Doxiadis, an "Ecumenopolis" would cover the entire earth's surface, an enormous universal city with no boundaries.[42]

"It's not smallness that's wanted," explained urbanist Robert Wood in 1959, "but intelligent bigness." While decentralization was inevitable, city leaders had a Keynesian faith that with proper centralized planning and regulation the expanding megalopolis could be harmonized. But for an enormous city to function intelligently, the modern city had to be integrated. Although their development projects often displaced thousands of impoverished African Americans, Robert Moses and other urban development figures described themselves as integrating New York and other cities. "[Moses] is a latter-day Paul Bunyan come to town," offered Cleveland Rodgers, "uprooting, demolishing, clearing, reshaping, rebuilding, refurbishing, and integrating the most crowded, chaotic conurbation on earth." "Throughout the city we are creating entire integrated neighborhoods," boasted Moses. "The process is slow. It appears haphazard, formless, even freakish to the uninitiated, to the wisecrackers, smart alecks and sidewalk superintendents, but in the end these seemingly isolated [projects] . . . are huge integrated improvements any one of which would be the occasion for huzzahs and superlatives in any other city."[43]

The builders of the modern city were not necessarily referring to racial integration. Before civil rights groups adopted the phrase in the 1940s, "integration" was a corporate organizational management term used by New Dealers to describe efficient communication between the disparate parts of a large bureaucracy. In the early twentieth century, the first national-sized corporations sought to vertically and horizontally integrate regional plants, production and distribution, and different levels of management. In an integrated firm, communication technology and progressive management negated the constraints of space and time. Geographically disparate facilities were assimilated into an interdependent standardized system. In the New Deal, the federal government championed integration, using the phrase to describe a new partnership between government and private business in national recovery, as well as between federal, state, and local governments. "'Washingtonese' isn't a difficult tongue to master, particularly if you speak English," wrote a *Washington Post* reporter in 1943. "Integrate, gear-in, over-all—Washington officials would be tongue-tied without these words."[44] "Integration" also did not always refer to an antidote to segregation. In fact, modernist planning strongly advocated zoning that segregated industry from residential neighborhoods, highways that segregated automobile traffic from pedestrians, and urban buildings built for segregated uses. Unplanned and mixed-use cityscapes, they believed, led to polluted industries sitting near homes, insufferable automobile traffic, and blight.

Instead, downtown leaders feared that the absence of integration would lead to disintegration. Not only were the crumbling, obsolete buildings surrounding

Brooklyn's central business district in danger of physically disintegrating, but the metropolis as a coherent entity threatened to dissolve into nothingness. Cities were entering "the stage of serious urban disintegration," lamented the Mortgage Bankers Association. "After a century dominated by the growth of enormous cities and the resulting increase of urban functions and responsibilities," explained housing activist Catherine Bauer Wurster, "the city is weaker as an entity than it has ever been in its history. It controls neither its shape, its function, nor its density. It is smothered and paralyzed by its own offspring: the suburbs and satellite towns. The latter are themselves equally weak and helpless" "An enfeebled [urban] structure," warned Ford Foundation president Henry Heald, "encourages disintegration and deterioration, characterized by ignorance, confusion, or lethargy on the part of the people, and represented in their surroundings by crime, accidents, disease, juvenile delinquency, racial tension, waste and excessive cost, and potential political corruption." Without a change in course, cautioned economist and New Dealer Miles Colean, "we shall have the continued failure of cities to meet the problems that lead to their disintegration."[45]

The disintegrated metropolis was a balkanized mess of local fiefdoms run by corrupt machine bosses, myopic homeowners associations, and provincial suburban town halls. In the New York metro area, fourteen hundred overlapping and uncooperative governments formed a labyrinthine bureaucracy incapable of mobilizing its vast resources. In an urban version of the prisoner's dilemma, the metropolis competed rather than cooperated with itself, resulting in cannibalistic decline rather than mutual growth. "Some of the horrors perpetrated by the absence of central jurisdiction are beyond the power of description to add or detract," complained real estate investor Robert Futterman. "We have towns that dump their sewage into the river used for water supply or recreation by towns downstream. One city closes its parks to residents of another. Public hospitals stand underoccupied beside boundary lines across which sick people are sleeping in hallways. Highways peter out suddenly into lanes. Adjacent small school districts run inefficiently small schools with inefficiently large administrative staffs, and cannot be persuaded to amalgamate."[46]

Brownstone Brooklyn and the surrounding metropolis thus could be "integrated" only if they were viewed in their entirety from the top down. Like the apartment dwellers atop Concord Village, city planners approached the vast metropolis from above. If one stood on the ground, the city appeared an unintelligible mess of blight and traffic, the suburbs an endless row of indistinguishable houses. Only from a bird's-eye view did the city take form. Swarms of scurrying ant-sized people and blinking lights coalesced into a functioning

"The modernist bird's-eye view." Borough president Abe Stark examining a three-dimensional model of the new Civic Center. *World-Telegram & Sun*, April 24, 1963. (Courtesy of the Library of Congress, Prints & Photographs Division, NYTWT&S Collection)

system. Millions of individual decisions became measurable trends. The hodgepodge of local streets came together into homogeneous zones. Approaching the city by plane, explained Cleveland Rodgers, one can see the "superb panorama of Greater New York." But when one steps onto the ground, "the picture quickly changes . . . a thousand details distract from the totality of the first impressions, making it impossible ever again to recapture or to recall the vision entire as it appeared before the city became real and alive. Transition is from oneness to multiplicity, from order to chaos, as panorama becomes pandemonium and distant murmurs grow into incessant roars punctuated by shrill clashes and alarms." "Through the airplane and camera we have acquired a *complete and precise view of our cities from above*," exclaimed CIAM architect José Luis Sert. "Air views have revealed to man a new 'urban façade,' a perspective which has never before been known."[47]

Surveying the landscape from atop a skyscraper or standing above a diorama of the city, downtown leaders used a series of metaphors to describe the integrated metropolis. For some the city was an organism, a body with a heart, arteries, lungs, and brain. For others the planned city was a garden. Still others borrowed the new technocratic language of large corporations, early computer technology, and cybernetics to describe an "urban matrix," "urban complex," or "urban system." If left unplanned, however, the harmonious whole became a cacophonous nightmare of disjointed parts. The urban body mutated into an "urban monster." Blight became a "cancer" eating away the city's heart and lungs. The urban garden gave way to an "urban jungle," "urban wasteland," or "urban desert." The matrix transformed into a "cobweb."[48]

If Manhattanization meant taking a regionalist, pan–New York City view of megalopolis, it also demanded a Manhattan-centric approach to political power. To politically integrate the sprawling city, postwar reformers hoped that a new and modernized central business district would streamline and centralize the thousands of local governments, bureaucratic agencies, school boards, fire departments, and park services that made up the new metropolis. Just as the coherent city could only be viewed from a plane or skyscraper, metropolitan leadership too needed to rule scientifically from the top down. A powerful administrative downtown could be the brain for a vast but harmonious regional metropolis. Cities were simply "too large to be governed 'from the grass roots,'" explained Robert Futterman. "Government must unify and integrate," said Cleveland Rodgers, "seek oneness, instead of multiplicity of interests." Special interests are capable of doing their own planning, he warned. "But the larger public interest is paramount and must prevail, not spasmodically, not in certain neighborhoods or sections, but for the entire community, for present and future generations."[49]

As they bulldozed nineteenth-century municipal buildings that they saw as nests of political corruption, liberal city planners envisioned Brooklyn's Civic Center as a modern command-and-control center for an empowered city hall. Strong executives and czars with centralized power and scientific administrative

skills would use the efficient buildings to rise above local politics, foster cooperation between labor and business, and act for the larger public good. In New
York City, a series of charter reforms starting in the La Guardia administration
in the 1930s diverted control over the city budget and operations from local
wards to the mayor's office. By 1961, a collection of centralized departments
headed by powerful commissioners who reported to the mayor ran virtually
all municipal services. A newly created city administrator coordinated departments and prevented overlap and waste. Where local bosses once dispensed
patronage positions to local supporters in exchange for votes, a Department of
Personnel headed by a commissioner allocated city jobs and set a strict pay
scale. With the start of the New Deal in the 1930s, federal and state grants
flowed to city hall rather than local districts, further solidifying the mayor's
role as the central administrator of an integrated public sector. Brooklyn's
Civic Center boasted new buildings designed to centralize, to rationalize, and
to Manhattanize. In 1955, a new Welfare Center opened in a modern concrete
and steel headquarters to efficiently run the area's services. In 1940, a new
Board of Education headquarters opened in a converted building on 110 Livingston Street with a mission to consolidate an unwieldy school system. New
federal and state courthouses, as well as a new house of detention, symbolized
a new scientific bureaucracy free of the cronyism and corruption of old.[50]

Even the most headstrong mayor remained bound by city borders and the
short-term demands of voters. Thus, city leaders created independent authorities led by powerful executives with the freedom to transcend local political
boundaries, integrate public and private sectors, and operate according to the
principles of science and efficiency. The nation's first public authority or
public benefit corporation was the Port Authority, founded in 1921 to administer the waterfront and build bridges and tunnels between New York and New
Jersey. With the power to issue bonds and collect tolls, the public benefit corporation was an autonomous government agency with its own operating budget and power of eminent domain. Not dependent on appropriations from the
state legislature, the Port Authority answered neither to the mayor nor to
voters, but instead was controlled by a permanent independent board of commissioners. Centralizing power in an impartial institution, Julius Cohen, a
Port Authority lawyer and drafter of the first public corporation, hoped to
initiate a new era of consensus between business, government, and labor.
"There is a reason for the word *corporation* and its resemblance to the word
cooperation. It is the bringing together of many units under a single managerial head." When it completed the majestic George Washington Bridge ahead
of schedule in 1931, the public benefit corporation received praise around the
city for its efficiency and scientific approach to city development.[51]

In 1956, the Port Authority, run by powerful czar Austin Tobin, turned to downtown Brooklyn with a seven-year, $85 million modernization program for the aging waterfront. Along the two miles of waterfront south of the Brooklyn Bridge, the authority purchased twenty-five obsolete docks and replaced them with ten modern steel-and-concrete piers. Forty-five acres of crowded lanes and aging buildings were cleared for open storage and freight traffic. Regional governments also hoped to modernize and centralize the informal and local labor arrangements along the waterfront as well. To fight widespread corruption, pilfering, and organized crime, New York and New Jersey in 1953 created a bi-state Waterfront Commission. Replacing the infamous "shape-up system" in which workers gathered on the piers hoping to get picked for a day's work by a Mafia-controlled foreman, the new commission required longshoremen to register in scientifically managed government hiring halls and information centers.[52]

Inspired by the success of the Port Authority and subsequent New Deal versions such as the Tennessee Valley Authority, city officials hoped to create a network of public authorities to build and administer the modern city from the Civic Center and Manhattan. In 1953, the New York City Transit Authority was formed to consolidate the city's disjointed and debt-ridden collection of private and public subway and bus lines, and it moved into a new headquarters in the Civic Center. The boxy building with simple glass and austere limestone free of pretentious cornices and columns, extolled Lewis Mumford, was "the very model of an efficient office building . . . a half-dozen Transportation Buildings would create a new kind of urban space, distinguished by composure and order." Robert Moses' powerful Triborough Bridge and Tunnel Authority operated the Brooklyn Battery Tunnel and other transportation arteries. The New York City Housing Authority (NYCHA) administered the area's vast public housing system. Created in 1934 to administer federal funds for public housing during the New Deal, NYCHA operated as an independent corporation with the power to issue bonds, collect rents, and use eminent domain to seize property for new projects. By 1959, the Housing Authority was Brownstone Brooklyn's largest landlord, operating five projects with almost nine thousand units in the area.[53]

Concord Village and the other middle-income housing that made up the Civic Center project were also centrally coordinated, public-private ventures. In 1938, New York State passed a law allowing life insurance companies to build and operate moderate-rent housing developments. After Metropolitan Life's Parkchester in the Bronx, Equitable Life's Clinton Hill apartment complex in Brownstone Brooklyn was the second project to be commenced under the law. Built between 1943 and 1955, the twelve brick towers with manicured lawns and more than twelve hundred affordable suites inspired the city to pass

the Redevelopment Companies Law. The new law permitted the city to condemn slums and to offer tax incentives to private redevelopment corporations
willing to build modern low- and middle-income housing. Private builders in
exchange had to agree to limit their profit to 6 percent of the equity investment, get projects approved by the city planning commission, and relocate
displaced residents in adequate dwellings. The first project built under the new
law was Met Life's Stuyvesant Town in Manhattan, an enormous eighteen-
square-block apartment complex housing twenty-seven thousand middle-
income renters. To make room for new construction, the city condemned
hundreds of dilapidated buildings and displaced more than eleven thousand
residents. Concord Village was facilitated by a subsequent amendment to the
law that allowed savings banks to participate in housing development as well.[54]

The Fort Greene, Pratt, and Atlantic Terminal urban renewal areas were also
public-private ventures centrally coordinated from Manhattan by a czar, city
construction coordinator Robert Moses. With the passage of the 1949 Housing
Act, the federal government hoped to stimulate public-private development on
a national scale. Under Title I of the Housing Act (colloquially referred to in
later years as "urban renewal," although technically that term referred to a
reformed version of the program created by the 1954 Housing Act), Washington sent New York City millions of dollars to acquire land and clear slums for
sale to private developers. With the federal government paying two-thirds of
the difference between the acquisition and sale prices of the land, the city
could offer creative discounts and incentives to lure investors into blighted
areas. Developers were free to build housing or the commercial property of
their choice, provided the project fit into a broader community plan and could
be constructed in a reasonable time frame. Developers too were required to
relocate residents to housing of the same or better quality at comparable rents.[55]

As millions of federal dollars poured into New York City, Robert Moses'
urban renewal board, the Slum Clearance Committee, took its place alongside
city planning agencies, NYCHA, and other public authorities as the brokers of
urban redevelopment in Brooklyn. The committee worked with private sector
leaders who also hoped to eschew competition and integrate development
efforts toward a common goal. A pro-growth coalition of banks, corporations,
universities, hospitals, and real estate developers formed private pro-develop-
ment authorities to encourage urban investment, slum clearance, and modern
urban planning. In Brooklyn, the Ford Foundation, Citizens' Housing and
Planning Council, United Housing Foundation, ACTION, and Downtown
Brooklyn Association avidly supported the Civic Center and pressured the city
to build new roadways, clear slums, construct parking garages, expand research
and office facilities, and build middle- and low-income housing projects.[56]

"The space of urban renewal." The city demolished the buildings and elevated train lines of Brooklyn's older downtown to clear space for the new Civic Center. Brooklyn Heights sits to the left. Concord Village was under construction off camera to the right. Photograph taken in 1952. (Courtesy of the Brooklyn Public Library, Brooklyn Collection, for image with the following call number: NEIG 0569)

As part of its geographic and political integration, some members of the pro-growth coalition aspired to Brooklyn's racial integration. While Robert Moses and many developers were unsympathetic to minorities, the postwar civil rights struggle remained an integral wing of a larger modernist movement. Brooklyn's civil rights leaders and housing reformers in the 1940s and 1950s were racial liberals with an initially hopeful attitude about postwar redevelopment. Though suspicious of developers, groups such as the Brooklyn Federation for Better Housing were advocates of principled slum clearance, public housing, and the centralization of power in an impartial bureaucracy. Even while criticizing development projects that displaced poor minorities or failed to admit African Americans as tenants, civil rights leaders protested in modernist terms. The NAACP, the National Committee Against Discrimination in Housing, and the Urban League sought to obliterate place boundaries, to render race obsolete, and to create an open city that was kinetic and impermeable to history and ethnicity. In the 1950s they worried less about preserving historic place and more about breaking barriers that kept African Americans "in place." They looked to the new Board of Education headquarters at 110 Livingston Street to administer scientifically managed, pan–New York City school integration programs that crossed neighborhood racial lines. They looked to powerful courts in the Civic Center to enforce anti-discrimination laws and give a mobile black population the freedom to participate equally in the process of suburbanization. With strong fair housing laws, "it will be the urban renewal of the Nineteen Sixties that will help Negroes escape the Ghetto," explained a hopeful Robert Weaver in 1961. Opponents similarly drew connections between urban redevelopment and civil rights. "Integration is like a super-highway," explained a white World War II veteran in 1956. "It's a wonderful thing—just as long as it doesn't run through my backyard."[57]

When Brownstone Brooklyn residents looked warily at Concord Village, they saw something more than three unassuming towers sitting on the periphery of Brooklyn Heights. The towers marked the arrival of a pro-growth coalition with massive public funds and plans to demolish and rebuild. Concord Village represented a liberal faith in government regulation, rational planning, and managed growth. It represented a modern urban ideal that sought centralized power, impermeability, disposability, integration, openness, and mobility. Against this backdrop, a new middle class would look to Brownstone Brooklyn for an alternative postindustrial landscape that they imagined was local, decentralized, historic, diverse, and unplanned.

The failures of the modern city have been well documented. As in other parts of the city, the first decade of postwar redevelopment in Brooklyn was clumsy and often cruel. Title I urban renewal projects were particularly riddled with problems. While the city quickly cleared land with bulldozers, the ambitious gleaming apartments and research facilities rarely materialized as planned. Even the infamously efficient Robert Moses had to scrounge for residents to fill his renewal sites, relying mainly on NYCHA, nonprofits, and a small handful of housing developers uniquely committed to his vision. As Long Island University and Brooklyn Hospital reneged on promises to build new facilities, much of the Fort Greene renewal site became dull parking lots. Other cleared sites remained empty for decades. Buildings that did go up took an average of eleven years to complete, leaving open scars across the cityscape. Despite exciting blueprints, modernist apartment towers such as Kingsview and University Towers looked drab. But most important, developers displaced thousands of residents, disproportionately poor residents of color, and made halfhearted attempts to find them alternative housing.

At the same time, the modern city had its share of successes. While NYCHA had plenty of problems, its low-income public housing projects in Brownstone

"Breaking free from the constraints of space and time." The modernist towers of University Terrace soar above the nineteenth-century landscape. Title I developments like this sparked local efforts to protect "Clinton Hill" from urban renewal. *World-Telegram & Sun*, October 5, 1964. (Courtesy of the Library of Congress, Prints & Photographs Division, NYTWT&S Collection)

Brooklyn offered well-managed and modern housing for the poor, and the projects continually had long waiting lists. High-rise cooperatives boasted attractive and affordable housing for middle-income families in an increasingly expensive city. The universities and hospitals that expanded became important sources of jobs in an emerging postindustrial economy. Modernist buildings were not obsolescence-proof, and over time they weathered with age and developed a patina of unique colors and contours. While the architects hoped to transcend history with their designs, the modern city slowly became as authentic as the city it sought to replace, a rich historic site with a strong sense of place worth preserving.[58]

Nor was the liberal growth machine as ideologically uncompromising as its critics portrayed it. By the early 1960s, in response to complaints, city agencies were tinkering with programs and experimenting with smaller "vest-pocket" projects, rehabilitation, and conservation of existing housing. But while willing to experiment with new programs in Brownstone Brooklyn, leaders remained committed to the core ideals of the modern city: that the obsolete cityscape should give way to the new; that local projects should be integrated in a bird's-eye view of the entire city body; that city governance should be both pan–New York City and Manhattan-centric; that competition between local institutions should cede to large-scale cooperation, regulation, and scientific planning; that government should cooperate with the private sector and labor unions to jointly reinvest in the city; that the city needed independent, powerful executives to integrate the disintegrating metropolis; and that Manhattan's booming postindustrial landscape provided the blueprint for future projects.

The greater failure of the modern city occurred not in its design or implementation but on the cultural front. For a new generation traumatized by the heavy-handed early years of urban redevelopment, the language of modern infrastructure—"master plan," "construction," "engineering," "institutionalization," "the system," "authority," and even "integration" itself—would come to represent not the progressive language of reform but the jargon of an alienating technocracy. To a new left, Concord Village represented the power of big business; to a new right, it demonstrated the excessive size of big government. The disposable and impermeable cityscape would represent to younger critics not liberation from space and time but an inauthentic throwaway society. The downtown skyscraper headquarters administering a pan–New York City system would inspire not the image of a garden but that of an imprisoning panopticon. The czars of development would appear not as unfettered public servants but as authoritarian. Not only would a new neighborhood movement turn against New Deal liberalism, but, dismayed by modernist projects, a new generation of activists would also begin to question the modernist project itself.

In Brooklyn, ironically, it was the successes of redevelopment that led to its demise. New York's growth coalition was the most active in the country, building internationally recognized symbols of postwar power and prosperity: the United Nations, Lincoln Center, and the skyscrapers and apartment towers of the Manhattan skyline. With the ambitious Robert Moses at the helm, urban renewal was really New York's renewal, as the city used more federal Title I funds than all other cities combined. But perhaps more influential a legacy for Brooklyn than modernist apartments or offices themselves was that Manhattanization birthed a romantic brownstone movement. One source of resistance would be the thousands of low-income renters, minorities, and small manufacturing firms displaced and galvanized by modernist projects. But more important, Manhattanization brought a new constituency to Brooklyn, a new urban white-collar class searching for authenticity that would radically reshape the borough's political and social agenda.

3 The Middle Cityscape of Brooklyn Heights

I live in Brooklyn, by choice.
—Truman Capote

In 1957, Truman Capote discovered Brownstone Brooklyn. In a travel article for *Holiday* magazine, the young author and new Brooklyn resident described his impressions of the "uninviting community" of Brooklyn, a vast, dreary proletarian space, "a veritable veldt of tawdriness where even the *noms de quartiers* aggravate: Flatbush and Flushing Avenue, Bushwick, Brownsville, Red Hook." Yet in this dreary space, Capote found Brooklyn Heights, a lovely, unique neighborhood that was a sharp contrast to its drab surroundings. Capote thought Brooklyn Heights to be an isolated island of culture and civility amidst a sea of urban blandness. "In the greenless grime-gray," he assured the reader, "oases do occur, splendid contradictions, hearty echoes of healthier days."[1]

Sitting in the shadows of the modern towers of Concord Village and the Civic Center, in a borough that was indistinguishably gray, Brooklyn Heights was a rare sanctuary of a simpler past: an age of Victorian nobility, brownstone mansions, carriage horses, small shops and bakeries, and handcrafts. "These houses bespeak an age of able servants and solid fireside ease, invoke specters of bearded seafaring fathers and bonneted stay-at-home wives: devoted parents to great broods of future bankers and fashionable brides."[2] In an era of new and sterile department stores and suburban malls, Brooklyn Heights had small antique stores run by elderly eccentrics. Their diverse offerings were delightfully disorganized and eclectic: "pink apothecary jars from an old pharmacy, English brass, Barcelona lamps, French paperweights . . . Spanish saints, Korean cabinets; and junk, glorious junk, a jumble of ragged dolls, broken buttons, a stuffed kangaroo, an aviary of owls under a great glass bell, the playing pieces of obsolete games, the paper moneys of defunct governments."[3] Surrounded by drabness, Brooklyn Heights was a mélange of ethnic color. "There is a street of Gypsies, with Gypsy cafés (have your future foretold and be tattooed while sipping tankards of Moorish tea); there is also an Arab-Armenian quarter sprinkled with spice-saturated restaurants." Along the waterfront there were sailors, "saronged East Indians, even the giant Senegalese, their onyx arms afire with blue, with yellow tattooed flowers, with saucy torsos and garish graffiti . . . [r]unty Russians, too."[4]

Capote was not alone in his discovery. As a wave of artists, writers, lawyers, and other white-collar professionals began to migrate into the area after World War II, Brooklyn Heights became the borough's first postwar revitalized neighborhood. The first new enclave would play a crucial role in the gentrification of Brownstone Brooklyn. In a district rapidly losing residents to emerging suburbs, the rehabilitated Gold Coast formed a middle-class base from which brownstoners in subsequent decades would springboard into the borough. But more than simply a new middle-class enclave, Brooklyn Heights was the birthplace of a new romantic urban ideal. Sitting on the edge of the modern Civic Center, the Heights was an imagined "neighborhood" located in the aging Victorian industrial districts surrounding the central business district. As they restored townhouses, wrote booster articles and historic portraits for local papers, and fought development plans, Capote and his peers recast Brooklyn's townhouses, waterfront piers, and industrial lofts as sources of anti-bureaucratic authenticity. In doing so, Heights residents formed a template for Brownstone Brooklyn's future neighborhoods. They also forged an alternative to the dominant modernist ideology of the 1950s and developed a distinctly urban (or anti-suburban) identity for a new middle class.

Perched on a hilltop across from river, the Heights was Brooklyn's oldest residential district, with large brownstones, majestic apartment buildings, and the borough's most prominent families. But like Boston's Beacon Hill and Chicago's Gold Coast, the neighborhood steadily lost middle-class families to emerging automobile suburbs starting in the 1920s. Working-class Italian and Irish immigrants who once lived south of Atlantic Avenue and north of Fulton Street migrated into the area. Landlords subdivided brownstones into rooming houses and railroad flats. A 1943 market study by four newspapers showed only a few blocks of high-rent housing surrounding the main thoroughfare of Montague Street. Rents four blocks away quickly dropped to among the lowest in the borough. Capote, writing in the 1950s, lamented what he imagined was the decline of a once patrician landscape. "Immigrant tribes, who had first ringed the vicinity, at once infiltrated en masse," explained Capote with literary flair. "Whereupon a majority of what remained of genteel old stock, the sediment in the bottom of the bottle, poured forth from their homes, leaving them to be demolished or converted into eyesore-seedy rooming establishments."[5]

The arrival of two new migrant groups starting in the 1940s further fueled the exodus of the Heights' white middle class. Spanish-speaking migrants from Puerto Rico replaced Italians in the rooming houses along Atlantic Avenue. African Americans replaced Irish residents in rooming houses, apartments, and new public housing complexes north of Fulton Street. "Many of the rooming houses are overcrowded with Puerto Ricans who can't afford space elsewhere," explained the *Brooklyn Heights Press*. "Neighbors in many cases resent the Puerto Ricans' appearance in the neighborhood. . . . Negroes are resented on the Heights as much . . . but there are very few living here. The owners won't rent to them." "Young people in the Heights can be divided into two fairly distinct groups," explained another editorial in 1959. "Those in the center of the Heights are from families with a comfortable standard of living.

Revitalized buildings on State Street at the southern periphery of Brooklyn Heights. Corner of Hicks and State Streets. Photograph taken June 7, 1959. (Courtesy of the Brooklyn Historical Society)

The average boy from this group lives perhaps in a two-family brownstone, and goes to a private school. . . . Those in the other group live in the Atlantic Avenue fringe of the Heights, and have a much lower standard of living. The average boy from this group is Puerto Rican, lives in a small apartment, and goes to public or parochial school."[6]

While residents fretted about the area's decline, Capote also excitedly described a countertrend. A new middle class was migrating to the area. Small numbers of artists and writers had begun to arrive during the Depression and settled on the periphery of the neighborhood. "The defeatists in our midst, the mourners of the 'lost' golden age, say cultural and scholarly refinement and adventurous contact with the world at large are at low ebb on Brooklyn Heights," explained a hopeful Brooklyn Heights Association in 1937. "We

A block away from Hicks Street, State Street's buildings remained more dilapidated. Corner of State Street and Columbia Place. Photograph taken June 7, 1959. (Courtesy of the Brooklyn Historical Society)

introduce our neighbors, the painters, the sculptors, the etchers, the lithogra-
phers, the illustrator of Brooklyn Heights *today*." "The enormous homes and
the fine rows, a steadily narrower area remains inviolable, the top drawer of
Brooklyn," wrote James Agee in 1939 of the center of the Heights, "[but on the
periphery] disintegration . . . great houses broken apart for roomers; a gradual
degeneration into artists and journalists, communists, bohemians and barbers, chiefly of Manhattan."[7]

After World War II, a new wave of white-collar workers and artists migrated
into the neighborhood. "Brave pioneers bringing brooms and buckets of
paint," exulted Capote, "urban, ambitious young couples, by and large mid-
rung in their Doctor-Lawyer-Wall Street-Whatever careers, eager to restore to
the Heights its shattered qualities of circumspect, comfortable charm." New
arrivals enthusiastically bought up old rooming houses to convert them to
single or dual-family use. Others moved into renovated tenement flats. Hundreds of prospective homebuyers combed the streets on Sundays. The Brooklyn
Heights Association reported rising membership. "Despite the two-way flow
of traffic between the suburbs and the Heights, most new Heights residents
come from Manhattan," concluded the local paper after conducting an informal survey of residents. "Many old Heights families, pressed economically,
moved out and their homes were converted into apartment buildings and
rooming-houses. In their stead came artists, writers, and professional men."
"People are swarming over from New York," explained local realtor Kenneth
Boss, adding, "More and more families are buying rooming-houses to convert
them to one-family dwellings." "If the current trend continues," explained
the *New York World-Telegram and Sun* in 1957, "in another 10 years the Heights
will be inhabited almost exclusively by artists, writers and sculptors, some
brokers, bankers and lawyers, and predominantly by commercial artists, press
agents and people in television and advertising."[8]

Although a London sociologist would not coin the term until 1964, the
Heights was being "gentrified." "A trend seems to be increasing for people
who are living in the suburbs to return to the city," explained realtor John
F. Hamlin in 1941. In his 1956 annual report, borough president John Cashmore spoke glowingly of a "return-to-Brooklyn" movement, as "bank executives and employees, engineers, economists, artists, member of the legal
profession, writers, and advertising agency employees" bought brownstones
and rented apartments in Brooklyn Heights. "For some time now, the
Heights has been drawing residents from the Village, the East 60s and Manhattan West," explained the *Herald Tribune* in 1957. "At least partly because
of this new infiltration, the fifty-odd blocks of mostly Victorian buildings
that make up the Heights on the eminence opposite downtown Manhattan

are looking up—property values are up, crime is down, and rooming houses are giving way."

The Heights would form an important anchor for the brownstone revitalization movement elsewhere in the borough. While white residents elsewhere were steadily migrating out of the borough, the return-to-Brooklyn movement marked the arrival of a new postindustrial white middle class. In 1960, residents who arrived before World War II occupied only 9 percent of the 11,457 housing units in Brooklyn Heights. A full 36 percent of Heights residents moved there in the years 1958–60 alone. New arrivals were overwhelmingly wealthier, more educated, and more concentrated in white-collar professions than residents in the rest of the borough. Between 1950 and 1960, the number of workers listed in the census as "professional and technical" or "manager, official or proprietor" rose from 40 to 48 percent, while in the rest of Brooklyn it fell from 23 to 20 percent. While the number of foremen and craftsmen stayed steady at 40 percent boroughwide, the Heights saw a drop from 21 to 15 percent. In the same decade, the number of Heights residents with some college education rose from one in three to 44 percent, compared to only 12 percent in Brooklyn as a whole.[9]

Written observations and informal surveys of residents also point to the growth of the white-collar middle class. Managers in banks, office headquarters, and insurance firms of Manhattan and downtown Brooklyn postwar central business districts, according to observers, were among the first to arrive. As early as the 1940s, brokers noticed that several Wall Street brokers and midtown executives were inquiring about houses in the neighborhood. "A trend seems to be increasing for people who have been living in the suburbs to return to the city," explained one local broker. "Part of this back-to-the-city movement possibly results from businessmen . . . who could formerly commute from suburban sections, are finding it more convenient, if not actually necessary, to be within quick access to these offices."[10]

Knowledge workers in media, law, and the arts also migrated into the area. Where Wall Street bankers and brokers were rich in financial capital, these "young men on the first rungs of success in the worlds of business, publication, advertising, art and broadcasting," explained the *Herald Tribune* in 1957, brought to Brooklyn Heights a high degree of cultural capital that compensated for their modest salaries. "The Bright Young Men are in the van of this trend, which might be called do-it-yourself on a somewhat grand scale, seeking the quiet neighborly life." "A lot of our friends are moving into the Heights," explained a twenty-nine-year-old new arrival, "many of them from Harvard Law School."[11]

The most visible settlers, however, were bohemian refugees from Greenwich Village. "The Heights was becoming a 'second Village,'" explained the local paper, "and displaced Villagers have been pouring in since. They are among the Heights' most fervent devotees." Word spread throughout the city that Brooklyn Heights was fast becoming "a neighborhood for displaced villagers," explained another editorial, "or a place where Village people live after they've married." "It's a kind of Greenwich Village with a little less noise and a little less dirt," boasted Bertram Wolfe.[12]

Brooklyn Heights had much to offer the new middle class. First, as an aging Brahmin district with depressed housing, Brooklyn Heights provided new residents with space. As young GIs returned from World War II and developers demolished older tenements, New York experienced one of the worst housing shortages in its history. In 1950, the city had a rental vacancy rate of 0.8 percent, the lowest on record. Home buyers found only 0.3 percent of the housing stock unoccupied and for sale. To rent or buy in Manhattan was particularly difficult. With the prohibitive costs of site acquisition and clearance, private developers could only afford to build high-rise luxury apartment buildings. With government housing aimed at low-income groups and unsubsidized housing increasingly accessible only to the very rich, Manhattan's real estate market of the 1950s began to displace the middle class. These college-educated middle-class refugees—writers, lawyers, artists, journalists, academics, brokers—poured into Brooklyn Heights hungry for affordable housing.[13]

A dilapidated brownstone in Brooklyn Heights was astonishingly large and cheap in a suffocatingly tight marketplace. To buy a new three-room cooperative apartment on the East Side of Manhattan in 1958 would require $15,000 and $175 in monthly maintenance charges. In Brooklyn Heights, whole brownstones with four floors, several bathrooms, large kitchens, private stoops, and small yards were selling for as little as $30,000.[14] In search of cheap, spacious townhouses, new arrivals moved both northward and southward from Montague Street. In the first four months of 1957, Sidney Place in the southern end of Brooklyn Heights had six of its rooming houses converted to single-family residences. Several of the new property owners banded together to buy three more rooming houses on the block, reselling them at reduced prices to families who converted them to private dwellings. On the northern end, Hicks Street between Cranberry and Middagh streets in 1953 had several boarded-up buildings and a rooming house. By 1959, all the buildings had been bought and renovated and were mostly owner-occupied.[15]

Brooklyn Heights was not just cheap space; it was a place with important cultural symbolic value for middle-class settlers. Brooklyn Heights was an alternative neighborhood that the new middle class juxtaposed to the Manhattan they had escaped and the suburban developments they refused to flee to. "Brooklyn, in short, is the place of the *via media*, the middle course," wrote

New York University English professor and Heights resident David Boroff. "Many residents of Brooklyn view themselves as a kind of Third Force between the city and the suburbs. Theirs is the vitality of the city without the penalties of big-city life, the grace of suburban living without its invasion of privacy. They dismiss the Great City as 'phony,' and the suburbs as 'conformist.' Brooklyn, they insist, has the best of both worlds."[16]

Lodged between the modernist landscape of the Civic Center and the slum periphery, the Heights represented a middle cityscape. The new middle class described an interstitial space where they had access to the cultural venues of the center city while maintaining a small-town feel. But the middle cityscape was much richer symbolic terrain that drew on long-standing tropes of American romanticism. In his classic work *The Machine in the Garden*, Leo Marx described the middle landscape as an in-between zone between the over-civilized city and untamed wilderness that reconciled the contradictory longing in American culture for both technological modernity and a connection to a primordial rural past. In Brooklyn Heights and similar gentrifying districts around the country, a new postindustrial middle class applied this romantic pastoral image to the belt of Victorian industrial districts surrounding the postwar central business district.

When Capote described the hidden oasis of Brooklyn Heights, he was not alone. A new cadre of Brooklyn-based writers created a type of urban local color writing that would play an important role in the gentrification of the borough: the urban discovery narrative. Writing in the local press, the writer-pioneer invited a white middle-class audience to participate in the process of exploration and discovery. As the author crossed the river by foot or by subway, he or she left the rational space of Manhattan and entered the forbidding interior of Brooklyn. Brooklyn was a homogenous and frightening wilderness devoid of culture, individuality, or a sense of place. "Brooklyn is a particularly amorphous place," explained *Fortune* magazine. "To the smart Manhattanite, [Brooklyn] has long been a kind of a joke; it is a place that once had a culture and aristocracy, and now is a no-man's land of factories and homes and gigantic tearing avenues—a place to get lost in—an unknown, unexplored land."[17]

"Brooklyn, by definition (of all those non habituees), is a maze," wrote one new settler in 1953 of her impressions before arriving, "populated by illiterate eccentrics bordering on the worldly limbo between insane Manhattanites and damfool commuters. I was looking forward to a grim stay." "An impenetrable jungle," explained another; "the borough is 'the end of the world,' a wild antipodes full of cemeteries and vast stretches of red-brick tundra with ungainly little houses pressed against each other. . . . Brooklyn is the home of the dead and the not-quite-alive, an illimitable and dreary bedroom of the glittering city." "At first I thought moving out here was like a great adventure—like moving out to the sticks," joked sculptor William Zorach. "I'm still wary of inviting people for dinner. They think you live in a jungle." Often settlers used dialect to accentuate the lack of sophistication of the outer borough: "And to think all I ever knew about Brooklyn was the Dodgers, Greenpernt, and toity-toid and toid." "According to folklore, Brooklyn is full of urban primitives, who speak an unintelligible patois, full of 'deses' and 'dems.'"[18]

While in a few cases the author was simply a travel writer, more often the explorer was in search of settlement. When moving to New York in 1956 to start his fledgling career as a writer, one settler found that exorbitant apartments rents in Manhattan were "evidently geared for a maharaja from Kapurthala rather than a guy from Saginaw, Mich." Priced out of Manhattan, he considered crossing the river into Brooklyn but felt intimidated. "People I met in Manhattan consider the spot just across the river a vast, forbidding and impenetrable wilderness. I gathered this jungle was inhabited by a race of barbarians. . . . I heard stories of Manhattanites who, after falling asleep on the subway, woke up in the middle of Brooklyn and didn't find their way home for a week. Terrible things happened to them. Some were never seen again."[19]

In other versions, the author-settler acted as a guide, leading a skeptical friend into Brooklyn. Having already settled beyond the confines of Manhattan, the writer pointedly juxtaposed his or her urban frontier savvy to the sheltered naïveté of his college-educated counterparts. "You live in Brooklyn?" asked one shocked friend, much to the author's glee. "They didn't know whether I was joking or threatening," crowed another settler about a tourist couple he invites to visit him across the bridge. "'Brooklyn!' Dottie gasped. 'What ever on earth for?'" As they travel across the river, one author reveled in seeing her more pampered friend unnerved:

My victim was fresh from Texas and ripe for the kill. . . . "Where're we going?" she cried in fearful anticipation. "To Brooklyn," I shouted. In the train she was silent, apprehensive. Her hands were busy opening and shutting her purse.

"Nervous?" I asked innocently.

She gave me a look that would have detonated an atom bomb.[20]

Much to his or her surprise, the author emerged from the subway to discover an oasis of local place. In a vast and placeless borough, Brooklyn Heights was a unique enclave with tree-lined streets, small cafés, and historic buildings. "Can you imagine my surprise when the first people I met were neither eccentric nor illiterate?" exclaimed one settler upon arrival. "Is this Brooklyn?" asked a surprised friend of her settler guide upon exiting the subway. "Yes," her friend mimicked her, "this is Brooklyn. Surprised, aren't you?"

Once an alienated white-collar worker toiling in bureaucratic Manhattan, the Brooklyn-based writer now rejoiced in a romantic feeling of reconnection to place. New arrivals walked through Brooklyn Heights "all eyes" and "full of the joy of discovery." Across the river in Manhattan, technocratic city planners and developers were crushing the city spirit with bulldozers, highways, and rationalist planning schemes. But in the Heights, the urban explorer could peripatetically wander the streets of a newly discovered local enclave. The narrator became a flaneur, meandering through Brooklyn's brownstone-lined streets without plan or purpose save the enjoyment of the area's eclectic gestalt. Rather than attempting to categorize or systematize, the narrator described a messy collage of places, relishing the area's disorder rather than feeling wary of it. New residents excitedly made intertextual references to other gentrifying districts in Europe, San Francisco, and New Orleans. "It's just like those ante-bellum homes down in New Orleans," exclaimed one. "Look at that charming little church. Like the picture post cards from Italy." "Romance! Perhaps it's the old mansions (now mostly multiple dwellings), reminiscent of a more luxurious age. . . . One has a feeling of completeness about the Heights one might have of San Francisco."[21]

Like the designers of the Brooklyn Civic Center, the authors of urban discovery narratives too described a modern city surrounded by a blighted periphery. But they offered a distinct rejection of the modernist project. Rather, they wrote romantic discovery narratives in which the explorer accidentally found an idyll unsullied by the forces of modernity. The romantic explorer traveled into the peripheral wilderness not to spread civilization but to escape its dehumanizing artificiality. Uncharted land represented not a site to be exploited in the name of progress but a fragile Eden, a vestige of the past not yet integrated into the grid space of the modern city. Although Eden, in reality, contained overlapping ecosystems in a constant process of change, the romantic explorer selectively excavated the layered terrain of the periphery to cultivate an anti-modern utopia. She or he relished the unprocessed terrain of hills, mountains, or wildlife, or admired the nomadic savages that still enjoyed the free and passionate lives of the primitive, a sharp contrast to bureaucratized urban life. He rhapsodized about older forms of manual labor—farm work, arts and crafts, fishing—in which the worker used his hands and saw the fruits of his labor, a fulfilling contrast to alienating forms of postindustrial labor.[22]

The phrase "This is Brooklyn?" was an expression of middle-class delighted surprise. But the surprise was not that Brooklyn Heights was as modern or civilized as Manhattan. Instead, settlers celebrated precisely its non-modernity. Echoing the themes of local-color writing, Brooklyn Heights was a distinct place that maintained its sense of independence, local flavor, and diversity in the face of universalizing, integrating, and place-destroying forces. The Heights appeared as a small urban village with cobblestone streets, quirky elderly residents, independent tiny shops, and an intimate face-to-face community. "[The Heights] is like a village and far away from the galleries," explained artist Noel Davis. "I like it here because it's folksy. People are readily identifiable." "Whenever I arrive from Manhattan," said Norman Rosten, "I feel like I've left the city behind. It's a smallish town. It has small community atmosphere."[23]

For enthusiastic settlers Brooklyn Heights was a brownstone oasis or island in an alienating desert or sea. The middle landscape sat surrounded by three non-places: impersonal and modern high-rise Manhattan, artificial and conformist postwar suburbia, and bleak and blighted working-class Brooklyn. In critiquing these three spaces—Manhattan, suburbia, and the ghetto—Brooklyn Heights residents invented Brownstone Brooklyn's first "neighborhood" and developed a cohesive identity as a new urban middle class.

To move to Brooklyn Heights was to reject a home in suburbia. When residents chose to live in Brooklyn instead of Long Island or Westchester, they ran counter to the dominant trend of postwar America. As they arrived, they met older residents who were already mulling over how to keep younger residents from leaving. As these two groups interacted in church groups and social clubs, they tried to articulate not just their reasons for arriving but also, and more desperately, reasons for current residents to stay. Brooklyn Heights was in a life-or-death competition with suburbia, and residents formulated a new pro-urban ideology that juxtaposed itself to the postwar suburban ideal.

In lectures, writings, and daily discussion, Brooklyn Heights residents participated in a growing critique of postwar suburban life.[24] While city planners hoped to integrate the city with the periphery, Heights settlers instead emphatically highlighted the differences between their enclave and suburbia. "We are no longer suburbia," proudly exclaimed a *Brooklyn Heights Press* editorial, "but we are, in the best sense of the pun, *superurban*."[25] To be "superurban" was to be urban to the utmost. Superurbanity was an idealized lifestyle for a new middle class that envisioned the city as a cultural center, rather than a blighted industrial center, with art galleries, museums, cafés, independent movie houses, and other cultural resources catering to their tastes. Superurbanites celebrated the messiness of the city, rather than lamenting its disorder. They promoted its close living, rather than criticizing its overcrowding. Superurban Brooklyn Heights was not just an alternative to the suburbs; for urban settlers it was better. By moving to Brooklyn, Heights residents felt they were morally, intellectually, and physically superior to their suburban counterparts.

Although a sharp break from a long-standing American tradition of hostility toward cities, superurbanity was not a celebration of urban modernity and rejection of rural nostalgia. Rather, Heights residents transposed the pastoral ideal to the city core, juxtaposing the inner city's older folkways to suburbia's excessive modernity. Suburbia was not underdeveloped or primitive, but overdeveloped, artificial, and bureaucratic. Whereas developers, planners, and suburbanites promoted the periphery as a clean, green, and modern alternative to unhealthy city life, Brooklyn Heights settlers offered a powerful counterargument: suburbia was in fact psychologically and physically damaging to individual creativity, community, and intimate family life. "We must recognize that disenchantment is taking place in suburbia," exhorted state commerce commissioner Edward T. Dickinson in an address. "There is real trouble in paradise as suburbia."[26]

Whereas postwar redevelopers celebrated speed and motion as liberating features of a kinetic city, Heights residents lambasted the effects of the automobile, highway, and commuter rail on family life. Locked in cars and tract homes, commuting for hours, isolated in detached homes, suburbanites, they believed, suffered from "commutensions"—the pressure and anxiety that arose from too much commuting. Coined by Dr. Fred Brown in 1958 and adopted gleefully by the Brooklyn Heights Press, the word contributed to the portrait of a nightmarish suburban existence characterized by "drinking by the parents," "instability," "emotional distance," and "pseudo-matriarchal" families. Brooklyn Heights with its superurban location suffered little from these ailments. "Here on the Heights where commuting is a mere matter of five minutes to Wall Street and 20 minutes to Midtown," boasted the Brooklyn Heights Press, "the 'commutensions' are small and the instabilities minimal. Families eat their dinners earlier than families in the suburbs, little children get to see their daddies before being put to bed . . . The father kisses the mother without a breath of whiskey (no clubcar on the IRT); and things in general hum along at the smoother and more leisurely pace."[27]

Heights residents were committed pedestrians. Whereas city traffic planners sought to build new highways and time stoplights to maximize urban speed, the walkers of the Heights purposely meandered slowly through their new enclave. Over the hum of cars speeding to the suburbs on the Brooklyn-Queens Expressway underpass, residents walked the narrow streets of the Heights, feeling reconnected to an earlier, more natural form of city life under assault by the relentless pounding of mass consumer culture. "I think your 'A Walk on the Heights' feature," wrote a resident to the local paper, "gives one heart to bear up under today's tempo of living with its *'multi-neon, next year's model, time payments made easy, duo-tone chrome, jet-propelled, get that buck emphasis.'*"[28]

Suburban life was deceptively comfortable. Rather than a pastoral sanctuary, the suburbs exacerbated the dehumanizing grind of modern capitalism. Under the veneer of green space and leisure, explained pastor Kenneth D. Miller to an audience at the First Presbyterian Church, was constant financial stress and indebtedness. "Life in the suburbs is a constant effort to keep up with payments, where the whole materialistic civilization finds its epitome," he stated. With no opportunity to rent, suburbanites must buy homes, finding themselves "carrying a terrifically heavy mortgage and buying everything else on time."[29]

Far removed from sophisticated superurbanity, suburbanites were in the eyes of Heights residents intellectually shallow. Unable to visit a museum or see a play, complained Miller, culture is limited to "Twenty-Minute Reading Clubs." They were "refugees from suburbia," explained two married couples, new Heights residents, to the Junior League in a talk entitled "Return to Urbanity"; "far from the city[,] we lived in an informational void." "High on the list of advantages to living in the city, as opposed to the suburbs," wrote the editors of the *Brooklyn Heights Press*, "are the many diverse opportunities to enjoy the arts."[30]

The most damning characteristic of suburbia was its homogeneity. In contrast, Brooklyn Heights appeared "historically diverse"—a new romantic urban aesthetic that recast older inner-city districts as sources of anti-bureaucratic authenticity. "There is more diversity apparent in the Heights," exclaimed a new settler, "than in probably any other area in the city." Some used the two words in a more concrete way to describe the area's eclectic architecture and antiquated street grid. In his series of articles on "what makes Brooklyn Heights a distinct community," Richard Margolis, the twenty-nine-year-old editor of the *Brooklyn Heights Press*, argued that the Heights' distinct mix of Victorian and Federalist architecture, narrow streets, and small garden plots had to be protected from being rationalized and destroyed in a modern world becoming bureaucratic and abstract. "Elsewhere we see the breaking down of neighborhoods, the blurring of differences," warned Margolis. "[Thus] every little curlycue in our wrought iron is to be treasured, guarded, fought for. Every tree is to be adored." Brooklyn Heights architecture assuaged the anxiety of a new urban middle class by providing a sense of rootedness and identity. It is to the new brownstone settler—"the young resident, often a fugitive from his hometown, . . . floundering in the vast formlessness of New York City"—that "the trees, the narrow lanes, the glimpsed gardens behind wrought-iron gates" say that "the neighborhood possesses a mythology all its own, accumulated secrets unimagined on the treeless, bull-dozed plains of New Suburbia."[31]

For others, historic diversity referred to the Heights' mix of ethnic groups and social classes. "When we moved from the Heights from a very satisfactory suburb, we were always embarrassed by the inevitable 'But why, *why?*'" mused one couple. "I like living in a neighborhood where races, nationalities, and social classes are gloriously jumbled, as they are in the Heights." "What's so exciting about front lawns and longer fins on cars?" asked Dr. Dan Dodson of New York University's Center for Human Relations at the National Conference of Christians and Jews held in the neighborhood. "Most of the really exciting things have always come out of the city . . . in the suburbs people tend to be alike." "This scene this past Sunday on Hicks Street was delightful," exclaimed Rona Schneider in her local arts column. "[I saw] Puerto Rican children, Chinese children, Anglo-Saxon types. I saw a mixture of economic classes, too, thanks to the artists. There were prosperous middle-aged folks looking in the galleries (prospective buyers), not-so-elegant young couples wheeling baby carriages (just lookers), quite-un-elegant artists, young, single aficionados of the arts, and numbers of the poorer inhabitants who live over the galleries."[32]

When Heights enthusiasts spoke of the area's diversity, they were not necessarily referring only to residents of the largely white neighborhood. In some cases, the new middle class looked excitedly to immigrant and black service workers as sources of ethnic authenticity. In a 1941 *Vogue* article entitled "Brooklyn Is My Neighborhood," new Heights resident Carson McCullers enthusiastically described meeting her "first native" when her electrician came to do work on her house. "He is a lively young Italian with a warm, quick face and a pleasant way of whistling operatic arias while on the job." The electrician invited her to a traditional party with "rich, wholesome Italian fare: *provalone*, cheese, salami, pastries, and more of the red wine." "It is strange in New York to find yourself living in a real neighborhood," she mused.[33]

Diversity also referred to the eclectic forms of consumption favored by a new urban middle class eager for alternatives to suburban middlebrow mass consumer culture. "We have Chinese, Indian, and Middle Eastern" could be either a delighted acknowledgment of nonwhite residents or simply a listing of the choice of restaurants. In a form of consumptive diversity, Brooklyn Heights residents contrasted colorful Arab spice shops, Italian bakeries, and antique stores to the deliberately universal, nonethnic, and ahistoric department stores and shopping centers of suburbia and downtown. "Had Dante lived where my wife and I lived years ago, in 14th Street, Manhattan, he would have rewritten the Inferno. Our apartment nestled between Klein's and Ohrbach's and we were trapped in a murderous crossfire of shoppers who were fighting to establish bargain basement beachheads," explained new resident Ira Wallach in a self-mocking version of the "urban discovery narrative." "Once we decided that we needed Status, the search for a new locale narrowed. We immediately ruled out the Bronx, Queens, and Staten Island. Greenwich Village, where we stood dry-eyed at the wedding of poetry and jazz, was already becoming too bearded for comfort. Furthermore, costume jewelry—particularly of hand-wrought copper—depressed us. . . . Then we discovered that in Brooklyn Heights Good Humors come wrapped in pages of Kirkegaard, people chew Sen-Sen to clear their intellectual breath, and public pressure forces the local advertising men to speak English. . . . We go out every night and rub against Triumphs and the carriage houses."[34]

As a new middle-class ideal, the concept of "historic diversity" uneasily mixed a progressive aspiration to transcend class and race barriers with the desire to draw a clear line between the sophisticated tastes of Heights residents and the pedestrian mass culture favored by lower classes. Brooklyn Heights residents were primarily highbrow or upper-middlebrow consumers who looked to the city as a center for the fine arts. "He watches the Ford Foundation's TV program *Omnibus*," explained journalist Russell Lynes (and inventor of the famous three "brows") in 1949 about the new urban middle class. "There is also a shelf of paper-bound French novels—most of them by nineteenth-century writers. The magazines on his table span the areas from *Time* and the *New Yorker* to *Harper's* and the *Atlantic*, with an occasional copy of the *Yale* and *Partisan Reviews*, and the *Art News*." "We have so many people here who work in cultured fields," joked Ira Wallach, "that even the most casual conversations are in hi-fi. In fact, no wolf whistles are permitted on the streets. When a beautiful girl passes, you have to hum the slow movement from Beethoven's Fifth."[35]

But Brooklyn Heights' residents pointedly rejected the notion that they were cultural snobs. Rather, they were cultural omnivores for whom one's superurban status was demonstrated precisely by one's willingness to consume diverse products from the urban poor. If Heights painters and musicians produced highbrow works, their poorer neighbors produced a seemingly equally authentic and non-bureaucratic "vernacular folk culture." Heights residents attended lectures and book readings, but they also relished the restaurants and pushcarts of Brooklyn's ethnic enclaves. They celebrated the aristocratic ambience of the neighborhood, but they also listened to jazz and took particular pride in feeling comfortable around African Americans. Just as Brooklyn Heights was both aging Brahmin neighborhood and gritty slum, Brooklyn's new middle class forged a cultural middle cityscape that mixed patrician and proletariat identities. "People in the Heights live in a bourgeois sort of way," explained Norman Rosten's wife in 1957. "But they haven't lost their Bohemian yearnings." "The highbrow's friend is the lowbrow," noted Lynes. "The highbrow enjoys and respects the lowbrow's art—jazz for instance—which he is likely to call a spontaneous expression of folk culture." "The Heights is everything the Village ever thought it was. It's a gathering place for civilized people. Many have traveled abroad, many more are widely read. They are interested in the spheres that matter," explained a Heights bookstore owner of his new clientele. "They are 'of the world' enough not to be shocked if they see a Negro walking with a white, and not to stare at a man in a turban. . . . My call at this book shop is for art, psychology, drama—what I call good material. Of course there is a market for the light novel and the common paperback, but that is not the bulk of the business. The people I see are young intellectuals, very much concerned with the world."[36]

Perhaps the term "cosmopolitan class" is more appropriate than "middle class" to describe the cultural landscape of gentrifying Brooklyn Heights. For if they celebrated a historically diverse landscape of highbrow culture and ethnic folk culture, Heights residents abhorred middlebrow mass consumer culture. As most of the new suburban areas they decried were lower middle-class, Heights residents' superurbanity mixed an anti-corporatist critique of bureaucratic "ticky-tacky" tract homes and a principled attack on reactionary racial politics with a veiled disdain for their provincial denizens. "Most of the people who have written about suburbia," lamented sociologist Herbert Gans, "come—like other writers—from the cosmopolite upper middle class. Their criticism of suburban life is actually directed at working- and lower middle-class, non-cosmopolite ways, which can be found in most city neighborhoods as well, but are not as visible there as they are in suburbia." "The highbrows would apparently like to eliminate the middlebrows and devise a society that would approximate an intellectual feudal system in which the lowbrows do the work and create folk arts and the highbrows do the thinking and create fine arts," joked Lynes. "All middlebrows, presumably, would have their televisions taken away, be suspended from society until they had agreed to give up their subscriptions to the Book-of-the-Month, turned their color reproductions over to a Commission for the Dissolution of Middlebrow Taste, and renounced their affiliation with all educational and other cultural institutions whatsoever."[37]

Lynes and Gans were not the only cultural critics to struggle to find a label for this new urban middle-class fusion of highbrow and lowbrow culture. While later critics would coin terms such as "radical chic" and "bohemian bourgeois," in 1950 Charles J. Rolo called it "the new Bohemia." "Out of the intermingling of today's *ersatz* Bohemia and patrician society," explained Rolo in an article in *Flair*, "there has burgeoned a fashionable metropolitan coterie which, its pace setters claim, has made Café Society if not obsolete rather old hat." Where in previous eras bohemians and patricians had regarded each other with disdain, the new cadre of white-collar professionals after World War II combined Ivy League degrees and prestigious jobs with anti-authoritarian cultural politics. They worked as lawyers for large corporations but retained artistic aspirations to write the Great American Novel. The result for Rolo was a new urban middle class that aspired to be part of high society while simultaneously rejecting it.

> In this canvas you find a picturesque fusion of blue blood and printer's ink; silver teapots and dime-store highball glasses; gowns by Jacques Fath and turtle-neck sweaters; interiors by Sloane or Robsjohn-Gibbings and junk shoppe classicism or Third Avenue dad; Groton accents and Southern accents and staccato, tough-guy accents . . . steelmen with investments in art, and art men with investments in steel; of art-consciousness and snob-consciousness[38]

But when Brooklyn Heights settlers spoke of historic diversity, they meant something beyond the concrete and the physical. More than the layout of streets and buildings, or people and restaurants, historic diversity was a gestalt. The Heights was an authentic place that was unplanned, organic, irrational, and free. Delighted settlers contrasted Brooklyn Heights, a "rare little island" of free expression, to the rational, bureaucratic world that surrounded it. "The organization bureaucracy, with its methodic and habitual ways of doing things[,] seem[s] the antithesis of the world of free-thinking art," wrote a recent arrival of the modernist civic center that neighbored Brooklyn Heights. "And yet, only a block or two away from imposing government buildings, I was introduced to a poet, a writer, and an artist . . . Brooklyn Heights is considered the 'Village' of Brooklyn, a haven for intellectuals, and artists, and performers."[39]

The most threatening "organization bureaucracy," however, was not located in suburbia. Sameness threatened to envelop Brooklyn Heights from all sides. More ominous than the conformist tract homes in Long Island was the technocratic landscape of Manhattan. Encroaching from the island were central planners, corporate developers, and bulldozers with ambitions to integrate and assimilate. In what would be a recurring trope in Brooklyn gentrification, set-tlers decried the Manhattanization of Brooklyn. "There is no place to hide," worried a local editorial. "At every point the city impresses its stamp upon us with high-rise apartment buildings and plans for large developments. . . . If official planners have their way, every street and every building will have its twin."[40]

If suburbia suffered from race and class homogeneity, a different form of sameness pervaded the modern city. Manhattan's skyscrapers, university cam-puses, and research centers represented a new bureaucratic society in which an alienated white-collar workforce worked in regimented anonymity. Brook-lyn's new college-educated managerial class agonized about the loss of indi-viduality and difference in a "rational, bureaucratic world." In book clubs, church sermons, and private discussions, Heights residents read and dissected works such as William White's *The Organization Man*, David Riesman's *The Lonely Crowd*, and other best-selling books by social scientists that lambasted the dehumanizing world of white-collar postwar America. In his speech "A Changing Social Order," Unitarian church pastor Donald McKinney in 1958 blasted the "cult of mediocrity" in New York. Citing the social theories of White, Riesman, C. Wright Mills, and Robert Lindman, the pastor encouraged his congregation to fight "conformity," to retain "integrity" and "awareness," and to fight "paternalism" at large companies. Another group of concerned residents invited a sociology professor from Westminster College to discuss Vance Packard's *The Status Seekers* at a church meeting. The threats addressed by these influential books of the 1950s—bureaucracy, status anxiety, confor-mity, and paternalism—resonated strongly with young, enthusiastic brown-stone settlers.[41]

For new Brooklyn residents, no neighborhood represented the horror of Manhattan more than its East Side. With its new office towers and luxury apartment high-rises, the area east of Fifth Avenue between 23rd and 96th streets represented both the aspiration and nightmare for New York's new urban middle class. Only minutes away from the new postwar midtown banking, insurance, and publishing conglomerates, the East Side was the pre-mier neighborhood for New York's white-collar middle class. When a Novem-ber 1956 survey conducted by the Regional Planning Association asked tenants in high-rent apartments in Manhattan subject to rent controls about their preferred next place of residence if they should move, 68 percent listed the middle East Side of Manhattan.[42]

But no place suffered from sameness more than the East Side. The apart-ments were small barracks-like units for which middle-class professionals paid exorbitant rents. The median rent per unit completed between 1947 and 1956 in the zone from 23rd to 96th Street was $229 compared with $181 for the borough as a whole. While the average household making $10,000 or more per year spent 7.7 percent of its income on housing, in Manhattan rent-controlled high-rent apartments in 1956 the average was 16 percent. For non-controlled units, the percentage was likely even higher.[43]

Even Greenwich Village, according to some Heights residents, had not escaped the bureaucratic monster that spread across Manhattan. Refugees from the Village described a former bohemian enclave that had been co-opted by tourists, developers, and poseurs. "Many who have moved from the Village to the Heights assure us that the Village is no more," explained a local editorial. "It is neither aristocratic nor artistic. Much of it is a slum. The rents are high, the streets are dirty and the tourists are noisy. Indeed it appears that Greenwich Village now exists only in people's heads—a bright, foolish memory that glows in the midst of the rubble." "Greenwich Village East, that is east of Broadway, has been taken over by the upper-bracket bourgeoisie," explained the leader of a busload of artists touring the Heights with plans to create a "Greenwich Village Far East." Brooklyn Heights was "a fine colony of artists, writers and sculptors," wrote the *New York Times*, "sort of a Greenwich Village without tourist traps."[44]

In contrast to the placeless landscape of midtown Manhattan and touristy Greenwich Village, new enthusiasts perceived Brooklyn Heights to have a sense of place. No feature captured this sense of authenticity more than the Brooklyn brownstone. In a kinetic modern city, brownstones were anchors, their heavy facades giving new white-collar workers a sense of rootedness and permanence in a transient urban environment. "Brooklyn Heights has been *solidly* present for centuries, and in much the same shape and dimensions that it exists today," wrote a young Heights enthusiast to the local paper. Where the modern city boasted of being impermeable to weather and age, Brooklyn Heights settlers relished the weathered surfaces of brownstones, treasuring the cracks from age that made their structures unique. If apartment developers sought to make their buildings flexible and disposable, settlers celebrated precisely what they imagined to be the non-disposability of brownstones, prizing their thick walls, monumental stone surfaces, and heavy wood ornamentation. If the modern city had replaceable, interchangeable parts, Brooklyn Heights residents imagined their machine-produced brownstones to be unique passion-inspired creations of individual architects with hand-crafted and irreplaceable decoration and design. New homeowners lovingly examined the intricate details of their Victorian buildings, cherished the ornamentation, and researched the biographies of former aristocratic owners. "There was a beautiful staircase floating upward in white, swan-simple curves to a skylight of sunny amber-gold glass," wrote Capote when seeing his friend's twenty-eight-room brownstone. "The floors were fine, the real thing, hard lustrous timber; and the walls! In 1820 when the house was built, men knew how to make walls—thick as buffalo, immune to the mightiest cold, the meanest heat."[45]

Brownstones were not simply old. They were distinctly Victorian, an era that for a new urban middle class represented a temporal middle cityscape. Neither pre-urban nor modern, the Victorian brownstone was an artifact from the city's most organic form, a primordial stage of urban industrial capitalism in which the Steel Age was still molten ore. "The past, the past was great: anything American, old, glazed, touched with dusk at the end of the nineteenth century, still smoldering with the fires lit by the industrial revolution, immediately set my mind dancing," wrote Heights resident Alfred Kazin in his peripatetic memoir *A Walker in the City*. "The present was mean, the eighteenth century too Anglo-Saxon, too far away. Between them, in the light from the steerage ships waiting to discharge my parents onto the final shore, was the world of dusk, of rust, of iron, of gaslight, where, I thought, I would find my way to that fork in the road where all American lives cross."[46]

For a new white-collar labor force in an emerging postindustrial landscape, the imagined Brahmin pedigree of buildings allowed residents to form an imagined communion with a Victorian gaslight bourgeoisie. Echoing a powerful romantic theme, residents were reinhabiting an organic landscape, fleeing university campuses and high-rise apartments to return to a brownstone landscape middle-class forebears once called home. References to the Gilded Age evoked an imagined era of middle-class autonomy and individual expression that no longer existed in the vast bureaucracies of postwar corporations. In contrast to the slabs of concrete erected by faceless technicians in midtown, Heights brownstones had "character" and "charm" and appeared "personal." Patrician men rather than plebeian developers from Queens had built the aging structures, leaving each with a unique imprint in the walls and floors. While they spoke vituperatively of contemporaries such as Robert Zeckendorf and Robert Moses, Brooklyn Heights residents savored the biographies of the real estate men of the nineteenth century, imagining the rapacious speculators to be aristocratic forefathers, their buildings inspired by good taste rather than profit, their homes refined rather than gaudy. New residents felt an intimate connection to the ghosts of the original owners, researching their lives, collecting artifacts, and in many cases referring to the brownstone itself by its builder's name. Whereas most in New York lived in buildings listed only as anonymous numbers, Heights residents enthusiastically talked of Litchfield Mansion or the Weld House. "Here, it seems is the real significance of the revival of Brooklyn Heights," argued new resident and writer John Cogley. "The community of Brooklyn Heights is determined to create, rather to re-create, a simple grandeur and way of life that may be just a memory before long if the attempt fails. The Heights community is trying to prove that the city, or at least one section of it, can be revived."[47]

For young artists and writers, living in townhouses rooted them in a gene-alogy of urban romantic writers. Residents imagined themselves reinhabiting the homes of Walt Whitman, W. H. Auden, Thomas Wolfe, and Henry Miller. "I could never walk across Roebling's bridge," explained Kazin, ". . . .or stop in front of the garbage cans at Fulton and Cranberry Streets in Brooklyn where Whitman had himself printed *Leaves of Grass*, without thinking that I had at last opened the great trunk of forgotten time in New York which I, too, I thought, would someday find the source of my unrest." "'Tropic of Capricorn' was the biggest influence on my life," said young writer Lou Seida about his move to a brownstone once home to Henry Miller. "It means more to me than the bible does to most people. It helped me tear down my inhibitions." Living among the ghosts of literary giants allowed one to take on the identity of a "Brooklyn-based author" regardless of one's output. "Tony, who is 31, is prob-ably the greatest writer of his generation in my opinion, which is by no means humble," explained Seida of his social worker roommate. "He's not too inter-ested in being published."[48]

The brownstone did not only embody a highbrow historic past. Their stoops, street-level windows, and human-scale design also evoked for new residents the gestalt of a working-class "urban village." Brownstones were part of an aging industrial landscape that for new settlers represented a gemein-schaft not yet destroyed by standardized mass consumer culture and regi-mented office labor. With its small manufacturing firms and wooden piers, Brooklyn's non-Fordist waterfront appeared eclectic and organic to white-collar workers and university students working in the planned central business dis-trict. The Heights' new middle class celebrated the area's petit bourgeoisie or old middle class of barbers, greengrocers, and other small business owners. At the same, they spoke wistfully of the waterfront's casual labor force of sailors and longshoremen. Artists, sculptors, and musicians alienated by new media conglomerates headquartered in Manhattan and the competitive art scene imagined themselves working by hand in a pre-mechanized and non-bureau-cratic artisan society. "The social makeup of the Heights is an unusual, organic unity of diverse elements: old Brooklyn families, young professional people, artists, musicians and writers, small shop owners and local employees," explained a local resident and art professor. If Manhattan was a "dead-level apartment house world, a one-class residential dormitory," Brooklyn Heights had "musicians and artists . . ., antique shops, signmakers, and cabinet makers."[49]

Brooklyn Heights represented for the Manhattan refugee a "real neighborhood," an authentic local place where genuine human contact and ethnic folk tradition remained uncrushed by alienating modernity and capitalism. "One can walk down the streets of Brooklyn Heights and feel its past. One can talk to its people and feel warm, cordial friendship without ever bothering to suspect the friendship of being a cover for material greed," explained a new resident. It is only in "old neighborhoods," explained Greenwich Village bookstore vendor and new Heights townhouse owner Eli Wilentz, where urban community still thrives. For in new and modern East Side apartment towers, "community as a social entity is non-existent. . . . [Residents] draw their social life from their friends anywhere, certainly not from those in the same building or even in their neighborhood. They don't do the shopping in local markets or walk their children who are off at private schools. The midtown restaurants, theatres, night clubs, specialty shops, are their proper domain. Transportation by car or taxi, of course. In the summer, off to East Hampton or Connecticut." Moving to Brooklyn Heights tenements and brownstones, however, allowed alienated white-collar East Siders to experience the more authentic folkways of the urban poor. "Imagine if the people on the Lower Fifth Avenue began acting socially like the poor," mused Wilentz. "At night the doorman would be putting out chairs for everyone to be sitting out front to gossip. Mothers would have pillowcases on the window sills from which comfortable vantage they could watch their children playing in the street. The corners would be crowded with groups of men discussing baseball or politics. The Fifth Avenue Hotel restaurant would be converted to a candy store, shoe-repair shop, open-air fresh-vegetable market, and a corner bar."[50]

Even the destitute evoked for new middle-class residents an earlier era when different classes cooperated in a face-to-face community. Mike, a seventy-four-year-old homeless alcoholic, for example, was for superurban residents the Heights' lovable "town drunk." Mike, explained one writer fondly, "is a respected member of the community, and is as much a landmark as the town hall. . . . In the town drunk are found all the attributes belonging to a kindly person, for never is he found without cheerful disposition and an ever-ready smile for anyone who passes by." With little interest in work, Mike chose his lifestyle and was happy with his lot. But "while he does little to help himself, he gladly aids those who will call upon him." Mike was intimately linked to the local place of Brooklyn Heights. While the poor elsewhere lived in barracks-like public housing, Mike was an old-timer well acquainted with the lore and history of the community in which he resided, "a walking encyclopedia."[51]

Perched on a hilltop across the river, Brooklyn Heights offered a view of Manhattan. It was a site where one could live close to the metropole but remain outside of it. It was a place where one could look upon the island of Manhattan with skepticism, wonderment, and disdain. Like Thoreau's Walden, Brooklyn Heights allowed residents to remain attached to the cultural amenities of the city but still remain authentically independent of it. "At times I think the Esplanade," wrote a settler of the boardwalk overlooking the Manhattan skyline, "was built to give inhabitants of the Heights an opportunity to look with pity on the heedless helter skelter struggles of their brothers across the river." "We get to appreciate New York so much more than New Yorkers do," said a young Heights housewife who grew up in Virginia. "We can see it from a distance."[52]

Brooklyn Heights offered a view in the other direction as well. While to the west lay the grid space of Manhattan, to the east, south, and north spread another imagined landscape of alienating sameness: blighted Brooklyn. For many settlers, Brooklyn Heights was an outpost in a forbidding borough, and a mix of Beat writers, journalists, playwrights, social workers, political organizers, and social scientists used the area as a middle-class base from which to explore Brooklyn's periphery.

These Heights writers and artists were fascinated and horrified by the tough neighboring boardinghouse district. Often renting or buying cheap property on the periphery of Brooklyn Heights, they lived in close contact with working-class white Catholics, Puerto Ricans, and African Americans. They were titillated by living close to danger and felt inspired by the rawness of the deindustrializing urban landscape. Laborers in the newly consolidated and integrated bureaucracies of the city center, they juxtaposed an imagined landscape of rebellion, freedom, and untamed wilderness to the institutional cityscape of the modern city. Often university students seeking relief from bureaucratic campus life, authors shunning the offices of new publishing conglomerates, and artists rejecting the inauthentic poseurs of galleries in the urban core, these self-acclaimed urban frontiersmen turned to the belt of older housing on the periphery for an imagined urban authenticity.

As they settled in the tenements and brownstones on the edge of Brooklyn Heights, they penned novels, plays, and poems and created visual representations of their surroundings to form a new and unique genre of Brooklyn-based urban romanticism. For some, the Brooklyn periphery was an urban naturalist landscape where the individual battled futilely against the overwhelming power of nature. For resident playwright Arthur Miller, Brooklyn was a tragic space where working-class men struggled unsuccessfully to exercise free will against the downward pull of brutal social and economic forces. During the

1940s and '50s, Miller used his Brooklyn Heights apartment as a base while he immersed himself daily in the lives of working-class Brooklynites toiling in the Navy Yard and later packing beers in the local beer factory. In his *A View from the Bridge* and *Death of a Salesman*, written while he lived in Brooklyn Heights, Miller used a bleak Brooklyn landscape both for realist commentary about social inequality and to reexamine Greek tragic form. With uncontrollable forces of poverty and social custom controlling their fate, Miller's Brooklynite characters try unsuccessfully to assert their individuality and gain pride and recognition in a demeaning and disempowering environment. The attempt is futile, and his plays climax with a final act of destructive violence.[53]

Yet along with its realism, Miller's Brooklyn-based works revealed some of the romantic aesthetics of Brooklyn Heights' new superurban middle class. In *Death of a Salesman*, the Lomans live in a decaying single-family house, struggling to survive the onslaught of the modern city. The small wood-frame home seems to be crushed by a "solid vault of apartment houses." The characters are "boxed in" by "windows and bricks." With the sun blocked out and developers uprooting trees from the soil, once fruitful backyard gardens are barren. Brooklyn is a desert of sameness. "The street is lined with cars. There's not a breath of fresh air in the neighborhood. The grass don't grow any more, you can't raise a carrot in the back yard," cries Willy as he looks at the towering cinderblock apartments that surround him. "They should've arrested the builder for cutting those down. They massacred the neighborhood . . . Smell that stink from that apartment house!"[54]

When Willy visits Manhattan, he enters a dehumanizing corporate world where an artificial bureaucracy has replaced the close human relationships of an older business era. As Willy pleads for relief from his unfeeling boss, his boss seems not to hear or care. He is more fascinated by the artificial voices on a new tape recorder he is playing with. "In those days there was personality in it," explains Willy of older business mores. "There was respect, and comradeship, and gratitude in it. Today it's all cut and dried, and there's no chance for bringing friendship to bear—or personality."[55]

Arthur Miller's plays were but one example of a slew of postwar Brooklyn-based naturalist fiction. Novels such as Albert Halper's *Atlantic Avenue* and Frank Paley's *Rumble on the Docks* shocked readers with their uncompromising depiction of life in the slums. Irving Shulman's sensational depiction of a Jewish teenage gang, *The Amboy Dukes*, although situated deeper in Brooklyn, was a wildly popular version of a similar genre. Like Miller's tragic play, the novels emphasized the futility of human agency in the face of overwhelming poverty. In a recurring trope, a male protagonist appears on the cusp of escaping the ghetto, but he is pulled by uncontrollable base emotions of lust, rage, and jealousy toward a tragic climax in which he commits either suicide or murder.[56]

Perhaps the most effective example of Brooklyn naturalism was Hubert Selby Jr.'s *Last Exit to Brooklyn*. In a series of brutal vignettes, Selby offered a raw depiction of Brownstone Brooklyn in which residents struggled to maintain a sense of dignity, but were driven by primitive instincts to commit murder, rape, sodomy, and suicide. Selby's work was a cut above the sensationalist slum novels produced by his Brooklyn-based peers. Despite what was at times a demeaning and sensational portrayal of Brooklyn's working-class residents, Selby was tuned in to the complexity of the blighted areas of the 1950s. His novel was meant to shock, but it remained an effective piece of anthropology, realistically capturing the homoerotic tensions in male street society, the intertwined relationship of union, street gang, organized crime syndicate, and political machine, the violent relationship between men and women, and the deleterious effects of crowded living on family life.[57]

For some writers, Brooklyn's slums were not repressive but liberating. While Arthur Miller lamented the depressed condition of the waterfront, resident writer Norman Mailer and white male Beat writers celebrated working-class South Brooklyn as "hip." These self-described "hipsters" hung out in local bars, drank heavily with longshoremen, and imitated working-class speech patterns. While the bachelor society of the waterfront terrified the homeowners of Brooklyn Heights, it was precisely that transience that fascinated Mailer and his peers. Brooklyn was a radically free space unencumbered by the artificial restraints of the corporation and the family. The boardinghouse district filled with single men was to Mailer sexually raw and spontaneously violent, free from the conformity of the 1950s that was deadening American life. By living a few blocks away from Montague Street, Mailer imagined himself a frontiersman boldly settling along a new urban frontier. "One is a rebel or one conforms," explained the young author. "One is a frontiersman in the Wild West of the night, or else a Square cell."[58]

In a revolt against new forms of white-collar labor, Beats and other hipsters selectively looked to Brooklyn's poor as sources of anti-bureaucratic authenticity. Self-described "white Negroes" turned to the city's growing African American population as a source of anti-institutional rebellion. They explored the black districts on the periphery of Columbia University, Greenwich Village, and Brooklyn Heights, listened to bop jazz, and imitated the speech and dress of black musicians. Drugs also pulled countercultural hipsters to the middle cityscape between skyscraper and slum. Wandering the streets for a fix, college-educated drug users became romantic urbanites, peripatetic explorers uncovering a hidden city invisible on abstract bird's-eye-view maps. As they left the safe confines of the university campus or middle-class neighborhood, Beat drug users described an organic, irrational, brutal cityscape that they juxtaposed to the phony, bureaucratic modern city they left behind. "I saw the best minds of my generation destroyed by madness," wrote Allen Ginsberg in the opening lines of *Howl*, "starving hysterical naked, dragging themselves through the negro streets at dawn looking for an angry fix."

No figure fascinated Brooklyn Heights hipsters more than the juvenile delinquent. While city educators and parents fretted about teenage delinquency and the heroin epidemic, Brooklyn's teenage gang members—"rebels without a cause"—personified alienation and provided a countercultural street language that Beats and hipsters relished. White middle-class hipsters were engrossed by "cool" slang: "zip guns," "bopping," "rumbling," "diddley bop," and "fish" dancing.

As they pushed into the poorer periphery of Brooklyn Heights, hipsters described themselves as lone crusaders in a philosophical and literary struggle against bureaucracy. Citing the writings of Jean-Paul Sartre, Heidegger, and postwar existentialists, Norman Mailer and other Brooklyn hipsters used the transient rooming house district as a backdrop for existential liberation. While many pointed to the Heights' history as an antidote to modernity, Mailer thought it was precisely Brooklyn's lack of history, lack of place, and lack of coherence that made it an ideal counter to the bureaucratic corporate world. In his novel *Barbary Shore*, Mailer used a Brooklyn boardinghouse as the setting for what he claimed to be the first of the existentialist novels in America. His main character was an amnesiac war veteran and a writer, unaware of his past, with no connections to family, tradition, or work. Filled with Godot-like impersonal dialogue, the book chronicled the existential conflict between characters in the empty space of Brownstone Brooklyn.[59]

Hipsters moved not into poor neighborhoods but near them. They insisted that living in a brownstone a few blocks deeper into the interior of the borough, or in a walk-up tenement instead of an elevator apartment, exposed one to a more authentic urban life than that available to peers a few blocks away. Whereas the center of the Heights had begun to soften with the inflow of too many white-collar professionals, the periphery retained a rawer form of urban verité. If one geographically contextualizes Mailer's list of "the Hip and the Square," it becomes clear he's describing the periphery and center of Brooklyn Heights: "wild" and "practical," "Negro" and "white," "Catholic" and "Protestant," "barbarians" and "bohemians." On the periphery of Brooklyn Heights, Greenwich Village, and the West Side, he explained, "the bohemian and the juvenile delinquent came face-to-face with the Negro, and the hipster was a fact in American life." The untamed authenticity of Brooklyn even allowed resident hipsters to one-up Manhattan-based Beats. "If you are talking about Jack Kerouac, I'd like to punch him in the nose," said Lou Seida, the twenty-three-year-old owner of a Beat café called Black Spring. "He's a phony."[60]

Hipster Brooklyn remained a middle cityscape. Beats and hipsters did not simply appropriate from Brooklyn's urban poor. They also unintentionally reshaped the landscape they imagined as authentic. Brooklyn gang members, for example, often cited movies such as *Blackboard Jungle* and *Rebel Without a Cause*, or novels such as *The Amboy Dukes*, as inspiration for their dress and walk. As one Park Slope gang member remembers: "Junior was the Don Juan of the neighborhood . . . walked around with a copy of Ginsburg's *Howl* in his back pocket . . . We combed our hair constantly, wore sunglasses, and all thought we were Marlon Brandos." Transcending the boundaries of a segregated postwar city, drug users also pioneered an interracial and interclass subculture. In neighborhoods such as Brooklyn Heights and the East Village, a college-educated middle class exchanged drug paraphernalia, slang, and techniques with the urban poor. Rural drugs such as marijuana filtered up from black, Puerto Rican, and Mexican migrants to the city's white managerial class. LSD and other chemical drugs produced in the research centers of the modern central business district filtered down from universities to peripheral urban slums.[61]

The line between those who looked to Brooklyn's slums as political activists and those who sought a countercultural refuge was blurred as well. While he did not share Norman Mailer's enthusiasm for the "freedom" of being poor, even Arthur Miller echoed some of the countercultural themes of the Beat movement. Miller's South Brooklyn was certainly not a liberating space, but economically and socially repressive. In *A View from the Bridge*, the South Brooklyn waterfront appeared as a primitive world of Italian Catholic longshoremen where free will clashes unsuccessfully against provincial Old World social customs, masculine codes of behavior, and oppressive economic conditions. Yet his male characters who successfully escape Brooklyn were countercultural misfits. Biff Loman wanders the West, working on farms with his hands. He is alienated, unmarried, and unable to hold a job. At the climax of the play, he breaks free from the corporate world by running out of a skyscraper and confronting his existential freedom and responsibility: "All I want is out there, waiting for me the minute I say I know who I am. . . . I'm nothing!" In *A View from the Bridge*, Rodolpho crosses the strict gender boundaries of South Brooklyn. Mocked by the other longshoremen, he sings jazz ballads, wears dandyish clothes, and has flowing blond hair. Yet his behavior is not disempowering but liberating. He is freer than Eddie, who is imprisoned by his own self-destructive machismo.[62]

Not all who explored Brooklyn did so for artistic inspiration. Brooklyn Heights was an outpost for the many "missionaries" who worked and volunteered in the area: social workers, settlement house organizers, journalists, charity workers, and social scientists. With roots in the settlement house movement of the nineteenth century, missionaries advocated a place-sensitive, grassroots approach to social work that differed dramatically from the top-down approach taken by the newly consolidated, mega-sized postwar philanthropic organizations of the modern city. In the 1950s, the Ford Foundation, the United Way, and other organizations attempted to integrate their disparate functions into large centralized institutions based in Manhattan or other downtowns, to rule top-down under strong executive boards, to standardize national programs, and to conduct empirically measured cost-benefit analyses of programs. The missionaries based in Brooklyn Heights were instead decidedly local, personal, and unstandardized. They customized programs to the specific needs of local communities, building on existing institutions and fostering a sense of neighborhood or block identity. Rather than viewing the city whole, from a bird's-eye view, they walked the streets and knocked on doors, developed intimate relationships with residents on a single block, and immersed themselves fully in the lives of the poor.[63]

The seminal example of this new postwar community organizing was the New York City Youth Board. Formed in 1948 by the city to respond to increasing public pressure to tackle the juvenile delinquency problem, the Youth Board offered a new hands-on approach to gang intervention, sending social workers to hang out with, gain the trust of, and give guidance to members of youth gangs. The Youth Board opened small offices around the city near gang hot spots and sent a cadre of idealistic men in their twenties to immerse themselves in the environment of the poor, to act as liaisons for social service organizations, and, they hoped, to convert street gangs out of their fighting culture. The South Brooklyn district, with one of the highest concentrations of street gangs in the city, had a branch.[64]

To develop intimate relationships with teenage gangs, Youth Board workers, referred to as "gang workers," became impromptu anthropologists and humanistic geographers who out of necessity developed a sophisticated and textured sense of local place. Starting from a bird's-eye view with an abstract neighborhood place name on an official map, the worker tried to immerse himself more deeply into the landscape and connect to unmapped community networks. "Although a worker knows the general area in which a gang operates, to find its exact location he must very often make use of various sources," explained a Youth Board guidebook. "He will get information, perhaps, from local agencies, schools and police. He will talk with people in the neighborhood. He will observe teenage groups at their various hangouts. Many times, he will get some names from writings on the walls, billboards and the like. Once the gang is located, the worker will begin to make contact with the group by 'hanging around' its favorite meeting places: for example, candy stores, street corners, or poolrooms. . . . Often the worker finds that he is aided in making and developing contacts by shooting pool, playing juke boxes or just in understanding local slang."[65]

Throughout the 1950s, a steady traffic of journalists, gang workers, artists, photographers left Manhattan and Brooklyn Heights to immerse themselves in Brownstone Brooklyn in search of the juvenile delinquent. To research his Pulitzer Prize–winning exposé on gang culture, *The Shook-up Generation*, *New York Times* journalist Harrison Salisbury spent a year accompanying gangs in South Brooklyn. Photographer Bruce Davidson similarly spent years hanging out with the Jokers, a Park Slope gang, producing a beautiful set of photos published in *Vanity Fair* in 1958; Norman Mailer wrote the introduction. Arthur Miller, too, spent the summer of 1955 hanging out with gangs in South Brooklyn to research a script for a Youth Board movie project. His screenplay proposal described the struggles of a social worker struggling to connect with a South Brooklyn street gang. The city accepted the screenplay initially, only to revoke its offer when the House Un-American Activities Committee deemed Miller too radical for the project. (The youth gangs of the West Side—another gentrifying middle landscape on the periphery of midtown—similarly inspired Leonard Bernstein's musical *West Side Story*.)[66]

Brooklyn Heights was home to a settlement house and other charity groups that brought middle-class activists in contact with the urban poor. Heights activist Richard Mendes, for example, directed the South Brooklyn Neighborhood House (SBNH) and taught sociology at Brooklyn College. Formerly known as the Little Italy Neighborhood Association when it began work in 1904, the settlement house offered free classes, a gymnasium, gang intervention programs, and a nursery school for children of the neighborhood. Located on Willow Place at the southern end of the Heights, the SBNH was used by many of the working-class renters who lived on the periphery of the neighborhood.[67]

Like HARYOU-ACT in Harlem and the Mobilization for Youth on the Lower East Side, Brooklyn's missionaries, such as Dick Mendes, were influential place makers who dramatically reshaped urban politics throughout the 1950s and 1960s. Settlement house workers and other community activists led fights against urban renewal projects and pushed the Ford Foundation and other philanthropic groups to experiment with community control experiments. Great Society administrators in the 1960s looked to anti-gang programs as a model for new participatory community action programs. By the 1970s, gang workers, teachers, social workers, and other community organizers formed a cadre of political activists that spearheaded a new "neighborhood movement" and led a reform insurgency in the Democratic party.

Urban missionaries pioneered a neighborhood-centric approach to urban space that humanized the poor and fought to recognize and protect authentic communities in areas dismissed as blighted. But as the first middle-class residents in poor neighborhoods, missionaries also created a middle cityscape, changing the environment in ways they did not necessarily expect. As they walked through blighted areas to make contact with the poor, community organizers were pioneers who unwittingly made areas more amenable for gentrification. In countering demeaning images of blight on behalf of poorer residents, missionaries rhetorically turned "slums" into "neighborhoods," imposing a middle-class place aesthetic that unintentionally embourgeoised urban space. Although in intent the settlement house sought to bring middle-class values to the poor, it often (as its name unintentionally suggests) brought middle-class settlers themselves.[68]

Obviously one cannot dismiss community organizers as gentrifiers. But it does demonstrate that the roots of gentrification can be found in unexpected places. Rather than in the boardrooms of urban developers and banks, gentrification was a grassroots movement that drew inspiration from Saul Alinsky and Dorothy Day. The migration to Brooklyn was one of contradictory intentions. Looking at a 1956 account by young Heights settler and settlement worker Katherine Coldwell, it is clear that even the most sensitive account of urban charity work can also function as urban discovery narrative:

Coming from West Texas, I lived for seven years in five localities in Manhattan, but so far as I know, I was never living in a *neighborhood*. No one spoke to anyone and no one knew anything about anyone, nor cared. We all lived a quiet, private and anonymous life. . . . Now living in Brooklyn Heights and walking to work at the Settlement . . . I know a lot of people and a lot of people know me. When the house across the street is painted green, it gives me pleasure, and when the beer cans a few doors down overflow onto the street—it gives me pain. . . . I have sat in the garden of a friend on Grace Court and have heard a fellow guest speak with displeasure of the wash tub on the back of an apartment on Joralemon. But in that Joralemon apartment I have seen the tub in use; have heard at close range the offensive radio; have even dandled the unclad child. I have carried a pair of unused pants from a home that owns a Renoir to a boy just out of prison who was wearing borrowed ones. . . . I see around me good and bad, growth and decay.

Coldwell's description is a humanizing, intimate treatment of slum life, yet it contains all the romantic themes of an urban discovery narrative. The social worker was once an alienated white-collar worker toiling in the modern city and yearning for something more. Rejecting the trappings of middle-class life, she became a community worker and discovered a real neighborhood on the periphery of the central business district. Once suffering from anomie, she feels emplaced and rooted among the poor, who despite their hardships live more authentic lives than the anonymous and atomized wealthy in midtown high-rises. Brooklyn's brownstones uniquely mix aristocratic elegance and working-class grit. Upon setting up the urban pastoral slum, the scene is interrupted by a symbol of modernity—in this case, the bulldozer—followed by the romantic lamentation that a fragile idyll she discovered is on the cusp of extinction.

> So now, hearing that part of this world I have found will be torn down to be replaced by handsome new buildings—new buildings where people will live anonymously, the way I used to live; buildings neatly set out so there won't be a pillared house that reminds me of an adolescent summer in New Orleans or a doorway with a brass knob reminiscent of London—when I hear this, I have a strange beat of the heart. And if then I stop to wonder what the new beat is, I realize that it is the fear of losing something that has become valuable to me, something I did not know before—a neighborhood.[69]

Bohemian artists and idealistic missionaries were not the only settlers to turn their eye towards the brownstone slums of Brooklyn. Another group of middle-class men quietly pushed past the periphery of the Heights as well. The Heights was an outpost from which gay men had access to a center of gay life in postwar New York City: the menacing but oddly tolerant sexual world of Brooklyn's working-class male street society. In a pre-Stonewall era when middle-class bars and clubs had strict prohibitions against homosexuality, Brooklyn's industrial waterfront had an active gay life. Along piers and in the Navy Yard, in Prospect Park and on the Promenade, working-class straight males, provided they were in the dominant position, regarded effeminate men and cross-dressers as an acceptable substitute for women if the latter were unavailable. Mafia-run dive bars, along with permitting prostitution and gambling, were among the few clubs that didn't prohibit male touching. With its culture of "circle jerks," "line-up" group sex, and "fag rolling" (luring a gay man into a secluded area with the promise of sex and then robbing him), postwar gang culture was highly homoerotic as well. Gang members often exchanged sexual favors with older gay men for cash. Others participated in same-sex relations in all-male environments: reformatory schools, prisons, and gang hangouts.[70]

Although home to an active gay scene, the rough-and-tumble cityscape on the periphery of Brooklyn Heights should not be mistaken as a tolerant area in the current sense, any more than one could describe the gay life in a contemporary prison as such. Participating in illicit sex in unpoliced, crime-ridden areas left men open to physical abuse and crime. The sexual relationship relied on the straight male's sense of power and control over his demi-female counterpart rather than mutuality. Flirtation could quickly change to physical and verbal abuse. In other cases, gay sexual consumers ran the risk of retaliation or robbery from their often underprivileged peddlers. Procuring sex from poorer young men at times could be exploitative as well.[71]

But in a postwar era where homosexuality had become strictly policed and punishable by law, Brooklyn social workers were flabbergasted by the casual attitude of working-class young men about gay sex. In one interchange, a social worker was stunned by a white Brownstone Brooklyn gang member's admission:

> Bop was proud in his new Marine uniform when I saw him. I congratulated him and said idly, "Thought you joined the Navy, Bop?"
>
> Bop replied, "I tried. I don't know what the hell happened. I had an interview with a Navy psychiatrist, and he says to me, 'Do you fool around with girls?' I answered, "I sure do, man. I sure do." Then this jerk asks me, "If there was a queer around, and you hadn't been laid for a long time, would you let the queer blow you?"
>
> "What did you tell him, Bop?" I asked.
>
> Bop answered, "I told him, 'Sure, if I hadn't been laid in a long time. I'd let a queer fool around with me.'"
>
> I showed my shock. "Bop, did you actually tell him that?"
>
> Bop replied, "Yeah. That's what I told him, Rick." A pause. "Hey Rick, do you suppose the Navy didn't want me because of that?" He was astonished. He went on, "What the hell's so wrong about having a queer blow you? All the guys around here do it." . . .
>
> "Are you [a queer]?" I asked. His answer to this was, "Well, fuck, man, everybody in the neighborhood does it."[72]

As solitary city explorers who meandered through the roughest sections of the city, middle-class gay men were romantic urbanists who forged a middle cityscape between skyscraper and slum. Trolling for sex, gay men descended from the bird's-eye view of the city to uncover an unplanned and place-centric hidden city of overlapping human networks. Although not necessarily inspired by racial or social idealism, white gay men were in practice some of the first white-collar professionals to transcend urban race and class boundaries. As gay men interacted with gang members, longshoremen, poor blacks, and Puerto Ricans, the language and culture of the urban poor filtered up to the white middle class.

Gay cityscapes also acted as a conduit for middle-class culture to filter down to the poor. Straight men in poor areas were often drawn as much to the cultural sophistication of gay men as to the prospect of sex. While "easy" girls or prostitutes often came from the lowest strata of Brownstone Brooklyn society, middle-class gay men spoke elegantly, wore expensive clothes and scent, bought pricey gifts, and exposed young working-class men to the cultural capital of middle-class Manhattan. "The homosexual provided them with many things," explained a Brownstone Brooklyn social worker about the white teenage gang he worked with. "He was a sex outlet. Good girls were few and required stratagems. Stratagems of speech which were beyond most of my kids. Girls were too much for Bugsy. He just couldn't get along with them. He got along fine with homosexuals."[73]

In the 1950s, gay men remained a noticeable presence throughout Brooklyn Heights. The Promenade, along with Montague Street bars such as Danny's, were known gay hangouts. "We have no complaints about those 'dears' who are also in the area (although not as many as in Greenwich Village)," mentioned the local paper in 1949. "They're a harmless lot, keeping pretty much to themselves." The rooftops of buildings, alleys, stairwells, and other hidden spaces also were also interstitial sexual spaces. "For the past several months the hallways and roof have become the playground for a band of youths, and a night spot for homosexuals," complained the residents of 2 Grace Court to the *Brooklyn Heights Press*. By the early 1960s, however, tensions in Brooklyn Heights began to rise as more gay men displaced by gentrification and police crackdowns in Manhattan began to frequent the area. At the same time, as the Heights became more upscale, a new crop of white-collar professionals with families had less tolerance for the interstitial working-class sexual landscape. In 1963, a series of morals arrests by police in local bars led to a heated exchange of letters by residents in the *Brooklyn Heights Press* attacking and defending the growing gay presence. "As to the Letters to Editor column last week, regarding the 'hounded and persecuted homosexual' etc., etc. . . . I remind the individual writing that the homosexual lacks basic morality. . . . Because their alliances are so brief, causing frequent apartment changing, they raise rents to exorbitant heights for those of us with families, who lead normal, moral lives. . . . Let them take their daisy chains, their makeup and tight pants out of the middle of Montague Street and the Central Heights." In her seven years on the Heights, the author continued, "I have seen it change from a Fag Haven to respectability and back again. Let's do something about it, mothers." By 1966, a flurry of vicious letters from angry residents complaining about the growing number of flamboyant "Village fags" and "Times Square queens" on the "Promenade of Pansies" led both the *BHP* and the Brooklyn Heights Association to issue separate statements condemning "exhibitionist" homosexuals and calling for more police surveillance of Montague Street bars, public lavatories, and other areas. In response, the Brooklyn Heights Chapter of the Mattachine Society, an early gay civil rights organization, tried to place an ad calling for a town hall meeting. The paper refused. The Mattachine Society subsequently organized a boycott of the *Brooklyn Heights Press* and businesses that advertised in it. The vituperative response by the *Press*, the Brooklyn Heights Association, and local residents to the boycott, and subsequent increased police crackdowns on gay men, sparked a more militant rights movement. By 1972, gay political activism had completely transformed the area. Despite never reversing its editorial, the *Brooklyn Heights Press* started a "Gay Voices" column, and a new newspaper, the *Phoenix*, openly recruited articles from gay writers. In fact, the neighborhood had such a strong sexual identity that one gay activist group had to stress to members: "We are the Gay Alliance of *Brooklyn*, not of Brooklyn Heights. . . . There's a lot of gay Brooklyn beyond Atlantic Avenue."[74]

Brooklyn Heights was Brownstone Brooklyn's first invented neighborhood. An eclectic new middle class of white-collar professionals, artists, journalists, editors, bohemians, social workers, and gay men looked to the Victorian townhouse district as an imagined authentic refuge from suburbia, the central business district, and the slum. Yet few residents fit neatly into categories. "Many hipsters are bisexual," explained Norman Mailer. Arthur Miller was both naturalist writer and missionary reformer. Kenneth Boss was both speculative real estate agent and member of the Socialist party. Eli Wilentz was both Greenwich Village Beat and historic preservationist. Lou Seida was both countercultural writer and full-time social worker. Artists lived adjacent to Wall Street brokers. All were members of a new middle class.

What united this new middle class was a collective urban identity. Bounded by overdeveloped Manhattan to one side and the undeveloped slum to the other, all agreed that they had discovered a historically diverse "real neighborhood" on the cusp of extinction and in need of rescue. Brooklyn Heights was a fragile middle cityscape that reconciled two competing visions of urban verisimilitude. For some it was a historic neighborhood that rooted residents in aristocratic past. For others the neighborhood was a gritty, diverse frontier

On the Esplanade in Historic Old Brooklyn Heights

"Young man, we folks on *The Heights* are no different from anyone else."

"On the Esplanade in Historic Old Brooklyn Heights." Frank Mack's 1968 cartoon captures well the urban aesthetic of Brooklyn Heights' new middle class. The Heights was "old" and "historic" with a dowager in the top left corner evoking the neighborhood's aristocratic past. Bohemians, gay men, cultural sophisticates (a young boy reading *War and Peace*), short hemlines, and tweed jackets point to the area's "difference" and "diversity." The colorful scene is set against the stark backdrop of downtown Manhattan. Missing from this celebration of Brooklyn's "historic diversity" are the area's African Americans, Puerto Ricans, and working-class whites. (Courtesy of the *Brooklyn Heights Press*)

that exposed middle-class residents to the authentic folkways of the urban poor.

With their paradoxical mix of populism and class snobbery, as well as a flair for self-aggrandizement, Brooklyn's new middle class made for an easy target for the more cynical. Even in the 1950s and 1960s, many critics had already began to poke fun at this new strain of urban romanticism. "A nostalgia for brownstones?" complained sociologist Bennett Berger. "Aren't all those delightful 'surprises' in old brownstones *standard* for old brownstones? Does the fact that air conditioning requires closed windows transform new office buildings into hygienic 'cages'? I wonder whether critics waxed sentimental a

hundred years ago when those darling eighteenth-century buildings were sac-
rificed to those monotonous rows of Victorian brownstones."[75]

Even if romantic urbanism was riddled with contradictions, however, it
was a pro-urban ideology at a time when most Americans were emphatically
rejecting cities. Its proponents intentionally moved into poor, increasingly
nonwhite neighborhoods when most whites fled the inner city and purposely
erected barriers to ensure that minorities couldn't follow. Certainly there were
those who saw their goal as making the area "nice" by displacing the poor as
quickly as possible. But often those same people earnestly imagined a mixed
community that transcended racial and class divisions. "Historic diversity"
was a paradox, and most residents simultaneously harbored affection and
hostility toward the poor, as well as self-righteous confidence and agonizing
self-doubt about their intentions.

Perhaps no figure better captured the contradictions of historic diversity
than Truman Capote. The acclaimed writer was both tough social realist and
urban romantic. He celebrated the aristocratic ambience of Brooklyn Heights,
but also participated, likely, in its gay subculture. He was an urban flaneur
who wrote excitedly of the area's diverse and colorful brew of Senegalese
sailors, Oriental bazaars, and antique stores, but was notably less enthusiastic
about the Heights' poor nonwhite residents living on the periphery. At the
end of his paean to Brooklyn Heights, Capote approaches Atlantic Avenue, a
border where "Brooklyn became Brooklyn again." As the flaneur crosses into
"a dark sector of the dockyards," he realizes he is no longer in "a true part of
the Heights neighborhood." "It lies . . . on the outmost periphery. Seedy hangouts, beer-sour bars and bitter candy stores mingle among the eroding houses."
The romantic flaneur has entered gang territory, and the sense of place he
detects here is less appealing:

> Here, the gutters are acrawl with Cobras; that is, a gang of "juvenile"
> delinquents; COBRA, the word is stamped on their sweatshirts, painted,
> sometimes in letters that shine with a fearful phosphorescence, across the
> backs of their leather jackets. The steep street is within their ugly estate, a
> bit of their "turf," as they term it; an infinitesimal bit, for the Cobras, a
> powerful cabala, cast owning eyes on acres of metropolitan terrain. . . .
> Their eyes, their asleep sick insolent eyes, swerved on me as I climbed the
> street. I crossed to the opposite curb; then *knew*, without needing to verify
> it, that the Cobras had uncoiled and were sliding toward me. I heard them
> whistling; and the children hushed, the skip-rope ceased swishing. Some-
> one—a pimpled purple-birthmark bandit-masked the lower half of his
> face—said, "Hey, yuh, Whitey, lemmeseeduhcamra."[76]

Capote's historic diversity had its symbolic and geographic limits. For the young writer and his new middle-class white neighbors, Brooklyn Heights was a refuge hidden from Manhattan's alienating modernity. But the middle cityscape had a border where the organic became wilderness, where the colorful ethnic mélange turned indistinguishably black, and where place dissolved into placelessness. From these two landscapes—hypermodern Manhattan and wild Brooklyn—Brooklyn Heights needed to be fiercely protected.

4 The Two Machines in the Garden

While new middle-class arrivals avidly described Brooklyn Heights in the mid-1950s, few formally outlined the boundaries of the enclave or listed systematically the exact characteristics that distinguished the "real neighborhood" from the inauthentic cityscape that surrounded it. With no legal or political definition, the Heights remained a vague in-between zone. On the northern periphery, the neighborhood transformed abruptly into downtown Brooklyn; to the south, it blended into the peripheral slums. By the mid-1960s, however, Brooklyn Heights had legally recognized boundaries, a new political party, new books commemorating its history, and a bevy of civic groups dedicated to preserving the area from development. Brooklyn Heights became Brownstone Brooklyn's first invented neighborhood.

In the history of the American city, the neighborhood has often coalesced when mobilizing against a perceived outside threat. The arrival of a new ethnic group or the threat of a development project inspired residents to exchange the class, ethnic, gender, and religious turf lines that divided an area for a collective neighborhood identity whose boundaries needed to be defended. For Brooklyn Heights—as well as the West Side of Manhattan, Greenwich Village, and other postwar middle landscapes throughout the city—the catalyst for neighborhood formation was the intrusion of the machine. The machine, although a metaphor, represented real political, architectural, and social forces. In fact, two machines threatened Brooklyn Heights in the eyes of new residents, each version encroaching from opposite sides. From the slum of South Brooklyn lurked the old machine: the industrial cityscape of polluted factories, corrupt ward politicians, violent youth gangs, and frightening crime syndicates. From Manhattan threatened a modern and more potent new machine—a matrix of centralized public authorities, city planning agencies, and private development groups spearheading a program of modernist redevelopment in Brooklyn. In defending the middle cityscape against these two machines, Brooklyn Heights residents along with the new urban middle class in Greenwich Village, the West Side, Morningside Heights, and other gentrifying districts in cities around the nation developed a new conception of urban place.[1]

More than just inspiring a new type of romantic urbanism, the battle against the two machines sparked the awakening of the young urban professional as a force in city politics. Lauded as the "New Politics" by enthusiasts or derided as "limousine liberalism" by critics, the new reform wing of the Democratic party forged by Brooklyn Heights' new middle class led an assault on the two pillars of the older New Deal liberal coalition. Heights residents were hostile both to working-class ethnic bosses who relied on patronage and personal relation-ships and to pro-growth liberals who believed in expertise, top-down plan-ning, and centralized executive power. Instead Brooklyn Heights' new middle class pioneered a new romantic version of liberalism that was antagonistic to bureaucracy and scientific planning but celebrated existential liberation, local place, decentralized government, participatory democracy, folk culture, preser-vation of historic communities, ethnic heritage, and individual rights. If the old machine divided politicians into those who were "loyal" and "disloyal," and the new machine categorized them as either "dirty" or "clean," the new urban professional liberalism distinguished between leaders who were "authen-tic" and those who were "phony."

The Old Machine in the Urban Garden

Brooklyn Heights is too uniform. I'd like to "unique" it with a few off-Broadway theatres.
                                        —Norman Rosten, 1958[2]

In 1957, Greenwich Village refugee Sylvia Taylor wrote a short letter to the local paper suggesting a few additions to her new neighborhood:

> My walks in Brooklyn Heights have decided my moving to that section. Here are four things I would like to see there:
>
> 1. An informal nite spot featuring good Jazz
> 2. A Café Espresso shop or two
> 3. A theater devoted entirely to foreign pictures
> 4. Spring art shows along the Promenade[3]

Outraged residents flooded the *Brooklyn Heights Press* with angry letters. "I would not like to see the four suggestions in the letter on the Heights," fumed one woman. "Evidently she would like to see the Heights converted to a Greenwich Village," complained another letter. "Feeling as she evidently does, we wonder why she doesn't live in the Village? Maybe she does." "The published letter brought forth a storm of abuse from residents," explained the paper, "who feared that Miss Taylor's brand of culture would turn the Heights into another Greenwich Village—a tourist trap and a haven for unsavory characters who dwelt on the lunatic fringe of the art world."[4]

Both Sylvia Taylor's letter and the hostile reaction it elicited highlighted a tension in the new romantic urban ideal. While they described a "real neighborhood" unmolested by the modern grid of New York City, Brooklyn Heights' new middle class was also transforming the environment they regarded as authentic. Just as *place* is a verb as well as a noun, "historic diversity" had to be cultivated rather simply discovered and preserved. Dull Brooklyn Heights had to be "uniqued." Dilapidated buildings had to be "historicized." Gray blight had to be "diversified."

Although they purposely transformed Brooklyn Heights, new residents were not modernists who decidedly wanted to reshape and exploit the obsolete cityscape in the name of progress. Instead they were romantic developers who envisioned themselves excavating an authentic cityscape hidden under an artificial layer of blight. Free expression, colorful diversity, and storied history all sat quashed by an oppressive industrial cityscape of dictatorial machine bosses, industrial smoke, and absentee landlords. Historic diversity had to be exhumed. Underneath the old machine—the Democratic clubhouse, the polluted factory, the rooming house, and the corner bar—lay a natural garden that needed only to be unearthed. They envisioned street fairs, block associations, and art galleries not as new institutions but as the revival of older and spontaneous forms of city life and folk culture.

On slum blocks with dilapidated townhouses and tenements, settlers started new block associations, playground committees, and tree-planting drives with the goal of cultivating a vibrant neighborhood that would benefit both white-collar and poorer residents. Still, to cultivate a sense of community, they had to navigate through a thicket of preexisting places. Settlers carved out a new neighborhood from the overlapping turfs that made up the area: the machine ward, the youth gang's territory, the union district, the parish, and the factory yard. Middle-class settlers clashed with indigenous bosses and chiefs in an acrimonious and sometimes violent struggle for control. The Heights was a battleground for conflict "between youth and age," warned Richard Mendes in a talk at the First Presbyterian Church. "Brooklyn Heights," he said, "is—and will become even more so—the arena of greater strife between the existing informal power structure . . . and the new, young and militant group of comparative newcomers to the Heights." Newcomers were changing the neighborhood in visible ways. "Women who wouldn't *dare* walk down Hicks Street in slacks 20 years ago now do it every day," Mendes pointed out. "[Adlai] Stevenson buttons were seen in the living rooms of some of the best homes on Brooklyn Heights during the last election." Yet despite these differences, Heights residents held out hope for a coexistence between old and new. As the local newspaper explained, "It would have to include a greater measure of tolerance between senior residents and newcomers, a recognition on the part of both that the Heights belongs to every resident, that is neither a second Greenwich Village or a private club."[5]

No part of Brooklyn Heights needed to be "uniqued" more than its physical landscape. If Brooklyn Heights was a historic neighborhood that settlers juxtaposed to the modern city, residents first had to "historicize" its brownstones and townhouses. New homeowners with a sense of mission bought the aging structures. In the eyes of new residents, absentee slumlords and poor tenants were abusing and neglecting the magnificent buildings. Dozens of renters lived transiently in homes meant to be privately owned. To convert a brownstone from a rooming house to a single-family home was to liberate it from misuse. Conversion was a restoration of both physical structure and class structure. Settlers described themselves as returning blocks to their original aristocratic character, allowing buildings to express their intended use, and uncovering the "real" neighborhood from the shroud of blight. "We were among the first couples to buy a house in the area," explained Milly Kantrowitz of her townhouse on the northern periphery of the Heights, "and in the beginning we were sort of discouraged by all the run-down property surrounding us. But all that's changed." In five years new residents had bought and converted two boarded up buildings, a vacant townhouse, and a "noisy rooming house" to owner-occupied homes. "I hope the trend continues," Kantrowitz added, "This end of the Heights has become a wonderful place to live—a real neighborhood."[6]

When Greenwich Village bookstore owners Jeanne and Eli Wilentz moved into 56 Middagh Street, they were excited to find a historic house with room for their three children. A former rooming house, the gray clapboard structure needed a significant amount of renovation, and the couple did much of it themselves—scraping floors, building closets, and rebuilding the decaying stoop outside. What drove the Wilentz family through the hardship was the rich history of the building. Clasping a yellowed piece of an 1832 newspaper she found in the cellar wall, Jeanne hoped her house "was one of the oldest houses on the Heights." (Although, she quipped, "everyone who lives in a frame house is sure *theirs* is the oldest one of all.") Eli Wilentz, fascinated by local history, kept a large collection of reference books on the Heights. By renovating, Eli hoped to restore the house to its original state: "We took off all the Victorian additions and have got it stripped down to pretty much its original condition," Eli explained. "All the architectural details and hardware are Federal. We had modern furniture when we moved in but it just didn't look right in this setting, so we've been slowly replacing it with antiques."[7]

The brownstone's historic character had to be evoked and excavated, rather than simply recognized and commemorated. If Brownstone Brooklyn was a layered landscape, settlers worked with their hands to delayer the brownstone of its modern history, hoping to pull off the fake and restore it to its authentic historical character. When settlers talked of renovation, they emphasized not the process of addition but that of removal. While adding new pipes, electrical wiring, and heating, they talked most excitedly about the action of taking away: "scraping," "exposing," "peeling." Brownstones, they felt, were covered by layers of grime and tacky paint, linoleum, and siding added by previous working-class residents. Brownstone renovators hoped to rip away the traces of recent history to reach a symbolic era—"long-vanished dignity"—that resonated with their present class aspirations. "The splendor of the New York row house stemmed from the wealth accruing to merchants and businessmen and the presence of a large prosperous middle class," wrote brownstone settler and historian Charles Lockwood. "In recent years, renovation-minded New Yorkers have reclaimed some of this vanished splendor from beneath layers of cheap paint and behind rooming-house partitions."[8]

Sometimes to restore the brownstone, the settler had to delayer both the inanimate and the human. When Tom and Ronnie Levin converted their brownstone to a single-family home, they had to take out an aging water heater and old wiring, and replace the decaying floor. They also had to remove the old tenants, notifying the residents of the rooming house that they had to leave in six months. "I'll never learn to think of myself as a landlord," joked Ronnie, "Of course, we won't be for long." With three young children, a Siamese cat, and a dog named Captain Nemo, the Levins needed the entire brownstone for bedrooms, a den, and a playroom in the basement. "It seems the more space we get," complained Ronnie, "the more we need."[9]

While avidly converting rooming houses to single- or two-family homes (or, in their words, "re-converting to original use"), brownstone settlers rarely relished the process of eviction. Upon buying a townhouse, some new homeowners found themselves reluctant landlords for several remaining tenants. Others rented out top-floor or basement apartments to create an income property that would pay for itself. "For 'John Purchaser,'" explained a frustrated new homeowner, "he may find several apartments of unevictable tenants protected under rent control. If he wants to convert the first two floors into a duplex, he must figure how to evict 'Mr. and Mrs. Like-It-Here.' He must go the Brooklyn Rent Control Office and obtain an eviction certificate by justifying that the apartment is of 'immediate and compelling' necessity for his family. For 'Mr. Rehabilitator' who buys a rooming-house and wants to create a duplex and two sets of apartments, he can't evict the tenants unless he can prove that more housing accommodations would result from his renovations. Thus one should do research before buying a house on the Heights."[10]

Residents who purposely moved to Brooklyn Heights to transcend the class stratification of suburbia found themselves members of a landlord class in an area sharply divided between landlords and renters. "The realtor through whom we bought the house had dwelt at length on the utopian aspects of this arrangement," complained a new owner of an 1845 brownstone, "pointing out that the money we collected from tenants would cover such expenses as mortgage payments, taxes, heat and repairs. It turns out later he had never owned a house. . . . [We were] like the old plantation owners of the honey-suckle South, we were land poor. [Karl] Marx also missed some of the subtleties in owner-tenant relations, possibly because he was thinking of serfs and feudalism, but more likely because he had never lived in a floor-through apartment on Brooklyn Heights. . . . [We] are much too inept as landlords to exploit *anybody*. At bottom, I think, we still feel like tenants. When our faucet leaks, our first impulse is to grab the 'phone and bawl out the landlord. It always comes as something of a shock when a tenant grows irate—can it be that he's angry with us?"[11]

In addition to collecting rent, owners of dilapidated brownstones depended on a casual labor force for home repair, placing them uncomfortably in the position of a bourgeoisie who managed and paid wages to workers. "We started the job with a contractor, but after a while we discovered nothing was getting done, so we fired him," explained frustrated new homeowner George Maroon. "I took a week off from work to round up my own crew of workmen, but it's hard to find good men. . . . They used sagging rulers, didn't even carry nails, and did most of the measuring by 'eye.' . . . [It's too bad I'm so Americanized.] I'm of Lebanese extraction, and I wish I had the old Lebanese technique of driving a bargain. It'd make dealing with workmen a lot easier!"[12]

The relationship between young college-educated landlords and older tenants—often poor or elderly—was filled with ambiguous feelings of guilt and displeasure. Often the same settlers who evicted residents from their individual townhouse also celebrated the diversity of the neighborhood as a whole. But the desire both to remove the poor and to celebrate their authentic folkways was an inherent tension in the ideal of historic diversity. In the eyes of the new middle class, the poor—particularly the nonwhite migrants arriving in increasing numbers after World War II—both embodied and destroyed local distinctiveness. In the historic city, the poor appeared toxic; they ripped away Victorian ornamentation, painted over natural wood, stored rusty bikes in marble fireplaces, left backyard gardens fallow and littered with plastic, and infested rooming houses that once had been aristocratic single-family homes. But in the diverse city, the poor were organic, an indigenous city folk on the cusp of elimination or assimilation by modernization. Sitting on folding chairs and peering out kitchen windows, the elderly poor spoke with a local twang, filled the air with the savory smells of ethnic foods, and watched over children at play. Their teenage grandchildren played loud music on street corners, littered the street with shards of broken beer bottles, and urinated on brownstone stoops.[13]

Just as the historic landscape had to be made historic, so too did Brownstone Brooklyn's diversity need to be diversified. Settlers attempted to "unique" the neighborhood by opening new stores, art galleries, cafés, and restaurants. If blight was dull and gray, the Heights boasted colorful new institutions that mixed an aesthetic of free expression with a refined taste for high culture. "Even as she was being pummeled for her apostasy," explained a local editorial, "[Sylvia Taylor's] suggested innovations were in the making. Now they are here—the café espresso house, the art galleries and fine films . . . Such citadels of Heights tradition as the Bossert Hotel and the Candlelight Restaurant are exhibiting paintings and culture and the patrons love it. The St. George Playhouse seems to be learning that good movies mean good box office, around here at any rate. On Montague Street Paul Meunier has fronted his ballet school with a fine arts gift shop, and across the street Sylvia Dwyer is running a new and vital art gallery. Down on Hicks Street the trend has moved swiftly. No less than six galleries have appeared. Together with Gina's Heights Espresso at 46 Hicks they are known as the Hicks Street Artists Group."[14]

The cafés and art galleries founded by Heights residents certainly catered to the new middle class. But many residents attempted to include poor residents in a grassroots effort to fix up the neighborhood by forming block associations, organizing street festivals, and building new play areas for local children. In early 1952, Richard Mendes and other members of the South Brooklyn Neighborhood House organized a committee of local volunteers to raise funds for a new playground on the roof of its Willow Place building. Sitting on the southern edge of the Heights, Willow Place was home to a mix of working-class Italians, new white middle-class residents, and a growing Puerto Rican migrant population. After hosting a successful block festival, the committee decided to expand into a permanent block association, renaming itself the

Willowtown Association. Along with organizing an annual street fair, the new group pressured the city to crack down on negligent landlords, demanded better street lighting, and alerted authorities about sanitary violations.[15]

Just as brownstone renovation at times entailed a stripping away of poorer residents, historic diversity also required a delayering of Brooklyn's industrial landscape. The new neighborhood cultivated by settlers was distinctly a post-industrial commemoration of the older economic landscapes. Antique stores, cafés, and art galleries made up a diverse landscape of consumption for white-collar workers eager to reestablish an authentic form of living in an increasingly technocratic city. They felt less enthusiastic, however, about the area's diverse landscape of industrial production. While Heights residents commemorated the area's non-Fordist industrial landscape as a non-bureau-cratic alternative to the modern city's large corporations, they remained selec-tive about which aspects of Brooklyn's economy they valued. Arts and crafts, shipping, pushcarts, and small shops evoked a village past. Block associations revived an older form of participatory town hall democracy. Even the aban-doned shells of industrial buildings formed a historic landscape eagerly rein-habited by artists.[16]

New Heights residents, though, were decidedly unreceptive to functioning industry. In a form of grassroots deindustrialization of South Brooklyn, Heights residents attempted to expel light manufacturing from the neighbor-hood and to prevent new industry from inhabiting unused factories and lofts. In January 1956, Heights resident A. J. Burrows bought an abandoned indus-trial building at 26 Columbia Place with plans to open a small factory. After rehabilitating the structure and cleaning the property of "old socks, beer cans, and garbage," Burrows and twelve employees began manufacturing electronic equipment. Outraged, both the Willowtown and Brooklyn Heights Associa-tions began protests to have the factory closed. Burrows, a dues-paying mem-ber of both associations, was dismayed: "Most of our work is by hand. We don't create any smoke or soot, and we're quieter than many of our neigh-bors. . . . I'm just as interested in the good of Willow Town as anyone else. After all, don't I own property there?"[17]

In November, the Willowtown Association brought a motion to the Board of Standards and Appeals to force the factory to move. The opponents offered an interesting advocacy of gentrification *avant la lettre*. Brooklyn Heights, the association argued, was a residential neighborhood undergoing a dramatic revival. If new manufacturing was allowed to open in abandoned factories, the process would be turned back. The historically diverse neighborhood would sink back into dull blight. The restored brownstones would once again become homes to the poor. "Houses that been converted to private homes will revert back to buildings exploited as rooming houses." The board allowed the property to stay, but imposed strict conditions: no signs on Willow Street, no loading or unloading on the street, and no use of street-side doors for business. It was "a partial victory," complained Richard Mendes, "[but] the day will come when we have no manufacturing in the neighborhood."[18]

When in July 1959 Love Lane Garage applied to the city for permission to build bigger doors on its plumbing supply storage facility, residents of the area and the Brooklyn Heights Association made similar arguments in opposition. Operating out of four Victorian carriage houses for years, Love Lane Garage was a creative and organic adaptation of industry to an older commercial landscape. To the dozens of new Heights residents living in the alleyway's recently renovated carriage houses and apartments, however, the arrival of trucks twice a month was a "flagrant abuse of the street." "We have worked very hard to make our little mews a more attractive place," protested spokesperson Harry Holtzman, artist and professor of art at Brooklyn College. "Outside of the initial cost of the property, six residents have put more than $100,000 in improving their homes. We clean the street ourselves, and we would like to plant trees along one side." The Board of Standards and Variance subsequently turned down the garage's plea. "I've applied for many variances of this sort and this the first time I've been turned down," explained the dismayed owner. "[We] just wanted to create a more efficient operation." "I'm very pleased about the decision," said a jubilant Holtzman. "Now we can continue to make this a prettier place." The battles were only the first of many that Brooklyn Heights' new middle class would wage to block the revitalization of industry in the area. Heights activists over the next two decades would block plans for a Consolidated Edison power plant, a new wholesale meat market, and a container port.[19]

Industrial operating equipment and trucks were not the only machines settlers wanted stripped from the Heights. The struggle against the old machine was a political one as well. On June 13, 1957, a collection of new Heights residents fed up with local politicians met in a brownstone to form a new Democratic club to represent the Third Assembly District, a broad district running from the Bush Terminal to Brooklyn Heights. The new West Brooklyn Independent Democrats (WBID) dismissed the existing Democratic club as a corrupt machine tyrannically controlled by local boss Frank Cunningham. "We are tired of one-man rule," explained club president Philip Jessup, a thirty-one-year-old lawyer and recent arrival to the Heights. "One-man rule is *the* rule in the regular Democratic organization," exclaimed the *Heights Press*. "Year after year the De Sapios and the Cunninghams are allowed to hold on to their positions as party bosses. No one in the organization would dare oppose them. They rule by decree. And now, suddenly we have insurgent Democrats like the WBID's, springing up all over the city, and insisting on democracy within the Democratic party." Frank Cunningham was unimpressed. "We're not afraid of this new group," he told the local paper. "They can oppose us if they want."[20]

The WBID was but one of many "reform" clubs to emerge in the late 1950s. Starting with the East Side's Lexington Club, a new white-collar middle class founded independent Democratic organizations to challenge local ward bosses in Greenwich Village, the West Side, Morningside Heights, and other middle cityscapes around Manhattan. The movement was national as well. In Chicago, Boston, and Philadelphia, reform clubs formed in inner-city Gold Coasts where a new urban managerial class lived in luxury apartment buildings and rehabilitated townhouses on the periphery of the central business district and major universities.[21]

Brooklyn Heights' new urban reform movement was not the first middle-class attempt to curtail the power of the borough's political machine. By founding an independent Democratic club, however, they distinctly rejected the party supported by reform-minded Brooklynites in decades past: the Republican party. As a minority party in a city run by a Democratic ethnic machine, New York City's Republican party had long been a upper middle-class Protestant "good government" party producing reform leaders throughout the twentieth century such as Seth Low, Fiorello LaGuardia, John Lindsay, and Robert Moses. Postwar Brooklyn Heights—like other silk stocking or Gold Coast districts in Manhattan, Chicago, and Boston—voted solidly Republican in both local and national elections. In 1952, 70 percent of Brooklyn Heights voters supported presidential candidate Dwight Eisenhower, and the district elected one of the two Republican representatives from Brooklyn to Congress (the other being in a specially gerrymandered district joined with Staten Island).[22]

For the younger and more liberal white-collar migrants arriving in the Heights, the postwar national GOP was too conservative, too hostile to Harry Truman's "Fair Deal," and too hawkish on foreign policy to remain attractive as a local reform party. "There was no possibility of a deal with Republicans," explained one reformer. "We are at the opposite ends of the spectrum when it comes to foreign policy." The new reformers populating the Heights had a new political sensibility that shared both the good-governmentism of Republicans and the liberal political views of the Democrats. Initially, residents experimented with a third party option: the Liberal party. Started in 1944 by anti-communist Jewish union leaders and supported primarily by lower-middle-class Jews, the Liberal party endorsed reform-minded candidates from either party to form fusion tickets, and occasionally ran candidates of its own.[23]

In 1957, LeRoy Bowman, a sociology professor at Brooklyn College, ran on the Liberal ticket for the council seat from the 13th Senatorial District. Although at seventy he was a generation older than most new residents, Bowman's resume was similar to those of many of the "missionaries" who moved to the Heights after the war. A specialist in race relations and juvenile delinquency, Bowman was active in community organizing, volunteering for the South Brooklyn Neighborhood House and directing both the Citizens for All Day Neighborhood Schools and the United Parents Association. As a candidate, he ran on a platform of a strong U.S. Supreme Court, civil rights, clean government, anti-McCarthyism, and increased government spending on social programs in the area. Most pointedly, however, he was independent of the local machine. "Everyone knows that I would stand up for what I believe," explained Bowman. "I'm really an independent. I think a councilman should represent his neighborhood, not just his party." Operating out of local real estate agent and supporter Kenneth Boss' office, Bowman ran a small campaign using a Liberal party sound truck, speaking on corners, and using $1,000 in donations to distribute mailers and handbills. Along with the Liberal party, an independent committee of local doctors, ministers, lawyers, businessmen, and teachers spearheaded his campaign.[24]

Bowman's campaign highlighted the radically different political approaches of new white-collar residents and the old machine. When Bowman and the Republican candidate arranged for a town-hall-style debate in the Heights to discuss "issues," the Democratic incumbent, Arthur Low, didn't show up. Heights residents were furious when they learned that Low had spent the evening socializing with other politicians elsewhere in the borough. When the League of Women Voters organized a second debate, Low sent word that he was too sick to attend. "In theory, he represents his neighborhood," complained the Brooklyn Heights Press. "In practice, he has represented no one." Further aggravating Heights residents, the rest of Brooklyn seemed not to care. Despite endorsements from the Brooklyn Heights Press and the Citizens Union, Bowman won only 7 percent of the vote, losing heavily to the Democratic incumbent.[25]

But rather than local elections, national politics—the failed 1952 and 1956 Adlai Stevenson presidential runs—sparked the formation of the WBID. In Brooklyn Heights and other gentrifying districts around the country, Adlai Stevenson was an inspirational figure who sparked the political awakening of the new urban middle class. The Illinois governor first gained national recognition when he gave a rousing speech at the 1948 Democratic National Convention. Young white-collar professionals who heard him speak described themselves as being transformed. Disillusioned by the cynical cigar chomping and backroom handshakes of city politics, young Stevenson supporters described the governor as an authentic political voice motivated by genuine passion rather than calculated self-interest. Where they saw local ethnic machine bosses such as Frank Cunningham and national politicians such as Harry Truman and Lyndon Johnson as crude and provincial hacks, Stevenson was witty and cosmopolitan. His speeches made references to Plato, Benjamin Disraeli, George Bernard Shaw, and William James. Working-class voters may have regarded him as an "egghead," but according to new urban middle-class enthusiasts, that was only because Americans were anti-intellectual. The Stevenson campaign did not rely on phony clichés such as Nixon's reference to his dog Checkers or characterizations such as those of Eisenhower as a military hero and golfer. Instead the governor spoke articulately about complex issues and was willing to embrace subtlety. "Mr. Stevenson's nomination introduces a refreshing figure in American politics and can bring about a new and higher level of political thinking and activity. In my estimation, his appeal to the intelligence, the high ethics and the individual responsibility of the citizen is a rare quality of political leadership," explained activist Pauli Murray to Arthur Schlesinger Jr. "I believe that his leadership will also attract hitherto unused talented people who have a keen sense of public responsibility but who have shied away from the rugged, hurly-burly methods of politics as practiced through traditional channels of party machinery."[26]

During the 1956 primaries, a group of Heights residents started the Brooklyn Heights Stevenson-Kefauver-Wagner Committee to mobilize local support for Stevenson. But they became increasingly frustrated when regular Democratic clubs made a backroom deal to support Governor Averell Harriman in the primaries. When Stevenson beat Harriman for the nomination, the machine made little effort to support his presidential campaign. Since Stevenson, unlike Harriman, offered no access to patronage, after the primaries the Democratic regulars focused instead on local elections. The perceived betrayal of Adlai Stevenson outraged the Heights' new middle class. Following the lead of dismayed Stevenson supporters in other gentrifying districts of Manhattan, Boston, and Chicago, the Stevenson Committee renamed itself the WBID and focused on defeating the local machine.[27]

"The West Brooklyn Independent Democrats, which rose last year out of the ruins of Stevenson's defeat, continues to grow in strength," lauded the *Heights Press*. "Its goal is nothing less than to control the regular Democratic party organization in this area, the Third Assembly District." "It was felt that the best way we could achieve our goals," explained Heights lawyer and WBID president Philip Jessup, "was by *becoming* the regular Democratic organization." In 1958, the WBID put up its first slate of reformers to challenge machine candidates in local primaries. While WBID candidates polled well in higher-income parts of the Heights, regulars won overwhelmingly in the district as a whole. "Naturally we were disappointed in losing the District-wide contests," explained Jessup, "but there were several encouraging signs." The declaration was an opening salvo in what would be a decades-long acrimonious fight between older machine leaders and in-migrating middle-class reformers in Brownstone Brooklyn.[28]

Commentators at the time called it the rise of the "New Politics." A new postindustrial wing of young white-collar professionals and college students had begun to break with the traditional Democratic party. On the surface, the rift between the New Politics and the old machine formed around specific political issues. The regular Democratic clubs took a view of government that was more in tune with the outlook of its largely Catholic and working-class constituency in its fusion of liberal economic policies and cultural conservatism. Machine candidates supported generous government expenditures on city programs but were hawkish on foreign policy and remained cool to the counterculture, civil rights, and other social movements emerging in the late 1950s. Reformers, in contrast, articulated a new urban white-collar version of liberalism that mixed an emphasis on fiscal responsibility with social libertarianism. The WBID complained that the machine was both wasteful and corrupt, as well as apathetic about civil rights. The regulars considered reformers to be libertines who were soft on communism and crime.[29]

The schism reflected more than different political stances. Regulars and reformers disagreed about the nature of politics itself. Regulars remained unenthusiastic about Adlai Stevenson not because they disagreed with his ideology but because the machine distrusted ideology altogether. Machine politics cared little about issues, focusing instead on personal relationships, patronage, favors, ethnic identity, and mutual self-interest. Voters supported politicians whom they knew personally and who provided them with jobs and city services. Politicians cared little about national or international issues, and instead were inextricably tied to a local web of institutions: small businesses, the unions, organized crime, the Catholic Church, local restaurants and bars, and ethnic fraternal organizations.[30]

The New Politics, however, rejected the secret backroom deal making of professional politicians. Reformers instead brought a romantic ideal to politics that emphasized direct democracy, free expression, and genuine passion rather than pluralistic compromise. In contrast to the hierarchical structure of the machine, reformers promoted an urban version of Jeffersonian democracy where local communities met in town hall meetings free of corruption and bureaucracy. The regular Democratic party, in their eyes, was a dictatorial machine controlled by a boss antithetical to democratic principles. They described their movement in revolutionary terms, envisioning themselves as liberating a captive population from despotic rule. "Slightly less than two centuries ago an American general was digging trenches on Brooklyn Heights in full and open rebellion against British tyranny," wrote the *Heights Press*. "Another 'rebel' group on the Heights is the West Brooklyn Independent Democrats. Their political aim is to overthrow the regular Democrats in the Third Assembly District. Like General Washington, they are seeking greater representation in government by the governed."[31]

The WBID believed that an authentic political club should be a forum for concerned citizens to discuss issues and causes rather than stations for dispensing building permits, jobs on the waterfront, visas, help with the court system, or the occasional bribe. "The WBID wants to be a political club, not a employment agency," explained one member of its policy of forbidding officers from accepting patronage. Instead of bartering services, the WBID held open debates, hosted lectures by invited speakers about national and international issues, and organized kaffeeklatsch discussion groups. The club purposely remained an amateur organization staffed by volunteers who worked out of a sense of civic duty rather than for power or financial rewards. Where regular clubs such as the one controlled by Frank Cunningham doled out staff positions to loyal supporters, the WBID held frequent elections for leadership. Where the local machine informally offered housing, jobs, and city services to constituents in exchange for votes and payoffs, the young lawyers who made up the majority of its leadership categorically rejected offering favors to constituents, believing instead that assistance to poor residents should stem from higher ideals of passion and justice, and creating community service and outreach programs to serve the needs of local residents. While in the regular club, constituents waited on line to meet with politicians or district captains to schmooze and ask for assistance, the WBID in 1959 opened a "consulting bureau" run by middle-class volunteers in which residents could ask questions about "individual neighborhood problems or issues affecting the area." They were characterized by "regular monthly meetings of the membership to hear speakers on subjects from air pollution to U.S. foreign policy in Ghana," explained Tammany politician Edward Costikyan sarcastically of the new reform clubs in Brooklyn and Manhattan, "forums, countless committees made up of members dealing with whatever problems they wanted to deal with (mental health, art tours, United Nations hospitality, problems of the aged), and a degree of self-righteousness."[32]

The differences between the party organizations represented a larger cultural and class conflict between the in-migrating new bourgeoisie of white-collar residents and the Irish and Italian Catholic old bourgeoisie of small businessmen who controlled inner-city politics. Political parties were social institutions as much as political organizations. For young white-collar residents migrating to Brooklyn Heights and Greenwich Village, participating in an Adlai Stevenson fund-raiser or going to a lecture series served as a way to meet neighbors, find possible dating partners, and feel a sense of community in a transient urban environment. College-educated lawyers, artists, and writers felt little social connection to the web of institutions that formed the old machine. New residents eager to get involved in local politics described feeling awkward and intimidated as they entered the local bar or clubhouse, often receiving hostile stares from older Italian or Irish club members. Others felt outraged when they had to wait for hours on line with poorer residents to meet with precinct captains whose qualifications they little respected. Young women particularly felt uncomfortable in clubhouses in which local working-class females rarely set foot. "In many clubs, the principal interest is the card game in the back room or the bar which pays the rent," complained one reformer. "Often a headquarters is operated from, or is very handy to the leader's saloon, undertaking parlor, or other business office. . . . Too often these old style political party headquarters, like old union headquarters, turn the stomachs of the majority of the 'unhardened' people who are not 'in.'"[33]

The fight between the old and new politics thus was a clash between an older male industrial landscape and a new mixed-gender postindustrial landscape. Brownstone Brooklyn machine politics was intricately tied to working-class all-male institutions: bars, storefront clubs, the Knights of Columbus and other fraternal organizations. Reformers, on the other hand, were a cross-section of the new urban professional class: young, white, Protestant or Jewish, college-educated, and disproportionately single or married without children. Unlike the all-male regulars, women were heavily represented at reform club events. To raise money and register members, the WBID organized kaffeeklatsches, lecture series, forums, and spaghetti and wine parties in rehabilitated brownstones and new apartment towers. Frank Cunningham's club instead rented a barge where politicians and loyal constituents drank heavily.[34]

This was not the first time local machines had to adjust to a changing constituency. With new populations constantly replacing old as neighborhoods filtered down in a constantly evolving city, the machine for decades had continually assimilated new immigrants into its organization to maintain power. By nominating "balanced tickets" with representatives from each ethnic enclave and distributing patronage among different communities, the machine attempted to keep stability through pluralistic compromise. With the arrival of thousands of blacks and Puerto Ricans to the city after World War II, the machine tried to digest the new groups by appointing loyal nonwhite leaders to token positions in city government. But when in a 1946 state assembly race, black female Republican and Urban League activist Maude Richardson lost by only two hundred votes to the white Democratic regular in Brooklyn's Fort Greene and Bedford-Stuyvesant, machine leaders realized that they could no longer ignore the area's growing black constituency. Nominating West Indian bookkeeper and clubhouse loyalist Bertram Baker, the party won handily against Richardson in 1948. Baker, Brooklyn's first black elected to the state legislature, soon became one of Tammany's most powerful politicians. In Harlem, J. Raymond "Harlem Fox" Jones and Hulan Jack followed similar career trajectories.[35]

While the machine was designed to accommodate neighborhoods filtering down to new and poorer migrants by offering them upward mobility, it was ill equipped to adjust to neighborhoods that were filtering up. Wealthy, college-educated urbanites had little need for patronage or favors. Their social and professional lives were linked to the offices, universities, and cultural institutions of the central business district rather than the union halls, bars, organized crime syndicates, and fraternal clubs in which the machine had influence. More important, they rejected the very core principles that underlay the machine. They believed in merit rather than patronage, clear morality rather than pluralistic compromise. Attacking the very core of machine politics, reformers categorically rejected any form of ethnically balanced tickets. Rather than an artificial quota system, they believed leadership should represent the authentic voice of the people as expressed in open elections.[36]

But just as the regulars failed to appeal to new white-collar residents, the WBID struggled to address the working-class constituency of the old machine. Although populist in intent, the very structure of the WBID catered to the tastes of the new urban middle class and made it difficult for poor or less educated residents to participate in club activities. By rejecting patronage and operating on a volunteer basis, reform Democrats ensured that only wealthy residents or their spouses with the time and funds to work for free could participate fully in club activities. In the debates, committees, and town hall meetings organized by the WBID, articulate lawyers and other college-educated residents familiar with Robert's Rules of Order and other parliamentary procedures dominated the proceedings. The WBID's categorical rejection of ethnically balanced tickets made it difficult to incorporate new black and Puerto Rican residents into the party. Beyond the structural impediments, the social environment of the club was distinctly upper middle-class. Just as reformers felt uncomfortable smoking cigars in a local bar, so too did working-class residents feel awkward attending a forum on "American relations with Cuba" or a cocktail party in a renovated brownstone.[37]

This is not to suggest that the WBID did not try to enlist Brooklyn's growing nonwhite population in its fight against the machine. If the regulars sought to cultivate a loyal cadre of black and Puerto Rican politicians from within the ranks, reformers looked hopefully to a grassroots Democratic insurgency led by a group of African American professionals in neighboring Bedford-Stuyvesant. In 1953, Wesley "Mac" Holder, a statistician working in the Brooklyn district attorney's office, became outraged when the local Democratic club nominated a white judge from outside the district to fill a vacancy on the Second Municipal Court. With political roots in the Garvey movement, a degree in mathematics, and a solidly middle-class upbringing in British Guiana, Holder was representative of Brooklyn's large and vocal West Indian professional class. When African American Lewis Flagg expressed interest in running for a municipal judgeship, Holder formed the Committee for the Election of Lewis S. Flagg, Jr. With the help of whites and black volunteers, the committee ran a hard-nosed campaign independent of the machine, even hiring private detectives to guard the ballot boxes on election night. Encouraged by the victory in the Flagg fight, Holder renamed the group the Bedford-Stuyvesant Political League (BSPL), an independent Democratic club with the mission of electing black representatives and judges. By the time it disbanded in 1966, the BSPL had led successful campaigns for four black civil court judges, three black state supreme court judges, two black criminal court judges, three black assemblymen, a black city councilman, and a black state senator.[38]

Brooklyn Heights and Manhattan's white reformers excitedly supported the black-led insurgency movements in Brooklyn and Harlem. When a group of black politicians, including the fiery Shirley Chisholm, broke from the machine to found the Unity Democratic Club (UDC) in 1960, the reform New York Committee for Democratic Voters, an umbrella group, endorsed their ticket. Eleanor Roosevelt spoke at one of their campaign rallies. Riding a wave of anti-machine sentiment in both the black and white communities, the UDC's theme was to "end boss-ruled plantation politics." Harlem's Adam Clayton Powell similarly rallied crowds by referring to the machine as a plantation and calling his opponent an Uncle Tom in his landslide 1958 primary victory over Tammany Hall candidate Earl Brown.[39]

But if black and white reformers shared certain rhetorical themes, their struggles in the 1950s and early 1960s remained very different. When Holder and Chisholm spoke of "bossism" and "plantationism," they criticized not the machine but the denial of black access to its spoils. The 1950s black reform movement was a fight for power rather than an ideological clash over the nature of politics itself. The "independent" BSPL demanded that regulars dole out a fair share of patronage to local blacks without questioning the concepts of patronage or backroom deals. From her beginnings decorating the cigar boxes that held raffle tickets in a local clubhouse, Chisholm, for example, rose through the ranks of and remained tied to the Brooklyn machine throughout her career. In Washington she championed issues that also appealed to reformist whites and civil rights leaders, but in Brooklyn she entrusted Wesley Holder with operating a gritty, issueless club that offered constituents favors, visa extensions, and housing in exchange for loyal votes. When Brooklyn's reformist whites and a new generation of black activists battled Chisholm in the 1960s and 1970s, even enlisting James Farmer of the Congress on Racial Equality as a candidate, they found themselves stymied by her ability to mix militant reform language with old-fashioned machine-style mobilization of local voters.[40]

One could easily romanticize the old machine and accuse reformers of simply attempting to engineer a middle-class coup d'état in Brooklyn politics. But many of the criticisms launched at the old machine by reformers—corruption, links to violent organized crime syndicates, inaction in stemming urban decline, ineptitude, and racism—were based in reality. And when Heights residents aimed to reorganize politics along principles of justice, openness and participatory democracy, they did so with the intention of liberating both themselves and the poor from the autocratic rule of "bosses." It was precisely their idealistic intentions that made the lack of support by working-class Brooklynites all the more frustrating. "The reform movement . . . is made up chiefly of college graduates and the wealthy, who are concerned with the conditions of the workers," lamented Zevie Schiver, vice president of the New York Young Democrats, in what would become a familiar refrain in decades to come. "Unfortunately it is the workers themselves, those with the economic problems, who vote against us."[41]

Through hard work, an openness to class and racial diversity, and a creative reimagination of the blighted cityscape, Brooklyn Heights' new residents cultivated a new urban neighborhood in an economically depressed part of Brooklyn. Yet Brooklyn Heights was an authentic place only insofar as it could be juxtaposed to the industrial blight that surrounded it. And to create a sense of place paradoxically required both an appreciation of the industrial landscape and an effort to clear it away. If the Heights was a historically diverse urban garden, it precipitated a clash between the gardeners and the urban industrial machine that lay atop it.

The New Machine in the Garden

On April 21, 1959, four hundred Brooklyn Heights residents jammed the Gold Room of the Hotel Bossert on Montague Street to attend a forum on urban renewal. Organized by the Community Conservation and Improvement Committee (CCIC), a new civic group dedicated to fighting development in the Heights, the meeting was unexpectedly large. As the packed crowd buzzed with anger and excitement, observers described an "electric atmosphere." When earlier that year Robert Moses had announced plans for Cadman Plaza, a massive redevelopment project on the periphery of the Civic Center, the news ignited a wave of protest. The city planned to demolish five square blocks of Heights housing to erect high-rise luxury apartment towers. The Heights' new middle class would have none of it. Over enthusiastic applause, Martin Schneider read a defiant letter drafted by the CCIC to Moses. Stop Cadman Plaza, read Schneider, for the Heights refused to become "a backdrop of the civic center." Keynote speaker State Senator MacNeil Mitchell, coauthor of New York's Mitchell-Lama middle-income housing program, assured the white middle-class audience of their new voice in city politics. "When I see this kind of crowd, I know that you have the voice and leadership to raise such a hue and cry that the city administration will have to listen." The Brooklyn Heights Association and other local civic groups endorsed the CCIC program. Even the "regular" Democrats of the Third Assembly District and the "reformer" West Brooklyn Independent Democrats put aside their differences to lend support to the campaign. Reporters from NBC, the *New York Times*, and the *New York World-Telegram and Sun* covered the event.[42]

While the CCIC criticized specific details, Cadman Plaza represented more to the audience than a poorly planned development project. Just as the old machine loomed on the poorer periphery of the Heights, Cadman Plaza marked for residents the arrival of an ominous new machine from Manhattan. Politically, architecturally, and socially, Manhattanization threatened to assimilate the pastoral oasis of Brooklyn Heights into a hypermodern, hyperrational, impersonal bureaucracy. Pushing outward from the central business district, private developers, city agencies, and nonprofit institutions such as the New York City Housing Authority, the Jehovah's Witnesses, and Long Island University hungrily demolished historic homes and mom-and-pop stores to build large apartments, public housing complexes, and office towers. A new and modern bureaucracy of public authorities, scientifically planned city agencies, and corporate administrators made large-scale plans and executive decisions with little regard for local communities and town hall democracy. The brownstone refuge only recently discovered and cultivated by young, middle-class Manhattan émigrés was transforming precisely into the air-conditioned nightmare they had fled from. "We don't want to become a transient backwater of the downtown business district," exclaimed one CCIC member to the enthusiastic crowd. Look at what had happened to Manhattan's Park Avenue, he continued. Once a family neighborhood, "now it's a dormitory for high-priced executives." "If the present trend toward large-scale, high-rise construction continues," warned CCIC chairman Otis Pearsall, "the Heights as we know it will disappear."[43]

The battle in Brooklyn Heights was only one front in a widespread anti-development battle spreading throughout postwar New York City. In December 1956, a group of middle-class residents inspired by Brooklyn Heights activists formed Gramercy Neighbors on Third Avenue in Manhattan to fight a local development scheme. In Greenwich Village and the West Side, new local organizations galvanized fights against Title I projects. Local newspapers, once unabashed supporters of city development, wrote a series of exposés about Robert Moses, corruption, and the abuses of urban renewal. "Within the past few years resistance to Public Housing has been growing stronger daily," wrote assemblyman Samuel Spiegel of the burgeoning anti-renewal movement in 1959. "Site tenants are united and working cohesively as a concerted group rather than as disorganized individuals. They are becoming bold and more aggressive. . . . Gramercy Neighbors, Harlem Housing and Tenants Group, Lincoln Square Chamber of Commerce, Lincoln Square Residents Committee, Queensboro Hill Community Church, Seward Park Site Tenants and Businessmen Committee, Washington Square Neighbors, Committee for the Preservation of E. 24th St. to East 28th St. . . ."[44]

But if Manhattanization endangered the middle cityscape, it also gave it form. Like the fight against the old machine, the struggle against the new machine and the city bulldozer acted as the catalyst for neighborhood formation. In the battle against development projects, residents developed new local political and civic organizations, defined clear boundaries of their neighborhood, promoted local democracy as an alternative to city-hall-administered programs, and formally articulated in print the romantic urban aesthetic that underlay the gentrification of the area. "We are not a slum!" cried the residents of Brooklyn Heights at Robert Moses, and in doing so were forced to develop a clear definition of the historic diversity they cherished. In criticizing the sterile towers of development projects, they drew detailed portraits of the historic neighborhood, and created new legal language to preserve its aristocratic architecture and Brahmin past. To battle both high-rent luxury apartments and low-income public housing, they articulated a middle-class aesthetic of urban diversity, commemorating privately owned small shops, non-bureaucratic artisan labor, and family-owned townhouses. In a revolt against scientific expertise and planning, they contrasted an organic Victorian landscape to one-dimensional, one-class modernist urban projects.[45]

The fight against urban renewal in Brooklyn Heights, as well as Greenwich Village and the West Side, also sparked a new political movement that united white, black, Puerto Rican, immigrant, middle-class, and poor New Yorkers. In the belt of Victorian housing surrounding central business districts and universities in New York, San Francisco, Boston, and Chicago, a new urban managerial class united with working-class white ethnics and new black and Latino migrants to revolt against urban modernism. As this tenuous interracial and interclass middle cityscape coalition fought against "city interests," "the system," "the master plan," "one-dimensional dormitories," and "bureaucracy," they forged the language that would form the bedrock of the neighborhood movement of the 1970s.

A closer look at the battle against the new machine reveals a conflict more complex than a simple struggle of the grassroots versus the system. Rather than a collection of scrappy underdogs holding back the bulldozer, Brooklyn Heights' anti-urban-renewal activists confidently exercised the power of a new urban professional class. And rather than a bullying Robert Moses attempting to crush local communities in the name of an abstract master plan, in Brooklyn Heights the city urban renewal agency was flexible, conciliatory, and often cowed by the increasingly intransigent demands of local activists.

If the fight against the old machine revealed a tension in the ideal of historic diversity, the fight against the new machine made transparent some of the class and race divides in the gentrifying middle cityscape of Brooklyn Heights. While there was much cross-pollination of anti-institutional ideas and political strategies between rich and poor, the most successful anti-development movements in New York City remained in Brooklyn Heights, Greenwich Village, the West Side, and neighborhoods with a powerful white middle class. The fight against Robert Moses in Brooklyn Heights was less a subaltern revolution than a silk stocking rebellion or a revolt of the artist colonies. While the urban poor often sought *more* modernist public housing and development projects, ones built for *them* rather than for luxury developers, Brooklyn Heights' new middle class fought an aesthetic battle against the sameness and alienation of the modern landscape. In the fight against luxury urban renewal projects they often forged valiant partnerships with the poor, but middle-class brownstone settlers dominated the movement. Their agenda often unintentionally, though at times purposely, served the process of gentrification.

When residents spoke of the encroachment of Concord Village on their Thoreauvian refuge, their fears were not simply symbolic. With the success of the new apartment complex, local banks and private developers excitedly contacted Robert Moses about the potential for similar developments deeper in Brooklyn Heights. "With the successful completion of the sale of Concord

Village," wrote Brooklyn Savings Bank vice president G. J. Bender to Robert Moses in August 1956, "perhaps the time has come to review the general idea of the possibility of Title I projects for the area of Brooklyn in which this bank is most interested. . . . If there is any way this bank can be of service or if there are projects which need sponsoring after due analysis, we shall be delighted to be of service to you or whomsoever you may designate."[46]

In July 1956, Moses' Slum Clearance Committee (SCC) announced plans for a small urban renewal project on the southern periphery of Brooklyn Heights. Moses discussed with city officials the possibility of clearing nine square blocks hugging the dilapidated thoroughfare of Atlantic Avenue. North of Atlantic Avenue, the city would commission private developers to build a high-rise apartment complex of luxury units renting at $60 a room. Residents displaced from the area would find housing in a low-income project south of the avenue. "We have in mind also for discussion a low rental project to the south, that is below Atlantic Avenue," explained Moses, "into which present, tenants, mostly Puerto Ricans with comparatively low incomes, in the Title One area could be moved without hardship."[47]

The six-block area chosen by Moses formed a typical cross-section of Brooklyn Heights' periphery, with a mix of white ethnics, Puerto Rican migrants, and a gentrifying middle class. On the corner of Joralemon and Hicks streets, a mix of elderly Italian pensioners and working-class families lived in decaying low-rent apartments and townhouses. Interspersed among the poor on Hicks Street and Willow Place, the Heights' new middle class lived in an assortment of renovated carriage houses and brownstones. South of Atlantic Avenue, a growing Puerto Rican population lived in tenements and rooming houses. On Joralemon Street, the South Brooklyn Neighborhood Houses offered classes, a playground, and nursery school to a mix of residents.[48]

Moses and the Slum Clearance Committee were unimpressed with the area's diversity, instead dismissing the area as a slum with obsolete housing and poor infrastructure ripe for redevelopment. Starting negotiations with the city and private developers, Moses brought his unique mix of high-handedness and secrecy to the project. As he lobbied the Board of Estimate to request a $275,000 research grant from the federal government, he hoped to cut through red tape, to make a deal with a developer quickly and secretly, and to start construction immediately, preempting local resistance with concrete facts on the ground.[49]

If in the 1930s New Yorkers lauded Moses' ability to get things done, the 1950s were the beginning of a new era in city politics. In Brooklyn Heights, Moses faced a new, powerful, and increasingly vocal urban white-collar class unwilling to accept city projects near their apartments and townhouses. When word of the project leaked to Brooklyn Heights in June 1956, the newly formed Willowtown Association met in the South Brooklyn Neighborhood Houses to organize resistance to the project. Led by settlement house director Richard Mendes, the mostly white middle-class activists wrote personal letters to politicians, drafted a petition, and contacted local newspapers. Though city projects might be useful elsewhere, the activists exhorted, Brooklyn Heights was a unique place that needed preservation. "I'm writing to you very informally about a project that is being planned for lower Joralemon St. and Willow Place," wrote the widow of influential lawyer and civic leader Otis Swann Carroll. "I've been told that Willow Place where there is a small playground and quite nice old houses is going to be demolished also. For the last few years, these small dwellings have been bought by young married people who prefer a small house and backyard where they can have flowers and shrubs to living in a huge apartment house. I do, myself, and so did my friend of long standing Genevieve Earle. . . . We are very grateful Mr. Moses for all the wonderful things you have done for our city and parkways, but Brooklyn Heights is unique. Please leave it the way it is."

"I knew Otis well and recall having been at your house when Gen [Earle] was there," responded an angry but deferential Moses. "All we designated at this early stage was an area for study included what you must agree are some very rundown slum buildings. . . . It looks as we must anticipate here another one of those general, premature, ill informed attacks on a proposal before it even reaches the publication stage. The rehabilitation of the area on either side of Atlantic Avenue is pretty far down the list of new proposals and can readily be abandoned in favor of other competing projects which have great support or less advance criticism." Moses was furious to find the interchange published the following week in the *Brooklyn Heights Press*. A series of articles criticizing the fledgling project appeared soon after in the *World-Telegram and Sun*.[50]

Along with pulling strings in city government and local newspapers, the Willowtown Association also pioneered a new strategy in the fight against urban development projects. If modernist city leaders privileged expertise over local sentiment, the association used its middle-class intellectual and social capital to challenge the city on its own terms. While poorer communities often felt intimidated and overwhelmed by the jargon and data of city planning agencies, the Heights had a deep pool of architects, lawyers, and academics eager to volunteer their services. Willowtown's white-collar volunteers collected data on the housing stock, conducted surveys, and dissected the legal and architectural shortcomings of Moses' project. In April 1957, the Willowtown Association presented an alternative redevelopment plan to the

city, calling for the rehabilitation of existing structures rather than demolition, spot clearance of a few abandoned buildings, and the relocation of displaced residents in any new buildings built.[51]

For Willowtown activists, the battle against Moses was larger than a few
buildings. While the threat to their homes was concrete, Willowtown's anti-
Moses activists described a war to protect town hall democracy, local folkways,
and cultural distinctiveness from bureaucracy, centralized authority, and scientific planning. "A city should be built for the people," exhorted local activist Richard Mendes, "not to satisfy the whims of some master builder." The
anti-renewal movement is "a sort of subway version of New England town
meetings," exclaimed the editors of the *Brooklyn Heights Press*. "And because
they are democratically organized to express the will of the entire neighborhood (including both property owners and tenants), their amateur efforts
often carry weight with professional politicians. In New York City, small
neighborhoods are often as isolated from each other as frontier towns. We're
glad that in this case Willowtown's dramatic example boosted the morale of
another neighborhood fighting to save itself."[52]

Frustrated by mounting opposition, Moses abandoned the project only a
year after plans were leaked to the press. "I don't see any useful purpose would
be served in any further discussion of the Brooklyn Heights area as Title I
project," wrote Moses to the president of the Brooklyn Heights Association.
"As you know, residents in the area, particularly in Willowtown, expressed
opposition to proceeding with the project and in absence of support from the
community, the Committee dropped it from the program." Elated at the
news, the Willowtown Association hung a sign on the front of the local Settlement House: "We Won." Moses, increasingly out of step with a vocal new
generation, was bewildered and angry at the stubborn resistance to his role as
a reformer and builder. At a 1957 United Neighborhood Houses dinner commemorating the seventieth anniversary of the settlement house movement,
Moses blasted the "Victorian" residents of "Willow Village" (the misstatement
was deliberate) for saving their own skins at the expense of the neighborhood
as a whole. "Heights projects should be put on a suspended list . . . because
there is much intemperate and uninformed opposition," he wrote to a supportive local bank. "The only suggestion I can make, or rather renew is that
Brooklyn develop some leadership in rehabilitation and reconstruction, and
that as to the Brooklyn Heights area specifically, the Heights Association be
revitalized with new blood and oxygen."[53]

The sense of victory for Heights residents was short-lived. With continued
pressure from developers and business leaders eager to expand Concord Village and the Civic Center southward, Moses turned his eye from Willowtown

to the northern periphery of the Heights. "[We] are deeply concerned over abandonment of plans for Cadman Plaza middle-income housing development in Brooklyn New York," wrote the Brooklyn Chamber of Commerce in April 1957. "This development is essential to our Brooklyn Civic Center." "In the Borough Hall area where we have our main office," pleaded Brooklyn Savings Bank president G. J. Bender, "the Cadman Plaza project is of vital interest to us."[54]

Like Willowtown, the northern section of the Heights eyed by the Slum Clearance Committee formed a middle cityscape of dilapidated brownstones, tenements, and small shops on the border of the modernist Civic Center and Concord Village. On the seven "primarily residential" but "mixed-use" acres selected by the SCC, two real estate firms determined only two buildings to be in fair condition. Nearby on Middagh Street, a hundred-year-old factory still produced candy. Along Fulton Street, large numbers of homeless congregated to form the borough's skid row. The Lyons House on Fulton Street was Brooklyn Heights' "last flophouse." Overcrowded tenements sat next to boarded-up homes and broken glass. A local reporter in a quick survey of a few dilapidated blocks noted seventy-eight For Rent signs. Yet along with symptoms of industrial decline appeared the early markers of gentrification. In the Ovington Building, Norman Mailer, Nathaniel Kaz, Truman Capote, and other writers and artists rented work spaces. On Monroe Place, newly renovated private homes surrounded a small church.[55]

Despite defeat in Willowtown, Robert Moses seemed unfazed by the prospect of local resistance, continuing to rely on Manhattan-based expertise and top-down executive power. In early 1957, he commissioned Helmsley Spear, Inc., a powerful Manhattan real estate firm, to make recommendations for the area. A year later, the SCC awarded sponsorship of the project to Seon Pierre Bonan, a developer with experience building Title I projects in Philadelphia, New Haven, and Boston. Harrison and Abramovitz, the architectural firm responsible for the United Nations and Rockefeller Center, tentatively agreed to design the tower.[56]

In April 1959, the Slum Clearance Committee submitted plans to the Board of Estimate for Cadman Plaza, a massive Title I project that required the clearance of seven acres along Fulton Street. Where a jumble of tenements (home to 263 families) and lofts stood, Moses proposed a modern twenty-story apartment tower surrounded by a cluster of five low commercial buildings and a landscaped terrace with an underground garage. Hoping to satisfy the demand of white-collar professionals for apartments close to the burgeoning financial sector in lower Manhattan, Moses described a fully taxpaying development with small, luxury-class rental units. The average rent of the 772 units would be $53. Forty-two percent of the apartments would consist of only two rooms. With open space, fluorescent light, central air-conditioning and air handling, superblocks, and soundproof windows, the project embodied the kinetic, impermeable, and integrated aesthetic of the modern city. "Through proper design and integration," explained Moses in a press release, "the project area will become part of the Brooklyn Civic Center Development program. . . . Construction of public buildings, expansion of educational facilities . . . parks, recreational facilities, local street improvements, improved traffic circulation, arterial improvements, expanded parking facilities which with large scale demolition of substandard sections in the 65 acre area will serve to create a better planned, integrated Civic Center . . . one of the largest and most comprehensive urban renewal programs undertaken in the United States."[57]

Modernist developers, bankers, and housing reformers heaped praise upon Cadman Plaza. The New York State Committee on Discrimination in Housing sent an enthusiastic telegram to Mayor Wagner urging approval of the project with a request to include low-income housing and a new school building. Moses tentatively agreed to add low-income public housing in an extension near the Brooklyn Bridge. (Overlooked by his critics is that Moses often insisted on placing low-rent projects and luxury developments side by side in his Title I projects. His stubborn modernist faith in "segregated uses," however, stopped him from considering mixed-income apartment buildings.)[58]

If Willowtown caused a splash of discontent, Robert Moses' Cadman Plaza unleashed a wave of local resistance. Along with statements of protest from the *Brooklyn Heights Press* and the Brooklyn Heights Association, hundreds of residents galvanized by the announcement met to form new organizations to combat city development in the area. In late 1956, a group of young recent arrivals to the Heights met in the basement of the First Unitarian Church to discuss the threat of urban renewal to their newly discovered enclave. "In 1956, '57 and '58 significant numbers of young professionals, Nancy and I among them, began moving into the Heights," reminisced lawyer and organizer Otis Pratt Pearsall. "These newcomers to gracious living in charming period houses on tranquil, tree-lined streets just across from Wall Street spotted serious threats to their new found way of civilized urban life, and they began meeting regularly. . . . The most important of these perceived threats were the well-advanced plan of Bob Moses' Slum Clearance Committee."[59]

In December 1958, Pearsall, lawyer William Fisher, and television producer Martin Schneider named the fledgling group the Community Conservation and Improvement Council, or CCIC (pronounced *kick*), and vowed to fight the Cadman Plaza project. "The community interests and unique charm of Brooklyn Heights may be seriously threatened," explained the CCIC mission statement. "Demolition of its fine old houses continues at a rate which must soon destroy the historic atmosphere of its quiet secluded streets. At the same time projects for Brooklyn Heights have been and continue to be proposed which fail to reflect the needs and interests of the community as a whole . . . Brooklyn Heights can not and must not stand still."[60]

Like the Willowtown Association, CCIC described a battle not just against a poorly planned project but against the underlying principles of urban renewal. If Robert Moses envisioned a project created swiftly and effectively by experts centered in Manhattan, CCIC believed development should be democratically administered by local communities. If Moses saw Brooklyn Heights as malleable space to be remade into new and improved forms, CCIC described a unique place in need of preservation and rehabilitation. "Fundamental principles underpin each of our objectives," CCIC exclaimed. "Any decision affecting the future of Brooklyn Heights or any part thereof shall be made with the advice, participation and consent of its residents . . . Our houses, historic structures and the architectural character of the Heights must be vigilantly preserved and safeguards must be developed to this end. Rehabilitation and, where required, spot clearance rather than whole-sale demolition shall be our theme. Relocation shall be held to a minimum and those involved assisted accordingly."[61]

Learning from the successful Willowtown fight, CCIC drew on the political and social capital of white-collar professional residents to stop Robert Moses in his tracks. Members with connections at city hall wrote official and personal letters to influential politicians. With a sincere faith in his role as principled and scientific public servant free from local corruption and cronyism, Robert Moses greeted these personal appeals with unveiled disdain. "We simply cannot remove pieces of property out of project areas because there are some objections on the part of owners and their representatives," Moses wrote to an assemblyman seeking protection of a "lovely" old building on Clark Street. "These projects must cover logical areas and in the process of determination of what is logical, the service of all agencies including the City Planning Commission is involved . . . If you have any evidence to support a contention that the plan which we have adopted is not sound or that we have included something which should be left out on the basis of proper planning, I would suggest you write me to that effect."[62]

If Moses championed logic and planning, in Brooklyn Heights he faced a new middle class willing and able to match his claim to expertise. With an abundance of lawyers, architects, businessmen, and academics at its disposal, CCIC set up three task forces to develop a multi-pronged attack on Cadman Plaza. The first, led by architect Herbert Kaufman, brought together local architects and housing experts to analyze closely the blueprints of Cadman Plaza and design an alternative plan. Another committee headed by Malcolm Chesney, an economist for the Brooklyn Union Gas Company, organized a group of twenty local architects to conduct a voluntary house-to-house survey of the entire fifty-block Brooklyn Heights neighborhood. The task force hoped to challenge the city's characterization of the area as a "slum" and to demonstrate the architectural value of many of the houses scheduled for demolition.[63]

While two committees of the CCIC battled the Cadman Plaza proposal, the last group explored new legal ways to protect Brooklyn Heights as a whole from future development projects. When researchers came across the Bard Law, the committee found a new weapon in the battle against urban renewal: historic zoning. The one-paragraph, never-invoked state law gave cities the power to protect through zoning or acquisition "place, buildings, structures, works of art and other objects having a special character or special historical or aesthetic interest or value." Inspired by the new Beacon Hill historic district established in Boston by the Massachusetts legislature in 1955, CCIC activists hoped to expand the law to protect not just individual landmarks but an entire neighborhood. When in 1958 James Felt of the City Planning Commission announced plans to overhaul the city's zoning laws for the first time since 1916, the CCIC saw a window of opportunity to establish New York City's first historic district.[64]

The drive to establish a historic district was a mammoth effort requiring dozens of Heights volunteers with architectural and legal connections and know-how. On one front, the CCIC lobbied the city's architectural, civic, and legal organizations for help in drafting the groundbreaking ordinance. In February 1959, Otis Pearsall cajoled the powerful Municipal Arts Society to create a special subcommittee of experts to spearhead the effort, including the ninety-two-year-old Albert S. Bard, after whom the law was named. In April, the committee dropped a note in the mailbox of Clay Lancaster, a respected architectural historian living in the Heights, explaining the historic districting effort. Lancaster volunteered to write a detailed house-by-house historic survey of more than six hundred Heights buildings.[65]

While one group sought to stall any further demolition, in April 1959, another CCIC subcommittee presented the city with an alternative plan for Cadman Plaza. In the place of high-rent studio and one-bedroom units, the CCIC version called for large family-sized, middle-income cooperative apartments. The Heights, the committee argued, was an area undergoing a grassroots revival. As a type of affordable homeownership, middle-income cooperatives would allow young Heights pioneers to continue the reclamation of the area. "[Both the CCIC and the Brooklyn Heights Association], deeply committed to the Heights, watched with mounting alarm the city's seemingly endless string of plans for the neighborhood: plans for high income housing at Cadman Plaza (and two years ago at Willowtown); the widening of Fulton Street, the Civic Center," explained the *Brooklyn Heights Press*. "How about middle income housing? What about converting rooming houses to family dwellings?" Discussing the Heights' enthusiasm for cooperatives, the editor of the *Press* explained, "In our passion to make the Heights a small town (just like the one all of us were born and raised in), we have nurtured a romantic belief in home ownership."[66] Along with detailed blueprints, the CCIC presented the city with alternative developers, Seymour and Jerome Berger, eager to build cooperative apartments without any tax abatements.

The city was moderately receptive. At a conference at the Slum Clearance Committee office on Randall's Island, the SCC promised Heights activists they would give equal consideration to the new developers, provided the new offer proved economically feasible. In February 1960, the SCC agreed to delay voting on Cadman Plaza and created a subcommittee to examine both Moses' plan and the CCIC plan. For an unbiased opinion, the city commissioned John R. White of Brown, Harris, Stevens, a private consultant, to conduct an independent study of the two proposals.[67]

The SCC's willingness to cooperate with Brooklyn Heights civic groups was indicative of a larger national shift in the politics of city development. Despite the characterization of redevelopment by critics as monolithic and rigidly ideological, New York City and the federal government for a decade slowly tinkered with redevelopment programs to correct the excesses of Title I of the 1949 Housing Act. The Housing Act of 1954 shifted the emphasis of Title I from "urban redevelopment" to "urban renewal." Unlike the blunt slum clearance program funded by Title I, new legislation required that urban renewal projects be linked to a comprehensive, workable plan for community development approved by the housing administrator. Along with acquisition and clearance, urban renewal also provided funds for conservation, rehabilitation, and the "voluntary repair of existing buildings." To ease the trauma of redevelopment for local populations, the federal government also pledged more money for public housing built specifically for the relocation of residents of urban renewal sites. In a further round of legislation in 1956, Congress authorized direct relocation payments to displaced residents and small businesses in renewal sites. In 1963, the Urban Renewal Administration published a guide, *Historic Preservation Through Urban Renewal*, explaining how communities could use Title I funds to conserve urban areas of historic significance. Fourteen historic neighborhoods took advantage of the program.

On the local level, New York City officials also modified the urban redevelopment agenda. In 1951, under pressure from middle-class Manhattanites for more community participation in city development, borough president Robert Wagner established twelve community planning councils. (In 1963, with Wagner as mayor, the city would create eight community planning districts for Brooklyn as well.) In 1957, the New York City Housing Authority announced a shift from superblock public housing to smaller vest-pocket projects less disruptive to neighborhood context. The following year, the city launched the West Side conservation program, an experimental Title I project with minimal demolition, rehabilitation of existing structures, on-site relocation of residents, citizen participation, and developments for a variety of income levels.[68]

The shift from redevelopment to renewal converted many former opponents. In 1957, Willowtown activist and settlement house worker Richard Mendes attended a two-day conference on urban renewal sponsored by the American Council to Improve Our Neighborhoods (ACTION). Once a harsh critic of urban redevelopment, he came back from the conference brimming with enthusiasm about the potential of the reformed federal housing program. "Perhaps the two most significant impressions I received from these men were their spelling out, (1) the government aids available to private builders to conserve, rehabilitate and rebuild neighborhoods, and, (2) the all-important role of the citizenry in planning with and stimulating Urban Renewal," Mendes wrote in a letter to the *Heights Press* entitled "Let's Support Urban Renewal." "In town after town, city after city, all over the country these programs have been sparked by the citizens and carried through by their acting in the closest kind of cooperation with the city officials. Baltimore, Oakland, Cleveland, New Haven and Philadelphia are only a few of the outstanding examples. . . . I hope that all will support and participate with the Brooklyn Heights Association and Willow Town Association in their work to bring portions of the Urban Renewal program to the Heights."[69]

One casualty of the changing times was none other than Robert Moses. In 1960, faced with public outrage about mismanagement and graft in city development projects, the city replaced Moses' Slum Clearance Committee with the Housing and Redevelopment Board (HRB). Headed by anti-Moses real estate leader J. Clarence Davies, the new HRB promised to bring reform to the urban renewal program. Rather than leaving the task to developers, the HRB took full responsibility for relocating displaced residents. To minimize dislocation and disruption of local communities, the agency replaced mass clearance projects with spot clearance of individual buildings and whenever possible funded the conservation and rehabilitation of existing structures. Aiming to be more open and accountable to the public, the HRB replaced Moses' unilateral deal making with developers with a transparent process of open auctions for potential projects. Breaking from Moses' insistence on planning projects only on a case-by-case basis, the HRB pledged to fit each development into an overall city plan approved by the City Planning Department. J. Clarence Davies, real estate agent Walter Fried, and African American New Dealer and civil rights activist Robert Weaver served as co-commissioners. Puerto Rican Herman Badillo was named the city's relocation commissioner.[70]

As their first order of business, the newly formed HRB faced a maelstrom of protest against Cadman Plaza. On July 19, 1960, seventy-five Brooklyn Heights mothers marched to protest the luxury development. Pushing baby carriages from the Long Island Historic Society to Borough Hall, the women, flanked by small children, attended a rally organized by a new civic group: the North Brooklyn Heights Community Group (NBHCG). The signs held by protesters juxtaposed the "homes," "history," and "intimacy" of the Heights to the encroaching Manhattan landscape: "We Don't Want to Move to the Suburbs," "Help Preserve the Historic Heights," "Public Funds for People, Not for Private Profit," "Homes Not Skyscrapers," "We Chose to Live and Work in the Heights and We Plan to *Stay!*" The group's spokesperson, *New York Times* classical music critic and composer Eric Salzman, gave the borough president a petition with 3,500 signatures.[71]

Seeking to distinguish itself from Moses, the HRB attempted to allay community concerns with a more conciliatory tone. In September 1960, the HRB proposed a compromise plan that divided Cadman Plaza into two sections of 400 cooperative apartments and 835 rental units split by a walkway. To make space for the larger cooperatives, the HRB architects eliminated plans for a suburban-style shopping center. In December, in attempt to answer criticism about the city's inadequate relocation program, the HRB sent Western Union messengers to ring the doorbells of every tenant on the Cadman Plaza site. The messengers delivered a bulletin with a report on the current status of the new project and a detailed description of their rights under the city's relocation laws. The bulletin explained that although relocation would begin in 1961, tenants had legal recourse and could not be forced to move without ample notice. Outlining the assistance available for new tenants, the HRB concluded, "It does not mean you will have to move at once. It does not mean you will have to move without notice. It does not mean you will have to move without help." In January 1961, the city announced plans for six new projects in outer Brooklyn and the Bronx, with 2,500 apartments for residents displaced by slum clearance projects in Cadman Plaza and Manhattan's West Side.[72]

By February 1961, the HRB happily described to reporters an agreement with Brooklyn Heights residents about Cadman Plaza. Along with 835 luxury rental units, the new plan included 405 middle-income cooperative apartments in a pair of twenty-two-story towers, forty-five duplex apartment town houses, a swimming pool, a play area, and two hundred underground parking spots. The Brooklyn Heights Association applauded the new proposal. As the plan moved toward approval, 375 members of the newly formed Cadman Plaza Cooperative Association excitedly made $50 deposits on future units.[73]

To the surprise of HRB leaders, their attempt at compromise sparked even more angry protest. Immediately after hearing reports of the new plan, the North Brooklyn Heights Community Group announced a new demand: 100 percent cooperatives for the entire Cadman Plaza project. Further, the civic group called for the city to scrap plans for any form of high-rise towers, instead pushing for rehabilitation and conservation of existing buildings. In June 1961, the NBHCG presented the city with a detailed critique of Cadman Plaza written by Martin S. James, a local resident and assistant professor of art and urbanism at Brooklyn College. The thirty-one-page report blasted the "clumsy, archaic, unprofessional administrative practice" and "scorched-earth techniques" of the city development program. Calling for the city to stop all forms of clearance and redevelopment and celebrating "organic" city life, the report was signed by a cross-section of the city's powerful intellectual class: local reformers LeRoy Bowman and Eli Wilentz, Nathan Glazer, Paul Goodman, Jane Jacobs, Staughton Lynd, Lewis Mumford, and several architecture professors from Columbia and the Museum of Modern Art. Lobbied by Martin James for further support, Brooks Atkinson, influential theater critic for the *New York Times*, wrote a lengthy "Critic at Large" column in May 1961 further criticizing Cadman Plaza and calling for the preservation of Brooklyn Heights' unique landscape.[74]

In December 1961, Clay Lancaster published *Old Brooklyn Heights: New York's First Suburb* with Charles E. Tuttle Press. With detailed descriptions of 619 century-old buildings in the area, based on three years of research, slide shows, and walking tours, the text was the first of its kind in postwar New York City and became the bedrock for the CCIC's increasingly powerful historic preservation drive. Armed with Lancaster's about-to-be-published manuscript, in October 1961, leaders of the CCIC met with city planning commissioner James Felt to discuss the possibility of using the new 1961 zoning laws to protect the historic landscape of the Heights. Felt, a post–Robert Moses city planner who, like J. Clarence Davies, was open to rehabilitation and preservation, enthusiastically endorsed the preservation plan. The Heights historic preservation movement received a further boost as public outrage grew over the planned demolition of Manhattan's Pennsylvania Station. With increased pressure from middle-class activists, in spring 1962 Mayor Wagner established the Landmarks Preservation Commission, a twelve-person committee of artists, architects, lawyers, and businessmen with the power to endow buildings and monuments with landmark status. Brooklyn Heights (excluding the Cadman Plaza Title I site) was on its way to becoming the city's first designated historic district in 1965.[75]

That same year, architect Percival Goodman, under the sponsorship of the North Brooklyn Heights Community and the Central Brooklyn Heights Group for Preservation, released his own plan for the area that preserved most of the historic structures, including the print shop where Walt Whitman printed *Leaves of Grass*. The plan also called for a twenty-story building of middle-income cooperatives at each end of the site and four six-story buildings built on vacant or sparsely used lots, to minimize dislocation. A nearby loft building would also be converted to sixty-five artist studios. The growing hodgepodge of Heights protest groups could not agree on the plan. When the Brooklyn Heights Association and Citizens' Housing and Planning Council dismissed it as unrealistic, a new group formed called the Citizens' Committee for the Goodman Plan.[76]

Faced with a cacophony of protest groups, the city continued to be accommodating. While the mayor supported Heights' residents demands for the historic districting of the area outside of the Title I site, in March 1962 the HRB unveiled a new compromise plan for Cadman Plaza. Answering local calls for more cooperatives, the new plan included 60 percent middle-income cooperative multi-bedroom units and 40 percent luxury rental efficiencies and one-bedrooms. In the addition, the city would rehabilitate a factory on the site, converting the loft space into artist studios. As with the previous proposal, a host of liberal groups endorsed the compromise. The New York chapter of the American Institute of Architects, the Citizens Housing and Planning Council, and the Citizens Union Planning Committee backed the new proposal. The Brooklyn chapter of the NAACP also enthusiastically championed the plan, perhaps due to city negotiations with NYCHA to include a low-income housing project somewhere adjacent to the site. Heights protesters were less impressed, calling the plan, in the words of a West Village Committee activist, simply "another attempt by the city to bulldoze an entire area."[77]

In its first two years of existence, the HRB claimed, it met almost a thousand times with local community groups in Brooklyn Heights and other neighborhoods around the city to offer compromises on urban development projects.[78] But in trying to bring a humane face to urban renewal, the HRB was missing the point. What the New Dealers in the HRB could not understand was that the issue for Brooklyn Heights' new middle class was not the details of the plan but planning itself. While the HRB was trying to tweak the numbers, Heights activists were attacking the impersonality of numbers themselves. If the HRB and other city planners sought to renew, rebuild, and rationalize the landscape, Brooklyn Heights residents were romantic urbanists, celebrating what they saw as the organic, subjective, local, historic, and spontaneous character of the Heights. The HRB hoped to integrate the Heights into a regional, kinetic city system, whereas the Heights residents deliberately sought to protect their "hidden enclave" from sameness. If the HRB sought to reshape the urban landscape on the principles of science and logic, Heights residents celebrated a urban landscape of passion, sexual freedom, and spontaneous growth. The HRB and CCIC weren't engaging in a debate about the future of Cadman Plaza; they were talking past each other.

When the HRB tried to incorporate community demands into blueprints of Cadman Plaza, they attempted the paradoxical goal of institutionalizing an anti-institutional critique. The HRB hoped to affirm the principles of modernist planning while acknowledging the localist aesthetic celebrated by romantic middle-class urbanites. After doubling the number of cooperative units in the project, the HRB explained in a statement that "every consideration was given to the many neighborhood groups which had expressed a need for additional units in the area. . . . We have been impressed by the proponents of cooperative apartments and, consequently, we are extending appreciably the land space immediately available for this type of housing. The Board is responsive to local community groups and their local needs."[79]

While heeding the calls of local groups, the HRB reconfirmed its commitment to scientific management, bird's-eye regional city planning, and the creation of an open, kinetic, and integrated city system. "However, it has, in addition, a responsibility to plan and develop projects which will make the maximum contribution of the city as a whole. . . . Our basic philosophy is one of considering the city as whole, developing a program which evaluates each project in relation to its impact upon a city-wide concept and plan for urban renewal and housing, and recognizing, that, while each neighborhood may and should have its own distinct character, it is fundamentally a segment in the totality which is New York. . . . We shall in attempt to develop a program which, when its various segments are considered in relation to each other, will yield a meaningful total. This composite will reflect the needs of many sections of the city, the variations in incomes and rent paying abilities, and the land use potentials of areas selected."[80]

The HRB acknowledged that Cadman Plaza was designed for high-income, white-collar professionals working on Wall Street. Only with the tax revenue from a fully taxable luxury unit, they argued, could the HRB build projects in poorer sections of the city. "Our studies indicate that Cadman Plaza is one of the city's prime residential sites for rental housing. It will provide much needed living accommodations for those who are employed in the downtown financial district of Manhattan, as well as those who work in the downtown Brooklyn area." Revenues from Cadman Plaza and other luxury developments made possible projects such as the Flatlands Industrial Park and a new industrial and commercial center in the Washington Street area. Title I luxury projects also produced funds for subsidized housing; without those funds, the city would run a crippling deficit.[81]

To residents who saw their neighborhood as rediscovered and unique, the attempt of the HRB to demonstrate how the Heights fit into an integrated city system was a contradiction in terms. Heights activists scoffed when planners added low-rise housing and walkways to their project models, making clear that any attempt by city planners to include the intimate streets, mom-and-pop shops, and rehabilitated artist studios of the Heights and Greenwich Village in renewal projects was doomed from the outset. Brooklyn Heights was a neighborhood because it was organic, the messy sum of a million private decisions, a repository of symbolic and cultural value developed naturally over time. Rational planning and abstraction, no matter how sympathetic, sterilized the cityscape and alienated its residents. "The rebuilding technique known as 'selective removal' or 'spot renewal' or 'renewal planning' or 'planned conservation' . . . is largely the trick of seeing how many old buildings can be left standing and the area still converted into a passable version of Radiant Garden City," concluded Jane Jacobs, Greenwich Village activist and supporter of the anti–Cadman Plaza movement. "[P]lans and drawings for projects and renewal areas in which, literally, room had been left here and there at great intervals for a corner grocery store . . . were accompanied by letters that said, 'See, we have taken to heart what you said,'" she complained, but these were a "corner-grocery gimmick."[82]

In fighting renewal, Martin James and Heights residents did not argue that the Heights should remain a slum. As urban pioneers in a gentrifying neighborhood, Heights activists, like Jane Jacobs in Greenwich Village, celebrated an "unslumming" process that was organic and unplanned. "Demand for the kinds of town houses that stand on the site were never greater," argued James. "These rare, original, early homes are considered especially desirable. In this market, the buyers outnumber the available dwellings. Open market conditions would quickly rehabilitate most of the area." "One-dimensional," "sterile," "transient," "scorched earth"—the florid rhetoric used by Heights activists obfuscated their main agenda. The real problem with government-funded luxury towers and low-income projects was not just their dullness, but also that they were gentrification-proof. "If government intervention cannot make a positive contribution that will benefit the area, the community, and the city, it has no business invading an area where private enterprise could do a better job! The city's intervention could be justified only by (1) a program of preservation and rehabilitation of all the historic homes, and (2) new construction and/or rehabilitation of other buildings where parking lots and garages now exist. All new housing units would be middle-income. Nothing short of this is even remotely justifiable."[83]

For an older generation of New Deal liberals with a modernist faith in large development projects, central planning, and cooperation between big government and big business, the attack on the public sector was puzzling. If Brooklyn Heights was rapidly "unslumming," wouldn't it be better for all parties involved if the process was managed by city officials? Wasn't urban renewal simply a form of "planned gentrification," and conversely gentrification a type of "organic urban renewal"? "Private money invested in rehabilitating small residence buildings—'unslumming' as [Jacobs] calls it," explained a bitter Roger Starr, New Deal liberal city planner and future neoconservative, "is equally 'cataclysmic' for the tenants who happen to be living in them. These tenants—who must have been paying low rents if the entire enterprise is to be financially possible—must make way for Mrs. Jacobs and her 'unslummers' just as surely as if a bulldozer knocked down their homes. In privately financed rehabilitation, the unsubsidized rise in rent is formidable. To be more precise, private rehabilitation is *more* 'cataclysmic' to those affected by it than is public renewal, at least if the public activity is in a designated 'urban renewal' area. In such areas, the government pays moving expenses for displaced tenants and provides assistance in finding new homes. And if the displaced tenants find their own homes—and if these meet normal community standards—they are paid a bonus."[84]

Populist language was easy to invoke when defending the neighborhood against luxury developers. But when the HRB finalized plans to add low-income housing to the Cadman Plaza project, the fight to preserve quaintness from the city bulldozer became much stickier. Whereas the sheer injustice of displacing poorer residents for luxury apartments united Brooklyn Heights in opposition, public housing for the nonwhite poor was far more divisive. In 1963, the HRB and the city housing authority agreed to add a low-income project to an extension of the Cadman Plaza luxury development. On a single block sitting between Public School 8 and the Brooklyn Bridge, the city planned to demolish about 50 units of tenements to build a single fifteen-story, 173-unit low-rent building. With the building likely to be home to a growing black and Puerto Rican population, the city received praise from civil rights groups and the Committee for Public Housing in Brooklyn Heights, a small Brooklyn Heights civic group committed to integrating the area. The WBID too voted to support the vest-pocket project.[85]

The issue of public housing was particularly dicey in a liberal Heights neighborhood with many residents strongly supportive of the emerging civil rights movement. Since the late fifties, a host of local community groups had been working with neighboring poor areas to integrate what they feared was becoming a "lily white neighborhood," or worse yet "Scarsdale on the East River." The Brooklyn Heights Fair Housing Committee collaborated with the NAACP to actively recruit black families from other parts of the city to move to apartments in the Heights. When the city initiated the "Princeton Plan" in 1964, pairing P.S. 8 with a mostly black and Puerto Rican public school in the neighboring low-income Farragut Houses, the Parents Association was the only white parents' group initially to vote to support the plan. (Although many parents voted with their feet, transferring their children to private or parochial schools. By 1973, only 14 percent of Heights Association parents sent their children to public schools).[86]

While a small group of Heights residents avidly lobbied for low-income housing, a larger group of Heights residents organized resistance. The Brooklyn Heights Community Council (BHCC), a new civic group formed specifically to fight the project, gathered three thousand signatures and threatened a mass demonstration on city hall. "Local proponents of the low-cost housing plan may continue to seek its adoption," warned a BHCC member and vice president of the Brooklyn Heights Association, "We won't let down to oppose this or any other attempt to impose poor planning concepts on the community." "The city is trying to put over public housing on us and overexploit the neighborhood," complained Paul Windels, Wall Street lawyer and president of the Brooklyn Heights Association. "This low-cost stuff is bunk." At an association membership meeting in June 1963, 766 members voted for a resolution against public housing, with only 39 in favor of the low-income project.[87]

While angry violent protests against low-income housing occurred in the outer boroughs, Brooklyn Heights' white-collar residents did not resort to the vituperative racial rhetoric of the city's working-class white ethnics. "It is probably only the residents' idea of dignity," suggested the *New York Times*, "that kept parents . . . from demonstrating in the streets." Instead of attacking the nonwhite poor, Heights residents described an aesthetic battle to maintain uniqueness in the face of sameness and to protect city life from the threat of sterile bureaucracy. They cast their opposition to public housing as a form of advocacy for the poor, pointing to the alienation and isolation of residents in planned modernist housing. "Low income housing is equated with the integration problem," explained a *Brooklyn Heights Press* editorial, ". . . although we don't necessarily agree. . . . We maintain the high-rise building, constructed in one corner of the Heights, would become a ghetto." "The solution to the problems of low-rent housing does not lie in the scaleless, intrusive, ill-designed brick monsters that we have come to know as 'projects,' whether they be built in our community or in any other," exhorted Heights architect and future Landmarks Preservation Commission vice president Elliot Willensky. "Until a comprehensive program of planning is developed which comes to grips with social and economic problems as well as those of the three-dimensional physical environment no further low-rent 'projects' should be foisted upon our citizens, regardless of the apparent nobility of the reason, whether those citizens be the articulate comfortable residents of Brooklyn Heights or our less articulate and less leisured neighbors in other communities whom low-rent housing is intended to benefit." Instead of institutional space, protesters called for a renovated public school, park space, and more recreational facilities for children.[88]

In October 1963, the HRB offered a compromise plan to satisfy both the supporters and critics of low-income housing. To meet community demands for an improved school and recreational facilities, the city would build a new building for P.S. 8, along with a playground and kindergarten play area. Run jointly by the Board of Education and the Department of Parks, the playgrounds would be open to the community on vacations and weekends. On the site of the old P.S. 8, the city would build a fifteen-story housing project for 150 low-income families. A new play area would be created on the site of a relocated police station, and Poplar Street would be closed to traffic. An old parochial school on the site would be allowed to remain standing.[89]

The Brooklyn Heights Association, the North Brooklyn Heights Community Group, and the *Brooklyn Heights Press* blasted the new compromise. Rather than acknowledging a racial or class conflict, protesters instead described an environmentalist crusade against the overexploitation of the landscape, a democratic revolt against authoritarian modernist developers, and a defense of the poor. "The proposed low-income project . . . which would be geographically isolated in the extreme northern corner of the Heights, would simply become one of the ghettoes," wrote an angry resident to the *New York Times*. "The facts are the overwhelming sentiment of the community opposed the low-cost housing project because the land involved in the Cadman Plaza development has already been grossly overexploited," explained Brooklyn Heights Association president Paul Windels. "Brooklyn Heights has pulled itself up by the bootstraps and is now one of the most attractive, middle-income areas in any city in the country. It is open to any who seek residence there without regard to race or color. . . . the low-cost housing project would have been a very poor, artificial attempt at integration." "Brooklyn Heights is an integrated community! . . . We have low income families living here," complained a "sick and tired" resident to the *Brooklyn Heights Press*. "Moreover, 375 families were recently unceremoniously shuffled out against their wishes by the city. We fought to keep them here! . . . Now suddenly, the cry arises that we are 'A rich lily-white community,' and that we are afraid of integration with low-income families. . . . The only way to achieve integration is when people live in a community by choice, not by being picked out as a number from a list, and being told, 'You are to go to district X,' by some impersonal, uninterested board."[90]

In another line of argument, residents protested that building a low-income project and new school would require the destruction of important historic buildings. "Brooklyn Heights has gained national attention by virtue of its remarkable degree of preservation, and its 19th Century amenities. Indeed, it is almost unique in the New York Metropolis in this respect," complained one activist group in a letter to Mayor Wagner. "Why, then, arbitrarily jeopardize an irreplaceable asset with a complete anomaly, when there are two hundred square miles of land area from which to select a much more suitable site for project housing." One Federal-style building at 55 Middagh Street, argued Eric Salzman, was the oldest house on the Heights. "I wouldn't mind so much if they were going to build another Brasilia," explained Gregory Rabassa, a professor of Spanish and Portuguese at Columbia University and a Middagh Street resident. "But I'm afraid they're planning another Stalinallee."[91]

Rather than demolishing buildings, some Heights protesters proposed that the Housing Authority instead rehabilitate five buildings scattered throughout the Heights for sixty low-income families. To avoid isolating low-income residents in a single building, they suggested setting aside a few apartments in the luxury towers of Cadman Plaza for low-income families. On the tract of land eyed by the city, protesters called for the conservation of all buildings, plus the transformation of empty lots into a parking lot, a small park, and a baseball field for children. In August 1964, borough president Abe Stark, under pressure from Heights activists, proposed a new plan to satisfy both sides that dropped the low-income tower and substituted ninety-five garden apartments for the elderly.[92]

Local civil rights leaders were furious. "You can't tell me that parking space and a ball field for the richest, most privileged white children in the borough of Brooklyn is more important than integrating Negro families into this community," complained Merrill Martin, chairman of the borough branch of CORE. "Here is a chance to create integrated schools and start breaking down ghettoes." "Distortion of the news . . . has been [the *Brooklyn Heights Press*] trademark for the last few years," complained former Willowtown activist and urban renewal convert Richard Mendes. "The proposed housing bears no resemblance whatsoever to the acknowledged deficiencies represented by Fort Greene, Gowanus, and Farragut [public housing complexes]. It is small—150 units, not 1500 plus—and it is in Brooklyn Heights. It will not be a self-contained ghetto, encircled by a slum, nor will it dominate the Heights." The Housing Authority already considered rehabilitation, added Mendes, and found the smaller existing buildings inadequate in size. "At least 500,000 people live in dilapidated dwelling units [in New York City]. . . . Low-rise, vacant houses are hardly the answer to a problem of such magnitude."[93]

Many Heights residents were simply ambivalent. "I suppose there is a high correlation between wanting to maintain our carriage houses and gas lamps and wanting to maintain our pristine population," mused Lee Adler, an advertising executive and "rediscoverer" of the Heights. "Heights residents don't want poor people and they don't want Negroes and Puerto Ricans in the area," sighed Kenneth Boss, a Heights real estate broker who kept a framed photograph of Norman Thomas over his desk. "There's no question about it. This will be a rich man's ghetto."[94]

In April 1964, after eight years of disputes, the city held a small groundbreaking ceremony for the Cadman Plaza project. In a small clearing amidst the rubble, the City Council president, Paul Screvane, and borough president Abe Stark made short speeches praising the project and celebrating the dawn of a new era of prosperity for Brooklyn. Behind the speakers stood eighty-six empty, dilapidated tenements, storefronts, and townhouses. While most of the families and businesses had already relocated, a hundred or so remained warily in their homes.[95]

The rhetoric of the event was a far cry from the confident chest-thumping of Robert Moses and city leaders of the past. The era of bold plans to reshape and rebuild the cityscape, to conquer the constraints of space and time, and to turn blight into light was nearing its end. Reading a speech on behalf of Mayor Wagner, Paul Screvane described the project in conciliatory terms. "The shining towers and green plazas that will occupy this area within a few short years will . . . be a worthy link between the quiet grace of historic Brooklyn Heights and the sturdy dynamism of the Downtown Brooklyn and the Civic Center areas . . . This project represents one of the first embodiments of the 'new look' in renewal and housing that the Housing and Redevelopment board, at my direction, has brought to our City. The diversity of housing types and the distinguished design of the structures have shattered once and for all the stereotype of urban renewal projects as dull repetitions of the same cookie-cutter design. . . . Most important of all, the long and stormy history of this project was finally brought to a constructive conclusion by a real dialogue between the community and the City Government—which we believe is essential to any worthwhile renewal activities."[96]

Sitting between the modernist Civic Center and "anti-modern" renovated brownstones, Cadman Plaza did in many ways embody a spatial and ideological middle landscape between two types of urbanism: "historic Brooklyn Heights" and "dynamic downtown." While the design of the tall towers looked similar, the final blueprints had evolved significantly from Robert Moses' luxury project a decade earlier. The final plan called for apartment towers of twenty-six and thirty-three stories. Between the two skyscrapers would sit eighteen townhouses with two or three bedrooms. With prices of $600 per room and monthly maintenance charges of $30–35, the project consisted entirely of middle-income cooperatives. In 1968, the city approved a third addition to Cadman Plaza. Brooklyn Heights Towers, later renamed Cadman Towers, consisted of a thirty-one-story building, a twelve-story building, and an assortment of twenty-four townhouses, with a total of 422 middle-income cooperatives.[97]

While born out of compromise, the tall, air-conditioned towers did not represent the dawn of a new era of enlightened urban renewal, as HRB leaders hoped. Instead Cadman Plaza was the swan song of urban modernism and pro-growth liberalism in Brooklyn. For the next decade, city planners would attempt to incorporate community planning, maximum feasible participation of local communities, and the conservation and rehabilitation of local architecture into model cities and other Great Society development plans. But, as with Cadman Plaza, the paradox of trying to maintain a sense of place through bureaucratic government intervention would be impossible. Attempting to institutionalize the anti-institutional rhetoric of critics, new development projects satisfied neither local communities nor government planners. By 1974, as the city and federal government turned to Section 8 subsidies, tax incentives for rehabilitation, festival marketplaces, and "mini planning," urban renewal and the centrally administered, regionally planned metropolitan system it strove for was dead.

If Cadman Plaza signaled the death of urban renewal, the project marked the birth of a new cityscape. Far from destroying it, as critics feared, Cadman Plaza gave historic Brooklyn Heights its form. In the battle against the towers, Heights residents drew formal boundaries around the neighborhood, conducted historic studies of the architecture, and wrote eloquent descriptions of their "historically diverse" enclave. Faced with the intrusion of a government-planned, technocratic, regionally integrated project, residents articulated a

The Whitman Close apartment tower and townhouses, seen here in 2010, were one of
the three compromise projects eventually built on the Cadman Plaza renewal site.
(Photograph taken by author.)

new type of urbanism that celebrated organic street life, aged surfaces, private
ownership, diversity, and local distinctiveness. The romantic urbanist literature produced in the fight against Cadman Plaza and urban renewal projects
elsewhere in the city—Jane Jacobs' *Death and Life of Great American Cities*, the

Martin James report—would inspire brownstone renovators in new neighborhoods sprouting throughout the borough.

As the city slowly demolished the tenements and brownstones for Cadman
Plaza, scores of Heights residents dug through the wreckage to salvage old ban-
isters, doorknobs and knockers, woodwork, stone ornaments, and marble—all
of which they used to help restore their brownstones elsewhere in the area. In
historic neighborhoods around the city, brownstoners scavenged the debris of
Title I construction wreckage to add to renovated townhouses. The historic
landscape was born in the wake of modern projects. One could not exist without the other.[98]

Critics of Robert Moses have often quipped that while the New Dealer
loved the public, he hated people. While city developers were enamored of
mass clearance projects, grand civic centers, public housing complexes, super-
highways, and mass consumer culture, they thought little about the effects of
their schemes on individuals. Standing over models and maps, they talked
easily of moving thousands of people with little regard for the psychological
effects of dislocation and the attachment to local place. If the CCIC, Jane
Jacobs, and the new young urban professionals in Greenwich Village and
Brooklyn Heights accomplished anything, they brought an important appreciation of the personal relationship of people to their environment, the messiness of city life, the intimacy of the street, the authentic sense of place, the
creative voice of local artists and musicians, and the idiosyncrasies of diverse
communities. Brooklyn Heights residents presented an important corrective
to the dehumanizing and authoritarian excesses of modernism.

Perhaps the anti-Moses movement deserves an inverted version of the charge
thrown at modern planners. If Brooklyn's new white-collar professionals loved
people, they hated the public. The romantic urban imagery of a historically
diverse Brooklyn Heights was privatist, celebrating the sanctity of home, small
shops, bootstrap renovation, and freedom from city intervention. They were
deeply hostile to social engineering, big government, and organized labor. They
sought to physically strip away the modern landscape to restore the Romantic-
era Olmstedian Victorian landscape, labeling as "phony," "sterile," or "alienating" the government-funded playgrounds, hospitals, highways, colleges, and
civic centers built since the New Deal. In the fight against urban renewal, they
celebrated the free market, extolling the authentically organic cityscape and
lambasting abstract regulation. In their fight against urban renewal, Brownstone
Brooklyn's ostensibly liberal new middle class would unintentionally become
bedfellows with an emerging New Right critique of government intervention.

But were the renovated brownstones, cafés, independent theaters, and
street carnivals becoming another form of sameness? Both Cadman Plaza and

historic Brownstone Brooklyn, urban renewal and historic preservation, modernist and anti-modernist urbanism were products of the same economic restructuring, two sides of the same postindustrial reshaping of an industrial landscape. Whether through planned gentrification or organic urban renewal, the Heights was slowly but surely becoming demographically indistinguishable from Scarsdale. "After World War II, a couple with $5,000 could put a down payment on a red-brick or brownstone house costing perhaps $15,000," explained the *NYT* in 1965 of the rapidly transforming area. "Today they have to put down $30,000 for a house costing up to $80,000—and more. With the increase in value, landlords who once found it profitable to run the brownstones as rooming houses have renovated the buildings for sale to eager families. This has pushed many former lodgers, mostly Negroes and Puerto Ricans, out of the neighborhood."

"We are in danger of becoming a middling neighborhood—full of middle class housing for middle income families who believe in a middle-road way of life," warned the *Brooklyn Heights Press* in a rueful moment. "We discriminate no less against the rich than against the poor. . . . Clearly there is no room at the co-op for the high income family . . . the City Authority is angrily upbraided for suggesting low income housing development. . . . We can, if we set our minds to it, create as barren an atmosphere of uniformity as was ever envisioned by the Great Neck Chamber of Commerce . . . and later wonder why things seem so dull around here. Is this *really what we want?*"[99]

In early 2005, when a brownstone only blocks away from Cadman Plaza sold for over $8 million, the irony was bitter. Brooklyn Heights was now "one-dimensional," high-income and white, while the modernist mass-produced monoliths—government-subsidized middle-income towers, public housing, the government offices in the Civic Center, fast-food joints, and even the ticky-tacky homes of suburbia—had become racially and socioeconomically diverse.

In the battle against the two machines, a hodgepodge community of Manhattan expatriates coalesced into the official neighborhood of Brooklyn Heights. The Heights was a dramatically new type of urban place that would inspire similar neighborhoods throughout Brownstone Brooklyn. New enclaves in Brooklyn would claim to be the "next Brooklyn Heights," or, alternatively, juxtapose themselves to "co-opted" or "phony" Brooklyn Heights. In new settlements such as Cobble Hill, Boerum Hill, and Carroll Gardens, residents would create civic groups, block associations, historic districting laws, and political organizations modeled after those in Heights. But the battle against the two machines sparked the class consciousness of the new urban middle class. If the industrial working class once forged an oppositional identity to the factory in saloons, fraternal clubs, and union halls, a new white-collar proletariat developed postindustrial class consciousness in antique stores, art galleries, cafés, renovated brownstones, waterfront piers, and empty factories. Derided by their enemies over the years as "yuppies," "limousine liberals," or "radical chic," this new constituency articulated a new type of anti-statist politics that was hostile to liberal centralized planning and bureaucracy, instead celebrating grassroots government, organic landscapes, existential liberation, creative expression, historicity and diversity, and do-it-yourself neighborhood revitalization.

5   The Highway in the Garden and the Literature of Gentrification

After the West End was torn down . . . the area's slightly
European atmosphere and the increasing sentimentality with
which ethnic areas began to be viewed starting in the 1960s
helped transform the remembered West End . . . the area was
recalled as a tight-knit, cohesive, even "primordial" community—
a place said to have avoided the anomie, anonymity and alienation often thought by intellectuals and writers to infect
cities—and since the 1950s suburbia too. I may not have helped
when I called the book I wrote about the area *Urban Villagers*.
                                                    —Herbert Gans[1]

In 1961, assistant professor of art and Brooklyn Heights resident Martin James released "Cadman Plaza in Brooklyn Heights: A Study of the Misuse of Public Power and Funds in Urban Renewal." To attack the city's high-rise develop-ment plan, the James report offered a scathing indictment of urban renewal and modernist planning. Where city planners relied on abstract statistics and scientific diagrams to label the area a "slum," James instead offered a romantic and colorful description of Brooklyn Heights that evoked its vibrant diversity and rich sense of place. Rather than simply a collection of dilapidated build-ings, the Heights was a rare vestige of an authentic neighborhood in a rapidly modernizing city. "The unique character is more than a sum of its parts," explained James. "It grows out of the complexes of handsome facades, the clean lines of short and narrow streets bordered with trees. It grows out of the suggestion of age and history, and the views of harbor and skyline. It grows out of the rim of small shops, galleries, artisan quarters and studios, out of glimpses of gardens and well-tended back yards full of trees and flowers." Not only was the landscape unique, but the community was diverse as well, as a new middle class mixed with the elderly poor. "The social makeup of the Heights is an unusual, organic unity of diverse elements: old Brooklyn fam-ilies, young professional people, artists, musicians and writers, small shop owners and local employees. There are also a number of single people, most of them elderly, living on benefits and pensions. People of many different backgrounds, origins, income and social conditions live together success-fully." The report also commemorated the semi-residential character of the blocks targeted by planners, which contained "besides the richness and variety of small, specialized shops, workshops and studios, a large number of houses of irreplaceable history and architectural value."[2]

Diversity alone was not the reason the blocks should be preserved. "The area, although less well maintained than the surrounding neighborhood, is not a slum, and has an unusual rehabilitation potential." Free from the inter-ference of government planners, the brownstone district was organically "unslumming." "Town houses, old but solid and distinguished, predominate," wrote James. "Many have always been maintained as private homes. Decay, which reached alarming proportions in the years between 1930 and 1950, has been dramatically turned back by a natural process of self renewal in the last decade. Young families, especially professional people, 'discovered' Brooklyn Heights and became property owners, restoring and rehabilitating the fine old houses, a process which is still going on." The James report was not simply defending the area against urban renewal. The anti-renewal tract was also an early promotion of gentrification *avant la lettre*.[3]

Upon setting up the urban pastoral, James strategically interrupted the serene scene with the intrusion of the city bulldozer. The unique enclave only recently "discovered" by middle-class pioneers, warned James, was in peril from encroaching modernity. Pernicious developers and city planners threatened to destroy the fragile middle cityscape between ghetto and sky-scraper. "This upgrading of the community has also introduced dangers," wrote James. "As elsewhere in the city, apartment house development threatens the irreplaceable old buildings which give the neighborhood its won charm. Speculators and developers are tastelessly destroying the old values that first attached them." The new project would not simply destroy a few buildings. Cadman Plaza would turn the area into midtown Manhattan. "The planning so far introduced, on false premises, intrusive 'downtown' conceptions into a tiny residential neighborhood." If the Heights emplaced residents in a historic past and offered an intimate sense of community, the hypermodern bureaucratic sameness embodied in Cadman Plaza towers threatened to alienate a fragile community. "[Towers] clash with the charac-ter of the area; they introduce cultural, spatial, and psychological disruptions which will severely damage the coherence of the community, its outlook, and its survival possibilities. Large architectural masses and the grandiose and impersonal scale will jar with the rest of the community." "Housing developments which seemed originally to solve so many problems in a rush," agreed critic Brooks Atkinson in his *New York Times* review of James' report, "treat human beings like statistics that can be tucked away in gigantic filing cabinets."[4]

James was not the only member of New York City's new middle class criticizing city planners. In the early 1960s, scores of artists, writers, academics, settlement house workers, and community activists living in the gentrifying townhouse districts in cities around the country wrote letters to the editor, issued pamphlets, drew cartoons, and produced academic reports condemning urban renewal. Some anti-renewal tracts such as Jane Jacobs' *The Death and Life of Great American Cities* have been canonized as classics. But Jacobs' book was only one of a tidal wave of protest documents: letters to the editors of local papers such as the *Brooklyn Heights Press* and *Village Voice*, children's books such as *Peter's Brownstone House*, satirical cartoon collections such as Richard Hedman and Fred Bair Jr.'s *And on the Eighth Day: Series of Essays and Tableaux on Planner and Planning*, short manifestos including Charles Abrams' "The Revolt of the Urbs," and local histories such as Clay Lancaster's *Old Brooklyn Heights*. "As you know, dissatisfaction with urban renewal in New York continues to grow, particularly in regard to the application of Title I," wrote Jane Jacobs and Heights activist Eric Salzman confidently to Park Slope congressman and future governor Hugh Carey in 1961. "Civic leaders, sociologists, and planners point out that projects such as Cadman Plaza are not merely inadequately planned and wastefully conceived, but will actually scar the city, the community, and their people." "Slum clearance has also come under fire from several prominent architectural and social critics, led by Jane Jacobs, who have been struggling to preserve neighborhoods like Greenwich Village, with their brownstones, lofts, and small apartment houses, against the encroachment of the large, high-rise projects built for the luxury market and the poor alike," explained Herbert Gans in 1965. "The intent has been to save the city for people (intellectuals and artists, for example) who, like tourists, want jumbled diversity, antique 'charm' and narrow streets for visual adventure and aesthetic pleasure."[5]

Jane Jacobs' book and other anti-renewal tracts sparked a paradigm shift in the way Americans talked about older industrial cities. In contrast to the universal, integrated, and modern cityscape championed by modernist planners, anti-renewal writers commemorated diversity, mixed-use buildings, historic architecture, ethnicity, and distinctive local neighborhoods. While each aimed to defend ostensibly unique and irreplaceable landscapes from assimilation into modern "sameness," the writers borrowed imagery from one another in a pan-urban intellectual network. To write her book, for example, Jacobs consulted with Herbert Gans as he conducted research in the West End of Boston. In his influential 1974 biography of Robert Moses, *The Power Broker*, Robert Caro cited Jane Jacobs as his primary inspiration. In fact, the anti-renewal writings were interwoven enough to form a genre of literature with common tropes and rhetorical devices. One might even refer to the works as forming a "literature of gentrification."[6]

To describe a literature of gentrification is not to insinuate that authors such as Martin James or Jane Jacobs had malicious intentions or that the process they depict was necessarily detrimental to postwar cities. In a postwar era of urban renewal and suburban flight, the literature of gentrification was a revolutionary form of romantic urbanist writing that humanized the inner-city poor and celebrated rather than disparaged the messiness of city life. Nor is it clear that the inflow of white-collar professionals into postwar areas such as Brownstone Brooklyn has been wholly negative for poorer residents. But the "gentrification" label does provide an important geographic and social context to works such as *The Death and Life of Great American Cities*. If writers such as Jane Jacobs sought to rescue place from modern capitalist assimilation, they also commemorated a specific locale in the metropolis at a fleeting moment in the city's evolution: a nineteenth-century industrial middle cityscape on the periphery of the postwar modern central business district or university campus, in the early stages of gentrification.[7]

In fact, the reformist spirit of the genre is precisely what makes the literature so richly representative of the contradictory impulses of gentrification. Just as postwar gentrification was a movement born of mixed intentions and unintended consequences, the literature paradoxically mixed real estate boosterism with a genuine advocacy for the poor. Settlement house workers and community activists wrote the literature of gentrification to protect impoverished and stigmatized urban areas from slum clearance plans. Yet the local-color imagery of the white ethnic "urban village" was often paternalistic and sentimental. The most eloquent critiques of urban renewal and modern architecture came from the left. But at the same time, the literature offered a conservative celebration of private space, free market capitalism, and home-ownership. The literature commemorated the local history and ethnic identity of inner-city districts. The image of the white ethnic urban village also disguised an anxiety about black migrants and public housing projects. The literature was a genuinely populist defense of local democracy and sought to protect the impoverished and disempowered from powerful real estate interests, but it was also thoroughly middle-class in its aesthetic. The authors earnestly sought to forge a countercultural space as an alternative to the homogenizing postwar central business district. Instead, the genre unintentionally offered a template for a different type of urban homogeneity.

What made the literature of gentrification so powerful was a common rhetorical device: a recurring trope of the "highway in the garden." Originating as a wonkish critique of particular public works projects, the trope described the dramatic moment in which a new piece of infrastructure, most often a new roadway, invaded and destroyed a bucolic urban landscape. The highway in the garden soon became more symbolic than empirical, however, a central archetype in an emerging middle-class myth about postwar urban redevelopment. What made this trope so powerful was that it tapped into long-standing themes in American mythology. The imagery of an idyll interrupted by modernity drew from Romantic-era pastoral writing and reflected a long-standing American anxiety about the conflict between modern technology and nature. But the highway in the garden was novel in applying this imagery to the declining postwar industrial city. With minor variations and not necessarily in this order, the narrative of the highway in the garden contained four acts: alienated modern abstraction in the high-rise central business district or university campus, the discovery of an authentic urban village in the surrounding Victorian cityscape, the violation of the urban village by the highway or other modern development project, and the death of place. The fifth act is sometimes included, but always implied: gentrification or the restoration of place.[8]

As a tale of a fragile Eden violated by modernity, the literature of gentrification represented both the best and the worst of romantic urban writing. At its best, the literature presented a complex pastoral vision of place. This strategically invoked the nostalgic image of the urban village to counter technocratic modernity, yet remained willing to explore the inextricable relationship between the two. Complex pastoral writing described dynamic, flowing streams of place tied to the specific contours of the landscape while also recognizing imagined or virtual places as legitimate, exploring both regional and local senses of place, and emphasizing how a sense of place is multiple in character, with the elements potentially either harmonious or cacophonous. At its worst, the literature offered a simple pastoral vision of place that was anti-modern, nostalgic, sedentarist, and paternalistic. Simple pastoralism described a fragile, quaint urban village geographically bounded, racially homogenous, and happily antiquated, whose sanctity was violated by the modern highway, housing project, or apartment development. Simple pastoral images were unselfconsciously middle-class, often erasing industrial production from the cityscape while preserving its working-class and ethnic ambience as a site of consumption.[9]

While the best gentrification literature contained elements of both, the simple rather than the complex pastoral tropes had the greater influence on the formation of Brownstone Brooklyn. This is not to say that writers such as Herbert Gans purposely were gentrifiers, and in fact he and others express a deep anxiety about the process. But the way readers interpreted the texts was

more important than the authors' intentions. Most of the middle-class enthusiasts inspired to move to Brooklyn by Jane Jacobs' *Death and Life of Great
American Cities* cited her sentimental "street ballet" or the passages where she
slipped into simple romantic nostalgia. Few could describe her guaranteed-
rent system or libertarian traffic proposals. Her other theoretical books went
largely unread. The impact of the literature of gentrification was on the level
of urban gestalt rather than concrete policy treatise. "Before I read your book,
I knew I loved the city," wrote a Brooklyn brownstone renovator and activist
to Jane Jacobs in the mid-1960s. "Now I know *why*." The goal, thus, is not just
to determine what the authors intended to write but to examine also how
they and their texts were understood.[10]

The literature of gentrification is difficult to label politically as distinctly
left or right. But the genre was fiercely critical of planning, bureaucracy, and
government regulation, a trenchant critique of postwar liberalism. Martin
Andersen, author of the influential *The Federal Bulldozer*, for example, was an
anti-government conservative. While the genre lionized do-it-yourself rehabilitation and homeownership, the literature also reflected the beginnings of
a political shift in New York's left—a transition that has been referred to as a
transition from "old" to "new," "reform" to "post-reform," or "materialist" to
"postmaterialist." Along with the Cold War, campus politics, and the rise of
the civil rights movement, urban redevelopment profoundly reshaped the
spatial outlook of New York's intellectual community. As rising rents, university expansion, and slum clearance threatened avant-garde enclaves such as
Greenwich Village, Morningside Heights, and Brooklyn Heights, the aging
"slums" surrounding the central business district and university campus took
on new meaning. Where postwar liberal planners looked to centralized planning and modern redevelopment to control a rapacious free real estate market, a growing chorus of critics on the left began to describe an expanding
administrative technocracy that threatened fragile and organic peripheral
communities. It was the alienation and anomie of new projects, rather than
the cold-water flats or dilapidated townhouses of old slums, that crushed the
human spirit. Abstract space threatened to wipe out an authentic sense of
local place.[11]

At the core of this new critique of urban redevelopment and postwar liberalism was the image of a white ethnic "urban village" located in a gentrifying
belt of center-city housing surrounding the central business district. In 1961
Dissent magazine released its first issue dedicated specifically to New York City.
With writers such as Herbert Gans, Percival and Paul Goodman, Dorothy Day,
Irving Howe, and Daniel Bell, the issue contained seminal critiques of urban
redevelopment and a new strain of nostalgia for the city's older European

immigrant districts. "The streets of New York were then safe at night. Happy days!" explained Lionel Abel in "New York City: A Remembrance." "Let's see what is missing today." Some authors critiqued the destructive capacities of an unregulated capitalist real estate market. "Wherever one goes—in the heart of old Manhattan or the farther outskirts of the Bronx and Staten Island— construction is seen," wrote Daniel M. Friedenberg. "Craters yawn in what were pleasant meadows, metallic booms and tiers of steel loom against the sky, overhead bridges span entire sidewalks with scaffolding and the pressure hammer constantly gnaws at the vitals of the pavement . . . for neither leafy elms nor elegant Park Avenue structures can withstand the path of progress as conceived by the builders. It must bewilder the sense of the spectator, this awesome chopping down and regurgitation of concrete and steel. Why are stately edifices barely thirty years old uprooted for squat ribbon-windowed office structures?"[12]

But when writers commemorated the older white ethnic slum, they did so to highlight the frightening features of the "new slum": the government-funded high-rise public housing projects that were more and more frequently becoming home to New York's nonwhites. "As it becomes increasingly clear that public housing has failed to make its tenants middle class," wrote Mike Miller and Carl Werthman, "a host of critics have appeared who seem almost to defend the slum." Some reformers wrote lurid, gothic descriptions of housing projects. In his bestselling expose of the city's juvenile delinquency problem, Harrison Salisbury described a visit to Brooklyn's Fort Greene Houses. Initially enthusiastic about the New Deal "great experiment in public housing," he found a "new ghetto": "shoddy shiftlessness, the broken windows, the missing light bulbs, the plaster cracking from the walls, the pilfered hardware, the cold, drafty corridors, the doors on sagging hinges, the acid smell of sweat and cabbage, the ragged children, the plaintive women, the playgrounds that are seas of muddy clay, the bruised and battered trees . . . the inhuman genius with which our know-how has been perverted to create human cesspools worse than those of yesterday . . . like Golgothas designed to twist, torture and destroy the hapless people condemned to their dismal precincts."[13]

A growing number of critics, however, pointed not to the baroque gro-tesqueness of the "new slum" but to its lack of character. Where the old slum was intimate and communal, the new slum represented the devastating effects of modernity on individual life. The problem for the poor was not material but existential. Mass production, air-conditioning, formalist architecture, and bureaucracy crushed the human spirit. If modernist reformers decried ramshackle housing and crumbling public facilities, the writers in *Dissent* pointed to a new symptom of poverty in a modern and affluent society: alienation. "The feeling of valuelessness, of futility—which oozes from our suburbs as much as it does from the city itself—is at the root of the *tedium vitae*, the listless and the restless boredom, the quiet or unquiet desperation which generates some many of our amusements, crimes and neuroses," wrote Ernest van der Haag. Not only was modernity not the solution, it was the problem.[14]

Brooklyn-based intellectuals in Brooklyn Heights offered similarly romantic accounts of the old slum threatened by modernization. In his 1951 memoir *A Walker in the City*, Alfred Kazin took a trip back to his childhood neighborhood of Brownsville. Stepping out of the subway, Kazin was dismayed to find an enormous public housing project cutting across the former Jewish slum. While reluctantly acknowledging the reformist impulse behind the new buildings and admitting he fled the poor neighborhood himself the first chance he had, the author waxed nostalgic about the neighborhood now lost: a local-color village of small shops, quirky ethnic characters, pre-Fordist forms of production, and aged buildings containing layers of historic memory. "I could not quite believe that what I saw before me was real. Brownsville in that model quarter looks like an old crone who has had a plastic operation, and to my amazement I miss her old, sly, and withered face," reminisced Kazin. "I miss all those ratty little wooden tenements, born with the smell of damp in them, in which there grew up how many schoolteachers, city accountants, rabbis, cancer specialists, functionaries of the revolution, and strong-arm men for Murder, Inc." But misguided planners had destroyed the warm industrial *shtetl* for aseptic modern housing. "To make that housing project they have torn away the lumber yard; the wholesale drygoods store where my dressmaker mother bought the first shirts I ever wore that she did not make herself; how many poolrooms; and that to me sinister shed that was so long a garage, but before that, in the days of the silents, a movie house."[15]

Kazin uneasily mentioned another homogenizing force that had spread across a once diverse landscape: Brownsville was turning black. "Negroes were the *shvartse*, the blacks. We just did not think about them. They were people three and four blocks away you passed coming home from the subway. I never heard a word about them until the depression, when some of the younger ones began to do private painting jobs below the union wage scales, and when still another block of the earliest wooden shacks on Livonia Avenue near the subway's power station filled up with Negroes. Then some strange, embarrassed resentment would come out in the talk around the supper table. They were moving nearer and nearer. They were invading our neighborhood."[16]

With his old ethnic neighborhood destroyed by liberal planners, Kazin looked longingly to gentrifying townhouse districts such as Brooklyn Heights to recover a lost sense of authenticity. He offered a neo-Romantic paean to the brownstone, powerfully articulating the emplacing power of Victorian housing in a landscape ravaged by modern development. With his native neighborhood violated by the bulldozer and the African American migrant, the rootless Kazin meandered lost through the cityscape. The memoir transformed into an urban discovery narrative. In a climactic moment, Kazin accidentally wandered into a Gold Coast district of the borough and "discovered" blocks of brownstones. Once adrift, the author was suddenly emplaced. The Victorian brownstone catapulted him into the past and rooted him in the city's place history. Echoing the themes of brownstone settlers, he was struck by their "thick," "solid," "textured" features. He relished the ornate details that distinguished them from the mass-produced, featureless structures of the modern city. "I had made a discovery," began Kazin. "I had stumbled on a connection between myself and the shape and color of time in the streets of New York. Though I knew that brownstones were old-fashioned and had read scornful references to them in novels, it was just the thick, solid way in which they gripped to themselves some texture of the city's past that now fascinated me. There was one brownstone on Macdougal Street I would stop and brood over for long periods every evening I went to the library for fresh books—waiting in front of it, studying every crease in the stone, every line in the square windows jutting out above the street, as if I were planning its portrait. I had made a discovery: walking could take me back into the America of the nineteenth century."[17]

Kazin and the writers in *Dissent* reflected a broader shift in the language of New York's reformist middle class. Where postwar liberal planners wanted to obliterate the ghetto, to smash its buildings and give its citizens the freedom and power to move freely in an open city, a new romantic reform movement disagreed with both the diagnosis and the cure. The problem with new slums was not that they kept people in place but that they lacked a sense of place. The old white ethnic slums "were dense and the housing utterly inadequate, [but] there was nevertheless a community of language, religion, and the spirit of self-help," explained Michael Harrington in a 1960 *Commentary* article that would later become a chapter of his bestselling *The Other America*. Provincialism and the inability to leave the old slum created a "closed community," a neighborhood island of "norms and values," as well as safety and support. "Even now, there is a unique feeling to life in the remnants of these old slums: one notices a concreteness, a kind of richness of existence, together with some of the old sense of identity and hope." Where the old slum was a community, Harrington worried that the "new concrete-and-steel, automatic-elevator slums" were non-places filled with "rootless transients," "victims of a bureaucratically produced rootlessness."[18]

Michael Harrington certainly was as far as one could get from the stereo-type of the yuppie gentrifier. That is precisely what made him so representa-tive of the conflicted impulses of the early gentrification movement. As a genuine advocate on behalf of the urban poor, Harrington turned to the same locale. A new middle-class resident moving to the slum on the periphery of the central business district on a mission of rescue, Harrington was surprised to discover an intimate urban village "dotted with the signs of the Old Coun-try" where elderly white ethnics shielded from mass consumer culture held on to a vanishing pastoral lifestyle. In the early 1950s Harrington "moved into a Jewish slum on New York's Lower East Side." He was astonished that on his first day there, a storekeeper was quick to ask, "You live in 740, don't you?" "The community was self-enclosed," Harrington explained. "It could figure out the street number of any stranger. On Saturday, its streets were deserted for the Sabbath; on Sunday there was an air of parade and excitement."[19]

This is not to say that the literature of gentrification was solely a product of the left. Rather than essays by Michael Harrington, the most influential of all gentrification texts was Jane Jacobs' quasi-libertarian *The Death and Life of Great American Cities*. If Le Corbusier was a guru for modernist urban planning students of the 1950s, Jane Jacobs was the founding mother of the New Urbanism and other place-centric schools of urban studies. Where a writer such as Reyner Banham described the multiple ecologies of Los Angeles, Jacobs was interested solely in one very particular ecology. Her romantic depiction of Greenwich Village commemorated a familiar locale: the belt of Victorian townhouses, tenements, and industrial lofts surrounding an expanding cen-tral business district in the early stages of gentrification. As Jacobs described the "historic" and "diverse" urban village, she tapped into the language of other middle-class pioneers in Brownstone Brooklyn, Greenwich Village, and the West Side of Manhattan. But if most new residents simply described a gestalt, Jacobs expanded her celebration of Greenwich Village into an intellec-tual manifesto.

Death and Life borrowed familiar tropes from other anti-renewal writings. Like the first act in many highway-in-the-garden texts, Jacobs began her nar-rative in a displaced state of modern abstraction. Starting from a bird's-eye view, she examined the city from a regional vantage that resulted only in emptiness and alienation. Where in some versions the author literally stood atop a skyscraper or highway overpass, Jacobs symbolically ascended with a scathing overview of the history of urban planning. From Ebenezer Howard's "garden cities" through Lewis Mumford's Regional Planning Association and the City Beautiful movement to 1950s New York City public housing, Jacobs described an arrogant and authoritarian tradition of urban planning rooted not in close observation of actual urban places but in "pseudoscience," "ideology" and "abstraction."[20]

The modernist bird's-eye, Jacobs argued, forced the viewer to see the city as only an agglomeration of statistics and abstract, geometric lines. Even when "instinct," "feeling," and intimate observation told a banker that Boston's "unslumming" North End was a vibrant district of ethnic shops and restaurants, the modernist was imprisoned by his or her abstract ideal of what a city *should* look like. "The pseudoscience of city planning and its companion, the art of city design, have not yet been broken with the specious comfort of wishes, familiar superstitions, oversimplifications, and symbols, and have not yet embarked upon the adventure of probing the real world."[21]

Descending from the lofty vantage point of abstraction, Jacobs introduced the reader to an urban discovery narrative. In the intimate shadows of city, she uncovered a place: a pastoral urban village filled with aging Victorian architecture and with elderly white ethnics, small shops, and eateries untainted by mass consumer culture. The street level revealed to the peripatetic pedestrian the mystic beauty of the city's messiness. In some of the most influential passages of postwar urban writing, Jacobs described the "street ballet" outside her Greenwich Village apartment.

> The stretch of Hudson Street where I live is each day the scene of an intricate sidewalk ballet. . . . Mr. Halpert unlocking the laundry's handcart from its mooring to a cellar door, Joe Cornacchia's son-in-law stacking out the empty crates from the delicatessen, the barber bringing out his sidewalk folding chair, Mr. Goldstein arranging the coils of wire which proclaim the hardware store is open . . . I exchange my ritual farewell with Mr. Lofaro, the short, thick-bodied, white-aproned fruit man who stands outside his doorway a little up the street, his arms folded, his feet planted, looking solid as earth itself. We nod; we each glance quickly up and down the street, then look back to each other and smile. We have done this many a morning for more than ten years, and we both know what it means: All is well.[22]

Jacobs' "street ballet" contained both the best and the worst of romantic urbanism. At its worst, the description echoed the simple industrial pastoralism popular among a gentrifying white-collar middle class. Her street ballet contained all of the clichés of local-color writing: elderly indigenous white ethnics intimately linked to the environment, a petit bourgeoisie inoculated from both mass consumer culture and bureaucratic labor, simple Old World peasant customs not yet assimilated by modernity, and antiquated vernacular architecture. Along with her own non-self-reflexive participant observation, her book relied heavily on interviews with middle-class settlement house workers. The result is a romanticized slum absent of tragedy. Hudson Street has no poverty, juvenile gangs, organized crime, catcalls, spousal abuse, anger, or alcoholism. Her factories have no smoke. Hudson Street was also lily white. While she described a neighborhood with "a fantastic ethnic variety from almost the whole world," African Americans and Puerto Ricans were conspicuously absent. She makes no mention of blockbusting, firebombings, gang warfare, and other manifestations of violent racial tensions tearing apart working-class areas of the city after World War II. Nor does she talk about the civil rights movement.

Although populist in its intent, Jacobs' description of Hudson Street's "diversity" was astonishingly superurban and upper middle-class. "Towns and suburbs, for instance, are natural homes for huge supermarkets . . . standard movie houses or drive-ins," she complained. "Cities, however, are the natural homes of supermarkets and standard movie houses *plus* delicatessens, Viennese bakeries, foreign groceries, art movies, and so on."[23] In another passage about the diversity made possible by old, low-rent buildings, the urban palimpsest she described was unselfconsciously upper-middle-class and bohemian:

> The floor of the building in which this book is being written is occupied also by a health club with a gym, a firm of ecclesiastical decorators, an insurgent Democratic party reform club, a Liberal political party club, a music society, an accordionists' association, a retired importer who sells maté by mail, a man who sells paper and who also takes care of shipping the maté, a dental laboratory, a studio for watercolor lessons, and a maker of costume jewelry.[24]

Hudson Street was not only filled with local color. It was distinctly *private*. Jacobs sharply contrasted the diverse block to the "dull" backdrop of the modern public landscapes built by New Deal and postwar liberal government planners. While she criticized the lifeless landscapes of high-rise downtown and sprawling suburbia, she reserved her greatest opprobrium for new low- and middle-income housing projects. Where Greenwich Village had life, spontaneity, and passion, government-aided housing complexes were in her view devoid of personality, individuality, or community ties. New slums suffered from the symptoms of overmodernity: planning, alienation, regimentation, and depersonalization. A totalitarian "papa institution" built government projects that replaced diversity with a bureaucratic "monopoly." Hudson Street, in contrast, was private, organic, and authentic. With her lionization of privacy, choice, individuality, small business, and freedom from government bureaucracy, Jacobs drew from both Greenwich Village reform Democrats and anti-government conservatives.[25]

To point to a strain of romanticism in Jacobs' writing is not to validate the dismissive and sexist reaction to her work by contemporaries such as Lewis Mumford in his infamous review, "Mother Jacobs' Home Remedies." Jane Jacobs was far too sophisticated to be dismissed as a sentimentalist. If on occasion she presented a simple pastoral rendering of the industrial cityscape, in her best writing she presented a flowing, dynamic vision of urban place that was both intimately local yet in a constant state of flux. She angrily dismissed concepts such as "neighborhood" or "ethnic enclave," arguing instead that the city was a shifting terrain shaped by multiple overlapping populations. Her historic landscape was a palimpsest in which buildings were repositories of symbolic value shaped over decades, offering multiple meanings to new residents. In the tradition of Walt Whitman, at times she zoomed in to the minute details of street life—a smile, the clang of a garbage can—but she also pulled back to view the city in its regionalist grandeur. She captured the stillness of a single moment, but also, like Whitman's urban ghost, hovered through the city, flowing along streams of people and memories in an urban sea.[26]

Much to her dismay, it was the simple rather than complex pastoral tropes that more often resonated with her new urban middle-class readers. At first glance, Jacobs seemed unaware of and at times even celebratory about the gentrification of Greenwich Village. In an area racked by tensions between Italian working-class residents and new white-collar professionals, and in the midst of a heated conflict between middle-class reformers and local Tammany boss Carmine DeSapio, Jacobs described a harmonious ethnic neighborhood that has "assimilated a great sprinkling of middle-class professionals and their families." She confidently celebrated the process of organic "unslumming," or the bootstrap renovation of old buildings by middle-class pioneers. "In Greenwich Village, almost no building is scorned by middle-class families hunting a bargain in a lively district, or by rehabilitators seeking a golden egg. In successful districts, old buildings 'filter up'. . . . What we need, and a lot of others need, is old construction in a lively district, which some among us can help make livelier."[27]

Beneath her Pollyannaish picture of working-class and white professionals in Greenwich Village, Jacobs revealed a deep anxiety about gentrification and frustration with how new middle-class urban enthusiasts were interpreting her work. In a revealing passage, Jacobs angrily described the efforts by her Greenwich Village neighbors to fight the expansion of a bakery. While Jacobs celebrated mixed-use neighborhoods, she pointedly insisted that light manufacturing had an important place in her eclectic vision of urban place. Much to her dismay, her new college-educated neighbors did not share her sentiment. "A bakery on this street, at one time mainly retail and small, has grown vigorously into a substantial wholesaler, and was applying for a zoning exemption," she wrote. "The street, which has long been zoned 'residential,' has been upgrading itself recently, and many of its property owners and renting residents, in their growing pride and concern with their street, decided to fight the exemption request." Jacobs was irritated at the hypocrisy of her gentrifying neighbors, noting that while they fought the bakery, the activists were quite receptive to the other nonresidential venues that catered to their middle-class tastes: "a real estate office, a small publishing company, a book-shop, a restaurant, a picture framer, a cabinet maker, a shop that sells old posters and prints, a candy store, a coffee house, a laundry, two groceries, and a small experimental theater." When she confronted the leader of the protest— a "principal owner of rehabilitated residential property on the street"—to ask him whether he wished to shut down the experimental theater, coffee shop, and other nonresidential uses along with the bakery, the owner simply responded in bemusement, "Isn't an implied choice of that kind absurd!"[28]

Gentrification was the central tension in her work, but in 1961 Jacobs did not yet have the vocabulary to make sense of it. Her Hudson Street in reality was not a quaint village but a dynamic middle ground lodged fragilely between an expanding postindustrial landscape and a declining industrial one. As one of the first middle-class "discoverers" of Hudson Street, she relished its unplanned, organic flavor. But the interstitial authenticity she craved was made fleeting by the organic free-market cityscape she celebrated. As more of her middle-class cohorts followed her, as developers began to build to answer growing demand, and as larger stores and clubs moved into an increasingly popular district, Jacobs worried that her enclave was beginning to "undiversify":

> Thirty-five years ago, [Eighth Street] was a nondescript street. Then one of its principal property owners, Charles Abrams . . . built on the street a small night club and a motion-picture theater unusual for its time. . . . These enterprises proved popular . . . and thus helped stimulate the growth of convenience and special shops. . . . [But soon] a diversity of clubs, galleries and some small offices were crowded out by blank, monolithic, very high-rent apartments. . . . Abrams watched, with dismay, bookstores, galleries, clubs, craftsmen and one-of-a-kind shops being pushed out. . . . Eighth Street was slowly but steadily starting to undiversify itself.[29]

Hers was the classic lament of the romantic urbanist middle class. Fiercely opposed to abstract government regulation or planning, yet fearful of the free market's rationalization of the landscape, Jacobs was faced with a paradox. Greenwich Village was not an eclectic enclave shielded from consumer culture. It was part of a dramatically restructuring megalopolis with a cutthroat, at times brutal, real estate market. Like a flawed anthropologist, Jacobs was an immersed observer unable to reflect on the way her own presence transformed the environment. She was precisely destroying the authenticity she craved. Her inability to resolve the paradox remained the greatest shortcoming of the book.

If there was an anti-renewal tract that matched the influence of Jacobs' *Death and Life* on Brownstone Brooklyn, it was Herbert Gans' famous eulogy of Boston's West End, *The Urban Villagers*. Before being demolished as part of a now infamous urban renewal project, the West End was similar to Brownstone Brooklyn, a middle cityscape of nineteenth-century tenements, warehouses, and townhouses on the periphery of Boston's expanding postwar central business district. Forty-two percent Italian American and largely blue-collar, the area was poor, with most residents renting small apartments or units in rooming houses. Gans' sensitive treatment of this impoverished district, powerless to fight destruction by developers, has since become one of the most powerful symbols of the failures of postwar redevelopment.

Gans' work, like Jacobs, remained a powerful piece of gentrification literature. While his description of a fragile white ethnic urban village destroyed by bulldozers has remained powerful in public memory, the West End he describes was also a gentrifying cityscape. A new and vocal pro-urban middle class was an overlooked and powerful presence in the book. With the postwar expansion of Massachusetts General Hospital and Boston's universities, doctors, nurses, and students rented apartments, providing a "smattering of professional middle-class culture to the area." Some "homosexuals who worked as male nurses" migrated to the West End "and were able to practice their deviant ways in an area which disapproved of them, but which tolerated them grudgingly." Bohemian artists and "would-be artists" were sprinkled throughout the parts of the neighborhood closest to Cambridge Street. If Jacobs ignored class tensions in her Greenwich Village, Gans found them incongruous to his narrative and downplayed them. "Deviant behavior, as displayed by the area 'characters,' the bohemians, or the middle-class residents was, of course, highly visible," he wrote ambivalently. "As long as the West Enders were not affected personally, however, they were tolerant. . . . Moreover, as Italians like to stay up late, and to socialize at high decibel levels, the bohemians' loud parties were no problem, at least to them."[30]

What made Gans' text such a rich example of gentrification literature was his own ambivalence about his project. Where Jacobs' lionization of gentrifying

Greenwich Village was unapologetic, Gans was much more circumspect about his participation in the wave of middle-class romantic urbanism. Throughout his writings of the 1960s and 1970s, one can detect in Gans a profound irritation at the snobbery of those he labeled as urban "cosmopolitan" white-collar professionals. While he sought to defend the poor from development, Gans went to great lengths to demonstrate that he was not an urbanophile and pointedly refused to celebrate the aesthetics of older inner-city districts. Bothered by the anti-suburban bias he detected among the city's new middle class, he later offered a deliberately contrarian defense of working-class Levittown. Elsewhere, he similarly defended the democratic potential of mass consumer culture. Only a few years after publishing *The Urban Villagers*, he became a defender of a reformed version of urban renewal that would relocate the poor in affordable, scattered-site housing on unused land in the center city, suburbs, and new towns. Once the poor were suitably relocated, Gans called for planners to raze and rebuild older sections of the city.[31]

Yet Gans remained a product of the Romantic era, albeit a reluctant one. He was well exposed to the body of anti-renewal writings emerging in the early 1960s and consciously hoped not to replicate their reverie for the authenticity of the slum. To write a defense of place that was complex rather than simple pastoral, Gans relied on his sociological training. He hoped to puncture any sentimentalism by employing a scientific methodology to determine how residents developed a sense of place in the West End. Despite his numbers, objective categories, and scientific description of "peer group" society, Gans' urban village remained too powerful an image to escape the sentimentality he rejected. It is precisely this ambivalent romantic urbanism, his desire to distinguish his intentions from his middle-class peers, and agonizing self-doubt that made his description so richly representative of gentrification.

Like most gentrification texts, Gans began with an urban discovery narrative. Initially approaching the neighborhood from a modernist bird's-eye view, Gans was unable to discern a distinct place in a sprawling cityscape. Examining the area from the "highways or elevated train lines that enveloped it," a "superficial observer" was only able to see a wasteland of "poorly maintained structures, some of them occupied or partially vacant . . . sullen looking adolescents and young adults who congregated on street corners . . . To the superficial observer, armed with conventional images and a little imagination about the mysteries thought to lie behind the tenement entrances, the West End certainly had all the earmarks of a slum."[32]

Upon descending to ground level, however, Gans discovered a hidden place, an urban village of colorful white ethnics, non-mass-culture stores, non-geometric streets, and aging unstandardized nineteenth-century housing. "My first impression left me with the impression that I was in Europe. Its high buildings set on narrow, irregularly curving streets, its Italian and Jewish res-taurants and food stores, and the variety of people who crowded the streets when the weather was good—all gave the area a foreign and exotic flavor." Gans, however, was too self-critical to resort to simple pastoralism and quickly caught himself from slipping into romantic reverie. "Looking at the area as a tourist, I noted the highly visible and divergent characteristics that set it off from others. . . . After a few weeks of living in the West End, my observa-tions—and my perception of the area—changed drastically."[33]

Although he arrived as a white-collar employee of a modern university, Gans was determined not to be seduced into pastoralizing the remaining blue-collar laborers in a declining industrial landscape. In a subtle rejoinder to his middle-class urban compatriots, he pointedly distinguished his research project from the local-color writing emerging from gentrifying Greenwich Vil-lage, Beacon Hill, and Brooklyn Heights. "Although it is fashionable these days to romanticize the slum, this has not been my purpose here. The West End was not a charming neighborhood of 'noble peasants' living in an exotic fashion, resisting the mass-produced homogeneity of American culture and overflowing with a cohesive sense of community. It was a run-down area of people struggling with the problems of low income, poor education, and related difficulties. Even so, it was by and large a good place to live."[34]

As a sociologist immersing himself in the slum on a mission of rescue, Gans was also aware that he was participating in a romantic urban tradition of "missionary writing" dating back to the nineteenth-century settlement house movement. Where Jane Jacobs uncritically took the observations of her middle-class social worker friends at face value, Gans remained highly critical of the sentimentalism and subtle embourgeoisement of the poor that he perceived in settlement house writings. Reading a contemporary settle-ment house memorandum describing the "warm," "multi-cultural" West End, Gans angrily wrote: "This is essentially a tourist's picture of the West End. While it would interest the visitor from middle-class suburbia who might come to the area for vicarious identification with exotic culture and the dense street life . . . West Enders themselves were not interested in the ethnic variety of the area. . . . And no West Ender in his right mind would have described the neighborhood as having charm."[35]

Gans acknowledged that "urban village" was his own invented term. None of the West Enders themselves recognized the existence of an "urban village," nor in fact did they consider themselves "West Enders." In fact, the central tension in the narrative was the indifference of "urban villagers" to the concept

THE HIGHWAY IN THE GARDEN   181

of neighborhood, community, or the "West End" that Gans sought to eulo-gize. For a place missionary such as Gans, the apparent lack of an indigenous sense of place was initially jarring. "Early in my study, for example, when asking people why they liked the West End, I expected emotional statements about their attachment to the area," he explained. "I was always surprised when they talked merely about its convenience to work and to downtown shopping. Then, after I had lived in the area a few weeks, one of my neighbors remarked that I knew a lot more about the West End than they did. This led me to realize that there was relatively little interest in the West End as a phys-ical or social unit." Even after the entire area, home to twenty thousand people, was demolished by the city, former residents "talked mostly about losing their apartment, and being torn from the people with whom they had been close so long."[36]

If Gans had also taken a regional vantage point, he could have described a more dynamic view of place that flowed from the West End to the suburbs as West Enders migrated outward and suburbanites symbolically "returned" to the ethnic city. By including the bohemians and white-collar professionals, he could have further thickened his description of a multilayered cityscape in a state of change. But since the study was a eulogy of a village lost and his goal to counter the unforgiving modernist rhetoric of urban renewal, Gans was geographically and temporally bound by his own project. His village had to be enclosed by fixed borders, and despite his misgivings he delved into simple pastoral reverie. While he qualifies each observation, his West Enders appeared much the "noble peasants" he warned against: warm, traditional, antipathetic to mass consumer culture, unbureaucratic and spontaneous, and happily place-bound with no desire to participate in the nationwide white working-class exodus to suburbia.

In lieu of any definition by residents themselves, Gans positioned the urban village as an oasis of place between two landscapes of sameness. The first way he claimed West Enders defined their turf was in contrast to the "out-side world"—namely, the government agencies, hospitals, and other institu-tional buildings that made up the neighboring postwar central business district. The second non-place against which he cast the urban village was a dystopic "urban jungle." If the urban village was a place "in which European immigrants—and more recently Negro and Puerto Rican ones—try to adapt their nonurban institutions and cultures to the urban milieu," the urban jungle was an urban wilderness populated by violent transients with no attachment to local place. The urban jungle was "populated largely by single men, pathological families, people in hiding from themselves or society, and individuals who provide the more disreputable of illegal-but-demanded services to the rest of the community. In such an area, life is comparatively more transient, depressed if not brutal." Lodged precariously between the sky-scraper and the jungle, Gans' urban village was precisely the middle cityscape described by Jane Jacobs and common to gentrification literature.[37]

His description of the neighborhood's demise followed this pattern as well. After setting the pastoral scene, Gans interrupted the serenity of the urban village with the intrusion of the city bulldozer. His last chapters describing the final months leading up to demolition are beautifully tragic, as powerless residents alternate between angry protest, denial, and fatalism. He ends with the image of a village rendered into a non-place: "I was told that before the West End was totally cleared—and even afterwards—West Enders would come back on weekends to walk through the old neighborhood and the rubble-strewn streets. The last time I saw the area, it had been completely leveled except for the buildings that had been marked for preservation. . . . The Catholic church . . . stood in lonely isolation in the center of the cleared area. . . . The cleared area looked very tiny, and it was hard to imagine that more than 20,000 people had once lived there."[38]

But questions remain. Had the working-class residents of the West End already been leaving before the bulldozers arrived? Would they have supported a renewal plan that included modern affordable housing? Along with his dismay about the inaction of the local poor to fight the destruction of the West End, Gans lamented that the Save the West End Committee was organized and run mainly by an upper-class civic leader from Beacon Hill. The urban villagers who participated were two artists and a young professional, as well as a handful of elderly ladies. Were poorer residents simply too uneducated, culturally fatalistic, and mystified by scientific authority and expertise to launch a defense of their homes? Or were they simply eager to follow the mass exodus to the suburbs? To determine the psychological effects of relocation, Gans relied on surveys of departed residents. But how much of the sadness was endemic to people who migrate, whether involuntarily or voluntarily? Were migrants who willingly left other slum areas similarly nostalgic for the "old days"? Did white suburbanites who left neighborhoods undergoing racial transition similarly feel sad and lonely in their new homes? Should all forms of reverie be given equal credence? Would the urban village have survived as Gans describes it even if the city had never demolished a single building? Would it have gentrified? Or would it have become a black or Latino district? To bring up these questions is not to defend callous forms of mass slum clearance carelessly administered by bureaucrats in the 1950s. Nor is it to deny the rhetorical importance of the sedentary urban village in an era of a modernist planning orthodoxy that held no regard for local place.

But answering these questions perhaps would have helped Gans avoid what he later felt was the biggest shortcoming of *The Urban Villagers*: the way middle-class enthusiasts misinterpreted it. "I shall resist the temptation to comment on misinterpretations of my work, except to regret that *The Urban Villagers* has sometimes been read as a romantic portrayal of ethnic enclaves and old-fashioned defense of *Gemeinschaft*," complained Gans in the introduction to the 1982 version of the text. "Authors cannot be held responsible for how readers interpret their work. . . . I tried to hard to report the cons as well as the pros of living in an ethnic goldfish bowl in which privacy and nonconformity were rare, although I should have said more emphatically that what I called 'the peer group society' was not a way of life one could choose freely."[39]

When Gans was writing *The Urban Villagers*, he never could have predicted the impact of his work. Initially a rhetorical device deliberately exaggerated to counter the excesses of urban renewal, his urban village by the 1970s became a mainstay of urban historical and theoretical writing. For example, Robert Caro's groundbreaking 1974 biography of Robert Moses, *The Power Broker*, relied heavily on the trope. Acknowledging Jane Jacobs as its primary influence, Caro's history read as a tragedy in which organic and cohesive ethnic urban villages fell prey to Moses' fanatic modernist ideology and hunger for power. As a political history, Caro's book offered a seminal and breathtaking critique of the transformation of the public-private authorities created by Progressive and New Deal reformers into heavy-handed and authoritarian regimes. As an urbanist, however, he strategically evoked the simple more than the complex romanticism of Jane Jacobs. To demonstrate the destructiveness of urban renewal, Caro used pastoral imagery to describe an older white ethnic industrial landscape. In a powerful section, for example, Caro described how Moses' Gowanus Parkway destroyed the neighborhood of Sunset Park, a townhouse district lying south of gentrifying Brownstone Brooklyn. Writing in the 1970s, when the area was an impoverished Puerto Rican area ravaged by housing abandonment and crime, Caro flashed back to 1940 to eulogize what was once a stable bastion of working-class white ethnics. While admitting that part of the neighborhood had been a real slum with dilapidated tenements home to "derelicts, winos, and whores," Caro described an Old World urban village filled with aging Scandinavian immigrants. "A slum! That wasn't a slum!" he quoted a former resident. "It was poor, but clean poor." As he eulogized the departed urban village, he drew heavily from the most nostalgic passages of Jacobs and Gans:

The brickfronts and brownstones were immaculate; one could walk by them any morning and see the housewives sanding and scrubbing their stoops; even the sidewalks were swept. . . . It was quiet and peaceful—there were many trees lining the streets, but few cars. . . . every summer brought a round of block parties, street lamps festooned with streamers, women and girls in gay peasant blouses from their native lands, folk singers with their accordions singing the old songs. . . . [Girls] married boys from the neighborhood and raised their own families there because "we wouldn't want to live anywhere else."[40]

With its eclectic mom-and-pop shops shielded from mass consumer culture and rustic Old World peasants, Caro's Sunset Park resembled the middle-class romantic descriptions of gentrifying districts of Brooklyn Heights and Greenwich Village. Along Third Avenue, he wrote, were newsstands selling *Nordisk Tidendes*, seven movie theaters, "tiny restaurants run by couples and featuring recipes from the old countries," "scores of small, friendly 'Mama and Papa' stores (the Northland Gift Shop, the Finnish Book Store, a hardware store that looked like a general store out of the Old West, a butcher shop that raffled off twenty-five big turkeys every Christmas)."[41]

After setting up the pastoral scene, Caro interrupted its serenity with the dramatic arrival of the modern highway. Caro inserted an isolated, powerful sentence: "If Third Avenue was the heart of the neighborhood, Moses tore it out." Although Caro admitted that the avenue already sat enshrouded by a noisy el (which is why the city chose it as a site for an elevated highway), he described beautifully how the modern highway tragically drained the life out of a once vibrant neighborhood. If the urban village had been an enclosed place, the highway was large, impersonal, dark, and arterial. "The parkway was something unfamiliar and strange. There were no lights underneath it and it always seemed damp there—condensation on the tubular steel supporting pillars caused a constant dripping on the street . . . 'It was noise, dirt, accidents, not lighted, a garbage dump, drag races along it in the night, wild kids, something totally negative.' . . . Once the avenue had been a place for people; Robert Moses had made it a place for cars."[42]

Once violated by modernity, the neighborhood began a slow death. "The vicious gyre of urban decay began—and widened." While he pointed to a few details about the size of the highway and the location of exit ramps, Caro described the effects of the new project more in epidemiological terms. Like a poison-tipped arrow, the highway interrupted the pastoral cityscape and released its venom. "For more than thirty years, the blight in South Brooklyn had been confined to the waterfront area. Now, thanks to Robert Moses and his parkway, it was on the loose, spreading across Sunset Park." Place in Caro's cityscape was akin to a walled-in Eden, or a dry space with fragile dikes holding back floodwaters. With the walls of the urban village punctured, the neighborhood was no longer able to fend off the encroaching dystopic urban jungle. Place was slowly engulfed by ghetto space. "Faster and faster, the residents of the side streets began to move out. . . . Along the avenue and on adjacent side streets, rows of brownstones and brickfront buildings that had held stores and apartments, the stores and apartments that had stood as a bulwark between Sunset Park and the slum to the west, began to be vacated." With the village swallowed by wilderness, Caro concluded with a nightmarish description of urban non-place:

> Drunks as well as whores roamed the avenue, cadging drinks until they fell asleep in doorways. Cheap saloons opened in some of the abandoned stores. Soon there were street gangs, fighting gangs, Irish and Puerto-Rican teen-agers, seeping down from the notorious Red Hook section to continue their racial warfare and prey on passers-by. The side streets off Third Avenue—streets whose apartments were now filled with families on welfare, families without fathers, and with poor Spanish-speaking families without clothes adequate for the cold New York winters—became places to dump and strip stolen cars; the streets began to be filled with their ravaged hulks. Rotting litter, rain-sodden mattresses and broken glass filled the sidewalks and gutters. Rats began to grow bold in the rubbish in vacant lots. There were even, to the horror of those residents who remained, drug addicts.[43]

In his more famous section describing how the Cross-Bronx Expressway destroyed the East Tremont urban village in the South Bronx, Caro invoked a similar trope. In fact, the image of the expressway destroying the white ethnic South Bronx has become one of the most powerful images in New York public memory.[44]

The most effective gentrification literature, however, was not nostalgic. In his rich, complex anti-development tract *All That Is Solid Melts into Air*, Marshall Berman relied on the trope, yet at the same time remained aware of its contradictions. He too described a cityscape destroyed by Moses and the unforgiving ideology of modernist development. Yet rather than beginning with the pastoral urban village, he started his scene postmortem, driving on the Cross Bronx Expressway and looking wistfully at the ghetto cityscape: "hundreds of boarded-up abandoned buildings and charred and burnt-out hulks of buildings; dozens of blocks covered with nothing at all but shattered bricks and waste." A former Bronx native, Berman was saddened to see the devastating effects of the highway on his once vibrant childhood home. "Ten minutes on this road, an ordeal for anyone, is especially dreadful for people who remember the Bronx as it used to be: who remember these neighbor-hoods as they once lived and thrived, until this road itself cut through their heart and made the Bronx, above all, a place to get out of. . . . We fight back the tears, and step on the gas."[45]

If the South Bronx lay victim to metrocide, Berman was clear about the culprit: "Robert Moses is the man who made all this possible." As he turned to the familiar highway in the garden narrative, Berman cited heavily the writ-ings of Jane Jacobs and Robert Caro to describe how the expressway punctured and deflated a once enclosed, stable white ethnic Bronx. "Miles of streets alongside the road were choked with dust and fumes and deafening noise. . . . Apartment houses that had been settled and stable for twenty years emptied out, often virtually overnight. . . . Thus depopulated, economically depleted, emotionally shattered . . . the Bronx was ripe for all the dreaded spirals of urban blight." In his brief history of Moses, Berman again borrowed most of his material from Caro. The city administrator in Berman's history is the last of a line of "titanic builders and destroyers" including Joseph Stalin, Goethe's Faust, Marlowe's Tamburlaine, Bugsy Siegel, and Peter the Great. Against his reveries about the lost quaint space of Coney Island or the white ethnic Bronx, Berman cast Moses' projects, from beaches to parkways, as megalomaniacal, dehumanizing, and sterile.[46]

Yet as he invoked the highway in the garden, Berman remained wary of the trope's seductiveness. After admiring Jacobs' description of Hudson Street, he noted the "undertow of nostalgia." He applauded Caro's portrait of the lost Jewish South Bronx for its rhetorical power, but he lamented its *Fiddler on the Roof* kitschiness. As his narrative returned to the devastated South Bronx of 1982, Berman recognized the hidden racial conservatism in his desire to eulo-gize the 1950s urban village. "It is the city before the blacks got there," he admitted sadly. Berman longed for the simplicity of the highway-in-the-garden trope and the clear villain it provided, but he recognized that the blame for the Bronx's decline hit much closer to home: he and his neighbors had left the Bronx willingly and enthusiastically. "We are not merely specta-tors but active participants in the process of destruction that tears our hearts. . . . It was the brutal truth: I had left the Bronx . . . and now the Bronx was collapsing not just because of Robert Moses but also because of all of us."[47]

Berman was not a simple sentimentalist. Rather than describing a seden-tary and anti-modern sense of place, Berman advocated a fluid, dynamic form of modernism that celebrated the disorder and diversity of a kinetic city. As he described the arrival of new Caribbean immigrants to the South Bronx, Berman noted that the city was changing. As in the best of Jacobs' writing, Berman evoked the "harmonious disorder" of an urban place, with its streams of people and ideas. His buildings were repositories of symbolic value that could be remembered and recycled for new uses.

But Berman's writing remained a form of gentrification literature, and like Jacobs, he returned to the same locale for his anti-Moses refuge: the middle cityscape of nineteenth-century industrial lofts and townhouses on the periphery of the central business district. If Jacobs celebrated the liberating possibilities of 1960s Greenwich Village, Berman concluded with an enthusiastic description of the gentrifying post-industrial lofts of SoHo. "This district of nineteenth-century workshops, warehouses and small factories between Houston and Canal streets . . . was scheduled to be razed for one of Robert Moses' most cherished projects, the Lower Manhattan Expressway. . . . But then, in the early and mid-1960s, a remarkable coalition of diverse and generally antagonistic groups . . . fought fervidly for years and finally, to their amazement, won and wiped Moses' project off the map. . . . In the late 1960s and early 1970s, thousands of artists moved in and, within a few years, turned this anonymous space into the world's leading center for the production of art. This amazing transformation infused SoHo's dreary and crumbling streets with a unique vitality and intensity."[48]

With his calls for recycling, reclamation, and redemption, Berman introduced the final act of the highway-in-the-garden narrative: gentrification. Some narratives stripped away the modernist highway to revive the organic cityscape that lay beneath. Other versions described the return of whites to the ethnic enclaves they once abandoned. Still others looked hopefully to artists and musicians successfully converting industrial space into sites of postindustrial cultural consumption. In his conclusion, Berman called for New Yorkers to transform the universalist, cookie-cutter highway into a historic place. He proposed that artists paint a giant mural on the Cross-Bronx Expressway, a timeline commemorating the borough's white ethnic past and concluding with the arrival of Puerto Ricans migrants and "Robert Moses and his dread road, smashing through the Bronx's inner life." Through color and history, the mural would reconnect the Bronx to its white ethnic past. "Children of the Bronx would be encouraged to return and put themselves in the picture." Through sweat equity, private rehabilitation, and bootstrap renovation free of government planners, returning residents would forge an exciting frontier of possibility. "It is a risky and precarious enterprise—we can feel the risks when we see the horror just around the corner." Berman's revitalized New York would be a bricolage of recycled items, references to the past, "a forest of symbols," "playful."[49]

The literature of gentrification was thus born out of the battles against urban renewal. To counter the technocratic language of city planners, writers cultivated the image of an urban village located in a nineteenth-century city-scape surrounding the central business district. Writers pastoralized the industrial cityscape in order to emphasize that stigmatized districts had social and historic value and should not simply be cleared away in the name of progress. While they fought on behalf of the poor, the writers also valorized the inner city as a site of postindustrial consumption for a new middle class. They articulated a new localist politics that was neither distinctly left nor right and which lionized sweat equity rehabilitation, freedom from government intervention and planning, and "organic unslumming." While ostensibly protecting the powerless from public urban renewal, Jane Jacobs, Herbert Gans, and others ironically provided a blueprint for private gentrification. Nowhere can this be seen better than in Brownstone Brooklyn.

6 Inventing Brownstone Brooklyn

In October 1973, Brooklyn Heights' Bossert Hotel, once the site for the seminal CCIC anti-urban-renewal rally, hosted the city's first Brownstone Fair. Organized by the Brooklyn Brownstone Conference, a new middle-class civic group, the fair advertised itself as a showcase for "Everything You Always Wanted to Know About Brooklyn Brownstones." More than two thousand attendees strolled past fifty exhibits run by enthusiastic volunteers. Instructional booths offered tips on old electrical wiring, stonemasonry, architectural ornamentation, and carpentry. Gardeners and horticulturists gave instructions on tree planting and care, community gardening, and negotiation strategies with the city park department. The Community Bookstore, started by Park Slope brownstoners, displayed more than a dozen "brownstone books" penned by Brooklyn's new middle class, ranging from local histories to renovation guides. Fledgling neighborhood and block associations invited potential home buyers to visit their new enclaves. The most popular exhibit was the mortgage information table, where experienced brownstone buyers offered tips on procuring financing from reluctant banks. To cap off the event, Brooklyn Union Gas sponsored a fleet of buses to take fair attendees on tours of Brooklyn brownstone neighborhoods.[1]

Much had changed in South Brooklyn in the fifteen years since the first battle against Robert Moses. Looking outward from the Bossert Hotel in 1973, fair attendees could see two seemingly contradictory landscapes produced by the same economic restructuring. On one hand, they could see a struggling industrial district becoming increasingly black, Spanish-speaking, and poor. Since the 1950s, black and Puerto Rican home buyers and renters had been steadily migrating into the tenements and brownstones surrounding Brooklyn Heights on the heels of white working-class residents departing for the suburbs. With choices limited by discrimination and little leverage to pressure landlords for better services, black and Puerto Rican residents of Brownstone Brooklyn quickly found themselves trapped in overcrowded, dilapidated, and paradoxically high-rent buildings. While individual buildings were over-packed, much of Brownstone Brooklyn appeared deserted. In the late 1960s, landlords saddled with high interest rates and taxes, increased pressure by the city to improve conditions, and poor relations with nonwhite tenants aban-doned their rental properties in droves. Scores of desperate owners seeking insurance, along with some frustrated residents, deliberately burned down dilapidated buildings. Merchants shut down stores. By the mid-1970s, black and Latino sections of Brownstone Brooklyn appeared a tragic patchwork of abandoned wrecks of buildings sitting next to overcrowded tenements. On once-bustling residential strips such as Fifth Avenue in Park Slope, scores of storefronts were empty. On other blocks children played in rubble-strewn empty lots. While entrepreneurial black and Latino migrants replaced some businesses with their own institutions, such as storefront Pentecostal churches, bodegas, and insurgent political clubs, the outflow of capital outpaced the influx. While Brooklyn Heights remained upscale, other sections of Brown-stone Brooklyn began to resemble a bombed-out city.[2]

As nonwhite migrants competed for housing and increasingly scarce manufacturing jobs with white ethnics, race relations in South Brooklyn dete-riorated. While decades earlier white Protestant residents had complained about the influx of impoverished Italian and Irish renters from the industrial slums of Manhattan, working-class white ethnics in the 1960s, already eco-nomically battered by a deindustrializing economy, lashed out against what they described as an expanding Brooklyn "ghetto." "[The area] is now in a state of deterioration because of the influx of Puerto Rican and negro Welfare Depart-ment families overcrowding houses, scattering garbage, holding drinking parties from Friday night to Sunday morning, and otherwise making living impossible for old time white families still there," complained an angry white Park Slope resident to a local precinct captain in 1963. "White owners . . . who paid 22,000–27,000 for their homes are being forced to sell out at any little price they can get. . . . one absentee landlord, who lives in Forest Hills, now owns 26 houses, all given over to welfare stuffing and deterioration."[3]

Blockbusters and other aggressive speculators only aggravated growing white working-class fear and resentment. After saturating the area with post-cards offering "quick cash sales with no commissions," blockbusters called or knocked on the doors of Brownstone Brooklyn families, hoping to spark white flight with ominous predictions of imminent racial decline. "Negroes are moving in nearby," explained one, "you had better sell before it's too late." After buying property cheaply from terrified white families, blockbusters rented the buildings at exorbitant prices to desperate blacks and Puerto Ricans. Others purchased several properties to become absentee landlords, chopping up the buildings into rooming houses and kitchenette apartments and charging exorbitant rents to a captive market of impoverished nonwhite tenants.[4]

Clashes between Italian and Irish working-class residents and in-migrating blacks and Puerto Ricans became increasingly violent. While juvenile gangs had long ravaged Brooklyn and were often organized along racial lines, 1950s gang culture could be surprisingly interracial. By the mid-1960s, however, gang violence hardened into a vicious form of racial warfare. In October 1964, police from three precincts had to be called to quell a riot in Park Slope when hundreds of white and black students fought with car antennas, stickball bats, and broken bottles outside John Jay High School. As they fled into the subways, angry teens assaulted bystanders and pummeled a local grocer. In other instances, working-class whites firebombed Puerto Rican and black tenements. Each racial assault fueled revenge attacks as the area sank into a deadly cycle of interethnic violence.[5]

But if one view from the Bossert Hotel was that of a devastated industrial cityscape, fair attendees could see another trend that was just as striking. Brooklyn was simultaneously revitalizing. In the 1950s, a few middle-class pioneers had "discovered" the small enclave of Brooklyn Heights. But two decades after middle-class residents first moved warily into the Heights, thousands of white-collar potential home buyers and renters fanned out into Brooklyn in search of cheap brownstones. Where in the 1950s Brooklyn Heights was an imagined oasis in an impoverished borough, by the 1970s Brooklyn boasted a bevy of "diverse enclaves" with "historic" names: Cobble Hill, Boerum Hill, Park Slope, Fort Greene, Clinton Hill, Carroll Gardens. Where once Brooklyn Heights residents cobbled together a handful of fledgling organizations to defend the area from urban renewal, Brooklyn's new brownstone buyers had at their disposal a powerful network of neighborhood and block associations, booster newspapers, reform Democratic clubs, park advocacy groups, and historic societies. If Heights activists once penned architectural histories and community surveys in response to city clearance studies, Brooklyn's new brownstone pioneers proactively wrote colorful community histories and neighborhood portraits of nascent middle-class enclaves throughout the area. Once a fragile middle cityscape between Manhattan and the ghetto, Brooklyn Heights had become a high-priced launching pad for pioneers pushing deeper into the periphery.

As they shopped for brownstones in Cobble Hill and Boerum Hill, middle-class fairgoers in 1970s could rely on new types of institutional support from both city officials and private companies. Insurance companies offered special policies for renovated townhouses. Local banks stopped redlining enclaves and excitedly gave out special mortgages for young pioneers. A collection of independent brownstone real estate brokers promoted areas on the upswing. New government programs offered tax incentives for home improvement and private rehabilitation. City leaders experimented with ways to decentralize municipal power to new neighborhoods. Housing reformers rejected modernist high-rise public housing and instead championed rehabilitation, sweat equity, cultural heritage, and historic preservation.

Brownstone renovation was no longer simply a renovation fad. By the early 1970s, the middle-class migration had blossomed into a full-fledged back-to-the-city movement. Local newspapers began to boast of a "brownstone revitalization movement" transforming Brooklyn and Manhattan. *Brownstoners* and *brownstoning* entered the popular lexicon to describe the young renovators. "Of their own free will, in the face of considerable odds and dire predictions, a growing number of younger people have been expending great amounts of psychic energy on the purchase and remodeling of old brownstones in beat-up neighborhoods," noted the 1969 New York City master plan. "The people are of all kinds—artists, writers, professionals, junior executives, civil servants, returned suburbanites . . . Their frontier is to be found in brownstone rows that have gone badly to seed as rooming houses. . . . The great reservoir is in Brooklyn. Brooklyn Heights has been almost completely renovated, splendidly so, but to the south and east lie large areas with potentials to be tapped: Cobble Hill, Boerum Hill, Carroll Gardens, Fort Greene . . . They are proud of being culturally in tune with the City, proud that their neighborhood has so many different kinds of people. They are proud most of all of the difficulties they face. They are, they like to believe, the new pioneers."[6]

The fact that brownstoners called themselves "pioneers" points up several striking features of the brownstone revitalization movement in its early years. The first was its grassroots nature. Although by the late 1970s downtown leaders championed brownstoning, gentrification did not originate in corporate skyscrapers or city hall. Boerum Hill was not created by pernicious developers and bankers pushing into poor neighborhoods to reap profit. Nor was Cobble Hill a scheme of downtown city officials to valorize central city neighborhoods and displace the poor. Rather, brownstoning developed with little support from the "growth machine," and at times outright hostility. Banks in the 1960s refused to grant mortgages in the largely redlined districts. Real estate agents were loath to advertise in areas with significant numbers of blacks and Puerto Ricans. City planners battled with brownstoners over urban development schemes. "In the absence of regular bank assistance, means of

Boerum Hill Creative Homes/ Creative People

11th Annual House & Garden Tour

Sunday, June 6/1 to 5p.m.

Featuring Work-In Homes
plus Historical Exhibit
St. Nickolas Cathedral
Arts & Crafts Fair
Flea Market
Entertainment and Refreshments.

Donation: $3.50
Tickets at Pacific Branch
Brooklyn Public Library
Fourth Avenue at Pacific Street
or $3.00 in advance.

For information
call 834-0510, evenings.

"Brownstone Brooklyn creatively reimagined by a new middle class." A 1976 home
tour poster by the Boerum Hill Association shows a "creative" brownstoner sculpting
a brownstone. (Courtesy of Robert Korn)

financing ranged from the peculiar to the bizarre, and improvements were
almost always financed out-of-pocket," explained writer and brownstoner
L. J. Davis. "People uncovered talents they had never suspected: one young
banker developed into a competent plumber, a social worker has become a
skilled ornamental plasterer."[7]

Brownstoners did not describe themselves as pioneers just for financial reasons. Cobble Hill and Park Slope represented not only an overflow of Brooklyn Heights white-collar residents but also the spread of its romantic urban ideal. Brownstoners envisioned themselves as place missionaries, moving into poor, increasingly nonwhite Brooklyn on a mission of rescue. Pioneers started block associations, organized street festivals, and opened food cooperatives as part of a countercultural search for authenticity in a bureaucratic and alienating society. Neighborhood organizers created new civic groups to foster a sense of community, place, and history. As they planted trees and dug community gardens in abandoned lots, others described themselves as "greening" the city and echoed the themes of a nascent environmental movement.

If brownstoners were place missionaries creating neighborhoods out of Brownstone Brooklyn's nineteenth-century landscape, Martin James' report, Clay Lancaster's *Old Brooklyn Heights*, Herbert Gans' *The Urban Villagers*, and other anti-renewal tracts from the early 1960s were their gospel. No bible was held more sacred than Jane Jacobs' *The Death and Life of Great American Cities*. "My husband and I live in the section of Brooklyn called Boerum Hill," wrote Patricia Snyder, artist and new Boerum Hill Association activist, in the mid-1960s, to Jane Jacobs, "having moved there just a bit over two years ago after falling in love with an ancient and decayed house there, which we have since been restoring. . . . We are presuming to write to you because we have used your book as our 'bible' in our effort to help our area; in convincing people to buy houses and join us in our fight to stay in the city rather than run away to the suburbs." "We had *all* read Jane Jacobs," explained another renovator.[8]

To spread the gospel of Jacobs, neighborhood organizers needed to physically transform as well as creatively reimagine a long impoverished landscape. Unlike the formerly aristocratic mansions of Brooklyn Heights, most of the area that became Boerum Hill consisted of cheaply built tract townhouses and tenements. Rather than a quaint urban village of white ethnic mom-and-pop shops, non-mass-culture trattorias, open-air markets, and pushcarts, the blocks south and east of the Heights were home to rooming houses, abandoned brownstones, and increasing numbers of impoverished Puerto Ricans and African Americans. Few current residents distinguished individual neighborhoods from the blocks that surrounded them. Brownstoners had to do more than simply discover communities; they had to invent them. New borders had to be established, new institutions formed, new independent community institutions opened. A sense of place had to be cultivated.

Pioneering was a term that mixed youthful idealism with problematic racial and class imagery. As they moved in poorer and increasingly nonwhite areas, brownstoners compared themselves to Western pioneers in covered wagons surrounded by hostile, nonwhite natives. As much modern Thoreaus as Buffalo Bills, brownstoners' frontier imagery drew as much upon the language of the emerging counterculture and environmentalist movements as it did the Old West. The back-to-Brooklyn movement was the twin of the back-to-the-land movement on the rural periphery; both reflected a desire for a new postindustrial labor force to reinhabit authentic landscapes from earlier, seemingly non-bureaucratic eras. College-educated brownstoners described the dilapidated industrial cityscape with much the same language as they did declining agricultural landscapes outside the city. Whether small farms and fishing villages on eastern Long Island or Victorian waterfront districts in downtown Brooklyn, white-collar enthusiasts recast former sites of production as landscapes of consumption with non-corporate mom-and-pop shops, non-assimilated ethnics, historic architecture, small streets, antiquated forms of transportation, and non-Fordist forms of labor.[9]

Brownstoning was a grassroots movement out of necessity, but also for ideological reasons. If the Brooklyn Civic Center once exemplified the high modernism of the 1940s and 1950s, the neighborhoods of Boerum Hill and Clinton Hill embodied the high romanticism of the 1960s and 1970s. Out of the skirmishes against urban renewal and redevelopment, brownstoning and other anti-development movements had burgeoned into a broader revolution of place. White-collar townhouse districts in Brooklyn and other cities were the epicenter of a national "neighborhood movement," "neighborhood revolt," or "community revolution." Neighborhood groups around the country led tumultuous protests to protect local communities from highways, urban redevelopment projects, and the expansion of modern universities culminating in the upheavals of 1968. On the periphery of Columbia University, students rebelled to prevent the university from building a gymnasium in a local park. In Berkeley's "People's Park," student activists and local merchants a year later planted trees and flowers on a university construction site to block plans for a parking lot. As they fought state police, protesters symbolically delayered the modern landscape to uncover hidden Costanoan Indian virgin soil. "The Costanoan Indians lived in this area called Berkeley. They had no concept of land ownership," exclaimed the student position paper. "Your land title is covered with blood. We won't touch it. You people ripped off the land from the Indians a long time ago. If you want it back now, you will have to fight for it again."[10]

Rather than directed from above by planners or the real estate industry, the first new district, Cobble Hill, emerged when a few families decided to cross the street. As Brooklyn Heights became high-priced, new middle-class residents sought cheaper rent and home prices on the periphery, crossing constructed boundaries that divided the Heights from the blighted space that surrounded it. Running along the southern end of Brooklyn Heights, with its collection of Lebanese and Syrian Arab shops, substandard housing, and a growing Puerto Rican population, Atlantic Avenue was known in the 1950s to be one of those boundaries. As one Heights resident explained in 1959: "Several years ago, as a newcomer to the Heights, I was warned that one simply did not venture south of Atlantic Avenue unless driven by a warlike urge to violate boundaries or an insatiable longing for *baba gannouge*. Indeed, the area 'across Atlantic' inspired much the same dread as a body in the closet, although delicacy and certain liberal pretensions prevented further discussion."[11]

Yet in the late 1950s new middle-class settlers slowly began to push across Atlantic Avenue in search of cheap brownstones. As they crossed into the poorer periphery, they drew upon the familiar tropes of urban discovery narratives. But in this case the narrators juxtaposed the wilderness not just to high-rise Manhattan but to the overgentrified Heights as well. "I was unable to buy a house in Manhattan or the Heights," explained one new arrival in 1959. "I came down to this area and saw Atlantic Avenue, I was scared to cross over. I told my wife 'We're going to cross this great big bugaboo, Atlantic Avenue.'" "My ostrich-type complacency lasted while there were still unexplored streets and alleys in the Heights," recounted another to the local paper. "Once these were exhausted, I gathered my courage and my baby carriage, and made a few cautious sallies to the Syrian food shops along Atlantic Avenue."

As in earlier urban discovery narratives, the narrators fled an overdeveloped modern city to become lost in a featureless peripheral slum. They were then surprised to discover a hidden "neighborhood": a middle-class imagined place where aristocratic Victorian architecture inhabited by an aging Old World ethnic petit bourgeoisie formed a refuge from mass consumer culture, bureaucracy, and public space. "The rich delights of Alwan's, Sahadi's and Malko's—rose petal jams, sesame rings, meat pies, hookas, nuts and honey—were unmarred by scimitar or switchblade. . . . [The] brownstones are reminiscent of an age of wealth and elegance. Old-timers recall when, in order to gain access to Amity Street it was necessary to have more than a nodding acquaintance with the bankers, ship-owners and financiers who dwelt on this once-private street."[12]

Living among a collection of working-class Italians, Arabs, and increasing numbers of Puerto Ricans, new middle-class residents did not assert an independent neighborhood identity, instead describing their area as a peripheral extension of Brooklyn Heights, or "South Brooklyn Heights." But if settlers situated themselves on a middle cityscape between gilded Brooklyn Heights and the slums of the Brooklyn periphery, the intrusion of the bulldozer sparked a cohesive neighborhood identity. When in 1958 the Bohack supermarket chain bought a small strip of land a few blocks south of Atlantic Avenue and applied for a zoning variance to build a new store, the prospect of a chain store violating their newly discovered enclave outraged new middle-class residents. Eager to protect the unique neighborhood from sameness, they founded a civic association modeled after the Brooklyn Heights Association.

Searching for a name that adequately reflected the area's historic import, activists pored over old maps in the Long Island Historical Association, eventually stumbling across a reference to a Cobble Hill Fort during the Revolutionary War. The neighborhood of Cobble Hill was born. "We are solid citizens of Cobble Hill," triumphantly cried a settler in the local paper, "a new and wonderful settlement south of the Heights, with a romantic 19th century heritage that is being reawakened." While a local newspaper fretted that many of the new group's proposals left "old-timers [in the area] either disinterested or in opposition," the new middle class that made up the Cobble Hill Association (CHA), along with the West Brooklyn Democrats, steadily campaigned on behalf of the neighborhood for the city to block new development projects. In 1962, the city agreed to acquire and convert the Bohack lot into Cobble Hill Park, a vest-pocket "leisure" park designed according to the principles of Jane Jacobs.

Cobble Hill was a bulwark not only against the sameness of corporate chain stores but against public development schemes as well. When in the spring of 1959, NYCHA announced planned for a small-scale low-income housing project on Atlantic Avenue, the young Cobble Hill Association organized rallies, wrote letters to local papers, and collected seventeen hundred names on petitions. While the city often disregarded local protests in other parts of the city, Cobble Hill's newly arrived white-collar professionals had muscle that could not be ignored. As one resident explained confidently to a city official during a heated meeting: "There is an overflow here from Manhattan and the Heights, a new element coming in that cannot be thrown out. They are professional people who want to build this area up." The city relented and abandoned plans that summer.[13]

"Cobble Hill" affixed a label on an existing new middle-class settlement. But in other cases, new neighborhood names anticipated rather than recognized the arrival of brownstoners. In 1962, Helen Buckler, a Greenwich Village writer and publicist, noticed an ad in the *New York Times* for a four-story brownstone in the "Borough Hall section" of Brooklyn. Several blocks east of Brooklyn Heights and Cobble Hill, the brick townhouse sat in an impoverished area few locals distinguished from the rest of South Brooklyn, although some called the vicinity North Gowanus after the industrial Gowanus Canal and low-income Gowanus Houses nearby. Like much of the area surrounding Brooklyn Heights, North Gowanus was impoverished and rapidly depopulating as white ethnics fled to the suburbs and nonwhite migrants replaced them. A 1960 study by the Pratt Institute showed a rise between 1950 and 1960 of Puerto Ricans from 8.7 to 39.8 percent and nonwhites from 9.7 to 14.4 percent. In 1968, another study showed that 53 percent of the area's households were either black or Puerto Rican. While wary of the location, Buckler was excited to find such a bargain only blocks away from the Friends meetinghouse in Brooklyn Heights, where she regularly attended services. Although warned by realtors that the area was a "mixed area," Buckler eagerly snapped up the rooming house for $18,500.[14]

Like most brownstoners, Helen Buckler was not a racial conservative. A writer for the *Nation* and biographer of Daniel Hale Williams, the first African American surgeon, she shared the intellectual roots of many activists moving to the area. Upon arriving in what she considered a non-place of seemingly transient African American and Puerto Rican rooming houses, however, she sought to excavate and restore the memory of place. With paint, Victorian antiques, tubs of forsythia, and eviction notices for her tenants, Buckler "restored" her brownstone to a two-family home, renting the top floor to a computer analyst and his artist wife. She also looked hopefully to the handful of elderly white homeowners remaining in the neighborhood ("little flowers one sometimes sees still blooming in an abandoned garden overgrown with weeds," suggested the *New Yorker*). Advised by real estate agents "that the first thing to do was name your neighborhood," Buckler invited eight of the remaining white families to her brownstone to organize a neighborhood association. Eager to find a name to replace the stigmatized North Gowanus, Buckler enlisted the help of the curator of Long Island Historical Society. As they both examined eighteenth-century maps of the area, Buckler noticed the name Boerum, a slaveholding family active during the Revolutionary War. Buckler excitedly coined the name Boerum Hill. The members of the new Boerum Hill Association (BHA) lobbied local papers and real estate brokers to use the name to attract new residents to the "reawakening" neighborhood. While some new arrivals took to calling the area Brooklyn Heights East, when an article about Boerum Hill appeared in the *World-Telegram and Sun* in 1964, the latter name stuck.[15]

Neighborhood names such as Boerum Hill symbolized more than catchy titles. While modernist developers unabashedly named their projects with the words *city*, *towers*, and *center* to emphasize their size, newness, and integration into a regional system, brownstone pioneers excavated the past to symbolically unearth lost community names buried under the modern cityscape. Some new arrivals borrowed existing place names used by locals. When in 1962 a group of brownstone pioneers eager to revive a neighborhood civic group renamed the South Brooklyn Board of Trade as the Park Slope Civic Council (PSCC), they chose the more commonly used "Park Slope" over names such as the "Prospect Park West area" or "Grand Army Plaza." In other cases, brownstoners unwittingly derived their historic names from titles of development projects, ironically underscoring the dialectical relationship between modern and romantic cityscapes. In Fort Greene, brownstoners relied on the name of a park and a large public housing complex in the area. Clinton Hill too was a name coined by Equitable Life for a middle-income housing project and later borrowed by neighborhood activists to describe the remaining Victorian cityscape. (Before both projects, locals used a variety of names for the area, including "Fort Greene Park area," "Navy Yard district," or "Brooklyn Hill.")[16]

Most important, Boerum Hill, Cobble Hill, and Carroll Gardens emulated the name of already gentrified Brooklyn Heights, adding value to depressed real estate through association. (Boerum Hill, the new Brooklyn Heights!) More than simply paraphrasing its name, new names hoped to capture the Heights' romantic urban gestalt. If *Boerum* and *Carroll* gave the "neighborhoods" an imagined aristocratic founding father, *hill* and *gardens* symbolically delayered the industrial cityscape to reach Brooklyn's agrarian past. Where modernist names celebrated the imprint of human development on the cityscape, *hill* evoked a formerly organic, natural, and uneven rural terrain with creeks, hills, and valleys not yet flattened by nineteenth-century laborers to build the city's street grid. (In reality, however, pre-grid-space Boerum Hill was and always had been flat.) *Hill*, like *heights*, also gave the area an aristocratic identity with imagined roots in the industrial cityscape where high land allowed wealthy families to avoid the noise and soot of the waterfront.[17]

Brownstoners did not simply affix historic names to the Brooklyn landscape. New residents eagerly penned histories of newly rehabilitated neighborhoods in the style of Clay Lancaster's *Old Brooklyn Heights* and printed them in pamphlets, home tour brochures, neighborhood guides, and other small publications. Brooklyn Heights had long been a high-income district of mansions and Brahmin institutions with a distinct identity, but the long-depressed landscape of other parts of the borough required a much more conscious reimagining of the past. To counter city planning slum designations, many local historians including Lancaster conducted assiduous archival research to produce much-needed accounts of Brooklyn's overlooked past. Some histories, however, were slapdash paragraphs on home tour brochures and real estate guides that relied on anachronistic place labels and offered a teleological three-act narrative in which an aristocratic enclave was born, died at the hands of city planners and nonwhite migrants, and was subsequently being revived by middle-class pioneers. In 1967, for example, the Boerum Hill Association printed a local history of the new enclave. While no residents in the past had ever distinguished the blocks of Boerum Hill from the area surrounding it, author L. J. Davis wrote a playful highway-in-the-garden narrative in which an aristocratic white Victorian enclave was slowly swallowed by blighted space. After relegating a paragraph to the dormant decades of non-place and non-history during which the area was home to nonwhite roomers, the history concluded with the recent arrival of middle-class pioneers who returned and rescued the neighborhood. Using a medieval-style font and adorning the booklet with pictures of stained glass, Davis wrote the history with a subversive sense of playful irony. Other home tour brochures were less self-aware.[18]

Yet neighborhood creation required more than simply drawing boundaries around an area and slapping on a name. To replicate Jane Jacobs' Hudson Street, brownstone pioneers had to create concrete facts on the ground by rehabilitating brownstones, opening diverse shops such as bookstores, and founding new democratic neighborhood institutions. But most importantly, a neighborhood needed people. In lieu of support from the established finance, insurance, and real estate (FIRE) industry, brownstone pioneers and local homeowners organized a grassroots FIRE industry to galvanize the revitalization movement.

With real estate firms refusing to advertise in the area, some frustrated brownstone pioneers became real estate agents themselves. Like Socialist realtor Kenneth Boss in Brooklyn Heights a decade earlier, a new cadre of 1960s brownstoner real estate brokers mixed New Left politics, countercultural aesthetics, and real estate boosterism to market fledgling neighborhoods. New grassroots agencies such as Old City Realty and Gaslight Realty fused anti-authoritarian rhetoric, free-market enthusiasm, and Victoriana to encourage middle-class Manhattanites to migrate to the area. In 1964, the Snyders, a young Greenwich Village labor lawyer and an artist, bought a brownstone in Helen Buckler's newly named Boerum Hill. While renovating their 1850s townhouse, they eagerly turned to community organizing and excitedly joined Buckler's fledgling Boerum Hill Association on a mission of rescue and a search for authenticity. "The neighborhood association in the slums appealed to a repressed sense of adventure in the new middle class homeowners," explained a future BHA president. "It offered them collective power, an opportunity for direct action, continual excitement. It gave them a chance to do something tangible." "We didn't think when we came here that such a tremendous amount of work would be involved," explained

Mrs. Snyder. "And I don't mean only on the house. I mean the work in the neighborhood, and the time it took from our personal lives—the meetings we had to organize and attend, the fight we had to make to turn this neighborhood around." By the end of the year, Robert Snyder replaced Helen Buckler as president of the Boerum Hill Association.[19]

As one of the new, young, and zealous brownstoners moving to the area, Robert Snyder brought a new mission to the BHA. If the association in its earlier years concentrated on pressuring the city for better services, Snyder decided to focus efforts on attracting new home buyers to the neighborhood. Much to his dismay, local real estate agencies were reluctant to direct white customers to an increasingly black and Puerto Rican area. At the suggestion of Buckler, Snyder decided to acquire a real estate license and advertise listings in the neighborhood himself. Working part-time out of his brownstone with his wife as an assistant, Snyder formed Boerum Hill Realty. Eager to forestall the arrival of blockbusters, the newly minted real estate agent walked through the neighborhood and approached the owners of rooming houses, offering to purchase their property with no commission. At the same time, he recruited middle-class white renovators from Manhattan to buy the homes. After Snyder turned over twelve townhouses in two years for no profit, local realtors caught on and started to advertise homes in Boerum Hill.[20]

Not all neighborhood organizers were new middle-class arrivals. "Native" homeowners and landlords were often the most active boosters for the brownstone revitalization movement. In the early 1960s, Salvatore "Buddy" Scotto, a young funeral home owner in a working-class Italian area south of Cobble Hill, decided to start a civic group after his aging parents refused to move with him and most of his peers to the suburbs. ("They said they didn't want to live with 'those people,'" he explained of their distrust of non-Italian suburbanites.) After unsuccessfully recruiting disinterested locals, Scotto met with a group of local businessmen in 1964 who, despite leaving for Bay Ridge, still owned stores in the area. Looking at what they called a "battle map," the group drew a line around the area where Scotto's father hung out and other Italians lived. Hoping to distinguish the area from impoverished Red Hook, they decided to call the area Carroll Gardens. While *Carroll* was the name of a Revolutionary figure, *gardens* sounded green and evoked the distinctive front lawns of the area's brownstones. Modeling itself after the Cobble Hill Association, the new Carroll Gardens Association (CGA) started a tree-planting drive.[21]

The fledgling CGA struggled. Working-class Italian American residents were family-oriented rather than neighborhood-oriented, as well as deeply distrustful of politicians who often had ties to the notorious waterfront. Local machine leaders were outright hostile and immediately tried to squash the new organization. One businessman quit the CGA after being offered a patronage post in the regular club. Others left after receiving subtle threats of violence from the Mafia-controlled Local 1814 of the longshoremen's union. Scotto's father received a menacing call from the union warning that "the fish stinks from the head." Only months after the founding of the CGA, Scotto found himself the sole member of the association.[22]

Scotto's effort to establish Carroll Gardens, however, received a shot in the arm from two new groups. An activist priest, Anthony Failla, introduced him to a cadre of young, college-educated Italian Americans from the area who had been galvanized by the antiwar movement and were eager to get involved in neighborhood organizing. When Scotto was named to the executive board of the South Brooklyn Community Antipoverty Corporation, he was exposed to white-collar professionals and black and Latino activists who taught him community organizing and coalition building skills. More crucial than government support was the migration of new white-collar professionals southward into the area from Cobble Hill. ("The people who hang plants in their windows instead of curtains," as Italian American residents referred to them.) Former Cadman Plaza activist Bill Winship and other Carroll Gardens pioneers buttressed the CGA and solidified the identity of the new enclave.[23]

In predominantly African American areas of Bedford-Stuyvesant, Prospect Heights, and Prospect-Lefferts Gardens, brownstoning was similarly spearheaded by local homeowners, many of whom were black women. Some of the first brownstoners were West Indian immigrants in the 1940s and 1950s who bought rooming houses and converted them to single-family homes. Starting in the late 1960s, groups of African American homeowners concerned about white flight and city redevelopment plans organized new civic groups and block associations to fight redlining, improve the image of the area, and encourage potential brownstone renovators both black and white to move to their area. Bedford Stuyvesant's Ruby Brent Ford, for example, founded the United Homeowners Association, which organized several block associations, a food cooperative, house tours for potential buyers, and a successful drive for a Stuyvesant Heights historic district. Founded in 1969 by an interracial group of homeowners, the Prospect-Lefferts Gardens Neighborhood Association (PLGNA) similarly created a new neighborhood name for a brownstone district between Crown Heights and Flatbush, organized home tours, and founded a newsletter. "I was originally from Bed-Stuy, which was a beautiful area—still is—but the minute a Black family moved in a white moved out," explained one of the African American founders of the PLGNA. "I felt that the only thing we could do was to try to publicize and let people know this area existed—and to try to get young whites to move in who would be interested in preserving the neighborhood, saving it from becoming a ghetto."[24]

Brownstoning in Park Slope was similarly encouraged by idealist "natives" who mixed gentrification boosterism with a sincere faith in community action and social justice. In the late 1950s, Joe Ferris, a local Irish American schoolteacher born and raised in Park Slope, returned from the army reserves dismayed to see the area being abandoned by his working-class neighbors and falling prey to blockbusters. In a Irish and Italian Catholic inner-city district divided among "college boys" and "street corner boys," the young idealist represented the former and was more drawn to the emerging civil rights and other social movements of the 1960s than many of his neighbors. Active in the Young Christian Workers and influenced by the writings of Dorothy Day, he hoped to stem the area's decline through direct action and the principles of the Social Gospel. Ferris traveled to Chicago to meet Saul Alinsky and came back with a strong conviction that community organizing could offer a potential cure for Park Slope's ills. Along with volunteering in a program for wayward teens, the young activist tried to mobilize church leaders, local politicians, and residents to work communally to stabilize the impoverished area. On a block eyed by blockbusters, he and Bill Jesinkey, another idealistic schoolteacher he met through the Young Christian Workers, bought a brownstone in 1961 and tried to start a cooperative. As they struggled to renovate the townhouse and begin a tree-planting program, they lobbied local churches to collaborate to establish a mortgage fund to help other struggling locals purchase and rehabilitate their homes. Saint Francis and other parishes declined. Local institutions had become increasingly fatalistic about the area's future in the 1960s. "It was not yet the fullness of time and circumstance," Ferris later explained.[25]

With little cooperation from local institutions, Ferris, Jesinkey, and Charles Monaghan, another college-educated Irish American Park Slope native and a writer for the *New York Times*, decided to look elsewhere. In the early 1960s, they turned to a new crop of white-collar renovators migrating to brownstones in the northeast section of the neighborhood. (Like Brooklyn Heights, Park Slope's Gold Coast formed an early anchor for postwar gentrification.) In 1966, the men met with a group of new middle-class pioneers in the basement of a renovated brownstone to start an organization to encourage prospective homeowners to move to the area. The newly formed Park Slope Betterment Committee (PSBC) collected funds to purchase a dilapidated brownstone before it could be "snatched up" by blockbusters and "mutilated into small compartments," organized an open house, and found a young Manhattan family willing to purchase it. Buoyed by their initial success, the PSBC began to put binders on dilapidated brownstones around the neighborhood with the goal of recruiting middle-class families to buy them. To publicize the stigmatized area, the organization conducted home tours of renovated brownstones. Using his position at the paper, Charles Monaghan wrote booster articles in the real estate section of the *New York Times*. The PSBC also sent publicity photos to newspapers of white Park Slope families in Victorian clothing walking in front of townhouses or riding in horse-driven carriages.[26]

A 1970s brochure for Brownstone Agency Inc., a new insurance company offering a special policy for brownstoners, reflects the ties between brownstone gentrification and the early environmentalist movement. (Courtesy of the Brownstone Agency Inc.)

Home tours were a revolutionary new tool for the brownstone revitalization movement. Originally fund-raising charity events among brownstone Brahmins in the 1920s, home tours in the 1950s became a political weapon used by anti-urban-renewal activists to forestall clearance plans. To counter an official designation of "slum," 1950s activists offered news reporters and city leaders tours of middle-class rehabilitated homes in condemned areas. By the 1960s, however, home tours transformed into a widespread promotional tool to recruit skittish brownstone renovators to Boerum Hill, Park Slope, and other revitalizing districts. Uncomfortably walking past rooming houses and empty lots, potential home buyers entered rehabilitated one-family homes where enthusiastic brownstoners greeted them and described the benefits of living in the area. "Boerum Hill is roughly the area comprising the colonial Boerum estate and the mid-nineteenth-century Nevins farm," noted the booklet for "The First Annual House Tour of Boerum Hill" in 1966. "Though long dormant, the area has recently been discovered by young professional and artistic people who have moved in and renovated houses, the ample proportions and structural graces of which reflect a standard of comfort that has become increasingly rare. Several of these homes are to be shown here." The BHA donated the proceeds of the tour to a local settlement house.[27]

While established real estate firms were wary about brownstoning, downtown finance and insurance leaders were outright hostile. When middle-class professionals moved into areas such as Park Slope, they were entering a zone redlined by banks and other lenders anxious about decline and often openly discriminatory against African Americans and Puerto Ricans. Even though brownstoners were overwhelmingly white and middle-class with good credit, few banks were willing to offer mortgages to home buyers moving to a racially mixed area with what they considered obsolete housing. Furthermore, most bankers were pro-growth supporters of urban renewal who viewed the attempts of local activists to rehabilitate districts as an obstacle to slum clearance. "Bank trustees are generally an older group of men in their 50s and 60s, many of whom remember the depression," explained a local insurance agent in 1971. "It was in the area of these brownstones where banks had the most trouble—the most foreclosures. These high prices for those same buildings are beyond their comprehension." "The Dime Savings Bank [advertises] for suburban developments, but not for Park Slope," lamented the Park Slope Civic Council in 1963. "Forward-looking Chase Manhattan, making pace-setting loans to Panama's cattle raisers, pioneering (and sometimes losing) on projects in Africa, encouraging corresponding banks to be more liberal with loans to good local risks, is cautious at home." "Sure one particular house may be good," explained the assistant vice president of the Williamsburg Bank to a prospective Boerum Hill brownstoner in 1966, "but we have to consider if it will lose in value from the neighborhood. Is a financial institution justified in putting money into something that is going to be degraded by what's next door?"[28]

With conventional mortgages expensive and hard to come by, brownstoners found creative ways to finance their purchases. Some simply emptied their savings, borrowed from relatives, and paid for the buildings mostly or completely in cash. "One fortunate family was able—by using savings, selling stocks, and begging that proverbial rich aunt upstate to give them an advance on her Last Will and testament—to raise $50,000 in cash," explained a brownstoner guide book. Others turned to expensive mortgage brokers who hunted for willing lenders among out-of-city banks and insurance companies. Still others relied on purchase-money mortgages, in which brownstoners borrowed money directly from the seller.[29]

Procuring home improvement loans for rehabilitation of the aging townhouses was difficult as well. Many brownstoners invested sweat equity into their dilapidated townhouses by doing renovations themselves. In 1971, a local civic group survey found that while 24 percent of brownstoners received conventional financing and 21 percent used FHA funds, 54 percent reported doing much of the renovations themselves. Along with the sense of danger of living in poor districts, the sense of being pioneers also came from the hardship of living in partially renovated dwellings. Living in a single room and slowly moving into other sections of the house as they renovated, brownstoners dwelled along an imagined frontier within their own homes.[30]

In the face of continued hostility and discouragement from banks and the real estate industry, Brooklyn and Manhattan brownstoners wrote dozens of guidebooks, manuals, and handbooks to encourage and support brownstone pioneers moving to the area, a new type of gentrification literature. With maps of brownstone neighborhoods, advice on procuring mortgages and insurance, tax guidance, tips on evicting remaining tenants, and a directory of contractors, masons, plumbers, and carpenters, books such as *You Don't Need to Be Rich to Own a Brownstone* and *The Home Buyer's Guide to New York City Brownstone Neighborhoods* were important resources for skittish new homeowners. Brownstone Biographies, a local publisher, printed *The House Research Guide* to help renovators research the "biographies" of their townhouses. In 1973, a new Park Slope brownstone owner and McGraw-Hill editor, Clem Labine, started a small magazine, the *Old House Journal*. Initially a small newsletter distributed from his brownstone, within a few years the magazine had readers in fifty states.[31]

Because many pioneers were Brooklyn-based writers and journalists, news-papers and magazines became important resources for neighborhood boosters to promote their new enclaves. Some newsletters, such as the *Brownstoner* or the *Gaslight Gazette*, specifically covered the brownstone revitalization move-ment. New arrivals such as Paul Wilkes and L. J. Davis and returning "native" journalists including Charles Monaghan and Pete Hamill also printed jazzy discovery narratives and local-color portraits of ethnic communities in major newspapers and magazines such as the *New York Times* and *Daily News*. New alternative newspapers such as the Brooklyn *Phoenix*, created in the mold of the *Village Voice*, paradoxically mixed anti-growth reform politics, highbrow cultural discourse, and countercultural critiques of mass consumer culture with real estate boosterism.[32]

Perhaps no magazine was more influential and better captured the diverse and contradictory impulses of gentrification than *New York*. Started in the mid-1960s as a Sunday supplement to the *New York Herald Tribune*, the maga-zine soon challenged the *New Yorker*, which had gained a reputation for being staid and establishmentarian, as the voice of Manhattan and Brooklyn's new and cosmopolitan middle class. With lists of things to do and articles with titles like "The Best Pastry Shops in Town," "A Guide to the Hidden Meanings of New York Parties," and "Facing Up to the Hamptons," *New York* offered clear standards of taste and cultural capital for white-collar professionals. At the same time, the magazine was an anti-institutional political reform weekly with articles that routinely attacked city hall power brokers and encouraged readers to fight development projects and bureaucracy. By the late 1960s, the magazine was primarily preoccupied with real estate. Articles such as "You Mean You Pay More than $50 a Month Rent? We Don't," "Condominiums vs. Co-ops," and "Now's the Time to Buy a Brownstone," as well as the "Urban Strategist" column, offered survival tips to Manhattan and Brooklyn's new middle class struggling with high rents and looking for cheaper housing in poorer districts. In 1969, *New York* dedicated an entire issue to the brownstone revival in Brooklyn. "Brooklyn: The Sane Alternative" featured romantic ur-banist articles by Pete Hamill, L. J. Davis, and Peter Blake inviting middle-class readers to explore newly gentrifying areas of Brownstone Brooklyn.[33]

While some brownstoners tried to attract other home buyers to new enclaves, other activists founded new participatory civic groups to forge scat-tered settlers into a cohesive community. In areas such as Park Slope and Cobble Hill, brownstoners founded hundreds of block associations. Created by new middle-class homeowners in cooperation with native landlords, block associations fought blockbusting, pushed absentee landlords to improve con-ditions on their property, and pressured the city for better delivery of services.

"Historic Park Slope." A 1967 publicity photo sent by the Park Slope Betterment Committee to newspapers shows brownstoner Evelyn Ortner in a turn-of-the-century period costume. (Courtesy of the Library of Congress, Prints & Photographs Division, NYTWT&S Collection)

"Our block association was formed in May 1965," explained the organizer of the Berkeley Place Block Association. "We have found that through the efforts of our organization, plus those of other organizations in our area, we are getting faster service from the police department, good cooperation from the sanitation department when it is requested, and some cooperation from absentee landlords. . . . More walks are being swept daily; more people seem concerned about the appearance of their property."

But while they hoped to lobby the city for better delivery of services, block associations more importantly aimed to develop a sense of local place. Echoing other social movements of the 1960s, block associations described a mission to bring participatory democracy, authenticity, and face-to-face communal life to a transient population in an alienating city. "Perhaps the most important accomplishment was psychological," explained the fledgling Garfield Place Block Association in 1966. "It has established a new community consciousness not there a year ago. With this has come a feeling among residents that they can solve their problems themselves, using their own resources."[34]

Block parties and carnivals were events that brownstoner block associations hoped could raise funds while building a sense of local community. With potato sack races, carnival booths, and homemade refreshments, the events attempted to restore the pastoral intimacy of a town fair or an imagined pre-television street society. In 1971, the Lincoln Place Association organized a "Victorian Block Festival." Along with visiting booths with games for children, participants could sip coffee at "Café du Park Slope," browse "the latest in unexpurgated novels" at the "Penny Dreadful Book & Poster Emporium," and buy fresh-baked cakes at "Ye Olde Lincoln Bakery." The event culminated with a dinner of coq au vin, vichyssoise, green salad, and wine. Other block associations started similar festivals, fairs, flea markets, and Spring Flings with plant sales, old-fashioned organ grinders and trained monkeys, performing dogs, magicians, and puppet shows.[35]

Tree-planting drives were another important activity that brownstoners hoped would both "green" the neighborhood and create a sense of community for participants as they worked together. In 1959, the Cobble Hill Association purchased twenty trees to initiate the first of a wave of planting programs in Brooklyn's new enclaves. In 1963, the Park Slope Civic Council organized Operation Appleseed, mobilizing hundreds of volunteers to plant trees along the streets and in backyards. By the early 1970s, Park Slope activists had reached their goal of planting one thousand trees in the neighborhood. The trend was not limited to Brooklyn. New York City activists planted more than four thousand sidewalk trees around the city in 1970 alone. Since New York City sidewalks had long been treeless, brownstoners had to experiment to find species that could survive the harsh conditions of city life. After trying gingko, honey locust, and oak, Brooklyn tree planters settled on the London plane, a hybrid of American and Asian sycamores. Along with shallow roots and high tolerance for pollution and cold weather, the tree grew quickly. By the mid-1970s, Brooklyn had one of the largest collection of sycamores in the country.[36]

Trees represented more than aesthetic improvements for brownstoners. Just as they stripped brownstones of paint and siding to expose their authentic character, brownstoners symbolically delayered the sterile, modern cityscape to uncover an imagined agrarian landscape. As they hammered through featureless concrete sidewalks, tree planters symbolically and literally hoped to sink roots into the earth, reconnecting the rehabilitated neighborhood to a pastoral past. "It's exciting. Something really happens to your soul when you realize you've had a part in planting a tree," explained a block association member in 1971.[37]

Along with planting trees along sidewalks, brownstoners and other new middle-class residents greened the blighted landscape by planting community gardens on empty, litter-strewn lots. In 1976, the Boerum Hill Association leased unused land from the fiscally strapped Urban Development Corporation. After raising $450 with a fund-raiser cocktail party, they created a one-acre garden with a cherry tree, small walkways, and vegetables. Throughout the late 1960s and '70s, on abandoned lots seized by the city, block associations and neighborhood associations leased land for $1 a year, cleared the rubble, and planted grass, tomatoes, beets, and lettuce. Groups such as the Green Guerillas offered tips on tree care, cutting through city red tape, and preventing vandalism. *New York* and other magazines and newspapers offered tips on "balcony gardening." The Brooklyn Botanic Garden initiated a course in the early 1970s on community gardening. Cornell University started a Brooklyn Urban Gardening Program and opened up an office in Park Slope.[38]

Brownstoners brought a similar romantic spirit to Brownstone Brooklyn's deteriorating parks. When new residents arrived in the area, they were shocked to find the large, majestic parks filled with wilting plants, decaying Victorian monuments, abandoned boathouses, and fountains filled with beer bottles and rubbish. Brownstoners in the 1960s formed the Friends of Prospect Park and the Friends of Fort Greene Park to pressure the city to clean up litter and broken glass, mend fences, and repair damaged trees and shrubs. As they explored what they described as the "hidden secrets" of the parks, they researched park histories and penned detailed walking guides. In the same spirit that they rehabilitated their brownstones, new park activists fought to restore damaged monuments, crumbling walkways and overpasses, and deteriorating buildings mostly dating back to the Victorian era.[39]

But while they worried about decay, brownstoners described a more urgent mission to save parks from the encroachment of modernity and bureaucracy. In a series of battles to protect parks from "the city," new middle-class residents clashed with Parks Department officials and city planners who held radically different assumptions about green space. Parks commissioner Robert Moses and his successor, Newbold Morris, were part of a New Deal generation of reformers with deep skepticism about Romantic park designers such as Frederick Law Olmsted. With roots in the Progressive playground movement, Morris and older city officials believed that parks were not refuges for solitary elites to meander leisurely but malleable public space with tennis courts, baseball diamonds, skating rinks, zoos, and swimming pools to be used constructively by "the people." Rather than fostering spontaneous self-expression and self-discovery, playgrounds encouraged cooperation and forged communities through structured play. Instead of "hidden gems," Robert Moses' parks were modern, integrated, and multiuse segments of a park system connected by transportation arteries. Morris brought a similar drive to modernize Brooklyn's parks. In 1961, Morris opened an outdoor skating rink in Prospect Park with plans to develop sports and recreational facilities throughout the park. In 1965, he excitedly announced that the Abraham & Straus department store had donated funds for a small farm in the park with active livestock to teach children about country life, à la John Dewey.[40]

While Moses and other city leaders dismissed Victorian parks as antiquated and elitist, young brownstoners instead cherished them. These activists hoped to recapture the historic authenticity of parks shrouded by blight and in danger of ruin by bureaucracy. Rather than demolish decaying buildings to build swimming pools and basketball courts, they hoped to rehabilitate the ornate, majestic monuments and buildings built by the nineteenth-century Romantic park designers. If Moses hoped to build standardized playgrounds throughout the city quickly and cheaply, brownstoners viewed their parks as inspired works of art created by the individual genius of historic figures. "People have no idea what the park represents as a work of art," explained Park Slope brownstoner and park activist Robert Makla in 1964. "It's a creation, just like a work of music or a theatrical piece. It is a range of unspoiled natural experience preserved for all time for the people of Brooklyn." "It is most regrettable that the integrity and serenity of Carroll Park have been marred by a Robert Moses, asphalt-paved, chain-link impaled slum 'playground' inside," complained Clay Lancaster. "In spite of this encroachment, century-old trees abound, and, with Prospect Park and Green-Wood Cemetery, it constitutes an historic three-part oasis of living verdure in nineteenth-century Brooklyn."[41]

Rather than draw up blueprints for new projects, brownstoners scoured maps in the Brooklyn Historical Society to determine Olmsted's "original vision." Most importantly, brownstoners rejected the notion that parks were places to be "used." Rather, they described parks much in the same way they did brownstone neighborhoods, as oases of tranquility and beauty in a alienating cityscape. "The city seems to think of the park as a place for skating rinks, museums, concerts and happenings," complained Makla in 1971. "All that is great, but you don't need a brilliantly designed park for that. You could have them in a parking lot." "Our parks too have a special purpose: to bring nature to city dwellers. There we can take a walk and enjoy trees, flowers, shrubs, and a breath of fresh air," complained another Park Slope park advocate in 1968. "Is [the park] a Fair Ground or nature in the midst of the asphalt jungle . . .?" Other brownstoners emphasized that rather than being "used," parks were places to be "experienced" and "felt." In a city that was rapidly modernizing, hippies and other countercultural brownstoners looked to Victorian parks as sites of "being." Rejecting the geometric shapes and structured rules of playgrounds, they conducted "be-ins" in Olmstedian meadows and "happenings" around ornate fountains.[42]

Brownstoners sparked a revolution in city park management. Horrified to see corporate commercial space and government bureaucracy in a public park, Robert Makla and other brownstoners fought the city to stop the opening of the A&S farm. When the city announced plans to raze a majestic but decaying seventy-year-old boathouse in Prospect Park to build a modern boat dock and parking lot, Robert Makla and other brownstoner park advocates contacted local politicians and wrote letters to the city endorsed by the Cobble Hill and Brooklyn Heights Associations, the Municipal Art Society, the Brooklyn Bird Club, and the Museum of the City of New York. The city abandoned demolition plans. In 1967, Clay Lancaster, with the help of a team of brownstoner volunteers, completed *Prospect Park Handbook*, a walking guide and history of the park, with a foreword by poet Marianne Moore. The Friends of Prospect Park, with the assistance of a volunteer horticulturist in the area, raised money to rehabilitate distinctive trees and flowers. In Fort Greene, the Friends of Fort Greene Park successfully blocked a modernization plan for sports facilities and playgrounds. Starting in the late 1960s, new parks commissioners Thomas Hoving and Albert Heckscher, under pressure from civic groups, agreed to abandon the building of new structures in city parks and concentrate on restoring existing structures.[43]

Brownstoners not only transformed residential blocks and parks but also brought a similar romantic spirit to Brooklyn's retail landscape. New arrivals hoped to breathe life into Seventh Avenue, Atlantic Avenue, and other shopping streets. But rather than the parking facilities and supermarkets championed by city planners, brownstoners hoped to revive what they imagined to be historically diverse Brooklyn institutions: open-air markets, pushcarts, farmers with wagons, small greengrocers, ethnic mom-and-pop shops, and street fairs. Some founded farmers' markets in parking lots, in empty lots, and on the edge of dilapidated public parks. In 1976, Greenwich Village architect and urban planner Barry Benepe founded the first Greenmarket on a lot on the East Side of Manhattan with the twin goal of reviving the center city and saving small farms threatened by suburbanization and mechanization on the periphery. The farmers' market marked a break from the open-air pushcart markets of the past. In the early twentieth century, pushcart peddlers were largely urbanized immigrants who bought their produce in town from large wholesalers. Benepe, with help from the Council on the Environment of New York City, instead creatively arranged for five small farms on Long Island, in upstate New York, and in New Jersey to transport fresh produce into Manhattan to sell directly to consumers out of trucks using crates and old-fashioned scales. In 1976, Brooklyn's first Greenmarket opened in the Brooklyn Academy of Music's parking lot. With ties to both the back-to-the-land and back-to-the-city movements, the rustic markets were a hit with the new middle class, and by 1980 more than fifty farmers sold produce at twelve markets around the city.[44]

Other brownstoners created new organizations together with local business owners, such as the Seventh Avenue Betterment Committee, the Atlantic Avenue Committee, and the Triangle Parks/Flatbush Avenue Improvement Committee, which planted trees, pressured merchants to spruce up the fronts of stores, published newsletters, and in one case raised money for a private street sweeper. They also organized art shows, wine and cheese parties, and other cultural events to encourage new middle-class residents to walk along stigmatized retail avenues. Starting in the mid-1970s, for example, brownstoner volunteers and local merchants organized annual street fairs along Seventh and Atlantic avenues to attract middle-class customers with neotraditional pushcarts, ethnic food stands, and carnival activities. In 1975, the Seventh Avenue Merchants Association (later known as the Park Slope Chamber of Commerce) hosted the first "Seventh Heaven." With the entire thoroughfare closed to traffic, more than 350 booths offered ethnic food, handicrafts, puppet shows, Renaissance music, belly dancing, theater, and relay races. "Park Slope is now ready for something like this," explained the coordinator, referring to the area's renovated brownstones and converted industrial lofts.[45]

New white-collar consumers dramatically transformed Brownstone Brooklyn's struggling retail landscape. Some older merchants suffering from a declining blue-collar customer base successfully made a transition to selling higher-end goods to the growing middle class. "In the wake of a great upsurge in residential renovation, is a new liveliness," explained the newsletter *Downtown Brooklyn* in 1975 about Park Slope's Seventh Avenue, "a heightened sense of style in shop windows and interiors and new types of merchandise aimed at the brownstoner's taste level." As their ethnic neighbors migrated to the suburbs, other immigrant merchants converted their Italian bakeries, Middle Eastern spice shops, and Irish bars into tourist sites that marketed ethnic authenticity to new urban enthusiasts. But the biggest impact was delivered by the new boutiques, antique stores, bookstores, pottery studios, bakeries, and restaurants opened by brownstoners. With names like Mélange, The Melting Pot, One Smart Cookie, and Little Things, brownstoner stores promoted romantic urban themes of anti-bureaucratic independence, ethnic diversity, intimate relationship to local community, arts and crafts, eclecticism, and intellectual sophistication.[46]

The brownstone revitalization movement also spawned new types of manufacturing. As more brownstoners poured into Brooklyn eager to restore aging townhouses, a local "heritage industry" slowly grew to accommodate a growing demand for gas lamps, brass doorknobs, hearths, window hangings, and other Victoriana. "Brooklyn could be to Victoriana what Williamsburg [Virginia] is to Early Americana," exclaimed a Park Slope newsletter in 1975. "There is a developing market for all types of Victorian reproductions. What better place to center such an industry than Brooklyn? . . . Such an industry—on a small scale—has already sprouted in San Francisco. But the 19th Century *belongs* to Brooklyn." The United Bronze Sign Company began selling special bronze plaques to mount on brownstones listing the date the house was built. Brooklyn Union Gas began manufacturing retrospective gaslights, "authentic Victorian charmers," to allow block associations to "enhance the nostalgic atmosphere." In Park Slope, the number of hardware stores increased in the 1970s by 19 percent, and by 1982 the area had three times as many as the rest of the city.[47]

In purely economic terms, the brownstoning of Brooklyn's shopping districts was remarkably successful. While most of the city experienced a massive flight of capital, the total number of businesses in Park Slope, for example, remained stable from 1970 to 1982. The results, though, were uneven. Rather than uniform growth, two distinct and stratified retail landscapes emerged. Seventh Avenue, near renovated brownstones, saw an increase in stores. Those gains were offset by shuttered stores and abandoned buildings on Fifth Avenue, farther away. (By 1982, northern Fifth Avenue had a 35 percent vacancy rate.) Nowhere was the difference starker than on Atlantic Avenue in the 1970s. East of Court Street sat a struggling industrial landscape, with

"Brooklyn: The Sane Alternative." *New York* magazine's July 14, 1969, issue introduces Manhattan's middle-class to "alternative" Brooklyn's "cheap brownstones" and "friendly natives." Vincent Ceci's cover design evokes the memory of the departed Brooklyn Dodgers. (Courtesy of Vincent Ceci)

more than 18 percent of its stores abandoned. Between Cobble Hill and Brooklyn Heights, however, Atlantic Avenue had transformed into a colorful, Jane Jacobs–esque white-collar consumptive landscape. As part of its "Turn Atlantic Green" campaign, the brownstoner-led Atlantic Avenue Committee planted scores of trees in the early 1970s. A struggling collection of Middle Eastern restaurants and bakeries benefited from an influx of new middle-class customers searching for the oriental ambience of "Brooklyn's Cabash." "More outsiders are coming here," explained the owner of a spice shop in 1974. "Near Eastern Food is very popular. This is the 'in' place now." Attracted by the cheap rents, new middle-class merchants and artists opened eclectic shops with quirky and diverse wares, including a batik shop, several antique stores, an occult shop, a restaurant specializing in "international cuisine," and a children's bookstore that specialized in "non-racist and non-sexist books" and operated out of a former barber shop. Closer to the waterfront, fifty artists opened new art galleries and tried unsuccessfully to rename the area "SoBro." In 1975, more than a dozen neighborhood groups from Brooklyn Heights and Cobble Hill successfully lobbied the city to create a special zoning district to protect the strip from high-rise development. That same year, the Atlantic Avenue Committee organized the first annual "Atlantic Antic," an enormous street fair with world music, ethnic cuisine, games, and art displays. To commemorate the area's historic diversity, middle-class organizers hired belly dancers, men dressed in Arab garb, and two camels for children to ride. "We want to remind people that we have things just like the 'Village' and Ninth Avenue and Fifth Avenue," explained a lawyer and Brooklyn Heights resident.[48]

Brownstoner activism soon expanded beyond single blocks or individual enclaves. As more neighborhoods sprouted throughout Brooklyn and Manhattan in the late 1960s and early 1970s, eager brownstone pioneers formed citywide organizations to represent what they realized was a spreading revitalization movement. In February 1968, a dozen representatives of block and neighborhood associations, local civic groups, and individual brownstone renovators from around the city met for what they referred to as a "revival meeting" in Park Slope resident Kenneth Patton's office at the Economic Development Council of New York. Made up of several writers, a magazine editor Everett Ortner, lawyers, a fund-raiser, and a minister, the group discussed the progress and obstacles of brownstone renovation. Excitedly pointing to "potential Georgetowns" developing around the city, Patton suggested that the group form a civic group to publicize fledgling communities and pressure the city and banks to assist brownstone pioneers. They decided to call the new civic group the Brownstone Revival Committee. "The BRC was a coalition of people interested in telling a story," explained Patton in 1973, "interested in modifying the city policies that related to the brownstone movement, interested in raising the banks' awareness of and contributions to the rehabilitation of city houses." The BRC was joined soon by a Brooklyn Brownstone Conference, a coalition of brownstoner neighborhood associations. The two organizations sponsored home tours, a series of lectures on brownstone history at the Brooklyn Public Library, and workshops on brownstone renovation, and started a small newspaper, the *Brownstoner*. In 1973, the Brooklyn Brownstone Conference organized the first Brownstone Fair, discussed at the beginning of this chapter.[49]

In 1974, the Brooklyn Revival Committee, along with the National Trust for Historic Preservation, the Economic Development Council of New York, the Municipal Arts Society, and the Brooklyn Union Gas Company, organized a "Back to the City" conference at the Waldorf-Astoria Hotel. With more than eleven thousand invitees, the conference attracted representatives of sixty-three cities from Savannah to Pasadena to attend panels on historic preservation, townhouse renovation, and neighborhood organizing. James Biddle of the National Trust for Historic Preservation, Robert Kenney, director of the Boston Redevelopment Authority, and other city leaders spoke of the national impact of townhouse renovation around the nation. Attendees watched films and slideshows with names like "Brownstones of Brooklyn," "Street of the Flowerboxes," and "New Old Town in Town." The conference culminated with a bus tour of New York neighborhoods and cocktails and dinner in renovated Brooklyn and Manhattan brownstones.[50]

Once considered by its participants to be an anti-authoritarian movement against corporate hegemony, planning orthodoxy, and city bureaucracy, the brownstone revitalization movement soon filtered up to corporate boardrooms and city planning agencies. By the middle of the 1970s, private rehabilitation, "neighborhood power," historic preservation, "organic unslumming," and the conversion of industrial space to residential space were no longer the language of dissent but ideas championed by finance and real estate leaders as well city policy makers. Many scholars point to the demolition of the Pruitt-Igoe housing project in St. Louis in 1974 as a paradigmatic moment, marking a shift from modern to postmodern urbanism. Rather than a sudden earthquake, however, the transition from Robert Moses to Jane Jacobs, from renewal to brownstoning, and from regional planning to neighborhood power was more gradual.

In some cases, brownstoners lured downtown real estate, banking, and finance leaders away from modern redevelopment and toward Jane Jacobs–style neighborhood preservation through friendly persuasion. As more home buyers pushed block by block further into the borough, some brownstoners organized efforts to woo reluctant local banks and insurance companies to support the movement. In 1966, the PSBC invited a group of bank officers for the first of many publicity cocktail parties in Park Slope. The gathering was held in a renovated townhouse, where middle-class brownstoners schmoozed with the bankers while Kenneth Patton, new Park Slope brownstoner and economic development administrator for Mayor Lindsay, gave a speech outlining the investment quality of the area. Several impressed bankers at the party promised to reconsider their policy. When in 1971 the Greater New York Savings Bank noted a $35 million increase in deposits in its Park Slope branch over only a few years, the bank was further assured that the neighborhood was on the upswing. By the early 1970s, Chase Manhattan, First National City, and Chemical Bank began to loosen their grip on brownstone mortgages.[51]

At the same time, a few insurance companies, once reluctant to cover non-fireproofed aging brownstones, began to recognize the potential profits in the brownstone revitalization movement. In 1974, John Cassara, a young Park Slope brownstone owner, became frustrated when he struggled to collect on a small claim on his home. Working in the insurance business himself, he founded the Brownstone Agency and designed a special home insurance policy tailor-made for brownstone pioneers. Most new owners were relegated to the state fire insurance risk pool or cobbled together individual plans at exorbitant costs, whereas the Brownstone Agency offered full coverage underwritten by the Insurance Company of the State of Pennsylvania. Along with recognizing the historic value of the aging townhouses, the policy covered unique features of brownstones such as old plumbing and "stained and etched ornamental glass." "The new Brownstone program has been designed taking into consideration the unusual efforts expended in revitalizing not only the city but Historical Landmark Housing in Brownstone areas," explained the new company. "The program is available to house-proud people maintaining their Brownstones in a manner consistent with the definition of a 'Brownstoner.'"[52]

Local companies also began to take notice of the brownstone revival as a possible way to stop customers from leaving for the suburbs and encourage incumbent upgrading in poorer areas. In 1966, Brooklyn Union Gas bought a vacant, dilapidated brownstone on Berkeley Place in a revitalizing section of Park Slope. As part of its "Cinderella Project," the company decided to convert the building into a two-family to showcase the possibilities of rehabilitation and to advertise the benefits of an all-gas-appliances house. After sandblasting off the paint, repairing the walls, and restoring the original front doors, the gas company placed two gas lamps at the doorway and in the front yard to

"Grand Opening of the Clay Pot, 1971." On Seventh Avenue in Park Slope, brownstoners like Robert and Sally Silberberg opened small stores like the Clay Pot. Originally a countercultural ceramics studio, the store transformed in later decades into a high-end designer jewelry and ceramics store. (Courtesy of Robert and Sally Silberberg)

establish a "Victorian atmosphere." Inside the house, the company refitted the brownstone with gas kitchens and laundries, and restored a marble fireplace with gas flames and ceramic logs. With Oriental rugs, a restored gas chandelier, a grand piano, a couch-bed, and a dictionary stand, the furniture was conspicuously Victorian-era. By 1974, Brooklyn Union Gas had completed four "Cinderella Projects" and opened a brownstone information center with free services for brownstoners. Other companies also began to support grassroots revitalization efforts in the city. In 1968, Bristol-Myers donated $40,000 to Mayor John Lindsay's administration to start the Operation Better Block program, which provided grants for citizens to start new block associations.[53]

Brownstoners also influenced the downtown growth coalition through formal political channels as well. Brownstoners were heavily represented in the Lindsay administration. Donald Elliott, Sam Azadian, Kenneth Patton, and other influential city administrators lived in areas such as Brooklyn Heights and Park Slope and were participants in or sympathetic to the movement. Brooklyn's growing reform democratic party also pushed downtown politicians towards a pro-brownstoning agenda. In 1968, Joseph Ferris, Charles

Monaghan, and new middle-class activists in the Park Slope Civic Council formed a new club, the Central Brooklyn Independent Democrats (CBID) (originally the Park Slope Independent Democrats), an offshoot of the WBID, and began to run for office. In Carroll Gardens, activists in the Carroll Gardens Association formed the Independent Neighborhood Democrats (IND).

Reform politics in new enclaves was inextricably linked to brownstone gentrification. On one hand, brownstoning brought to Brooklyn a new middle-class constituency drawn to the antiwar and environmentalist movements. Decrying technocracy and imperialism, antiwar rhetoric dovetailed with a growing critique of the militarist language of urban renewal and celebration of local place. In some cases, political organizing itself was the catalyst for brownstoning. In Park Slope, several members of the new club were former residents of Brooklyn Heights or University Towers who discovered the area while canvassing for the WBID and moved there. But reform politics in new enclaves primarily grew out of brownstoners' frustration with the lack of support by local machine politicians for their neighborhood revitalization efforts. When young PSCC members went to local boss Joseph Mangano to ask for help, he "blew them off," remembered Monaghan. CGA activists similarly approached Mangano with an environmental study detailing the level of pollution in the Gowanus Canal. Unused to the new confrontational style of politics, the perplexed machine politician became enraged and accused the group of trying to intimidate him. Like the Progressives earlier in the century, middle-class civic groups soon transformed into political organizations.[54]

While some tried to convert downtown leaders to the gospel of Jane Jacobs, larger numbers of brownstoners launched an assault on city development projects through collective action. Brownstone Brooklyn in the 1960s and 1970s was a hotbed of protest campaigns against hospital expansion, urban renewal, and new highways. Throughout the 1950s, urban renewal projects, city expressways, school integration plans, public housing, and other centralized government development schemes had sparked widespread and scattered protests throughout the city, but by the late 1960s, thousands of anti-development neighborhood organizations coalesced into a powerful neighborhood revolt against city bureaucracy. Throughout the city, local communities angrily battled city officials in the streets and courts to halt city redevelopment schemes.

Faced with growing opposition from city neighborhoods, the new machine did not simply collapse. Despite widespread protests in the 1960s and early 1970s, downtown leaders did not abandon their faith in modern redevelopment as a way to revive cities. Instead, a new generation of city leaders and urban planners tried to incorporate the anti-bureaucratic ethos of young brownstoners and other neighborhood activists into urban renewal projects.

This shift was not limited to New York City in the 1960s. Although remembered as an era of expanded government intervention, the Great Society marked not the golden age of New Deal liberalism but an awkward attempt to reconcile a New Deal faith in scientific government programs with neighborhoodist demands for local distinctiveness and community control. The result was an intriguing in-between stage that one could refer to as the era of "local modernism."[55]

As a typical reform mayor of the late 1960s, New York's John Lindsay was a prime example of a local modernist hybrid uneasily straddling two paradigms of urban reform. As a Cold War liberal, Lindsay was entranced by new computer technology and cybernetics, hiring McKinsey consultants to use Planning, Programming, and Budgeting System (PPBS) technology to centralize and rationalize city bureaucracy. At the same time, he spoke in spiritual terms about alienation and the need for community. Lindsay both created superagencies, centered in city hall, and experimented with "little city halls," precinct community councils, and school decentralization programs. While he maintained a faith in highway building, his plans for expressways called for community involvement, minimal dislocation, pedestrian walkways, and residential space. His first urban task force included archenemies Jane Jacobs and urban renewal power broker Edward Logue. His urban task force program mixed an emphasis on building intimate local communities with Cold War military rhetoric: Operation Beat the Heat, Operation Play Streets, and Operation Puerto Rican Repertory Theater, for example. This impulse to both centralize and decentralize was the core tension in the Lindsay years. "After years of Lindsay watching, I'm convinced that the man's a schizophrenic," complained Greenwich anti-renewal activist and *Village Voice* reporter Mary Perot Nichols in 1970 of the "two Mayor Lindsays."[56]

Throughout the 1960s, local modernists experimented with new hybrid projects in Brooklyn that hoped to mix centrally planned public redevelopment schemes with incentives for private brownstoning and neighborhood decentralization initiatives. With the success of the West Side Improvement conservation district, city planners in the 1960s turned to Brownstone Brooklyn with the hopes of using government funds to stimulate the private conservation and rehabilitation of existing buildings. "The City [is seeking] ways of meeting the challenge with more than a 'bulldozer' approach," explained Milton Mollen, coordinator of housing and development, in 1965. "Where renewal is required, the approach is governed by two considerations: first, the treatment should be fitted to the need—as much as possible saved and improved, as little as possible demolished or displaced. . . . We are trying to find ways of preserving neighborhoods not only physically but in terms of the people living there, not only through a single sweeping approach but through a many-sided, flexible approach."[57]

In 1958, a coalition of forty-three local religious, political, and business organizations launched the Downtown Area Renewal Effort (DARE), a conservation and rehabilitation program for 120 blocks south of Atlantic Avenue. At the behest of DARE, the city in 1961 agreed to begin a study of Cobble Hill as a potential site for "urban renewal." Seeking to work with community groups and facilitate grassroots community revitalization, the city promised to eschew large-scale clearance and promote rehabilitation of existing structures. "For the bulk of the site," the City Planning Commission proposed "private conservation and rehabilitation of private structures with some spot clearance. . . . For the badly blighted area east of Court Street, redevelopment is suggested with 1,300 new apartments, both privately constructed middle-income and low-rent housing." Impressed with the city's new approach, the Cobble Hill Association warmly endorsed the study.[58]

At the behest of several local institutions, city planners also targeted Park Slope. In 1965, a coalition of thirteen Park Slope organizations including several block associations, two local churches, two hospitals, and the Park Slope Civic Council formed a Committee on Neighborhood Conservation to apply to the city for status as a neighborhood conservation district. Started in 1959, the conservation program brought New York City housing inspectors to inspect dwellings and force landlords to adhere to city codes. City and federal funds aided the private rehabilitation of homes, supported block association tree-planting and cleanup drives, and developed youth programs for local teens. While the Committee on Neighborhood Conservation pushed for district status, in 1967 Senator Robert Kennedy, St. Augustine's and St. John's churches, a local machine politician, and local millionaire John Richmond launched a showcase rehabilitation project for St. John's Place. Home to an impoverished African American and Puerto Rican population, the targeted block was lined with some of the most notoriously dilapidated tenements in Park Slope. Designed by Victor Gruen Associates and executed by the Tishman Realty Corporation, the project won a HUD award in 1968. When locals witnessed the successful modernization of twenty buildings with no relocation of residents, eleven more local organizations endorsed the Neighborhood Conservation District, including several churches and the local YMCA.[59]

In neighboring Bedford-Stuyvesant, Robert Kennedy, Mayor Lindsay, and local religious institutions and civic groups brought a similar hybrid faith in both modernist slum clearance and community participation and rehabilitation to an array of new and ambitious anti-poverty programs. The Bedford-Stuyvesant Restoration Corporation (BSRC), founded in 1967, was a nationally recognized community development corporation that uneasily tried to reconcile two different planning philosophies. In one section, the Superblocks program was a vintage urban renewal initiative that shut off several blocks to traffic and built a fifty-two-unit FHA-financed apartment building, along with a modernist park, concrete benches, and playgrounds designed by I. M. Pei. In another area, the Scattered Rehabilitation Program renovated abandoned houses to sell to low- and moderate-income buyers as well as give homeowners funds to fix up their homes. A rehab program converted 198 rental units in three apartment buildings to affordable co-ops to encourage homeownership. When the area was declared part of the federally funded Central Brooklyn Model Cities district, new programs similarly incorporated overlapping and sometimes conflicting planning agendas. When Model Cities planned to clear several blocks to build modern public housing, Project Weeksville (also funded by Model Cities) fought the clearance plan to preserve several old wooden homes that were remnants of a historic nineteenth-century African American community.[60]

The Lindsay administration also had ambitious plans to revive downtown Brooklyn's languishing urban renewal program with a new humanized approach to redevelopment that avoided the mistakes of the past. At a first glance, the 1968 plan for the Atlantic Terminal Urban Renewal Area looked like a vintage slum clearance plan of the 1950s. The city would acquire and demolish more than 460 buildings and relocate 750 families and 375 businesses, including the notoriously unsanitary Fort Greene Meat Market. On the cleared land, the city hoped for 2,400 new low- and middle-income units in high-rise towers surrounded by two parks, day care and other community facilities, and a new fourteen-acre campus for City University's Baruch College. But the Lindsay administration assured the public that this was not going to be the top-down and heavy-handed urban redevelopment of the past. The project included local community leaders in decision making at an unprecedented level. Rather than recruit an outside developer, the city named the Fort Greene Non-Profit Improvement Council as the sponsor for the project. With the majority of its members residents of the Atlantic Terminal Area, the council included elected representatives from neighborhood organizations such as Grassroots, Inc., the Pratt Area Community Council, and the Willoughby House Settlement. Along with approving the construction of high-rise towers, the Fort Greene Non-Profit Improvement Council acquired federal funding for the rehabilitation of brownstones. "This isn't going to be a bulldozer project," Paul Kerrigan, one of the community liaisons, explained. "We want to avoid the tragedy of past urban renewal projects, where the residents have been driven out and the community has had no say in planning the new construction."[61]

City planners experimented with community participation and mixed uses in their highway program as well. In 1966, Lindsay proposed building a Cross-Brooklyn Expressway across Brooklyn. But if Robert Moses had bludgeoned his expressway across the Bronx years earlier, John Lindsay proposed a reformed program for building and designing roads. After consulting with community groups to determine the best location, the city planned for the expressway to replace little-used railroad tracks to minimize the relocation of residents. Rather than dividing neighborhoods, the "linear city" would proactively attempt to stitch together two segregated white and black sections of Brooklyn. In an interesting hybrid of modernist arterial space and romantic enclosed place, the "linear city" would be a mixed-use highway with cars and rapid transit relegated to underground lanes, topped by a pedestrian walkway, two community colleges, a shopping center, six thousand housing units, and light industrial space. Throughout the planning process, Lindsay promised to include community groups in decision making.[62]

Once enamored by the gigantic open space of the modernist Civic Center, Brooklyn's downtown business leaders also began to incorporate the principles of rehabilitation, intimacy, and walking into their retail development plans. In 1968, a coalition of businesses and nonprofit institutional leaders formed the Downtown Brooklyn Development Association (DBDA) to lobby the city for more investment and planning in Brooklyn's central business district. While the DBDA looked much like the pro-growth coalition of previous decades, the new group abandoned the space-age modernist rhetoric of the 1950s and began to adopt the romantic language of the brownstone renovation movement. Rather than looking at Brownstone Brooklyn as a symbol of obsolescence, downtown boosters celebrated the area's history and heritage as potential draws for new customers and investors. In 1972, the DBDA invited five hundred city officials, businessmen, and civic leaders to its first annual luncheon. The theme of the luncheon was to celebrate downtown Brooklyn's "being." Times had changed since the era of Robert Moses. Even the power brokers were now staging a be-in.[63]

In 1973, together with Mayor Lindsay's Office of Downtown Brooklyn Development, the DBDA finalized plans to turn the aging retail district along Fulton Street into Fulton Mall, a pedestrian mall closed off to private and commercial traffic with eclectic kiosks, planters, and walkways covered by a plastic and steel canopy. The mall would be "a pacesetter in the worldwide trend toward planning downtown areas for the man on foot," announced Mayor Lindsay. Rather than setting up a deliberate contrast to the surrounding Victorian cityscape, downtown business leaders designed the new mall with the aim of tapping into the neighboring brownstone revitalization movement.

Hurt by decades of white flight, local merchants hoped a walkable mall would attract the area's new racially liberal whites to the increasingly black and Latino shopping area. "[It's] the natural shopping area for a new middle class that's coming up fast in Brooklyn Heights, Carroll Gardens, Boerum Hill, Park Slope, Cobble Hill, and probably soon in Fort Greene as brownstone restoration spreads there," explained an enthusiastic local restaurant owner. "I don't see how the mall can fail to attract them because they're young and not alarmed by the racial mix—let's face it, why mince words?" Brownstoner civic groups, however, were apathetic during the planning process, aside from lobbying for historic landmark status for the restaurant Gage & Tollner. After ten years of red tape and unexpected construction problems, developers finally finished renovating Fulton Mall in 1983. The mall's two hundred discount stores and fast-food joints catered mostly to low-income and working-class Latino and black Brooklynites. Despite begin shunned by surrounding brownstone neighborhoods, however, the mall was quite successful and became one of the ten most profitable downtown shopping centers in the country.[64]

In 1971, the Office of Downtown Brooklyn Development brought a similar hybrid approach to a small declining waterfront strip between the Manhattan and Brooklyn Bridges. Once a thriving industrial district and the borough's downtown before the building of the Brooklyn Bridge, the area had a rich assortment of nineteenth-century warehouses, lofts, and tenements on the periphery of Brooklyn Heights. While the area was largely in disuse by the 1960s, 110 small manufacturing firms remained, as well as a small residential population of Puerto Ricans, elderly white ethnics, and increasing numbers of artists in search of cheap studio space. In 1963, Con Edison bought many of the empty warehouses and waterfront property with plans for building a power plant. Heights residents successfully blocked it and a subsequent plan for a relocated Fort Greene meat market. With industrial development plans thwarted, the city in 1969 tentatively declared the area the Fulton Ferry Renewal Area and announced plans for a classic urban renewal project of fifteen hundred units of subsidized middle- and low-income high-rise housing and new parks. When the city faced protests from manufacturing firms and the Citizens for Artists Housing, a group of private developers in 1971 offered a reformed proposal for a "Ghirardelli Square type" plan with restaurants, museums, and art galleries in rehabilitated buildings, as in San Francisco. Facing continued pressure from neighborhood groups, the city issued a report supporting private conversion of empty industrial buildings in the area to residential use. A pioneering developer bought the Berglass Toilet Seat Factory to create the first luxury lofts in the area in 1974. Another entrepreneur opened the popular River Café along the water. By the mid-1970s, after a series of internal battles, city and state officials, despite objections from Con Edison, rezoned Fulton Ferry for artist housing and a historic district, as well as opening up the Maritime Museum. Brooklyn's version of South Street Seaport took shape more from grassroots protest than the schemes of outside developers.[65]

While the intentions were good and the results promising, local modernism only delayed a paradigm shift. Despite city attempts to incorporate community input into city projects, New Yorkers had fully turned against the language of infrastructural development: "the system," "engineering," "power," "public authority," and the "master plan." Brownstoners fueled by a mix of anti-authoritarian politics, a faith in bootstrap renovation, and residual bad blood from the anti-urban-renewal wars of the late 1950s were hostile even to supportive forms of government intervention and centralized planning.

In both Cobble Hill and Park Slope, activists launched an assault on both the DARE and Neighborhood Conservation programs. With a deep hostility to centralized authority, activists attacked city officials and even the middle-class leaders of their own civic groups. Despite endorsements by the leaders of the Park Slope Civic Council and Cobble Hill Association, independent brownstone renovators rallied to fight what they perceived to be a "Trojan horse," a ruse to allow city bulldozers to wreak havoc on a fragile cityscape. In Cobble Hill, the veterans of the fight against the Bohack supermarket organized the Boro Hall Community Group to fight urban renewal. "Encouraged by her triumph against a project of doubtful parentage and intent," complained the chairman of the Pratt Institute's Department of City and Regional Planning, "Jane Jacobs crossed the East River into Brooklyn and helped a few articulate groups in Cobble Hill defeat a project conceived by the community, whose sole purpose was solely that of helping its residents rehabilitate their homes." In Park Slope, dissidents attacked the leadership of the PSCC, organized rallies, distributed flyers, and wrote letters to politicians and newspapers.[66]

The campaigns reflected a new urban professional politics that mixed a seemingly conservative celebration of bootstrap renovation and the free market with a socially liberal celebration of difference, anti-authoritarianism, countercultural aesthetics, and "historic diversity." "Our reputation for 'charm and quaintness' . . . make[s] us a perfect target for greedy, unscrupulous real estate speculators. Our quiet streets and small houses (easy to knock down and bulldoze away) invite the speculative high-rise apartment builder," charged the Boro Hall Community Group in a series of flyers. "The slum-designation is only the first scene of the first act . . . What do conservation and rehabilitation mean? . . . These are propaganda words that sound good. . . . A behind-the-scenes group of realty interests, social planners and do-gooders, brain-trusters, and their political henchmen . . . have succeed in brain-washing a handful of officers of the Brooklyn Heights Ass'n and the Cobble Hill Ass'n into endorsing the proposed study." "We believe this [program] may prove to be a Trojan Horse," exhorted a dissenter to the PSCC. "Housing is really only part of the story. The major part—social work—will make our neighborhood a testing ground for social engineering operated by the Municipal Welfare and related City Department." "This group has voted the power to ITSELF to conclude and the sign the contract for this Conservation program for the WHOLE COMMUNITY," complained the editor of *Civic News*. "Is this RUSSIA?"[67]

For activists who hoped to apply the anti-bureaucratic principles of brownstoning to aid poorer residents as well as new white-collar residents, the reflexive hostility to any form of government intervention was frustrating. "Don't be frightened and misled by emotional splinter groups who distort facts," pleaded the Brooklyn Heights Association in a pamphlet. "With community support and supervision, urban renewal can assure a bright future for our neighborhood for years to come." "I am deeply upset and troubled by your biased handling of the conservation issue," wrote Park Slope social worker and Betterment Committee founder Bill Jesinkey to the editor of *Civic News*. "Your 'Erosion of Freedom,' 'The Dignity of Self-Sufficiency' and 'Cobble Hill Do-It-Yourselfism' are beyond the obvious. . . . [Conservation] is not a hand-out. . . . It is not urban renewal. . . . It is an attempt to put into the hands of the community the major responsibility for enforcing the building, health, and sanitary codes. . . . [Critics] seem to state that this community can fight the spread of decay with a strictly volunteer program. It is indeed strange to find the paid professional editor of the *Civic News* among such critics."[68]

Neither renewal plan ever came to fruition. In Cobble Hill, under pressure from activists, the city halved the size of its urban renewal study and eventually abandoned it. In Park Slope, as more white-collar professionals migrated to the neighborhood and ascended to power in the PSCC, the organization in 1969 withdrew its endorsement of the code enforcement program. "In the years since the original conservation program was requested, extensive private investment had taken place in our community," explained the new PSCC president. "Park Slope is currently a leading neighborhood in the brownstone restoration movement. . . . Many neighborhoods in Brooklyn are not as fortunate as Park Slope in being a historic community. . . . It is these areas which are truly lacking in institutions, community organizations and resources that need Federal assistance. Park Slope is not a community threatened by economic or social problems. Private initiative is swiftly improving housing, streets, commerce, and public services. . . . [G]overnment resources should be used in more critical areas in the borough." "The ultimate meaning of this fiasco was unmistakable," complained the dismayed head of the Pratt

Institute's planning department in 1964 about the Cobble Hill defeat. "Unless public understanding could be achieved, there would be no objective evaluation of the merits of individual urban renewal proposals. This eventuality would not have proven too distasteful to various and sundry aspiring lawyers, who found in the fomenting of emotionally charged opposition to urban renewal a sure-fire issue in their battle for political recognition . . . [as well as] a host of self-styled leaders who tried to use people's fears of change as a stepping stone to revolution or to the resurgence of the more virulent forms of so-called 'conservatism.'" With the assistance of a three-year grant from the Rockefeller Brothers Fund, the Pratt Institute founded a new Pratt Community Education Program to encourage citizen participation and improve communication between renewal agencies and local communities.[69]

The Atlantic Terminal urban renewal plan similarly stumbled. Finding a site to relocate the Fort Greene Meat Market was difficult in a minefield of increasingly cantankerous neighborhood groups scarred by the earlier era of urban renewal. Initial plans to locate the market next to Brooklyn Heights in the Fulton Ferry industrial waterfront area between the Manhattan and Brooklyn Bridges caved under pressure from Heights protesters. After facing resistance from five other neighborhoods, the city placed the market near a largely Puerto Rican area of Sunset Park in a former Bethlehem Steel shipyard. As the city entered its fiscal crisis in the mid-1970s, Baruch College abandoned plans to move to the area, leaving a swath of empty land. Despite promises by the city that local community groups would have control of the planning process, state officials had a different agenda. In 1974, officials in Albany, upset by the move of the Giants football team to New Jersey, created a New York State Sports Authority to encourage stadium development throughout the state. When the authority began to formulate plans for a new stadium on the Atlantic Terminal site, the Fort Greene Non-Profit Improvement Council got a temporary court injunction to halt the study. New groups such as Brooklynites Against the Downtown Stadium and Brooklynites Against Downtown Sports, made up of local block associations and neighborhood civic groups, began to hold rallies. While the Improvement Council did successfully build several high-rise low- and middle-income apartment towers, in the early 1980s the site remained largely vacant and sown with discord.[70]

The city's reformed highway program met a similar fate. With anti-expressway groups halting projects around the city and country, advocates of Lindsay's Cross-Brooklyn Expressway pleaded with protesters not to confuse it with the clumsy and destructive roadways of years of past. Support Lindsay's new highways, begged *New York Times* architectural critic Ada Louise Huxtable. "[Protesters in years past] stopped the renewers and blocked the roadbuilders, and in many cases they were right. But they were not all right. . . . The status quo, unfortunately and inelegantly, is not so hot. . . . None of this can be rationalized by nostalgia, rugged individualism, or the mystique of some brand of modern urban romanticism." Despite Lindsay's efforts to answer community complaints, his highway program never got off the ground. In April 1969, fifteen busloads of residents from Brooklyn arrived in Albany to protest the formation of the Cross-Brooklyn Highway Authority. With neighborhood groups challenging every step of the planning process, the city abandoned the project for both political and budgetary reasons.[71]

Faced with widespread protests and decreasing political support, an older generation of liberals in the late 1960s organized a final surge to reenergize the city's faith in government planning and publicly sponsored housing projects. In 1968, Governor Nelson Rockefeller, frustrated by the city's inability to overcome community resistance and attract private developers for middle- and low-income housing, created a new state public authority, the Urban Development Corporation (UDC). With the power to issue bonds and negotiate with private investors, unencumbered by local zoning ordinances and citizen participation clauses, the UDC, headed by power broker Edward Logue, was a throwback to the New Deal. The agency built more than a hundred housing projects and "new towns" around the state (mostly on unoccupied land to avoid relocation issues), including the comprehensive planned community of Roosevelt Island. In 1972, the UDC turned its eye to Brooklyn, announcing plans for a 1,750-unit mixed-income apartment development on the long-empty Schermerhorn-Pacific site on the edge of Boerum Hill. With five connected buildings, a 250,000-square-foot mezzanine with three levels for shopping, and 70 percent middle-income and 30 percent low-income units, the project design won an award from *Progressive Architecture*. The project sparked an immediate backlash from opposing Boerum Hill activist groups fighting for both more and fewer low-income housing units. As the UDC struggled with fiscal problems in the mid-1970s and searched for a compromise that would satisfy angry locals, the site continued to sit fallow for years.[72]

By the 1970s, the neighborhood revolt against City Hall had become a rout. After protesters halted the construction of the Cross-Brooklyn Expressway and held up Manhattan's Westway in legal battles, the city abandoned its highway development program to concentrate on the rehabilitation of existing roadways. Faced with rising debt, empty cleared sites, local resistance to displacement, and an inability to relocate tenants, the city in 1970 announced that it would no longer initiate new urban renewal projects and instead would concentrate on finding investors for previously cleared sites. In 1965, the city, state, and federal governments assisted with or built more than 23,600 units of housing. By 1970, the number dropped to just over 4,200. In 1972, the Nixon administration issued a moratorium on all federal subsidies for city housing production. In the mid-1970s, the Mitchell-Lama subsidy program for construction of middle-income housing quietly ended. Private residential construction dropped precipitously, particularly in areas with growing black and Puerto Rican populations. Landlords with apocalyptic fears of poor non-white tenants and dwindling municipal services abandoned their properties in droves. By the early 1970s, the city was losing housing units to demolition and abandonment faster than either the private or public sector could replace them. Blocks of repossessed tenements and brownstones stood boarded up, as the city had no money to rehabilitate them or rebuild something in their stead. The final blow came in 1974 when Edward Logue's UDC nearly declared bankruptcy and defaulted on its municipal loans. The era of the modern city had ended, and both conservative and liberal reformers had abandoned the New Deal faith that government could build model housing for its citizens.[73]

As the New Deal liberal planning regime collapsed in the 1970s, brownstoning and romantic urbanism emerged as the new bedrock of state and federal policy. In the 1960s, community activists knocked heads with a downtown establishment who still believed strongly in state-sponsored redevelopment

Abandoned buildings and boarded-up stores on Park Slope's Fifth Avenue in the 1970s. (Courtesy of the Brooklyn Public Library, Brooklyn Collection, for image with the following call number: NEIG 1699)

plans. But in a country struggling with high oil prices, inflation, and debt, 1970s neighborhoodism dovetailed seamlessly with a new conservative skepticism about government bureaucracy and fiscal waste. Volunteerism, sweat equity rehabilitation, neighborhood power, cultural heritage, and historic preservation replaced modernization and renewal on the urban agenda. In New York City, with catastrophic debt and rows of abandoned brownstones and tenements sitting empty in a city with a crushing housing shortage, a new generation of officials who saw themselves as "Jane Jacobsians" turned to sweat equity brownstoning and private rehabilitation as potential solutions to the urban crisis. In 1973, the city started a Neighborhood Preservation Program providing tax incentives and low-interest loans to neighborhood groups involved in rehabilitation. In 1975 the city amended its J-51 law to provide tax incentives for developers to convert industrial space into residential units. The city also experimented with urban homesteading programs modeled after programs in Wilmington and Baltimore, in which low- and moderate-income "homesteaders" could buy city-owned abandoned property for a minimal price provided they rehabilitate it to meet set guidelines. In 1976, Chemical Bank, Morgan Guaranty Trust, and the New York Bank for Savings also began to provide seed grants for homesteading and other "self-help" low-income rehabilitation projects. In 1973, new city planning commissioner and self-described "neo-Jacobsian" John Zuccotti announced a shift from master plans to "mini-planning," with a particular emphasis on "diversity, community preservation, humanistic 'streetscapes' and a view of the city as a composite of neighborhoods." In 1975, voters overwhelmingly supported a referendum to make revisions to the New York City charter to give neighborhoods more power over city planning, development and municipal services. Fifty-nine powerful community boards were given official input in approving new development plans with the Uniform Land Use Review Procedure (ULURP). In 1977, the mayor's office added a further requirement that developers provide an additional environmental impact statement when seeking approval for new projects.[74]

"Thinking small" was the new mantra in Washington as well, as federal policy shifted toward decentralized power, volunteerism, choice, local control, and market-driven reform. After a year-and-a-half-long moratorium to reevaluate federal housing programs, the Housing and Community Development Act of 1974 replaced the centrally administered Model Cities with the Community Development Block Grant (CDBG) program, in which grants were given directly to cities to spend on local projects with minimal guidelines. The act also initiated the Section 8 rent subsidy program and support for private development of low-income housing, as well as funding for urban homesteading programs. The 1976 Tax Reform Act offered new tax incentives for the private rehabilitation of buildings on the National Register of Historic Places. As they lionized small traditional enclaves, conservative officials attacked "big government" expenditures for cash-strapped cities. Shortly after he threatened to veto a federal bailout of New York's impending bankruptcy ("Ford to City: Drop Dead," read the famous *Daily News* headline), President Gerald Ford appropriately declared 1976 the "Year of the Neighborhood."[75]

On the eve of the city's first Brownstone Fair in 1973, the brownstone revitalization movement was widely celebrated by liberals and conservatives alike as an economic, spiritual, and social boon. After decades of flight that had left the city on the verge of financial collapse, a white middle class was moving back to the city, voluntarily rebuilding and integrating ghettos with little financial help from the government. More important, in an alienating society, Brownstone Brooklyn marked the potential rebirth of community. In 1972, Vance Packard looked with hope to gentrifying Brownstone Brooklyn as a powerful antidote to American modernity. In his *A Nation of Strangers*, the pop sociologist and bestselling author warned of "the increasingly rootless nature of Americans," a nation with "great numbers of inhabitants unconnected to either people and places . . . a breakdown in community living." "There is a general shattering of small-group life," he warned. "We are becoming a nation of strangers."[76]

But in Park Slope, he found "an important lesson in community-building" in a city of "hopeless sprawl." "What started as a thousand or so families seeking a 'buy' in a home became . . . a true community of interacting neighbors. The block organizations or other groups now have gala cookouts with each neighbor contributing a native dish. There are champagne breakfasts in the park in the spring and block festivals for young and old. . . . Park Slope is not unique in New York. The 'brownstoners' have recently been creating authentic communities out of rundown areas on the Upper West Side, in Chelsea, on the Lower East Side in Manhattan, and at Cobble Hill, Boerum Hill, and Fort Greene in Brooklyn."[77]

But while Packard brimmed with enthusiasm about the rebirth of community, Brownstone Brooklyn simmered with race and class tensions. The brownstone revitalization movement was part of a broader interclass and interracial neighborhood movement that united rich and poor, black and white, elderly and young in the fight against urban renewal projects. But while white-collar professionals and the urban poor at times worked together, the brownstone revitalization movement was sparking new tensions in a postindustrializing city. And no one seemed as troubled by the changes as the brownstoners themselves.

7   The Neighborhood Movement

In 1972, after a series of acrimonious and increasingly narrow defeats, Brownstone Brooklyn reform Democrats finally won their first campaign against the regular Democratic clubs. Cobbling together a coalition of brownstoners, blacks, Latinos, and working-class ethnics, Michael Pesce and Carol Bellamy eked out primary wins against two incumbents for state assembly and state senate, respectively. With strong support from Brooklyn Heights and Cobble Hill voters, the victories marked a demographic tipping point: brownstoners now outnumbered the local working-class machine vote. While both candidates benefited from a heavy turnout by the area's white college-educated supporters of the McGovern presidential campaign, the West Brooklyn Independent Democrats enthusiastically described the beginning of a political revolution. The corrupt blue-collar machine that once formed the bedrock of urban Democratic politics had begun to collapse. Ascending in its place was a new postindustrial liberal coalition forged in the middle cityscape that united college students, white-collar urban professionals, and the poor. "The Reform Democratic victories in the 52nd Assembly District that had occurred in the June primary election resulted from a coalition that heretofore had been only a theory," noted Ben Tenzer, vice president of the WBID. "[A] coalition of liberals (mostly white), blacks, Puerto Ricans, working-class ethnics (mostly Italian) . . . Political theorists from Schlesinger to Buckley have promoted or discussed the idea of such a coalition. The mythology of Bobby Kennedy is based upon the notion that he commanded the joint affections of the left and the right, of laborer and intellectual and ethnic and racial minorities. Yet no one has achieved 'VICTORY,' for example, the elected office, until now." Reform candidates would continue to win in Brownstone Brooklyn throughout the decade.[1]

Reformers had reason to feel heady. Not only had it beat the old machine, but the "Bobby Kennedy coalition" had also turned the tide in its battle against the technocratic new machine in city hall. In 1970, neighborhood activists successfully halted a New York State plan for the formation of a new Atlantic Avenue Development Authority. When news of the proposed bill reached Brooklyn, eight hundred largely white middle-class protesters from Brooklyn's revitalizing enclaves halted traffic on Flatbush Avenue for a half hour with signs saying "Save Our Homes" and "No More Rocky Roads." When a few days later six hundred protesters took buses to Albany, the State Senate withdrew the bill. The Atlantic Avenue Development Authority battle was only the first of many triumphs in Brownstone Brooklyn. Throughout the 1970s, brownstoners joined with poorer residents to block city plans for the expansion of two hospitals, a waterfront urban renewal scheme, a Seventh Avenue pedestrian mall, a new container port, and a host of other projects. The citywide neighborhood revolt against city bureaucracy was approaching victory. "The Cobble Hill struggle has become everyone's struggle," wrote the *Brownstoner* about the fight against Long Island Hospital in 1973. "Cobble Hill has joined the citywide 'Save Our Homes' coalition. . . . [C]ommunities can avoid being gobbled up by institutions in the name of progress."[2]

While in renovated brownstones residents spoke excitedly of a new political coalition, a few blocks away in working-class Brownstone Brooklyn the old New Deal liberal coalition was in a state of crisis. On a hot July afternoon in 1973, only months after the reform victory, Park Slope exploded in the worst outbreak of racial violence in the area's history. The incident that sparked the riot began on Union Street, a block residents referred to as "the DMZ," dividing Puerto Rican and Italian sections of impoverished Fifth Avenue. Violent clashes between the two groups had been slowly escalating for years. On this particular day, a group of Puerto Rican teenagers angry about Herman Badillo's loss in that year's mayoral runoff crossed Union Street to attack gloating Italian teenagers with bottles, knives, and guns. Later than evening, a group of Italian men drove past the DMZ for a revenge attack on the headquarters of the Machetes, a Marxist Puerto Rican political club dedicated to Puerto Rican independence and neighborhood improvement. Jumping out of the car and firing pistols, the men wounded three while screaming, "If Badillo had won, we would have killed all of you Puerto Ricans." The next night twelve Puerto Rican teenagers fired a shotgun across Union Street, hitting a pair of Italian twenty-two-year-olds.

While Machete and Italian political club leaders begged for residents to remain cool, events spun out of control. As helmeted police tried to keep order, five hundred Italian and Puerto Rican teenagers gathered at the DMZ swinging bats and knives and hurling bottles and rocks. Teenagers positioned on fire escapes along the block fired into the crowd. Someone tossed a fire-bomb. After forty-eight hours of violence, Union Street was devastated. Piles of garbage from overturned cans and broken glass from the smashed windows of the Manufacturers Hanover Trust building covered the bloodstained concrete.[3]

Two blocks away, across another DMZ, in the official historic district of Park Slope, the area's new middle class, still heady from the recent reform victory, watched warily. "A few short blocks away, seeming unaffected by the poverty and the violence, the brownstoners of Park Slope go about their upper middle-class existence," lamented a local brownstoner paper. "They are not consciously ignoring the problems so painfully evident a few hundred feet away, not turning away in hopes that if they don't see the problem then perhaps it doesn't exist. No, to the people east of an imaginary line drawn down the middle of Sixth Avenue the area below that demarcation is, if not another world entirely, then certainly a place remote from Park Slope's brand of reality. A harsh generalization of an area having a liberal density perhaps as great as that of any community in the country?"[4]

Some brownstoners did not remain aloof from the violence. Reform Democratic leaders and brownstoner activists throughout the decade worked with city officials and a local parish to organize regular peace meetings between the two communities. Yet some who watched the intervention of Brooklyn's new white-collar residents in the racial battles between their neighbors wondered if they were making things worse. When a group of Park Slope Italian teenagers firebombed a black and Puerto Rican tenement, Village Voice writer and increasingly cynical Slope resident Jim Sleeper unfairly caricatured the response of his peers. "Down the Slope came a hundred of its resident lefties," a bitter Sleeper remembered years later, "'another curse,' the Italians called them—marching to 'smash racism' and handing out leaflets to black and Hispanic tenants advising them of their rights as 'national minorities.' Liberals clucked their tongues and pondered stronger enforcement of fair-housing laws and prosecutions of 'hate crimes.' Senator Vander Beatty, a black politician whose district included a corner of the block, showed up at a 'peace meeting' with white community leaders at the local parish, and he skillfully played both sides. The Italians boycotted the meeting, feeling they'd done what they'd had to do—and would do it again."[5]

Both the reform victory and the 1973 riots complicate any simple depiction of gentrification as a bipolar class and racial conflict between gentrifiers and the gentrified, or white and black. The middle cityscape cut across class and racial lines in complex ways. In a restructuring city with a burgeoning

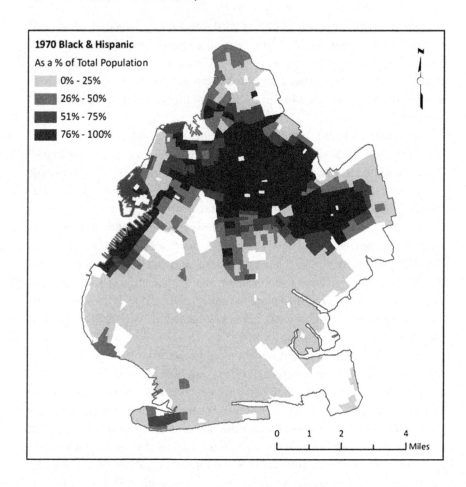

1970 Black & Hispanic
As a % of Total Population
0% - 25%
26% - 50%
51% - 75%
76% - 100%

0   1   2   4   Miles

postindustrial economy and declining industrial sector, two groups migrated simultaneously to Brownstone Brooklyn. White middle-class professionals arrived in tandem with black and Latino migrants, each competing for the same space and clashing with remaining white ethnics. The result was a tripartite landscape in which postindustrial white-collar professionals formed uneasy coalitions and conflicts with nonwhite migrants and blue-collar white ethnics.

"A most important social phenomenon is now occurring in the Park Slope area of this borough and I would like to present the following descriptive analysis of it," explained a writer in the *Home Reporter and Sunset News* in 1967. "A 'new group,' mostly professional people ranging from corporate executives and lawyers to poets and architects, has discovered the brownstones of this area. They are spreading their habitations outward from the axis of Eighth Avenue. Until their arrival a few years ago, real estate values in the area were

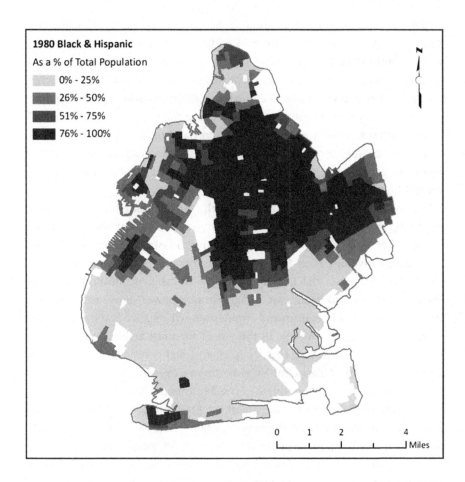

1980 Black & Hispanic

As a % of Total Population

0% - 25%

26% - 50%

51% - 75%

76% - 100%

0   1   2   4

Miles

also steadily declining." As they moved into the area in tandem with poorer African Americans and Puerto Ricans, race and class tensions were high. "Picture the dynamics of the situation: The area was being invaded by new minorities, wealthier ones above Seventh Ave., poorer ones below, but both having cultural values differing somewhat from those of the aboriginal dwellers who interpreted the activities of this 'new group' as an attack on their autonomy (which they never really exercised)." A cynical Park Slope brownstoner gave a blunter assessment in 1971: "The three groups you have here have damned little in common. The blue-collars hate the blacks and view the brownstoners as weird kids with money and no brains; the blacks hate the blue-collars and at the very least resent the brownstoners; and the brownstoners try to ignore the blue-collars and strain their liberalism all out of shape trying to adjust to the blacks and their culture of poverty." A more succinct summary of the collapse of the New Deal Democratic coalition would be difficult to find.[6]

Yet the 1972 reform victory showed that gentrifiers and the gentrified did more than just come into conflict. Whether referred to as the "Bobby Kennedy coalition" or the "Save Our Homes coalition," brownstoners formed political coalitions with African Americans, Latinos, and working-class white ethnics to battle both machine clubhouse politicians and city development projects. Rather than simply aiming to displace the poor, brownstoning both shaped and was influenced by the "neighborhood movements" of the urban working class and poor. Brownstone Brooklyn sat on a fault line between three insurgent landscapes: Manhattan's white-collar professional reform belt, black central Brooklyn, and white ethnic, largely Catholic, southern Brooklyn. As white-collar professionals interacted with African American and Latino migrants, the brownstone revitalization movement dovetailed with a new black power insurgency. As angry white ethnics lashed out against the two new groups invading their turf, a new conservative backlash similarly influenced and borrowed the language of brownstone gentrification. Together these three groups forged a new "neighborhood power" movement that was hostile to New Deal liberalism and emphasized self-reliance and freedom from centralized planning. "We live in the one of the most active, neighborhood-oriented areas of New York City," explained Heights resident Celene Krauss and member of the Alliance for Neighborhood Government.[7]

While historians have pointed to the 1960s and 1970s as the decades in which New Deal liberalism came apart, in Brownstone Brooklyn and other gentrifying districts around the county a new postindustrial "slow growth" movement was born. Whether brownstoners, black power insurgents, white ethnic reformers, or conservative backlash politicians, Brownstone Brooklyn residents together in these decades espoused a "new localism" that was anti-statist but neither exclusively right nor left. African Americans calling for community control of schools, white ethnics resisting scattered-site housing and busing, middle-class whites fighting the demolition of townhouses, and mixed-race coalitions fighting hospital expansion and expressways all shared a deep distrust of mega-institutions, expertise, planning, executive power, and private-public consensus. They shared a dislike for big business, big labor, and big government, championing instead voluntary service, self-determination, and do-it-yourself, bootstrap neighborhood rehabilitation. All questioned the metanarratives of modernist highways, master plans, and universal government programs. All described Brooklyn as a diverse mosaic of independent neighborhoods rather than an integrated modern system.

Spearheaded primarily by the new middle class, Brownstone Brooklyn's neighborhood movement offered a new and potentially vibrant form of democratic politics in a postindustrial city. But like the New Deal liberalism it

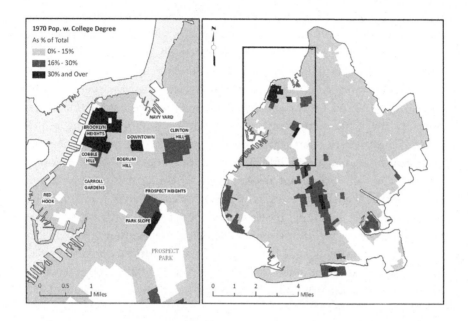

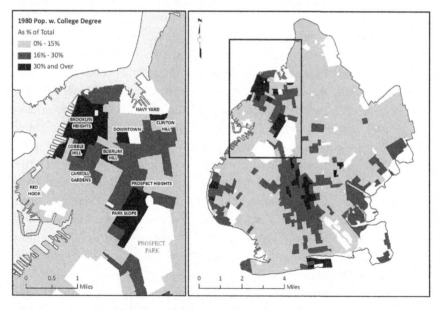

"The Reform Belt." From 1970 to 1980, the percentage of college-educated residents rose significantly along a belt of neighborhoods running from Brooklyn Heights through Park Slope, Prospect-Lefferts Gardens, and Prospect Park South.

replaced, the nascent coalition had fatal fault lines. As well intentioned as many of their efforts were to form partnerships with the urban poor, the white-collar urban professionals who dominated the movement made brown-stoning and the postmaterialist search for authenticity their central focus. Brownstoners were continually frustrated by working-class residents who looked to politicians for the concrete delivery of services and personal rela-tionships rather than espousing broader social issues. When fighting against hospital expansion or other urban redevelopment schemes, brownstoners had congruent interests with the urban poor. But in battles over fast-food joints, supermarkets, and waterfront development schemes, they fought projects that poorer consumers and workers often supported. When they fought banks on issues such as redlining, brownstoners joined forces with working-class homeowners. But when they critiqued municipal unions, they attacked insti-tutions that white ethnics and increasing numbers of African Americans relied upon. The biggest source of tension in Brownstone Brooklyn, however, would be over housing. Gentrification birthed the neighborhood movement but would also tear it apart.

With white ethnic homeowners eager to protect their territory from African American migrants, poor white and nonwhite renters anxious about gentrification and harassment by landlords, and brownstoners eager to upgrade the neighborhood, it was amazing that a political movement formed at all. Yet throughout the late 1960s and early 1970s, brownstoners continued to form partnerships with low-income tenants and local homeowners to defend enclaves from the encroachment of the new machine. In a series of vituperative battles, interracial neighborhood groups vigorously fought to protect private enclaves from the expansion of institutional public space. Rather than against private luxury apartment complexes, most of the battles pitted local residents against public universities and city hospitals. In 1971, Park Slope's Methodist Hospital announced plans to demolish seventeen brown-stones to build a high-rise staff residence hall. An interclass and interracial coa-lition of brownstoners and rent-controlled tenants formed the Community Council of Methodist Hospital to protect their homes. In Cobble Hill, low-income and white-collar professional renters and homeowners battled the ex-pansion of Long Island Hospital. In both cases, the hospitals halted plans and agreed to create permanent positions for community representatives on the administrative boards.[8]

In a city long divided between renters and landlords, renters formed a class that unified Brownstone Brooklyn's middle-class artists and professionals, white ethnics, and nonwhite poor. "In their willingness to take concerted action, relatively well-to-do citizens are taking cues from ghetto-dwellers," explained *New York* in 1970 of the growing radicalism of high-income renters. In Brooklyn Heights in 1970, for example, a group of tenants in six dilapidated brownstones formed the Clark Street Tenants Council after getting no heat or hot water for four weeks. After hiring a lawyer, the council contacted tenants to inform them of their rights and lobbied the city to intervene. In Park Slope, as tenants associations multiplied, activists from the fight against Methodist Hospital organized the Park Slope Tenants Council in 1971. Led by a group of young interracial activists, the council created a newsletter, organized tenants to protest for improved services, and joined forces with the city-wide Metropolitan Council on Housing to protect rent control laws. The West Brooklyn Independent Democrats along with other reform Democratic groups around the city also lobbied for tenants' rights. In a city where nearly 80 percent of the population rented their homes, New York had a long-standing tradition of tenant activism. Along with the ingenuity of poor tenants, New York City's large number of white professional renters gave the movement muscle unmatched in other cities. Eighty-five percent of the members of the Clark Street Tenant Council were unmarried college students or college graduates working in professions. A cadre of young, white college-educated volunteers also organized the Park Slope Tenants Council.[9]

Brownstone gentrification also emerged alongside the squatters' movement, a grassroots phenomenon that many brownstoners pointed to as the possible beginnings of nonwhite "organic unslumming," or for more radical brownstoners a form of "guerilla architecture" resisting the spread of sameness. When in 1970 several Puerto Rican and black families desperate for housing moved into condemned buildings scheduled for demolition in Manhattan's Morningside Heights, Lower East Side, and Upper West Side, they received support from reform Democratic organizations and anti-poverty neighborhood groups. While the city eventually cracked down on the squatters and the movement fizzled after a few years, enthusiastic reformers in city government toyed with the possibility of encouraging squatting, sweat equity, homeownership, and self-help as a solution to the city's abandonment problem and growing stock of in rem (owned by the city due to tax foreclosure) buildings. In the early 1970s, the city initiated the first of several pilot programs that converted low-income, rent-controlled buildings into co-ops owned by former tenants.[10]

If rent control brought together the area's wealthiest and poorest renters, redlining, or the refusal of local banks to grant financing within impoverished inner-city districts, was an issue that unified South Brooklyn's white-collar professionals and working-class aspiring homeowners. In the late 1970s, an interracial group of activists in working-class areas of East Flatbush and

Prospect-Lefferts Gardens started pressuring local banks to grant mortgages in their neighborhoods. Armed with a study conducted by the New York Public Interest Research Group (NYPIRG), an organization funded by college student donations, anti-redlining activists picketed banks, lobbied politicians, gathered signatures, and contacted local papers. The anti-redlining movement gained a crucial boost when a Park Slope brownstoner, Herb Steiner, founded Against Investment Discrimination (AID) in 1977. After picketing local banks and handing out flyers, AID met with local bank representatives and demanded more mortgages in Park Slope, increased advertising for the area, quarterly reports on lending activity to community leaders, and a community committee to review rejected mortgage and improvement applications. Brownstoners with positions in the media wrote editorials and articles condemning the effect of redlining on black and Puerto Rican families as well as celebrating brownstone neighborhoods as a source of anti-institutional authenticity. "You are young and you are black and Puerto Rican," complained Pete Hamill in a 1977 *Daily News* column. "You work hard through high school, you go to college . . . So you go to Brooklyn . . . This place of stately 19th century brownstones, with solid walls, not the cheesy cardboard of the projects . . . Forget it. Forget the dream." If they could dismiss the pickets and marches in poorer neighborhoods or offer small concessions, local banks bowed to the pressure of Brooklyn's powerful brownstoners. Frustrated with one bank's inaction, AID organized a "withdrawal week" during which Park Slope residents withdrew $875,000 from Greater New York Savings Bank. Greater immediately agreed to their terms. Citibank in 1977 also announced a pilot program to commit $10 million in mortgages for one- or two-family homes (most of them brownstones) in Prospect Heights, Park Slope, and Flatbush.[11]

Not all brownstoner activism was simply self-interested. A significant number of Brooklyn's idealistic new middle-class residents engaged in a war against the new machine primarily for the sake of their poorer neighbors. Young lawyers volunteered for South Brooklyn Legal Services throughout the 1960s and 1970s. Brownstoners were heavily represented in the interracial Christians and Jews for Social Action, a tenants' rights group in neighboring central Brooklyn. Operating out of Presbyterian churches in Brooklyn Heights and Greenwich Village, the Task Force for Justice sent "court watchers" to downtown Brooklyn courts to monitor fairness and to explain proceedings to the poor. Many of these organizations founded by brownstoners would, in an interesting twist, spearhead the fight against gentrification in the 1980s.[12]

Middle-class residents conducted many of their neighborhood improvements in cooperation with poorer residents to the benefit of both groups. While one survey showed that 70 percent sent their children to private schools, a number of influential white brownstoner parents sent their children to local public schools with nonwhite students. In Park Slope, for example, brownstoners united with poorer residents in 1964 to successfully pressure the city to demolish the dilapidated P.S. 77 schoolhouse and build the new and expansive P.S. 321, despite four thousand signatures collected by the Seventh Avenue Merchants Association in an attempt to protect the forty-two homes and twelve stores that would need to be razed. The new P.S. 321 soon became a hotbed of parent activism. "In a school which is roughly a third Black, a third Spanish-Speaking (Puerto Ricans, Cubans, etc.) and a third 'other' (Board of Educationalese for White)," explained brownstoner and new PTA president of P.S. 321 Jennifer Monaghan in 1969, "we introduced, funded and staffed a breakfast program for children who were coming to school without breakfast, elected our candidate to the first elected Community School Board, and introduced two phonetic reading programs."[13]

Although overwhelmingly white and much wealthier than the city average, brownstoners' strong faith in local control and aversion to centralized bureaucracy made them allies with the most militant wings of Brooklyn black politics. In the 1950s, Brooklyn Heights reformers had formed partnerships with middle-class black insurgents in neighboring Bedford-Stuyvesant. But in the late 1960s, a new generation of African American activists linked to the passionate politics of the civil rights movement revolted against two groups of regulars who had taken control of Brooklyn black politics: an older generation of reformers who had since become incorporated into the county machine, and a new powerful organization led by Sam Wright that emerged to control the distribution of Great Society federal anti-poverty funds. Pastors of Baptist and Presbyterian churches such as the Reverend Bill Jones and the Reverend Gardner Taylor, as well as members of groups such as Clergy Concerned for a Better Fort Greene, provided some of the inspiration for the insurgency. Inspired by the activism of southern churches in the civil rights movement and the direct action campaigns of Brooklyn CORE, Brooklyn pastors pushed their congregations to participate in picketing and sit-ins at Downstate Medical Center and Fulton Street retail stores demanding more jobs. The insurgents themselves were largely made up of young anti-poverty workers who entered politics through Great Society community action programs (CAPs) and other decentralization initiatives. Librarian Major Owens and former Brownsville teacher Al Vann gained a foothold in city politics without any ties to the local machine. Where civil rights pastors brought a passionate faith in direct action and protest politics, CAP leaders brought a strong belief in decentralization and community control. Regarded by mainstream civil rights organizations as "militants," this new generation of black leaders forged a new style of black power politics that was suspicious of centralized power, hostile to machine politics, firm in its belief in participatory democracy, ambivalent about government intervention, passionate about cultural authenticity, and rooted in a belief in neighborhood self-determination rather than integration.[14]

In a seemingly paradoxical partnership between black militants and a new white bourgeoisie, middle-class residents in Park Slope, Boerum Hill, and Brooklyn Heights provided crucial support to this new cadre of black insurgents and their calls for the decentralization of schools and municipal services. During the 1968 teachers' strike, which pitted the teachers' union against a black and Puerto Rican local school board in central Brooklyn, Brooklyn's brownstoners largely sided with the black activists. Describing a battle of local democracy against a corrupt "big labor" teachers' union, white middle-class parents in Park Slope formed the Brooklyn Committee for Community Control and crossed picket lines to keep P.S. 321 open. "No one in New York City—not even prosperous white men—can do anything about the thorough domination of education by would-be aristocrats of 110 Livingston Street and the education unions," explained Charles Monaghan.[15]

Brownstoners did not solely support school decentralization out of sympathy to the civil rights movement. As advocates of "parent power," they also borrowed the language of black militancy in their own contentious battles against the Board of Education "bureaucracy" headquartered near the modern Civic Center. Park Slope's new white middle-class parents were known by teachers and administrators to be particularly combative. When in 1969 the Local School Board elected a new superintendent, for example, the brownstoner-controlled P.S. 321 PTA tried to bring a lawsuit that their candidates had been unfairly blocked. Parents also objected when the board appointed a principal they found unqualified. "Parents got rid of the old principal at PS 321 by making things so unpleasant for him that he left all by himself," explained PTA president Monaghan to the Park Slope Civic Council in 1969. "It seems to be a sad fact that you have to be unpleasant to the bureaucracy to get things done."[16]

For some romantic urbanist brownstoners, black activism had more of an aesthetic appeal than a political one. The separatist rhetoric of black power offered young white middle-class enthusiasts another form of anti-bureaucratic urban authenticity. Since the Beat movement in the 1950s, a portion of New York's white bourgeoisie had long been drawn to African American figures who they imagined represented an untamed form of spontaneity and rebelliousness, in contrast to the "square" leaders of mainstream civil rights organizations. While cynics unfairly painted a caricature of silk stocking liberals inviting Black Panthers to wine-and-cheese parties, the interest of Brooklyn's new middle class in the politics of their nonwhite neighbors did at times contain an element of "radical chic." In August 1968, the Brooklyn Heights Peace and Freedom Party invited three Black Panthers to a Brooklyn Heights church to "tell it as it is." To a titillated white crowd, the speakers, dressed in dark glasses, black berets, and leather jackets studded with buttons, described plans to "burn [the city] to the ground, without a brick left standing, or a steel beam left standing." Dismissing "Lindsay and his staff of homosexuals," they invited the crowd to join their struggle. "If you white people want to do anything, you can stand with us and fight, side by side. You can go into your communities and tell all those people who are buying guns for themselves to ship those guns to us instead. Or you can give us money to buy those guns ourselves." "I doubt if there was one among us who, despite being scared to Hell, couldn't say 'They're right,'" admitted a white Heights attendee.[17]

While they overwhelmingly described themselves as liberal, most brownstoners were not radicals or revolutionary romantics drawn to the authenticity of black activists.[18] Critics relished contrasting the dichotomous life experiences of wealthy sentimentalists and the black poor they championed, but white professional brownstone renovators and central Brooklyn black activists in fact had congruent concrete interests. Black militancy oddly dovetailed with brownstone gentrification, and as a form of urbanism, black power shared many of the localist themes of the brownstone revitalization movement. Black insurgents in Brooklyn were not simply lobbying for more power like the previous generation of reformers, but instead offered a broader spatial critique of liberalism and the relationship between core and periphery, modernization and preservation, and scientific expertise and participatory democracy. Like the brownstone revitalization movement, black militants emphasized the sanctity of local place specifically situated in the Victorian landscape surrounding the central business district, community control free from the intrusions of city hall's planners, organic folk culture, historic neighborhoods, calls for the middle class to return to the inner city, and a new formulation of the ghetto as a "place to be protected" rather than a prison that "kept people in place." Both brownstoners and black militants were suspicious of scientific regional planning and universal government programs, as well as hostile to local ethnic ward bosses. Both groups shared a vision of the city not as an integrated, kinetic system but instead as a diverse patchwork of cohesive ethnic enclaves.

Rather than inviting Black Panthers and revolutionary nationalists to dinner parties, middle-class civic organizations looked hopefully to small grassroots black and Puerto Rican activist groups on impoverished blocks as potential allies in battles against development projects, as partners in neighborhood rehabilitation projects, and as a potential stabilizing force for Puerto Rican and African American young adults. In 1968, the Park Slope Civic Council and several block associations formed the Ad Hoc Committee to Help Grassroots, a local black power activist group run by local teenagers and young adults in their twenties with nationalist leanings. The Civic Council helped arrange for P.S. 321 to be opened in the summer and after school for the group to meet and run a community center. Other Park Slope activists formed the Martin Luther King Coalition that year, which organized "brotherhood parades" and international folk music concerts in the neighborhood to raise money for grassroots anti-housing-discrimination groups, and a boycott of local stores selling grapes in order to support striking migrant workers.[19]

In electoral politics, brownstoner reform clubs reached out not to revolutionary nationalists but to black insurgents whom they considered to be "responsible militants." Al Vann retained ties to black nationalist activist groups such as the East, but he also built a neighborhood improvement organization called Vannguard and was willing to form coalitions with white reformers. A Morehouse graduate and city librarian, central Brooklyn politician Major Owens in the 1960s was held in particularly high regard by brownstoners for being a firm believer in community control while remaining free of the patronage and corruption associated with rival Sam Wright. Owens was a dedicated activist in the Brooklyn Tenants Organization and Rent-Strike Coordinating Committee and for two years was chairman of Brooklyn CORE. In 1966 he helped found and led the Brownsville Community Council and soon gained citywide recognition for his excellent administration of the CAP program. Mayor Lindsay appointed him the head of New York's Community Development Agency two years later. When Owens entered electoral politics, he organized an insurgency group, Central Brooklyn Mobilization for Political Action, to take on Wright's machine. After a series of losses to Wright, Owens won a state senate seat in 1974.[20]

Brownstoner populism did not only draw inspiration from black power activists. A conservative backlash among the area's working-class white ethnics similarly contributed to the neighborhood revolt against city government. Park Slope's Republican assemblyman Vincent A. Riccio, for example, was a conservative insurgent who joined brownstoners in opposing the Atlantic Avenue Development Authority and Seventh Avenue pedestrian mall. A former social worker specializing in youth gangs and dean of boys at John Jay High School, Riccio shared the background of many of the young political activists of the area. His frustration with city bureaucracy led him to a different type of populist politics from those of rival reformer Joseph Ferris. Riccio and other Brooklyn white ethnic conservatives articulated an angry and racially

charged version of romantic urbanism. As they attacked the Lindsay administration and what they perceived to be the excesses of 1960s liberalism, they
spoke nostalgically of pastoral Old World urban villages destroyed by public
housing, busing programs, and state subsidies to African Americans. Attacking
downtown power brokers and eulogizing safe enclaves threatened by crime,
white backlash politicians echoed brownstoner and black power celebrations
of Brownstone Brooklyn's "neighborhoods."[21]

While sharing in the language of the "new localism," however, Brownstone
Brooklyn's white ethnic backlash developed more in reaction to the "Bobby
Kennedy coalition" than in partnership with it. As industrial jobs declined,
tax and interest rates rose, and crime rates skyrocketed, frustrated working-
class Italian American and Irish American Brownstone Brooklynites who were
once the bedrock of the New Deal coalition lashed out at the two new groups
of migrants moving to the area: white-collar professional whites and the nonwhite poor. Park Slope, warned native journalist Pete Hamill in *New York* in
1969, was experiencing a "revolt of the white lower middle class." "Encroach-
ments of blacks and Puerto Ricans from the northwest, beautiful-people
McCarthy-Kennedy brownstone-renovators from the northeast, and homegrown pill-popping dippy-hippies lolling in Prospect Park to the southeast,"
explained the *New York Times* in 1969. "The only direction from which the
proletarian whites of Park Slope do not feel imperiled is the southwest: Green-
wood [*sic*] Cemetery."[22]

Along with a feeling of being invaded by new migrant groups, several contradictory issues fueled Brooklyn's white ethnic populist revolt. Anger about
their children being bused to nonwhite schools in other parts of town, scattered-site public housing, and other state-mandated integration initiatives
sparked attacks on city bureaucracy and calls for more neighborhood autonomy. In other heated fights, white ethnics fiercely defended organized
labor from city decentralization initiatives. When brownstoners and black
activists fought for community control of city institutions, they battled with
nascent municipal unions formed after years of tough labor battles. In a tragic
rift in New Deal urban liberalism, white ethnic workers fused pro-union rhetoric with vituperative racial attacks on the black poor. Similarly, white-collar
professionals and black power activists mixed conservative assaults on municipal unions and organized labor with passionate support for civil rights.

No issue more fueled the conflict between brownstoners, African Americans,
Puerto Ricans, and white ethnic working-class residents than Brownstone
Brooklyn's rising crime problem. The nation's crime rate began to rise dramatically in the 1960s. Deindustrializing urban areas with high rates of abandoned property, unemployment, poor policing, and segregated facilities were

particularly hit hard. After a surge in the late 1960s and early 1970s, urban crime rates stabilized at distressingly high levels. By 1978, seven out of ten New Yorkers expressed fear of walking a block away from their homes. Why the nationwide crime rate rose, plateaued, and suddenly dropped in the early 1990s remains unknown. But as even the most conservative law-and-order mayors struggled unsuccessfully to put a dent in robbery and murder rates, by the mid-1970s politicians and residents had resignedly accepted crime as a permanent feature of the urban landscape.[23]

As the city's crime rate began to rise in the 1960s, Brooklyn's most expensive brownstone blocks were hit as hard as other parts of the city. In 1971, the Better Brooklyn Committee organized an emergency town hall meeting in a Brooklyn Heights hotel to discuss safety in the area. Five hundred residents attended with angry complaints about muggings and attacks. In 1974 alone, burglaries in the Brooklyn Heights precinct rose 37 percent. The same year, one Cadman Plaza subway station reported an average of one mugging a week. "Crime, crime, crime," exhorted Benjamin Rosenberg, vice chairman of the Better Brooklyn Committee, "is the greatest problem today in the streets, in the schools, and unfortunately, in your homes." In the early 1970s, a new type of "historic architecture" began to appear on the windows and doors of renovated brownstones: ornately designed, black-painted iron bars and gates. Locksmiths reported a thriving business as residents installed double and triple locks on the doors.[24]

For Brownstone Brooklyn's white ethnics, rising crime and disorder represented only another example of the insidious partnership between the area's two new migrant groups. A new breed of ethnic law-and-order conservatives such as Staten Island's John Marci painted a powerful and poisonous narrative in which once-stable neighborhoods were destroyed by lawless African American and Puerto Rican migrants, hippie brownstoners who undermined moral values and privileged the rights of criminals over victims, and cowed politicians who would rather handcuff police than risk an urban riot. They proposed more aggressive police tactics, stronger sentencing for convicted criminals, fewer rights for suspects, and a no-tolerance approach to public protest and civil disobedience. "I want MY CIVIL RIGHTS," angrily complained a white Brooklyn Heights resident in 1968 as part of the growing backlash. "I want the civil right not to be mugged as I walk to the subway. I want the civil right not to have my purse snatched on the street. I want the civil right not to be terrified each time I walk into my apartment. . . . Don't we, the decent citizens who pay all the taxes deserve civil rights too?"[25]

While conservatives quipped that college-educated "limousine liberals" were hypocritically tucked away in safe suburbs, brownstoners in Brooklyn had as much exposure to crime as white ethnics. But brownstoners approached the issue with the same localist principles that underlay the revitalization movement: hostility to centralized bureaucracy, a faith in participatory democracy, and a belief in the sanctity of local neighborhoods. Brownstoners believed that cops should walk the beat, develop face-to-face relationships with local residents, and work out collective strategies with community leaders in town hall meetings. In Brooklyn Heights, Cobble Hill, and Park Slope, brownstoners in the spirit of Jane Jacobs organized an "eyes on the street" program and a "block watchers program" where citizens watched their streets and reported unusual behavior.[26]

The localist approach of brownstoners appealed more to Brownstone Brooklyn's Puerto Ricans and African American residents than did than the get-tough strategy of working-class conservatives. More often the victims of street crime than white residents, African Americans and Latinos formed neighborhood groups that were quite supportive of public safety efforts and pressured the city to increase the police presence in the area. In 1969, for example, a group of largely African American block associations in Clinton Hill organized a "narcotics-free zone" and successfully pushed the police to conduct a sweep to halt an influx of junkies. Nonwhite residents were also quite worried about police brutality. As early as 1959, Puerto Rican teenagers in Willowtown and Cobble Hill complained to settlement house workers about harassment, being roughed up, and racial name-calling by police. During the long hot summers of the 1960s, the sparks for explosive unrest in neighboring Bedford-Stuyvesant were clashes between police and local youths and subsequent allegations of brutality. Two years before the Park Slope riots of 1973, Puerto Ricans and Italian residents battled for days after a police officer shot a Puerto Rican Vietnam veteran as he left a check-cashing store on Union Street. By allowing for community oversight and personal relationships between the police and citizens, leaders hoped to balance security concerns with more humane treatment of local residents.[27]

Along with a concern for the civil rights of Puerto Ricans and African Americans, Brooklyn's new brownstone middle class shared those groups' anxiety about police corruption and brutality. When they moved into poor areas, many new middle-class residents dealt with urban police for the first time, and while in principle they liked the idea of the neighborhood cop, they had little patience for the subtle system of payoffs that police arranged with local merchants and organized crime syndicates. Police crackdowns on juvenile delinquency sometimes spilled over into confrontations with a new countercultural middle class sharing the same space with nonwhite teens. When Mayor Lindsay ordered high-profile cleanup campaigns of New York City parks, police clashed not only with Puerto Rican and black youth but also with hippies and college students. The result was an increasing sense among white middle-class brownstoners that they, like African Americans and Puerto Ricans, represented an "oppressed class." As early as 1959, Brooklyn Heights white-collar professionals, perhaps naively, drew parallels between their struggle against excessive police force and that of the area's nonwhite poor. "Two instances of arbitrary police action [occurred] on the Heights last week," angrily wrote the editors of the *Heights Press*. "In one case, police have been arbitrarily arresting teenagers on Atlantic Avenue. . . . Thousands of New York teenagers are being deprived of their basic American rights. . . . The other instance of police arbitrariness occurred last Sunday on lower Hicks, when four [art] galleries and [antique] shops were shut down because of the Sabbath law. . . . They did it crudely and without ceremony. . . . Back where we come from that's called a police state."[28]

With outdated equipment, patronage posts, ethnic cronyism, and widespread corruption and racism, the New York City Police Department in the 1960s was a vestige of the old machine in desperate need of reform. In previous decades, modernist reformers made efforts to centralize and scientifically manage the department. In the 1960s, however, local modernist city leaders mixed centralized technocratic solutions with a romantic urbanist emphasis on walking the beat, town hall meetings, community control, and participatory democracy. Although often maligned by contemporary critics as an ineffectual sentimentalist, Mayor Lindsay was an example of this hybrid. During the mayoral race, he campaigned as a law-and-order candidate with a call for a "computerized" police department that by "centralizing and modernizing its communications system" would shorten police response time to emergency calls. When in office, Lindsay launched the first centralized police computer system for dispatchers, initiated a universal 911 emergency number, modernized police radios and communication systems, added almost eight hundred new officers, and expanded from 75 to 944 officers the size of the Tactical Patrol Force, an elite commando unit of six-foot-tall, zealous jujitsu experts under direct control of the commissioner.[29]

While Lindsay entered the mayor's office with modernist plans to centralize, professionalize, and computerize an inefficient law enforcement bureaucracy, he was also influenced by the new localist version of urban reform championed by black, Puerto Rican, and white-collar residents of the West Side, Greenwich Village, and Brownstone Brooklyn. Lindsay walked in his shirtsleeves through black and Puerto Rican neighborhoods and attempted to bring the principles of community-based planning and participatory democracy to law enforcement. Before Lindsay, in 1965 the Wagner administration, under pressure from local civic groups, had established precinct community councils where community leaders and precinct captains met to exchange ideas. But when Lindsay added civilian representatives to the Civilian Complaint Review Board in 1966, the issue of community policing became much more explosive.

The Civilian Review Board was the culmination of a decades-long grass-roots police reform movement centered in gentrifying neighborhoods in Brooklyn and Manhattan. The impetus for the change was growing racial tension between police and African American and Latino residents in the city's poorer neighborhoods. In 1953, at the request of a coalition of religious, civic, and civil rights groups, the city had created the Civilian Complaint Review Board, composed of police representatives, to investigate charges of police misconduct. In 1964, after numerous allegations of abuse by police and complaints of inaction by the board from black and Puerto Rican civil rights groups, Theodore Weiss, a Manhattan reform Democrat from the West Side, introduced legislation for an independent nine-member review board run by appointed civilians rather than police department members. Far from a radical proposition, the idea of adding civilian oversight to the review process received widespread support from moderate city leaders. As the Association of the Bar of the City of New York, the American Jewish Committee, and other organizations pushed for civilian representation during the 1965 mayoral campaign, all of the major candidates in the Democratic and Republican primaries endorsed some version of the plan (with the exception of William F. Buckley and maverick Brooklyn Republican Vito Battista). Six months after taking office, Mayor Lindsay, a moderate fusion politician, established a compromise version of the review board, manned by four civilians and three policemen. The board had limited power, with the authority only to make non-binding recommendations to the commissioner after conducting independent reviews of reported police misconduct.[30]

An angry Patrolmen's Benevolent Association (PBA) began a referendum campaign to have the new board abolished. Just as in the teachers' strike, white ethnic municipal union advocates tragically fused a pro-labor stance with the rhetoric of racial backlash. To white ethnic union members, "Lindsay liberals" not only wanted to streamline the labor force, cut salaries, and undermine job security with community control initiatives but also looked the other way as African Americans and Puerto Ricans attacked teachers and police, committed crimes, and verbally abused municipal workers. The result was a pyrrhic victory for municipal labor in New York City. By labeling Lindsay as an anti-police, bleeding-heart "criminal coddler," the PBA was able to rally support to establish itself as a powerful union. But in doing so, it relied on racial rhetoric that alienated a generation of young African Americans and Latinos. PBA law-and-order rhetoric also successfully deflected the public's attention from much-needed administrative reforms and crackdowns on corruption.

Just as they sided with local schools against the teachers' union, brownstoners had little sympathy for the PBA, and they widely supported civilian review of police misconduct. In Brownstone Brooklyn, the local branch of the Liberal party issued petitions in 1964 demanding that the City Council place citizens on the board. During the referendum campaign, middle-class civic groups in Brooklyn Heights, Cobble Hill, and Park Slope rallied to support the beleaguered institution. A week before the referendum, two hundred prominent Heights residents raised money to place an advertisement in local papers. Support for the board transcended the divide between Democratic regulars and reformers. Old machine leaders such as Anthony Scotto, president of the powerful Brooklyn Longshoremen's Union, endorsed the board, along with Abe Lindenbaum, president of the Brooklyn Jewish Community Council, and Kings County Liberal party leader LeRoy Bowman.[31]

In familiar reformist spirit, brownstoner supporters of the Board remained confident that they could allay the fears of white ethnic voters by organizing town hall meetings and open debates free of machine control or bureaucracy. Instead they were shocked to confront a populist conservative insurgency led by their angry neighbors. When in 1966 a brownstoner civic group sponsored a town hall debate between Norman Frank of the Patrolmen's Benevolent Association and Aryeh Neier of the American Civil Liberties Union, two hundred angry residents pushed into the Methodist Hospital auditorium. As Truth About Civil Turmoil (TACT) and the American Patriots for Freedom passed out flyers warning of "ominous left-wing forces," Frank commenced with an attack on the review board. Dragging on a Pall Mall cigarette, Frank described to cheers from the crowd how "Lindsay's board" would make police officers hesitate a "split second" with their finger on the trigger, risking their lives. When Neier began his rebuttal, he struggled to finish the speech over a chorus of boos, catcalls, hoots, and nose thumbing. During the question-and-answer session, the first questioner, Michael Mahoney, angrily questioned the ACLU speaker's "Communist ties." "You are reading from a biased, ugly, non-factual account," stammered a flushed Neier as the audience yelled, "Go back to Russia" and "Lindsay liar."[32]

The leaders of Park Slope's middle-class civic groups were furious. "We go out and sponsor a debate on the Civilian Review Board," fumed the president of the Park Slope Civic Improvement Association. "We obtain the P.B.A.'s best spokesman, Norman Frank, and then we sit there like lace curtain people while the opposition stacks the hall, shouts and bullies anyone who differs from their point of view. Mr. Neier had the grace to give up his time and attend what he thought was going to be an exchange of ideas, and he gets greeted with boos, catcalls, and is called a 'communist.'" The group promised to match the aggressiveness of their opponents, but many worried that convincing their working-class neighbors might be a lost cause. "If Lindsay passed a bill to give free milk to Girl Scouts they would claim he was trying to kill off future Conservatives by putting too much cholesterol in their diets." That November, the referendum passed citywide with overwhelming support from outer-borough white Catholics and working-class Jews. The review board was abolished.[33]

While white ethnic conservatives and leftist brownstoner reformers seemed to be on opposite sides of the political spectrum, their shared populist hostility to city government and calls for decentralization of power led also to unexpected coalitions. In their fight for neighborhood autonomy, brownstoners often supported conservative attacks on bureaucratic programs such as school busing and scattered-site public housing. In 1972, about 150 Brooklyn Heights activists belonging to the area's multiple block associations, civic groups such as the Environmental Coalition and the South Brooklyn Citizens for Local Democracy, and the WBID met for the first Brooklyn Heights Town Meeting, organized by Lorna Salzman, an environmental activist and a veteran of the fight against Cadman Plaza. The participants hoped to form a "Brooklyn Heights Township" with a permanent neighborhood assembly free of city control, made up of local citizens, and dedicated to "democratic self-government." In their newsletter, the *Township*, the new coalition attacked the school pairing of P.S. 7 and P.S. 8 in the Heights and other busing programs and supported calls by black activists in central Brooklyn for community control. At the same time, the newspaper strongly endorsed the battle of white residents of Forest Hills, Queens, to block the opening of a scattered-site public housing project. The low-income project, according to the newspaper, was an example of a "fascist move" by bureaucrats to undermine neighborhood political power. "I have been asked about the paper's political affiliations, explained the editor. "Some said [it] was leaning toward the 'Left,' and others, on the contrary, felt they had detected some very 'Conservative' utterances by some of our writers. . . . We strongly support the Jeffersonian precept of a government of the people, by the people, for the people. We advocate local government, the right of each community to determine what is best for its people."[34]

With an open hostility to centralized bureaucracy and yet a socially liberal outlook and genuine support of minority rights and the fight against poverty, brownstoners espoused a postindustrial version of liberalism that transcended older divisions between left and right. Brownstoners were equally suspicious of "big government," "big labor," and "big business." Rather than conservatives or leftists, the eclectic collection of young Wall Street professionals, media executives, artists, historic preservationists, hippie communalists, and New Left activists were militant localists. "Lindsay liberals" was a misnomer. Instead, Norman Mailer's failed 1969 mayoral run better captured the militant place ideology of brownstoning.

The pugnacious and self-promoting Brooklyn Heights politician certainly was not the typical brownstoner. While on occasion he delivered drunken, profanity-laced speeches, by most accounts Mailer's campaign was sincere, and with Joseph Ferris as his campaign manager he ran on a platform that called for radical decentralization of all political power to local neighborhoods. The first step would be for New York City to secede from New York State. Within the new city-state, local neighborhoods would have complete control over their own services. "Each neighborhood could decide to incorporate itself as a village and use city services if it wants, set up its own services, or mix them any way it wants," he explained to an audience of Brooklyn College students.

Led by an artistic novelist-mayor, the loose confederation of independent urban villages would allow alienated New Yorkers to recapture an authentic sense of community lost in an increasingly technocratic society. "People have lost faith in the experts. . . . Man has created a technical structure and we've lost our sense of intimacy," explained Mailer. "People once had a sense of being better men or lesser men—of what's good and bad. Now our minds are whirling around so we don't know what's good or bad." In defense of local place, Mailer lambasted spatial, institutional, and racial integration. "Each neighborhood would be allowed to forge its own destiny. . . . Every neighborhood should be able to set up their own conditions to live their own life. If whites want to set up a neighborhood and exclude Negroes, that's okay, if blacks want to exclude whites, that's okay, if people want an integrated neighborhood, that's okay."[35]

While Mailer's campaign never took off, the new localist revolt against liberalism also undergirded the politics of the WBID and other reform Democratic groups. Pointing enthusiastically to a "Bobby Kennedy coalition" in 1972, reformers hoped they had begun to tap into white ethnic, African American, and Puerto Rican disenchantment with city politics to forge a new and progressive neighborhood movement. In many ways, however, the reform victory over the regulars was due more to the collapse of the industrial political landscape than to the unity of a new postindustrial coalition. Reform politics, in contrast to machine politics, rallied around inspiring causes, rather than brokering votes from constituents. In the late 1960s and early 1970s, two issues in particular galvanized both the reform and conservative insurgencies and devastated the county machine: the Vietnam War and race.

Starting in the late 1960s, Brownstone Brooklyn became a hotbed of antiwar activism. In Park Slope, white ethnics, African Americans, Puerto Ricans, and brownstoners joined together in several peace marches and rallies in Prospect Park. Young Italian American college students and teenagers in Carroll Gardens began neighborhood organizing against the war. While the WBID and other reform clubs passionately became the antiwar party, "regulars" such as Congressmen Hugh Carey and John Rooney disinterestedly and loyally supported President Johnson. In primary races where low turnout normally helped the machine, Vietnam brought large numbers of independent, antiwar voters to the polls. In response to increasingly close races against antiwar candidates in 1968 and 1970, John Rooney, Hugh Carey, and other old-timers uneasily shifted to moderate opposition of the war. But Vietnam was too divisive for the deal-making style of machine politics. As the militantly antiwar WBID picked off young white ethnics worried about the draft, fence-sitting regulars alienated the large hawkish portion of their base.[36]

Race rather than Vietnam remained the most devastating issue for machine politics. For decades, the regular Democratic party had successfully allayed the political demands of a growing African American and Puerto Rican population by incorporating them into the workings of the machine. But by the late 1960s, racial tension was tearing apart the working class that formed the bedrock of machine support. On one flank, white-collar professional reformers and new black insurgents drew black and Puerto Rican voters away from the machine with their passionate support of civil rights. On the other side, conservative and Republican law-and-order politicians siphoned away white ethnic votes.[37]

The devastating effect of race for regular Democrats first became evident in the two mayoral campaigns of reformer John Lindsay. The victorious Lindsay won a narrow plurality by forming a fusion reform coalition of new machine business and real estate leaders, idealistic students, young urban professionals, African Americans and Puerto Ricans. At the same time, racial tensions tore apart the old machine Democratic party in the outer-borough neighborhoods that formed its base. New Republican and conservative backlash candidates lured white working-class voters from regular clubs by aggressively fueling a growing resentment toward low-income African Americans and white-collar professionals. In 1965, Lindsay was able to win Park Slope only because white ethnics divided their votes between party regular Abraham Beame and the surprisingly powerful Conservative party candidate William F. Buckley. As desperate white regulars turned up the racial rhetoric to curtail the flight of angry blue-collar whites from the party, alienated black voters who had favored Abraham Beame in 1965 turned to Lindsay in 1969. Lindsay again benefited in 1969 when Staten Island Republican state senator John Marci ran on an anti-crime platform and cut heavily into machine candidate Mario Procaccino's base in white Catholic Brooklyn.[38]

In the late 1960s and early 1970s, Brownstone Brooklyn's machine put up stiff resistance to the reform movement, black power, and white backlash, using both hard and soft power to stave off all three insurgencies. In some cases, local leaders resorted to intimidation and violence. In 1971, a group of college-educated Italian American activists and brownstone pioneers in Carroll Gardens worried about the limited appeal of the WBID opened up a storefront Independent Democrat organization with the goal of pushing southward into the largely Italian American district. Criticizing the links between local machine regulars and organized crime, the Independent Democrats announced plans to "serve the community by providing to the people the help that has long been lacking." A week before the inaugural party, in the early hours of morning, the storefront was bombed. Many suspected the act was linked to organized crime. "I don't know why they picked us," Independent Democrat Joseph Bruno told local papers carefully, without naming any suspects. "We represent change. Maybe that's it."[39]

But more often regular Democrats tried to use soft power to undermine reform efforts or assimilate the movement into the workings of the machine. The county organization led by Meade Esposito engineered a complex array of redistricting throughout the 1960s and 1970s to try to divide up reformist enclaves. Regulars also impeded reform campaigns by challenging voter registration drives in local courts, where, to the frustration of young activists, machine-appointed judges routinely rejected lists of new voters on technicalities. The threats of criminal prosecution also successfully intimidated working-class residents from supporting insurgents. In other cases, regular clubs lured insurgent politicians to the machine with promises of patronage posts or campaign support. To the chagrin of the WBID, Brooklyn Heights millionaire maverick and onetime reformer Fred Richmond became a John Rooney loyalist in 1972 after nearly beating him four years earlier. Other machine politicians reluctantly tried to adopt the militant rhetoric of their challengers. When community protests in Carroll Gardens against development projects neared victory, complained Michael Pesce in 1972, local machine politicians often joined activists at the last minute to take credit. Other machine politicians such as Vander Beatty and Shirley Chisholm skillfully adopted the cathartic protest rhetoric of militant reformers while remaining loyal to the regular Democratic organization.[40]

Regular clubs also maneuvered to take control of new councils, school boards, "little city halls," and anti-poverty agencies created by city decentralization initiatives. When Park Slope brownstoners and conservative insurgents both battled to get representatives on a new precinct community council, for example, local regulars initially outmaneuvered them. In 1967, the 78th Precinct Community Council held an election for a board of directors. The meetings deteriorated into shouting matches between old-timers, conservatives, and young professionals. "The two hours of combat were even more like a scene from a wild west movie," a local newspaper commented. "The place was jammed . . . pretty close to 500 in attendance." Leading the brownstoner slate was Ethel Owens, a white humanities professor, community activist, and wife of Major Owens, who claimed to represent "the new democracy—of the little people, little property owners." The "old-timers" belonged to the local machine.

"The political bosses (who I will continue to identify in rather mysterious terms)," explained a frustrated brownstoner, "began to experience castration fears, having misinterpreted the aims of the 'new group' as power aspirations rather than policy aspirations." As the presiding chair intentionally interrupted brownstoners' speeches with his gavel and procedural objections, machine leaders mobilized hundreds of local constituents to pack the house and vote them onto the board. Many brownstoners in attendance were dismayed. "As part of the 'new group,'" complained Bernard Strassberg. "I am constantly dismayed to find politics immersed and firmly entrenched in every aspect of this community. A simple request or action of any kind sets on the merry-go-round of the inner workings of the local politicos. A desire to improve a section of this city by means of community action by any group of people should be encouraged by long time residents, as being motivated for a common goal." Another brownstoner grumbled that "the political factions by prearranged manipulations, gathered together their chief cohorts to act as 'Judas Sheep,' leading their friends and neighbors to vote, even if they knew nothing of what they were voting for." By the late 1970s, however, white-collar brownstoners had successfully taken control of Park Slope's 72nd and 78th precinct councils.[41]

But if the machine maintained power by co-opting some of the themes of reform, the "Bobby Kennedy coalition" came together best when reform candidates borrowed the political techniques of regulars. When idealistic middle-class brownstoners or well-recognized national activists swooped into poorer neighborhoods to lead passionate issue-based campaigns, they often lost the working-class vote. When national civil rights figure James Farmer moved to Brooklyn to run in a 1968 congressional race, a scrappy Shirley Chisholm surprisingly walloped him by emphasizing his outsider status, relying on a network of regular clubs to turn out loyal voters, and mobilizing local black women. When Brooklyn reform Democrats invited the famous antiwar and civil rights activist Allard Lowenstein to challenge the aging and seemingly vulnerable congressman John Rooney in 1972, Lowenstein similarly suffered a devastating loss.

Although he was not from the area, Lowenstein was a product of the new politics and was confident that he could eschew cynical politics and tap into a deep yearning for social change. While some advised him to concentrate on his Brooklyn Heights brownstoner base, Lowenstein hoped to appeal openly and honestly to the African American, Hasidic, Puerto Rican, Italian, and Polish communities included in the congressional district. A cadre of young, enthusiastic college students from around the country volunteered for the cause and flooded the area, handing out flyers, manning new storefronts, and conducting door-to-door registration campaigns. Lowenstein himself moved into an all-black section of Fort Greene and organized kaffeklatsch meetings with community leaders throughout the area.[42]

John Rooney, on the other hand, hardly campaigned and relied on local club leaders to mobilize loyal voters. Dismissing Lowenstein as a "liberal boid" flying in from Manhattan, Rooney painted a portrait of a condescending outsider invading ethnic neighborhoods he knew little about. Many locals agreed. While Rooney rallied a base of loyal white ethnics, Lowenstein clumsily angered everyone. While his inspirational speeches galvanized college student volunteers and brownstoners, he was less adept at Brooklyn realpolitik. Black community leaders didn't trust him. Hasidic Jews resented his "shiksa wife." Catholics hated him because he was Jewish. Lowenstein's choice to live in Fort Greene signaled to white ethnics that he was on "the side of the blacks." Even the Grassroots Independent Democrats, a small and primarily African American and Puerto Rican reform club, became frustrated that his soaring rhetoric was disrupting their delicate efforts to build ties with local Italian clubs and white ethnic senior citizens groups and withdrew support. On election day, Lowenstein's idealism was no match for Rooney's veteran machine. Long lines of Lowenstein's supporters waited helplessly as dozens of voting machines mysteriously broke down in Brooklyn Heights and pro-Lowenstein districts. Brownstoners couldn't find where to vote when voting stations were moved to unmarked buildings at the last minute. After years of going to the polls, black and Puerto Rican voters were turned away because of technicalities with identification cards. Rooney edged out a furious Lowenstein, who, against advice, got a court order demanding a runoff. With no presidential ticket to boost turnout, Rooney mobilized his local cohorts and beat a crestfallen Lowenstein by an even greater margin months later.[43]

Brownstone Brooklyn's reform movement was more successful when it turned to homegrown ethnic activists with biracial, bi-ethnic, or bi-class appeal. Young, college-educated veterans of community action programs in particular had enough cultural capital to speak fluently in the language of the new politics and gain the support of young urban professionals. At the same time, by virtue of their ethnicity and neighborhood ties, they could attract working-class ethnics who would normally vote for the machine. Carroll Gardens' Michael Pesce, for example, was a Legal Aid lawyer and passionate reformer who was also a neighborhood-raised first-generation Italian immigrant from the town of Mola and the son of a longshoreman. While his antiwar stance appealed to brownstoners, he won by also relying on a local immigrant clubhouse to bring out a strong Molese vote to protectively support one of their own. A few years later, Joe Ferris in Park Slope also formed a similar bridge between middle-class brownstoners and the area's Irish working class.[44]

Brownstoners hoped that that this cadre of young activists would translate middle-class reform politics to apathetic working-class African Americans, Puerto Ricans, and white ethnics. Reform groups in Brooklyn and Manhattan provided candidates with outside political support and adulating press coverage. When running for office, Buddy Scotto received visits from Norman Mailer and "Eleanor Roosevelt types" from Manhattan, and both he and Ferris were the subjects of enthusiastic articles by the *Village Voice*. (Scotto, explained the *Voice*, was the "Zapata of the waterfront," Ferris the "Irish Johnny Appleseed.") While they welcomed the support, some reformers became frustrated that they were being placed in the role of liaison between middle-class reformers and hostile natives. "They proceed to identify us as 'ethnic leaders' and assign us the job of selling their platforms and their candidates to our 'people,'" grumbled Pesce.[45]

Ethnic reformers often strategically balanced two distinct types of politics. Brownstoners were thrilled that Ferris, for example, was a passionate advocate for environmental issues in Albany. At home, however, they were dismayed that he operated an old-fashioned clubhouse that concentrated more concretely on the efficient delivery of services to his poorer constituents. In one case, he helped an elderly woman who upon applying for her first passport to visit Poland discovered she had never become a U.S. citizen. (Ferris went to the Ellis Island archives to dig up the passenger manifest of the ship she arrived on.) Some disillusioned brownstoners began to refer to him dismissively as a "pothole politician." But ethnic reformers countered that middle-class activists were solely concerned with abstract issues and were oblivious to, if not dismissive of, the material needs of their neighbors. "Much of the reform movement in New York has been turned on by ideological, philosophical questions," explained Pesce of his efforts to forge a "blue-collar reform movement." "And the chic reformers never related the war to the home issues–the bread and butter issues of jobs, pensions and crime. The working man, the neighborhood guy, has been hit hardest by the war." By the 1980s, in a familiar pattern, brownstoners grumbled that Brooklyn's black and white ethnic reformers once again had become "regulars."[46]

Blue-collar white ethnics remained a minority of reformers. At the core of the "Bobby Kennedy coalition" and the neighborhood movement was a tenuous relationship between the two postindustrial migrant groups of white brownstoners and the nonwhite working class and poor. Here also was the greatest tension. While at times gentrifying whites and poorer black and Puerto Ricans had common interests, the competition for the same Victorian landscape also led to conflict.

When brownstoners started new block associations and neighborhood improvement groups, many did so with the goal of fighting bureaucracy for poor and wealthy residents alike. But as they renovated townhouses and planted trees, some began to notice uncomfortably that block association meetings had few black or brown faces. In 1975, the United Block Association of Park Slope conducted a study of the forty-one block associations in the area. Seventy-three percent of members interviewed were white, with a median education of sixteen years, and 85 percent of those employed had white-collar professions. Sixty-nine percent were homeowners who had lived on the blocks for a median of only three and a half years. Association activists talked of reviving a Jacobsian sense of community that thrived on short street blocks. But they had trouble attracting poorer residents to participate in their "street ballet." The paradox was one that brownstoners continually struggled with.[47]

A few block associations tried to recruit poorer renters. When a group of white professionals in 1969 migrated below Seventh Avenue into a nonwhite section of Park Slope, for example, the Berkeley Place Block Association (BPA) offered them trees, discount gaslights, and some brochures on home renovation. "Shortly after the expansion [however] this self-satisfaction began to curdle," explained a dismayed organizer. "The two and a half blocks covered are racially mixed with whites, Negroes, and Puerto Ricans, yet meetings continued to be almost entirely white." The Berkeley Place Association developed a campaign to knock on doors of poorer tenants and organized a carnival on the new block with booths, a rock band, and a "nutty little play" by resident

Claire Labine, a writer for the television soap opera *Ryan's Hope*. Not surprisingly, few nonwhites attended. "Unsuspected ills of the urban psyche were uncovered: animosity, fear, timidity, suspicion," concluded one the organizers. "Clearly the BPA would have to do more than make itself available; it would have to change its whole approach to doing business, perhaps even its idea of what its business was."[48]

Although native landlords and property owners were often boosters of the brownstone revitalization movement, tensions at times emerged between old and new homeowners as well. While brownstoners celebrated the local color of ethnic enclaves, they felt less enthusiastic about the paint and ornaments working-class residents added to the exteriors of buildings. Groups such as the Carroll Gardens Brownstoners and the Society for Clinton Hill formed to pressure locals to stop altering the surfaces of their buildings. As they sent pamphlets, organized home tours, and gave talks to older residents, brownstoners drew upon the populist language of the social movements of the 1960s and 1970s to inspire their efforts to impose their standards of taste on working-class residents. "The consciousness raising of Clinton Hill homeowners will protect them from their neighbors," explained a real estate broker. "People will not be able to install aluminum sidings over their historic facades or paint their brownstones chartreuse."[49]

Brownstoner efforts to revive retail areas also led in some instances to conflicts with poorer residents. In some cases, black and Latino residents relied on the low-end retail stores that renovators saw as a sign of blight. In other cases, brownstoners attacked large corporate chain stores that poorer residents relied upon for cheap goods and jobs. When reform leaders joined with local businessmen and potentially displaced tenants to fight supermarkets from opening in Cobble Hill and Park Slope, low-income minorities in neighboring areas objected. Brownstone Brooklyn's black and Latino residents were not averse to confronting local retail establishments. A group of African American activists in Fort Greene, for example, led a successful community boycott of the Myrtle Avenue A&P in the 1960s after a local guard shot a resident during an argument about a bag of potatoes. (The A&P replaced the managerial crew with a predominately African American one.) African American and Latino activists, however, often protested for more jobs in bigger and better-stocked supermarkets. Brownstoners instead hoped to protect small independent shops on struggling retail thoroughfares such as Fifth Avenue. Pathmark and other large chain stores, they argued, destroyed the healthy diversity of the area, displaced local tenants and small businesses, and created anomie. For poorer residents in public housing, supermarkets provided more jobs and affordable produce than mom-and-pop grocery stores.[50]

Nowhere were race and class tensions about retail more evident than in the battles over fast-food joints. When brownstoner civic groups in the 1970s launched a series of campaigns to block the opening of chain restaurants along Atlantic, Fifth, and Seventh avenues, they did so sincerely to protect mom-and-pop shops from corporate power. In 1974 when Burger King announced plans to open a new restaurant on Montague Street in Brooklyn Heights, the proposal sparked the largest community protest in the area since the fight over Cadman Plaza. Angry Heights residents wearing "Whopper Stopper" T-shirts picketed the corporation's Manhattan office, issued petitions, and lobbied the Landmarks Preservation Commission to block the project. The architecture of the restaurant was not the issue, though. Working with an architect and the Landmarks Preservation Commission, the franchisee, Morris Bailey, planned to retain the historic facade of the original 1925 building. Instead, Heights residents pointed to the fast-food joint as the encroachment of an alienating corporate landscape onto a diverse and organic landscape. "I am violently against the establishment of a Burger King on Montague Street," explained one protester. "The littering and loitering will destroy the quaintness and quietness that has made the Heights a haven from the impersonalized city. The easy, almost European flavor, is being destroyed by the hustle of super-junk and saw-dust burgers."

But the protests soon took on a more uncomfortable theme. Because of its bureaucratic ambience, Burger King would attract "undesirables" from the neighboring Civic Center. "Purse-snatchers, muggers, and criminals use these outlets as a base of operation," complained one protester. "BURGER KING! Everywhere this outfit tries to open in city environs they are met with furious rejection," claimed a pamphlet by a "historic" Montague Street florist established in 1853. "Why? Because they attract a type of customer and condition which generates filth, litter and hanging out which soon turns the area into a slum." Compared to the "lovely small shops" of Montague Street, the pamphlet exhorted, Burger King had "big store coldness" and an "indifferent anonymity." "This kind of 'food' factory will become a magnet attracting all the sad, sick human debris," it concluded. "[We] are on the razor's edge of destruction. You know how tenuous is the balance that tips a neighborhood onto a downward path."[51]

The racially charged attacks on fast-food customers made some Heights residents uneasy. "The Burger King issue strikes some people as showing racist or too exclusivist overtones," wrote one to the *Heights Press*. "Beneath all the rationalizations, what people really fear may be the 'other element' coming in. . . . So we have banded together. . . . We call ourselves the Committee Against Racism and Elitism in Brooklyn Heights." With many members wary of the race and class overtones of some the protests, a divided WBID could not agree on a position. "If the WBID wishes to maintain its good relations with the Heights community," complained *Heights Press* columnist Bob Side in 1974, "then it should cease being scared stiff of the possibility that passing a resolution in defense of our neighborhood might be construed as anti-minority. Fortunately, Carol Bellamy, Michael Pesce, Don Elliot and other Reformers spoke up at Grace Church against Burger King and they haven't been called anti-black."[52]

Brownstoner support of community control of schools also led in some cases to conflict with black and Latino parents. In Park Slope, brownstoner parents who supported school decentralization forged an interracial coalition to demand better services from the Board of Education. In Brooklyn Heights, however, parents used the rhetoric of community empowerment to fight a struggling school integration program. In the mid-1960s, the city paired Brooklyn Heights' P.S. 8 with the largely African American P.S. 7 a few blocks north of the neighborhood. As noted earlier, a vocal group of liberal and dedicated white Heights residents joined with Farragut public housing parents to support the program. For the next ten years, the pairing of P.S. 7 and P.S. 8 became a contentious issue that sharply divided the neighborhood. While the WBID was consistently in favor of the program, the Brooklyn Heights Association and a new group called the Brooklyn Heights Neighborhood School Association was steadfastly against it. Residents in opposition to the pairing cast the debate as a battle against a bureaucratic school system that forced children into large classrooms disconnected from their neighborhoods, with outdated educational techniques and a non-progressive curriculum. "Pairing reinforces the bureaucratic power of the Board of Education and the State Education Commission," explained a former anti-Cadman Plaza activist in 1971. "It insures the subservience of parents and children to bureaucratic interests and mass society. Pairing is racist in concept and practice because instead of recognizing children as individuals, it sees and treats them solely as members of an ethnic group, black or white." (The busing program ended abruptly in 1974 when a mysterious fire burned down P.S. 7.)[53]

The institution that best embodied this localist mix of anti-busing rhetoric and countercultural critiques of technocracy was the new private school St. Ann's. Founded the year after the pairing decision primarily, some argued, for parents seeking to avoid the paired schools, St. Ann's described itself as a progressive refuge for creative children in an increasingly bureaucratic society. The student body represented the "broadest possible spectrum of ethnic and religious groups," explained the headmaster defensively in 1965 when accused of drawing white students away from the integration experiment. "Many of the very parents who vigorously battled for pairing of P.S. 8 left it. Their complaint was not against integration; it was against inadequate education." When one couple moved to Boerum Hill in 1966, for example, they looked for a "flexible and culturally diverse school that wasn't beyond the means of a middle-income family." "There was news of a school just beginning in Brooklyn Heights which, at that time, was not too expensive and which had pity on middle-income families," explained the father of his decision to send his child to the private school. "St. Ann's was small and already had pupils whose parents were the most adventurous of my long-time friends. The school had an optimistic approach and welcome people from every background–the direct opposite of our experience in Westchester. St. Ann's wanted each student to discover his own uniqueness."[54]

Some activists became increasingly cynical about white middle-class support of community control. "The most blatant Southern segregationists, for all their distasteful fanaticism, deserve more respect than their Brooklyn Heights counterparts," charged a Heights resident to the local paper in 1964. "They don't offer hypocritical lip-service to integration, nor do they resort to half-baked psycho-analytical or social rationalizations to conceal their resentment of the nonwhite." "It would control its own schools, police, etc. Sounds great doesn't it?" complained activist group EQUAL in 1971 of the Brooklyn Heights Township. "Contents of the corridors? Brooklyn Heights. Cobble Hill and *Boerum Hill* . . . What is particularly painful is that this kind of 'power to the neighborhoods' is being vigorously promoted by white radicals who fought the good fight for black dignity in Ocean Hill. . . . This is not the first time that strategy of black liberation has been turned inside out for the benefit of whites and detriment of blacks."[55]

The highly localized focus of the neighborhood movement could lead to conflicts that cut across race and class lines as well. When white-collar professionals, small business owners, and poorer residents joined forces against a new development on a particular set of blocks, they sometimes faced opposition from poorer and working-class residents of neighboring areas who looked to the same project as a potential source of employment. When the city in the early 1970s announced plans for a container port along the waterfront adjacent to Cobble Hill and Brooklyn Heights, for example, the acrimonious battle over the project divided Brownstone Brooklyn into industrial and postindustrial camps. In opposition to the container port was the Ad Hoc Committee to Save the Waterfront. Organized by poverty worker Ramon Ruguiera and reform politician Mike Pesce, Save the Waterfront was an eclectic anti-development coalition of environmental activists from the Pratt Institute Center for Community and Environmental Development, the Brooklyn

Heights Association, Heights white-collar professionals eager to block industry from the area, and more than five hundred largely poor Puerto Rican and Italian households threatened with displacement by the new project. Supporting the container port were the International Longshoremen's Association, machine politician John Rooney, and working-class residents of Carroll Gardens and Red Hook desperate to revive the dying shipping industry along Brooklyn's waterfront. Drawing from their powerful academic constituency, the Brooklyn Heights Association and the Pratt Institute presented the city with an alternative plan for a container port in Red Hook. To demonstrate that the waterfront should be a site of green recreation and cultural consumption for local communities rather than industrial production, Save the Waterfront in 1972 organized a romantic urbanist festival on Pier 6 with ethnic food stands, folk music, and a visit from the sloop *Clearwater*. Allard Lowenstein and other reform politicians attended in support. The city compromised and shifted the bulk of the container port south to a more sparsely populated section of Red Hook. On the local level, the neighborhood movement scored a victory that addressed the concerns of environmentalists about pollution, the desire of brownstoners for a recreational waterfront, the search of artists for cheap rents, and the fear of the poor of losing their homes. The regional benefits of limiting shipping activity in the area were more mixed.[56]

Competition for housing, however, remained the greatest area of conflict in Brownstone Brooklyn. As the brownstone revitalization movement expanded in the late 1960s and early 1970s, newspapers began to describe growing tensions between white-collar professionals and nonwhite tenants in neighborhoods such as Manhattan's Upper West Side and Brooklyn's Park Slope. "Many will find themselves trapped in a rapidly escalating, no-holds-barred battle of wills that can last for years, a Kafkaesque nightmare that will cost the new owners thousands of dollars and leave them disillusioned, bitter and guilt-ridden," described the *New York Times* in 1974. "In this drama, the tenant plays The Eternal Loser: he will eventually have to go, usually to less desirable quarters at a considerably higher rent. The buyer-tenant warfare, an unhappy consequence of the largely successful brownstoning movement, is little publicized. But it is much discussed at New York parties where cheerful couples who bought and renovated empty buildings listen uncomfortably to the anguished tales of those who have been caught in the quagmire of eviction."[57]

Some battles between brownstoners and poorer tenants were nasty. In one case, a brownstoner bought a rooming house and strategically didn't collect rent from her eighteen tenants for six months. Knowing the low-income tenants would not be able to pay, she then demanded back rent and evicted them. Tenants responded by stuffing the toilets with paper towels and throwing bottles out of the windows. In another brownstone bought by a middle-class couple, three tenant families filed with the city to fight eviction and refused to let the couple in to begin renovation. After a year, the tenants left but broke all the windows in protest. "In the war game known as owner versus tenant, both are losers," lamented the *Brownstoner*. "The tenants will, in the end, have to go. And it usually a bitter victory for the owner."[58]

But brownstoning was a conflicted movement that struggled with its own inner contradictions. As they evicted residents, socially liberal brownstoners were often, ironically, the most strident critics of the displacement of the poor. The result was a series of increasingly heated exchanges within the movement. In March 1967, Diana Foster, a Brooklyn Heights interior decorator and antique store owner, wrote an angry column to the *Brooklyn Heights Press* entitled "Protecting the Perimeter." She fretted that the fledgling brownstone settlements surrounding Brooklyn Heights were under threat by rising crime. "There are a great deal of rooming-houses in, to name one place, Boerum Hill. Unfortunately, many of these places house dope addicts and other criminals. . . . I have heard, year after year, of the 'bad' run down neighborhoods. . . . But common sense and facts, are important. First of all, the 'houses' didn't dirty, or 'desecrate' themselves. Only people can chip off plaster, write on walls, throw garbage in the halls and let water overflow causing ruin. Trash, black or white, ruin property. . . . Minorities don't want trash, black or white, for neighbors either."

Foster assured readers that there was hope. Although now a trendy white enclave, Brooklyn Heights had once been a dangerous frontier. "When I first moved to Brooklyn Heights, about 25 years ago, even streets like Willow St. and Columbia Heights, which are supposed to be in our 'best' neighborhood, housed many rooming houses, just as bad as some of the places we now look on with horror, as slum neighborhoods," Foster assured. "Year by year, these places have been eliminated. Personally, I renovated over twenty houses, here in the Heights, many of which were really run down rooming houses, and made them into places where people were proud to live." Just as a new middle class had "rescued" Brooklyn Heights years earlier, so now could ambitious settlers revive and fortify new neighborhoods deeper in the urban periphery. "There are other territories that can be made just as beautiful, and most important, that it is necessary for these close localities surrounding us, to improve . . . Cobble Hill has 'Come-Up' greatly in the past few years. It is my belief that Boerum Hill has even greater potential."

Foster concluded with a battle cry for young brownstoners. "What I'm trying to do, is to get some of our young people, who cannot afford the high prices of Heights homes, but who want city town houses, to get up enough 'guts' to move into these beautiful town houses, because that is what they once were, and will be again, and push out all the undesirables. It can be done, and more importantly, it can be done much easier, and much cheaper, than people think. I'll be here, in my Antique Shop at 62 Hicks St., every Saturday and Sunday, from noon to five o-clock, to help anyone who wants, and needs, advice to get their own home, in the future 'Historical Boerum Hill Beautiful.'"[59]

The Boerum Hill Association was mortified. "The idea of protecting a perimeter in an urban environment smacks of setting up machine-gun emplacements along Court Street," wrote association president David Preiss in a response entitled "Perfecting the Perimeter." "'Pushing back the undesirable' ghetto elements, as Miss Foster proposes, is neither very kindly nor smart. It is the solution proposed by the monkey who decided he would see no evil. We propose to work with the people in this community, undesirable or otherwise." In an angry letter, Boerum Hill brownstoner Daniel Icolari was more direct. "Miss Foster's aggressive, unabashedly chauvinistic remarks such as 'We've been kind to these people too long' smack of the kind of bulldozing racist tactics we newer Boerum Hill residents are deeply committed against. We want to retain the truly integrated, multi-class status our community enjoys, rather than ascribe these problems to a group or groups of people, and banish these people from our community."[60]

The association instead tried draw on the language of the new politics to affirm the ties between brownstoning and a broader social movement against bureaucracy. The blame for Boerum Hill's poor conditions, argued David Preiss, should be pointed not at rooming house residents but at the old machine of crony slumlords and the new machine of indifferent city hall bureaucrats. "The matter of blockfront beauty is a concern that has less to do with tenants than it does with absentee landlords and the Department of Sanitation, the police, and the Traffic Department. For instance, on our block of State St., from Nevins east to YWCA, there are no posted parking regulations. On the other blocks, which have signs posted, parking regulations are not enforced by the police—and the police are themselves the greatest violators of parking regulations on State St., near the courthouse. The Sanitation supervisors shrug that they can't clean the streets under these conditions, but they don't issue summonses to landlords, either, when refuse is piled high in front patios for weeks on end. And landlords are responsible for peeling paint. . . . If residents of the Heights are really worried about protecting their perimeters, they might concentrate first on Cadman Plaza. I find it ugly."

The mixed intentions of brownstoning permeated popular culture as well. The earliest brownstoner television show was the Brooklyn Heights–based

Patty Duke Show in the mid-1960s. By the late 1960s and early 1970s, however, a bevy of new back-to-the city movies, television shows, and novels announced the arrival of a white-collar labor force searching for social liberation in reno-vated center-city apartments and nineteenth-century homes. Some sitcoms, such as *Mary Tyler Moore* and *One Day at a Time*, presented a benign relation-ship between new urban professionals and quirky ethnics who already lived there. In Brooklyn-based *Welcome Back Kotter*, a countercultural teacher returned to his old neighborhood in Brooklyn to fight school bureaucracy on behalf of an appreciative and harmless collection of white ethnic, Puerto Rican, and African American gang members. Roman Polanski's horror film *Rosemary's Baby* (1968), however, hinted at deeper tension between young new arrivals and older tenants.

By the early 1970s, brownstoner urban discovery narratives began to change. A new genre of Brooklyn local-color writing expressed a deeply embit-tered and ambivalent version of Jane Jacobs' Hudson Street. Brownstoner writing retained romantic urbanist motifs but increasingly infused them with discussions of class and race tension, poverty, anger and guilt. Where Jane Jacobs and Herbert Gans ingenuously described a white ethnic neighborhood gemeinschaft, a new generation struggled to reconcile their desire for historic diversity with an antipathy for the urban nonwhite poor. Written from the perspective of brownstoners, the works captured the growing tensions in a restructuring city that was growing both poorer and wealthier, both ghetto-ized and yuppified, as the industrial landscape declined and a new white-collar postindustrial landscape expanded.

Brooklyn-based novels such as Paula Fox's *Desperate Characters* and L. J. Davis's *A Meaningful Life* or Hal Ashby's 1970 film *The Landlord* turned the urban discovery narrative on its head. Rather than new arrivals discovering an oasis of neighborhood place in a frightening urban wilderness, the protago-nists pushed out from Manhattan with a coherent vision of Brooklyn's Jacob-sian urban villages created by hip magazines, young real estate brokers, and residents of revitalized neighborhoods. The dramatic moment in the narrative was the discovery not of place but of non-place, as the urban explorers realize to their dismay that the "urban village" was in fact a slum, that their renova-tions required the eviction of the nonwhite poor, and that the locals appeared angry and menacing. In some cases, the writers simply reworked their roman-tic urban vision to include the nonwhite urban poor as a new set of quirky local color characters. But more often, the new gentrification literature was infused with a sense of irony or a dashed romanticism.[61]

Brownstone Brooklyn in the 1960s and 1970s, thus, offers a complicated picture of the early politics of gentrification. Rather than simply engaging in a battle between gentrifiers and the gentrified, brownstoners and poorer residents formed coalitions to fight development projects, protect rent control, and decentralize city bureaucracy. In electoral politics, new middle-class residents forged political alliances with white ethnic, African American, and Puerto Rican residents to win victories for an emerging reform wing of the Democratic party. At the same time, these groups engaged in contentious battles over housing and political control over neighborhood institutions.

Brownstone Brooklyn also presents a political narrative of the late 1960s and 1970s different from the one usually recounted by historians. Rather than simply the collapse of New Deal liberalism and rise of conservatism, Brownstone Brooklyn saw the emergence of a new and dynamic type of localist politics that was both anti-statist and anti-corporatist, and which emphasized neighborhood autonomy, private rehabilitation of existing housing stock, devolution of municipal services to community nonprofit groups, miniplanning, ethnic power, and bootstrap do-it-yourselfism. As the 1970s came to a close and the city emerged from fiscal crisis, however, the direction this new localism would take was unclear. Did the neighborhood movement have an agenda beyond stopping development projects and dismantling bureaucracy? Or was it simply an anti-regime? Could Brooklyn's anti-growth coalition of angry white ethnics, black power insurgents, Puerto Rican activists, and white-collar countercultural brownstoners transform into a new, vibrant form of postindustrial liberalism? Or would the emphasis on local control, self-help, and private market solutions to housing development evolve into an anti-statist neoliberalism? Or were they two sides of the same coin?[62]

Conclusion: Brownstone Brooklyn Invented

In 1983, a young filmmaker released the first "anti-gentrification" documentary about Park Slope. *Where Can I Live?* described an emerging battle between low-income tenants and landlords on Thirteenth Street between Seventh and Eighth avenues. In 1982, a developer converted the vacant Ansonia Clock Factory to luxury cooperatives on the corner of Seventh Avenue, setting off a wave of speculation in the area. The Slope South Realty Development Association soon bought eight low-rent buildings next to the factory with the hopes of warehousing them until they could convert them to cooperatives. As six apartment buildings sat boarded up, the largely Puerto Rican and African American tenants in two remaining tenements complained that landlords were pressuring them to leave with menacing threats, arson, reduced services, sabotage of facilities, and even occasional violence. An interracial coalition aided by two young brownstoners who recently moved to the block publicized their struggle in local newspapers, lobbied for help from South Brooklyn Legal Services, organized a march, and held a block party to unify tenants. "We see it like an invasion. Because that's what it is," complained community activist Ibon Muhammad. "They've come along like some invading army and just took over."[1]

Park Slope activists were not the only activists mobilizing to fight gentrification in the late 1970s. The term was originally coined by a London sociologist in 1964, but American sociologists loosely adopted it at the end of the seventies to describe a growing back-to-the-city movement and beginnings of downtown revival in many American cities. Newspapers soon used the term in quotation marks to describe optimistically what seemed to be a surprising reversal of decades of white flight and economic decline for American cities. "Hard as it is to believe, however, New York and other cities in the American Northeast are beginning to enjoy a revival as they undergo a gradual process known by the curious name of 'gentrification,'" explained the *New York Times* in 1979. "Have the nation's older cities really regained their health?" asked the *Washington Post* that same year. "One could conclude as much from all the tales of an 'urban renaissance' and surges of middle-class investment in formerly rundown neighborhoods—a process that has produced the new mouthful word 'gentrification.'" As reports of evictions and harassment spread, however, newspapers and protesters soon began to use the term to specifically describe the displacement of low-income, predominantly non-white tenants in townhouse and tenement districts surrounding the central business districts of revitalizing cities. Some newspapers described a specific type of racial neighborhood transition that seemed the mirror image of white flight. "Whites are taking back Black neighborhoods," complained *Ebony* in 1978 about gentrification in cities from San Francisco to Atlanta.[2]

The charge of gentrification sent shock waves through Brownstone Brooklyn. Once lionized for rehabilitating neighborhoods and fighting city hall, brownstoners found themselves cast as villains. Many veterans of the fight against urban renewal became defensive. "The people attempting to revitalize our cities' declining neighborhoods have long faced several natural enemies: negligent city agencies, indifferent or conflict-ridden legislators, and extreme political groups," complained the *Brownstoner* in 1978. "But now comes opposition from a new quarter. The sociologists, whose past recommendations to politicians helped lay waste our urban landscapes, have invented a new field of study. . . . It is termed gentrification." "Good news? You would think so. But many people do not think so. Invoking that dread term of urban affairs, they say it is 'gentrification,'" sarcastically complained William H. Whyte, one of the founding fathers of the anti-renewal movement. "There is not a conference on city problems that does not ring with protestations of guilt over gentrification. Shame on us for what we have done. What displacement?"[3]

Whether called gentrification or brownstoning, however, all could agree that Brownstone Brooklyn began to dramatically change after 1977. As it emerged from near bankruptcy, New York City began a dramatic economic revival. "Whatever happened to urban crisis?" asked T. D. Allman in a 1978 *Harper's* article about the unexpected downtown boom of New York City and other cities around the country. While manufacturing continued its steady decline, Manhattan's service economy dramatically expanded, with employment rising annually for a decade. From 1977 to 1989, corporate services such as legal and consulting firms, advertising, and investment banking added 271,000 jobs. Private health, education, and social services added 527,000 jobs. Entertainment, tourism, and culture industries added another 68,000.[4]

New York City's emergence as a white-collar city both benefited from and fueled Manhattan and Brooklyn's brownstoning movement. Expanding firms brought to the city a new wave of postindustrial workers who migrated to Brownstone Brooklyn's enclaves eager to search for affordable rentals, buy cooperatives, renovate townhouses, and start new neighborhood groups. But more unexpectedly, the 1960s neighborhood revolt had created fertile soil for the flowering of the 1980s corporate landscape. In their search for anti-bureaucratic authenticity in the inner city, brownstoners acted as pioneers for the bureaucratic institutions they reviled. Boosters excitedly pointed to the rebirth of Brooklyn's neighborhoods. New corporate services firms moved to the center city to tap a growing pool of educated and cosmopolitan workers. Expensive chain stores looked to open in areas with rising incomes. Risk-averse developers found safe, improving areas to convert older buildings into new condominiums.

As New York City experienced a real estate boom after 1977, brownstoning transformed from the plucky and beleaguered grassroots movement of the 1960s. Where once renovators had to cajole reluctant banks and insurance companies to invest their enclaves, Brownstone Brooklyn was now awash in speculation. During the abandonment crisis, housing activists had pressured the city to offer incentives for low-income residents to engage in homesteading projects and conversion of empty buildings to co-ops. Now luxury apartment developers used those same programs to create high-priced co-ops. Park Slope, for example, saw a dramatic surge in co-op conversions after 1977. In the years from 1977 to 1984, 130 buildings, or over 7.5 percent of the area's housing stock, were converted to co-ops. In 1974, after a decade of brownstoning, the price of a one-family home in Park Slope had risen to 16 percent higher than the borough average. By 1981, however, the number had skyrocketed to 100 percent higher. The average sales price for a two-family house rose from 8 percent lower than the borough average in 1974 to 56 percent higher in 1981. Rents also rose dramatically, from 6 percent lower than the borough average to 8 percent higher. According to a 1983 Regional Plan Association report, every neighborhood in the area saw a drop in low-rent and moderate-rent units from 1970 to 1980. While Park Slope had 40 percent fewer, Cobble Hill, Carroll Gardens, Boerum Hill, and Prospect Heights lost 50 percent of their low-rent units. At the same time, medium- and high-rent units grew by 36 percent and 38 percent, respectively, in the area. One Park Slope real estate agent even received calls from foreign investors eager to buy buildings sight unseen with hopes of flipping them for profit.[5]

The late 1970s and early 1980s were particularly difficult for the poor. Before housing activists successfully lobbied the city to reform J-51 and other co-op conversion laws in the mid-1980s, speculators and landlords in Brownstone Brooklyn and Manhattan evicted tenants, warehoused rent-stabilized buildings, reduced services, and in some cases committed arson to free older structures for higher-income tenants. In the most extreme cases, former residents of rooming houses and other single-room-occupancy units became homeless. Because of the efforts of housing activists, the city in the mid-1980s corrected many of the abuses of city rehabilitation programs. Yet even with protective legislation, complaints about displacement grew throughout the decade.[6]

As rents and home prices skyrocketed in Brownstone Brooklyn and low-income residents lobbied for affordable housing and anti-displacement legislation, the fragile neighborhood coalition between white-collar professional improvement groups, incumbent upgraders, and poorer renters began to crumble. New anti-gentrification coalitions of low-income tenants, poverty workers, artists eager to preserve cheap rents, bohemians searching for authenticity, and concerned white-collar professionals protested home tours, organized marches, and lobbied the city for protection against evictions. In response to the new attacks, many brownstoners who were once staunch McGovernites defensively turned to the right. Some organized new conservative pro-gentrification groups, such as the Park Slope Action Democrats, that championed the free market and pilloried any sort of government regulation of the housing market. Other improvement groups began to split into hostile factions in support of and against the brownstoning movement. The rhetoric was heated, with groups accusing one another of being "fascists," "reactionaries," "extremists," "racists," "an apartheid regime," and "radical chic." "The Voice of the New Politics . . . Protecting the values of the brownstone movement: individual enterprise, freedom of expression, and neighborhood self-help. These values rebuilt Park Slope," argued a Park Slope Action Democrats pamphlet expressing the new conservative version of the area's once countercultural "new politics." "That's why we are so opposed to the reactionaries who want to keep the middle class out of Park Slope. They want to destroy the spontaneity and creativity that makes Park Slope special. Already these extremists have harassed house tours and citizen patrols. They've stopped vital development of abandoned buildings. And they've captured the hearts and minds of elected officials."[7]

In Boerum Hill, brownstoning similarly took on an angry tone. White-collar residents who once moved to Brooklyn as an outgrowth of the counterculture and environmentalist movements began in the late 1970s to launch vituperative attacks on their low-income neighbors. In 1978, for example, the Urban Development Corporation finally began to develop new plans for the long-languishing Pacific-Schermerhorn urban renewal site. On the largest parcel, the UDC approved a plan by private developer Cauldwell-Wingate for market-rate, unsubsidized apartments. On the two other parcels, the Gowanus–Boerum Hill Housing Association, an advocacy group founded by two local settlement houses, was given approval to put up low-rise, low-income Section 8 housing for residents displaced by gentrification in the area. When news reached Boerum Hill of the new plan, a group of brownstoners formed the Neighborhood Action Coalition to lobby for only middle-income units. "The GBHHA is a group of 12 middle-class citizens suffering from the strain of left-wing fantasies left over from the era of radical chic," charged one member, in the spirit of the new brownstoner conservatism. "Their group is not in any way connected to or supported by the Boerum Hill Association." "Before the brownstoners came, there were transients here—we're turning it around, why don't they just leave us alone?" complained another resident. "Why invest government money where private dollars are working?" "Yes I'm concerned with the people who've left. But, why when middle-class people move out of an area, is it called 'market force' and when the poor move, it's called 'racism'?" complained a brownstoner and owner of a fabric-dyeing store on Atlantic Avenue called the Melting Pot.[8]

No figure better represented the new brownstone conservatism than former Greenwich Village reformer Ed Koch. By the late 1970s, the neighborhood movement in cities throughout the country began to elect an eclectic array of reform mayors ranging from Marion Barry and Dennis Kucinich to Ray Flynn and Buddy Cianci. Elected mayor in 1977 by a mix of young urban professional reformers in Manhattan and Brooklyn, outer-borough white ethnics, gay voters, business and real estate leaders, and black middle-class incumbent upgraders, Koch stitched together many of the localist wings of the 1970s neighborhood movement into a new conservative coalition. His housing policy was an outgrowth of brownstoning that emphasized the private reha-bilitation of in rem housing, the devolution of low-income housing develop-ment to Saul Alinsky–inspired nonprofit groups, and an emphasis on encouraging homeownership among the poor. He also reveled in ethnic kitsch and cultivated a folksy image of a neighborhood New Yorker. At the same time, by attacking "poverty pimps" and black leaders in central Brooklyn and Harlem, he rhetorically tapped into the angry neighborhoodist language of white ethnic backlash. In an angry version of back-to-the-city romantic ur-banism, Koch was a reformer who hoped to reverse what the "city was be-coming" and instead "take the city back"—back to a pastoral white ethnic industrial city before the racial transition of the 1960s and 1970s. Koch cele-brated the most progressive vision of Jane Jacobs' street ballet. He also located in her Hudson Street an older and angrier theme of American romanticism: racial fall and redemption.[9]

Rather than becoming either pro- or anti-gentrification activists, however, most Brownstone Brooklyn residents—rich and poor, black, white, and Latino—remained much more ambivalent about the changing landscape. The anti-gentrification movement was not simply pointing to an affordable housing issue but also challenging the fundamental principles of brownston-ing itself. Residents of Park Slope, Cobble Hill, Brooklyn Heights, and Fort Greene in the late 1970s began an agonizing debate that would last for decades. The word *brownstoning* evoked a search for a sense of place in the central city. *Gentrification*, however, suggested that the project was actually one of displacement. Brownstone Brooklyn's neighborhoods were increas-ingly vibrant and prosperous, as well as islands of political tolerance for diverse lifestyles. But the anti-gentrification movement was growing precisely in these neighborhoods that had birthed the counterculture, reform Democratic, and antiwar movements and led the interracial revolt against urban renewal and expressways in the 1960s and early 1970s: Brownstone Brooklyn, Atlanta's Inman Park, Chicago's Hyde Park/Kenwood, and San Francisco's Western Ad-dition. How had former radical spaces become sites of protest by the poor? Even more puzzling, low-income residents drew on the enclave names coined by renovators to mobilize against displacement ("Gentrifiers, keep out of Boe-rum Hill!"). Had the Jane Jacobs–inspired neighborhood movement uninten-tionally produced a new version of "Negro removal"? Had the experiment of Brownstone Brooklyn that began in Brooklyn Heights in the 1950s ended up a success or failure?[10]

Certainly brownstoners had reason to feel defensive about charges of gen-trification. In three decades of overwhelmingly bad news for American cities, decimated by white flight, racial unrest, and deindustrialization, how could the brownstone revitalization movement be considered anything but a re-markable and unexpected success? In a decade in which New York City lost almost 800,000 residents and areas such as the South Bronx were devastated by housing abandonment and arson, a socially liberal and taxpaying middle class moved into depopulating areas of Brownstone Brooklyn and formed partnerships with poorer residents to battle destructive development projects and lobby for local control over municipal services. Considering that Com-munity District 2 (approximately the neighborhoods of Brooklyn Heights, Boerum Hill, Fort Greene, and Clinton Hill) had lost 15 percent and Park Slope about 20 percent of their populations in ten years, brownstoning was a coun-tertrend that made the area more integrated and economically viable. Despite the drop in the total population, the number of households remained stable as singles and small families moved into the area. While in the 1970s the median income of the city dropped by 7 percent, in Park Slope the median income actually rose by 17 percent. Moreover, rather than bulldozing tenements for luxury apartment towers, much of the revitalization had been done by grassroots block associations, civic groups, and individuals using sweat equity. Brownstone Brooklyn's blocks now had newly planted trees, restored brownstones, ethnic festivals, and street fairs. While retail districts in other parts of the borough sat shuttered and boarded up, Brooklyn's Seventh Avenue, Court Street, and Atlantic Avenue were bustling with new shops, studios, and small restaurants. Would the area have been better off if brownstoners had not moved to the area? Certainly depopulated cities such as Detroit or Buffalo would have benefited from even a quarter of the sweat equity investment poured into Brownstone Brooklyn. Nor was it clear whether brownstoning had displaced or replaced the poor. Stories abounded of renters being pressured by landlords to leave revitalizing areas. But non-revitalizing blocks with high rates of abandonment and demolition saw rates of displacement that were just as high. The debate about whether gentrification causes displacement remains unresolved.[11]

Brownstoners could point to more than simply financial reasons to call their movement a success. Brownstone Brooklyn was for enthusiasts a vibrant political landscape that represented the triumphant culmination of the populist and democratic revolts of the 1960s. More than simply reversing the trajectory of white flight, the Jacobsian neighborhood revolt had revolutionized the language of urban planning and city governance. The era of Robert Moses' heavy-handed and top-down master planning lay in the distant past. At the start of the 1980s, in the midst of another development boom, Brownstone Brooklyn's enclaves had in place new and powerful safeguards against slum clearance. A strong landmarks preservation commission protected the area's twelve designated historic districts. Because of the efforts of neighborhood activists in the 1960s and 1970s, developers seeking approval for new projects had to go through a round of environmental reviews, the Uniform Land Use Review Procedure, and presentations to community district boards led largely by powerful and engaged white-collar professional residents. Despite the boards having only advisory capacity, one study in 1980 showed that the city planning commission adhered to their recommendations about 90 percent of the time. Unlike the urban renewal era of the 1950s, in which the government built massive highways or bulldozed dozens of city blocks for public housing, new projects in the 1980s rarely involved massive slum clearance. Developers largely built on previously cleared urban renewal sites, infill sites between existing structures, and landfill along the waterfront.[12]

But the greatest triumph of Brownstone Brooklyn for enthusiasts was that it represented a bold and revolutionary new type of postmodern urbanism. Once dismissed by planners in 1950s as slums, Jacobsian neighborhoods such as Park Slope and Brooklyn Heights were now templates for human-scale and mixed-used cityscapes that developers and city planners eagerly tried to replicate. In the place of the stark towers of the 1950s and 1960s, new projects made contextual references to surrounding landscape and historic references to the past. Developers preserved important landmarks, emphasized mixed uses, incorporated eclectic and contextual designs into their buildings, and embraced the waterfront as a site of consumption. Rather than razing old structures for Cadman Plaza–style apartments, a new generation of Brownstone Brooklyn developers hoped to recycle industrial buildings such as the Ansonia Clock Factory or Empire Stores in Fulton Ferry into luxury apartments that retained historic surfaces and commemorated the legacy of Brooklyn's past. Along the waterfront, new festival marketplaces with sloops, wooden piers, pushcarts, and historic buildings tried to replicate the romantic bazaars pioneered by anti-development groups such as Save the Waterfront in the 1970s. "As we approach the 1980s, the future, as conceived in the '50s, is at last behind us. The 'Star Wars' sets are out. A new sensitivity to human values and historic continuity is in," exclaimed former urban renewal critic Wolf Von Eckhardt. "Fast food chain restaurants are changing their décor to warm colors, imitation wood and brick . . . [a new style] moving away from glass, steel and concrete abstractions and which grows from the roots of the past."[13]

While many residents looked to Brownstone Brooklyn as a glowing success, another group of critics saw the gentrifying enclaves evolving into something more troubling. As an economic landscape, they argued, Brownstone Brooklyn was a mixed bag. While the area was becoming more prosperous, the benefits of that growth remained unevenly distributed. Rather than reviving the industrial economy, Park Slope and Boerum Hill were highly stratified postindustrial landscapes in which wealthy white professionals lived adjacent to increasingly poor African Americans and Latinos. In Community District 2, per capita income in 1970, at $2,765, was below the borough average. By 1980, the number had jumped to $7,557, almost $2,000 above the borough the average. In a borough where the median white family income was $20,000 in 1980, the median in Community District 2 was $29,000. At the same time, however, black and Latino families in the district sat below the white median, at about $13,000 and $12,000, respectively. Park Slope similarly saw a proportional increase in the 1970s of families with incomes under $10,000 and over $30,000.[14]

Others began to question whether Brownstone Brooklyn was in fact a successful political experiment. Critics once enamored of the neighborhood revolt against technocracy in the late 1960s became increasingly disappointed by Brownstone Brooklyn's localist politics of the 1980s. Rather than evolving into a new and vibrant liberalism, critics complained that brownstoner activism had become a limited and parochial form of middle-class NIMBYism. Where in earlier decades government master planners presented bold if flawed visions for the city future, Brownstone Brooklyn residents now wrote myopic articles celebrating the "hidden secrets" of "my neighborhood" or debating whether residing on Sixteenth Street "really counted as living in Park Slope." As they concentrated on local issues such as lobbying for speed bumps on individual blocks, Brownstone Brooklyn residents passively waited for individual private developers to initiate new projects on scattered and unconnected sites. "With the fall of physical planning [in the 1970s]," complained Ada Louise Huxtable in 1987, ". . . the Planning Commission is no longer the proposer of plans and projects, is no longer the initiator of ideas and interventions, the agency responsible for evaluation of the multiple effects of massive constructions. It functions reactively to the proposals of others." Neighborhood activists, limited to an advisory capacity, by and large made only reactive contributions to new developments. A new 1980s ritual of "creative obstruction" replaced the top-down urban renewal schemes of the 1950s. After an individual developer announced plans for a gargantuan complex, community boards and activist groups dominated by middle-class brownstoners eager to preserve a Jacobsian sense of urban authenticity would subsequently filibuster the project with ULURP, environmental review procedures, and threats of legal action. Developers would compromise by adding park space or atriums, preserving individual buildings, adding affordable housing, pasting on faux historic imagery, and offering to rehabilitate subway stations or other public amenities. The result was a new cityscape designed and administered by private developers with no relationship to a broader integrated civic vision. With new supermarkets boasting rustic pushcarts, nostalgic festival marketplaces, and retro-Victorian office developments, a new generation of critics began to wonder if the city was in fact becoming a postmodern and private theme park. "What is missing today in New York is the spirit that inspired Hugh Ferriss's vast pictorial idealism and the Regional Plan Association's initial farsighted goals," argued Huxtable wistfully of a previous era when young urbanists dreamed of building an egalitarian city of tomorrow. "It does not matter that Ferriss reached unrealistically for the stars. . . . It is the reach that is important, the sense of a larger destiny than the bottom line."[15]

Perhaps the most damning critique was of Brownstone Brooklyn as a form of urbanism. The brownstoning movement originated not simply as a search for cheap townhouses but as part of a larger middle-class search for authenticity in a Cold War society entranced by technology, modernist redevelopment schemes, and mass consumer culture. Brownstoners hoped not simply to move to Brooklyn but to challenge class hierarchies, reject suburban conformity and consumption, and foster a new counterculture that reconnected participants to nature and older forms of community. In 1976, historian Robert Berkhofer Jr. wondered if the brownstone revitalization movement would result in a broader cultural shift:

> Does the back-to-the-city movement betoken a fundamental change in the cultural and economic values held by most Americans? . . . By choosing to restore old houses when they can afford new housing, do they reject the culture of novelty and the economy of obsolescence? Lastly, do they seek to reestablish the sense of community in America through the literal restoration of old communities? Are these "urban pioneers" repudiating the individualistic life patterns of the old-time pioneers who settled the frontier for a new ethic of togetherness? In short, does the movement reveal future economic, cultural and ecological outlooks of the American populace in general, or is it just the passing fancy of the privileged?[16]

Eight years later, a famous *Newsweek* cover offered its answer. Nineteen eighty-four was the "Year of the Yuppie." The yuppie represented a striking new public image of the brownstoner. In the 1960s, the new middle class looked to food cooperatives, farmers' markets, balcony gardens, independent bookshops, ethnic restaurants, and renovated brownstones as sites of authenticity in an increasingly technocratic society. In the 1980s, as former countercultural pottery shops and antique stores became high-end boutiques and ethnic restaurants became loci of gourmet cuisine, the same accoutrements had seemingly become symbols of a materialistic yuppie culture. Rather than subverting class privilege, Brownstone Brooklyn to some disappointed critics had simply reworked the standards of taste for a new white urban bourgeoisie. In 1987, *Dissent* put out its second New York City issue to reflect on the changes in the city since its last such issue in 1961. Twenty-five years earlier, the magazine had contained seminal articles celebrating local place and critiquing modern urban redevelopment. In 1987, Ian Rosenberg instead offered a description of Park Slope's Seventh Avenue. While the writing was still Jacobsian, Rosenberg's Park Slope had become a dystopic version of her street ballet:

> Stroll through Park Slope on a warm Saturday night, past young middle-class crowds patronizing a cornucopia of chic new restaurants offering the latest in trendy cuisine: sushi, Tex-Mex, "continental," five types of

Chinese, Thai, and various gourmet take-out shops. A lone shoemaker hangs on, but for a dime store or bodega where you can still get an ice cream sandwich for under a dollar, you have to literally go down the Slope, an avenue or two away. Interspersed among the restaurants are numerous real estate offices and nearly as many "new wave" florists. . . . New craft shops display expensive, elegant *objets*. Completing the ambience are those emblems of yuppiedom, Benetton's, a nearly-completed D'Agostino's, and a recently arrived "closet designer" . . . this is a place to be, and to be seen. This is *New York Magazine*'s Park Slope.[17]

Brownstone Brooklyn was committing the cardinal sin of middle-class romantic urbanism: it was becoming "inauthentic." But was this a sign that brownstoning was a failure? In subsequent decades, new middle-class pioneers including a new generation of African American professionals would continue the search for authenticity by moving deeper into the borough on a mission of discovery and rescue. Would they find the "real" Brooklyn? Or perhaps the romantic question itself needed to be questioned. It is safe to say that Seventh Avenue represented both the remarkable potentials of the politics of authenticity and its limits.

Abbreviations

AL	*Apartment Life*
AM	*American Magazine*
ASP	Adlai E. Stevenson Papers, Princeton University
BCBPL	Brooklyn Collection, Brooklyn Public Library
BCCC	Brooklyn Committee for Community Control papers, in possession of the author
BCSP	Brooklyn Council for Social Planning Papers, Brooklyn Public Library
BE	*Brooklyn Eagle*
BHAB	*Brooklyn Heights Association Bulletin*
BHS	Brooklyn Historical Society
BHT	*The Boerum Hill Times*
BSRCN	*Bedford Stuyvesant Restoration Corporation Newsletter*
BT	*Brooklyn Today*
BWT	*Brooklyn World-Telegram*
CN	*Civic News*
CORE	Congress of Racial Equality papers, Columbia University
DB	*Downtown Brooklyn*
ELP	Edward Joseph Logue Papers, Yale University
FL	*Flatbush Life*
GABNYPL	Gay Alliance of Brooklyn Papers, New York Public Library
GG	*Gaslight Gazette*
GN	*The Good News*
HCP	Hugh L. Carey Papers, St. John's University
HDMBHS	H. Dickson McKenna Collection, Brooklyn Historical Society
HRSN	*Home Reporter and Sunset News*
HT	*Herald Tribune*
NB	*Nation's Business*
NBQ	*New Brooklyn Quarterly*
NY	*The New Yorker*
NYAN	*New York Amsterdam News*
NYJA	*New York Journal American*
NYCHA	New York City Housing Authority Papers, LaGuardia Wagner Archives
NYCMA	Municipal Archives, New York City
NYDN	New York *Daily News*
NYHS	*New York Herald Sunday*

NYM	*New York Magazine*
NYNYS	*New York Navy Yard Shipworker*
NYP	*New York Post*
NYT	*New York Times*
NYWTS	*New York World-Telegram and Sun*
PPP	Pratt Planning Papers
PSCC	Park Slope Civic Council Archives
PCL	*Protestant Church Life*
Phoenix	The Brooklyn *Phoenix*
RERBG	*Real Estate Record and Builder's Guide*
RMP	Robert Moses Papers, New York Public Library
RPN	*Regional Plan News*
RWPMA	Robert F. Wagner Papers, Municipal Archives, New York City
SM	*Skyscraper Management*
SU	*Standard Union*
TB	*The Brownstoner*
TT	*Triangle Tribune*
VFBCBPL	Vertical Files, Brooklyn Collection, Brooklyn Public Library
VFBHS	Vertical Files, Brooklyn Historical Society
VFMANYC	Vertical Files, Municipal Archives, New York City
VIPMA	Vincent Impellitteri Papers, Municipal Archives, New York City
VV	*Village Voice*
WP	*Washington Post*
WSJ	*Wall Street Journal*

Notes

Introduction

1. "Protests Delay Razing of House," *NYT*, November 22, 1966, 40.
2. Ibid. A few of the signs described are from another demolition protest by the BHA a few months later; see "A Brooklyn Carriage Brigade Routs Town House Wreckers," *NYT*, April 15, 1967, 1.
3. "The Consequences of Brownstone Fever," *NYM*, March 31, 1969; "Brownstone Fever in Park Slope," *TB*, November 1, 1968; Michael Armstrong, *The Phoenix Brownstone Guide, 1980–1981 Edition* (New York: Michael Armstrong, 1980).
4. "Responsible Approach to Saving Abandoned Brownstones: Save Social 'Mix' in Your Neighborhood," *TB*, April 2, 1969; "Landmark House and Garden Tour," *BHT*, supplement to the *Phoenix*, May 2, 1974.
5. "Responsible Approach to Saving Abandoned Brownstones."
6. "Displacement Report to the Gowanus-Boerum Hill Community," unpublished booklet, August 1980, BCBPL.
7. "Manhattan: The New Brooklyn," *Time Out New York*, April 4, 2002.
8. Caroline F. Ware, *Greenwich Village 1920–1930: A Comment on American Civilization in the Post-War Years* (Boston: Houghton Mifflin, 1935), 9–15; Chad Heap, *Slumming and Racial Encounters in American Nightlife, 1885–1940* (Chicago: University of Chicago Press, 2009); National Urban Coalition, *Displacement: City Neighborhoods in Transition*, 4; J. Thomas Black, Allan Borut, and Robert Dubinsky, *Private-Market Housing Renovation in Older Urban Areas* (Washington, DC: Urban Land Institute, 1977), 1, 7–37.
9. Since discovering the phenomenon in the late 1970s, geographers and sociologists have produced a copious amount of literature theorizing gentrification and analyzing contemporary case studies. Few can agree on a definition of the term, why it happens, or whether it is a benefit or detriment to cities. Most agree, though, that the debate has reached a stalemate. Rather than attempting to retheorize gentrification, this book draws on the theoretical work of social scientists to take a historical approach of examining the process over time. For a comprehensive overview of the literature on gentrification, see Loretta Lees, Tom Slater, and Elvin Wyly, *Gentrification* (New York: Routledge, 2008). For a description of the "stalemate," see Sharon Zukin, "Gentrification: Culture and Capital in the Urban Core," *Annual Review of Sociology* 13 (1987): 129–47. Several works have been particularly useful to this study. For a scathing critique of frontier imagery in gentrifying districts, see Neil Smith, *The New Urban Frontier: Gentrification and the Revanchist City* (New York: Routledge, 1996). For an analysis of the culture and politics of the "new middle class" and links to the counterculture in gentrifying Canadian cities, see David Ley, *The*

New Middle Class and the Remaking of the Central City (New York: Oxford University Press, 1996). For a description of gentrification as a revolt against urban modernism in Toronto, see Jon Caufield, *City Form and Everyday Life: Toronto's Gentrification and Critical Social Practice* (Toronto: University of Toronto Press, 1994). For a balanced treatment of the benefits and detriments of gentrification in contemporary Brooklyn, see Lance Freeman, *There Goes the 'Hood: Views of Gentrification from the Ground Up* (Philadelphia: Temple University Press, 2006).

10. Thomas Sugrue, *The Origins of the Urban Crisis: Race and Inequality in Postwar Detroit* (Princeton, NJ: Princeton University Press, 1996); Arnold Hirsch, *Making the Second Ghetto: Race and Housing in Chicago, 1940–1960* (Chicago: University of Chicago Press, 1983); Robert A. Beauregard, *Voices of Decline: The Postwar Fate of U.S. Cities,* 2nd ed. (New York: Routledge, 2002).

11. Craig Steven Wilder, *A Covenant with Color: Race and Social Power in Brooklyn* (New York: Columbia University Press, 2000); Harold X. Connolly, *A Ghetto Grows in Brooklyn* (New York: New York University Press, 1977); Wendell Pritchett, *Brownsville, Brooklyn: Blacks, Jews, and the Changing Face of the Ghetto* (Chicago: University of Chicago Press, 2002); Jonathan Reider, *Canarsie: The Jews and Italians of Brooklyn Against Liberalism* (Cambridge, MA: Harvard University Press, 1985); Jim Sleeper, *The Closest of Strangers: Liberalism and the Politics of Race in New York* (New York: W. W. Norton, 1990).

12. For the landscape of "posts," see Ley, *The Making of the New Middle Class;* Richard Edward DeLeon, *Left Coast City: Progressive Politics in San Francisco, 1975–1991* (Lawrence: University Press of Kansas, 1992); John Hull Mollenkopf, *A Phoenix in the Ashes: The Rise and Fall of the Koch Coalition in New York City Politics* (Princeton, NJ: Princeton University Press, 1992).

13. City of New York, *The City in Transition: Prospects and Policies for New York: The Final Report of the Temporary Commission on Finances,* June 1977, 23, 104–6; Saskia Sassen, *The Global City: New York, London, Tokyo* (Princeton, NJ: Princeton University Press, 2001).

14. For an example of a multidirectional narrative and emphasis on regional restructuring in both the center city and suburbs, see Robert Self, *American Babylon: Race and the Struggle for Postwar Oakland* (Princeton, NJ: Princeton University Press, 2003). Historians influenced by the "LA School" of urbanism have led calls for new multiethnic, multiclass, and polyglot histories of urban space; see Raúl Homero Villa and George J. Sánchez, eds., *Los Angeles and the Future of Urban Cultures: A Special Issue of American Quarterly* (Baltimore, MD: Johns Hopkins University Press, 2005). For an analysis of the deindustrialized city as a repository of historic memory, see Jefferson Cowie and Joseph Heathcott, eds., *Beyond the Ruins: The Meanings of Deindustrialization* (Ithaca, NY: ILR Press, 2003); Christine M. Boyer, *The City of Collective Memory: Its Historical Imagery and Architectural Entertainments* (Cambridge, MA: MIT Press, 1994). For the importance of culture, symbols, and discourses in shaping postwar urban space, see Self, *American Babylon,* and Eric Avila, *Popular Culture in the Age of White Flight: Fear and Fantasy in Suburban Los Angeles* (Berkeley: University of California Press, 2004). For an analysis of the 1970s as a moment of transition rather than denouement of the civil rights movement and urban liberal politics, see Thomas

Sugrue, *Sweet Land of Liberty: The Forgotten Struggle for Civil Rights in the North* (New York: Random House, 2008); Matthew Countryman, *Up South: Civil Rights and Black Power in Philadelphia* (Philadelphia: University of Pennsylvania Press, 2006); Bruce Schulman, *The Seventies: The Great Shift in American Culture, Society, and Politics* (New York: Free Press, 2001). For new studies of neighborhood revitalization efforts in postindustrial cities, see Alexander Von Hoffman, *House by House, Block by Block: The Rebirth of America's Urban Neighborhoods* (Oxford: Oxford University Press, 2003); Howard Gillette, *Camden After the Fall: Decline and Renewal in a Post-Industrial City* (Philadelphia: University of Pennsylvania Press, 2005).

15. For an excellent example, see Jon C. Teaford, *The Metropolitan Revolution: The Rise of Post-Urban America* (New York: Columbia University Press, 2006).

16. Leslie Elish, "Brownstone Revival in New York City: A Report for the Brownstone Revival Committee Financed by the Fund for the City of New York," April 1971, NYCMA; "The Membership from 'A' to 'Z,'" *TB*, June 3, 1976, 7; Kenneth Jackson, *Crabgrass Frontier*, 302.

17. David Ley, *The New Middle Class*; 14–15; Barbara Ehrenreich, *Fear of Falling: The Inner Life of the Middle Class* (New York: Harper Perennial, 1989); B. Bruce-Briggs, *The New Class?* (New Brunswick, NJ: Transaction Books, 1979); Alain Touraine, *The Post-Industrial Society; Tomorrow's Social History: Classes, Conflicts and Culture in the Programmed Society*, trans. Leonard F. X. Mayhew (New York: Random House, 1971); Daniel Bell, *The Coming of Post-Industrial Society: A Venture in Social Forecasting* (New York: Basic Books, 1973); Richard Florida, *The Rise of the Creative Class: And How It's Transforming Work, Leisure and Everyday Life* (New York: Basic Books, 2002); David Brooks, *Bobos in Paradise: The New Upper Class and How They Got There* (New York: Simon and Schuster, 2000); Richard Barbrook, *The Class of the New* (London: OpenMute, 2006).

18. "A Brownstoner Defines One," *TB*, February 2, 1969.

19. Doug Rossinow, *The Politics of Authenticity: Liberalism, Christianity and the New Left in America* (New York: Columbia University Press, 1998); Manuel Castells, *The City and the Grassroots: A Cross-Cultural Theory of Urban Social Movements* (Berkeley: University of California Press, 1983).

20. For excellent histories of the origins of conservatism, see Lisa McGirr, *Suburban Warriors: The Origins of the New American Right* (Princeton, NJ: Princeton University Press, 2001); Matthew Lassiter, *The Silent Majority: Suburban Politics in the Sunbelt South* (Princeton, NJ: Princeton University Press, 2006).

21. Nan Ellin, *Postmodern Urbanism* (Cambridge, MA: Blackwell, 1995); David Harvey, *The Condition of Postmodernity: An Enquiry into the Origins of Cultural Change* (Cambridge, MA: Blackwell, 1989); Ley, *The New Middle Class*.

22. For an analysis of inequality in the postindustrial city, see John Hull Mollenkopf and Manuel Castells, eds., *Dual City: Restructuring New York* (New York: Russell Sage Foundation, 1991).

1   Urban Wilderness

1. Harrison Salisbury, *The Shook-Up Generation* (New York: Harper and Brothers, 1958), 1–4.
2. Ibid., 4.

3. This discussion of the relationship between material and represented space draws from the work of postmodern geographers such as Edward Soja and Doreen Massey. "Brownstone Brooklyn" was a "thirdspace" between real and imagined landscapes. See Soja, *Thirdspace: Journeys to Los Angeles and Other Real and Imagined Spaces* (Cambridge, MA: Blackwell, 1996); Doreen Massey, *Space, Place and Gender* (Minneapolis: University of Minnesota Press, 1994).

4. Herbert J. Ballon, *Brooklyn Neighborhoods: A Basis for Neighborhood Studies and a District Plan for a Neighborhood Council Program in Brooklyn* (Brooklyn: Brooklyn Council for Social Planning, 1941).

5. "South Brooklyn–Red Hook," chap. in *Brooklyn Communities: Population Characteristics and Neighborhood Social Resources* (New York: Bureau of Community Statistical Research Department, September 1959), 2:1; "Research and Church Planning," *PCL*, April 6, 1957; Salisbury, *The Shook-Up Generation*, 3; "Delinquency Rates," map by New York City Youth Board, 1954, Box 123, Folder 2141, RWPMA; memorandum from H. M. Currier to Miss Farra, January 25, 1944, Box 18, Folder 3.3.011, BCSP.

6. Ballon, *Brooklyn Neighborhoods*, "In South Brooklyn, Vagueness of the Descriptive Term," *BE*, October 17, 1886, 6; "South Brooklyn, the District Defined by Elastic Term," *BE*, March 21, 1886, 6; residents of Prospect Hill to editor, *BE*, March 17, 1889, 17.

7. For a Marxist critique of urban nostalgia and the reactionary politics of place, see David Harvey, *Justice, Nature and the Geography of Difference* (Cambridge, MA: Blackwell, 1996); Sharon Zukin, *Landscapes of Power: From Detroit to Disney World* (Berkeley: University of California Press, 1993). Rather than dismissing "place," Doreen Massey instead offers an alternative progressive, anti-essentialist and global definition of place that is heterogeneous, porous, a product of social relations, and in a constant process of change; see Massey, *For Space* (London: Sage Publications, 2005), 9–12.

8. For one of the most influential discussions of the "city as text," see Michel De Certeau, "Walking in the City," in *The Practice of Everyday Life*, trans. Steven Rendall (Berkeley: University of California Press, 1988); see also Tim Cresswell, *In Place/Out of Place: Geography, Ideology, and Transgression* (Minneapolis: University of Minnesota, 1996), 12–13.

9. Consolidated Edison Company of New York, Economic Research Department, *Population Growth of New York City by Districts, 1910–1948* (Con Edison Company: New York City, 1948).

10. New York City Market Analysis, compiled by the *Daily News*, *New York Times*, *Daily Mirror*, and *Journal-American*, 1943.

11. For the concept of place "layers," see Doreen Massey, *Spatial Divisions of Labour: Social Structures and the Geography of Production* (London: Macmillan, 1984), 117–18; Daniel Bell, "The Three Faces of New York," *Dissent* 8 (Summer 1961): 223. The seminal discussion of the "legibility" of older cities was by Kevin Lynch, *The Image of the City* (Cambridge, MA: MIT Press, 1960), 47–48.

12. Colin Rowe and Fred Koetter, *Collage City* (Cambridge: MIT Press, 1984). For an analysis of the dialectic between modernity and preservation in New York City's landscape, see Max Page, *The Creative Destruction of Manhattan, 1900–1940* (Chicago:

University of Chicago, 1999); also M. Christine Boyer, *The City of Collective Memory: Its Historic Imagery and Architectural Entertainments* (Cambridge: MIT Press, 1994).

13. The goal is here is not to undermine Brownstone Brooklyn's legitimacy as a historic landscape. Rather, it is to suggest that modernist urban renewal sites, rooming houses, and even highways are also historic and worth preserving. Rather than arguing tritely that "historic" Brooklyn is simply "invented," the book argues that all of Brooklyn's layers are both modern and historic.

14. The goal is to bridge the gap between critical cultural geographers, who see places as social constructions by the powerful, and humanistic geographers, who see place as something real, important, and inherent to human identity. Brownstone Brooklyn was socially constructed from a richly layered place-text. For a good overview of this debate over place, see Tim Cresswell, "The Genealogy of Place," chap. in *Place: A Short Introduction* (London: Blackwell Publishing, 2004). The image of the "hard" and "soft" city is borrowed from Jonathan Raban, *Soft City* (New York: E. P. Dutton, 1974).

15. Jeanette Jeanes, "A History of Carroll Gardens," 1970, Carroll Gardens Folder, VFBHS.

16. "Community Planning Study: South Brooklyn, Red Hook, Carroll Gardens, Boerum Hill-Gowanus, Cobble Hill, Brooklyn Heights, Fort Greene, Central Business District, and Civic Center," prepared for the New York City Planning Commission, Manuel S. Emanuel Associates, December 1967, L-1; Map A-354 of Brooklyn in October 1869, BHS; Jasper Dankers and Peter Sluyter, *Journal of a Voyage to New York and a Tour of the American Colonies 1679–1680*, ed. and trans. Henry Murphy (Brooklyn, 1867); see map of Brooklyn in 1776–77 in Henry McCloskey, *Manual of the Common Council of the City of Brooklyn for 1864*, BHS. Boerum Hill's flat topography is described by Philip Kasinitz, "The Gentrification of 'Boerum Hill': Neighborhood Change and Conflicts over Definitions," *Qualitative Sociology* 11 (Fall 1988): 169.

17. "Farmers Market," *TT*, September 1, 1976; "Clinton Hill: Spring House and Garden Tour," pamphlet, May 4, 1975, Clinton Hill Folder, VFBHS; Jeanes, "A History of Carroll Gardens," 1970; Carroll Gardens Folder, VFBHS; Marc Linder and Lawrence S. Zacharias, *Of Cabbage and Kings County: Agriculture and the Formation of Modern Brooklyn* (Iowa City: University of Iowa Press, 1999), 80–81; Philip Kingle, "King's County During the American Revolution," in *Brooklyn USA: The Fourth Largest City in America*, ed. Rita Seiden Miller (New York: Brooklyn College Press, 1979), 78.

18. Ron Miller, Rita Seiden Miller, and Stephen Karp, "The Fourth Largest City in America— A Sociological History of Brooklyn," in *Brooklyn USA: The Fourth Largest City in America*, ed. Rita Seiden Miller (New York: Brooklyn College Press, 1979), 17–18, 20; Ira Rosenwaike, *Population History of New York City* (New York: Syracuse University Press, 1972), 49–52.

19. For the image of the Victorian city as a "heteroscape" formed by real estate commodification and uneven development, see David Scobey, *Empire City: The Making and Meaning of the New York City Landscape* (Philadelphia: Temple University Press, 2002). For descriptions of Brooklyn Heights, see Brian J. Danforth, "Brooklyn Heights: New York's First Suburban Community," *Journal of Long Island History* 13, 1 (Fall 1976): 43–51; William R. Everdell and Malcolm MacKay, *Rowboats to Rapid*

Transit: A History of Brooklyn Heights (Brooklyn: Brooklyn Heights Association. 1973); David Ment, *Building Blocks of Brooklyn: A Study of Urban Growth* (Brooklyn: Brooklyn Educational and Cultural Alliance, 1979), 64–66.

20. Charles Lockwood, *Bricks and Brownstones: The New York Row House, 1783–1929* (New York: McGraw-Hill, 1972), 141; Kenneth Jackson, *Encyclopedia of New York City* (New York: Yale University Press, 1995), s.v. "Brownstones," by Joel Schwartz.

21. Ibid.

22. Lockwood, *Bricks and Brownstones*, xii–xv; Richard Plunz, *A History of Housing in New York City* (New York: Columbia University Press, 1990), 60; Eleanora Schoenbaum, "Emerging Neighborhoods: The Development of Brooklyn's Fringe Areas, 1850–1930," Ph.D. diss., Columbia University, 1976, 110, 121.

23. Lockwood, *Bricks and Brownstones*, xiii, 26; Clay Lancaster, *Old Brooklyn Heights: New York's First Suburb* (New York: Dover Publications, 1979), 23–25; Harmon H. Goldstone and Martha Dalrymple, *History Preserved: A Guide to New York City Landmarks and Historic Districts* (New York: Simon and Schuster, 1974), 27–28; Joy and Paul Wilkes, *You Don't Have to Be Rich to Own a Brownstone* (New York: Quadrangle, 1973), 1–2.

24. Lockwood, *Bricks and Brownstones*, xii, 74–75, 141; Carolyn Loeb, *Entrepreneurial Vernacular: Developer's Subdivisions in the 1920's* (Baltimore: Johns Hopkins University Press, 2001), 43; "Profit in Wrecking: Materials from Old Buildings Are Used Again," *Washington Post*, December 22, 1910, 13. Boston's rowhouses were similarly slapdash; see Sam Bass Warner Jr., *Streetcar Suburbs: The Process of Growth in Boston, 1870–1900* (Cambridge, MA: Harvard University Press, 1978), 76, 117, 130–31. Rowhouses in Montreal, Philadelphia, London, Baltimore, and other cities have a similar history; see Michael Doucet and John Weaver, *Housing the North American City* (Montreal: McGill-Queen's University Press, 1991), 62–63.

25. Quoted in Lockwood, *Bricks and Brownstones*, xiv, 225. In Boston, Henry James similarly found the brownstone landscape of Back Bay "rich and prosperous and monotonous. . . . oh, so inexpressibly vacant!" As quoted in Bainbridge Bunting, *Houses of Boston's Back Bay* (Cambridge: Harvard University Press, 1967), 20.

26. "Brooklyn's Growth, Some Interesting Facts About New York's Sister City," *Washington Post*, October 18, 1886, 3.

27. J. E. D. Cantwell, "Should They Bring Back the Trolley?" *NBQ* 5, 3 (1983): 12–16; "Trolley Lines' Deadly Trail," *NYT*, June 13, 1893, 9; "Indignation in Brooklyn," *NYT*, May 28, 1895, 9.

28. The Buttermilk Channel legend was debunked by Henry McCloskey, *Manual of the Common Council of the City of Brooklyn for 1864*, 145–47. For a description of pastoral nostalgia and Victorian "bourgeois urbanism," see Scobey, *Empire City*, 11, 120. For examples of nostalgia for Dutch New York, see Philip Lopate, "The Days of the Patriarchs: Washington Irving's *A History of New York*," and Roger Panetta, "The Hudson-Fulton Celebration of 1909," both in *Dutch New York: The Roots of Hudson Valley Culture*, ed. Roger Panetta (New York: Hudson River Museum, 2009).

29. Plunz, *A History of Housing*, 52–57; Scobey, *Empire City*, 136–41; Warner, *Streetcar Suburbs*, 5–13; "Proposal to Make a Park out of Jackson's Hollow," *BE*, March 16, 1881; "Darby's Patch," *Brooklyn Eagle*, March 16, 1883; "Spring Moving in Darby's

Patch," *BE*, March 25, 1884; "City Survey," *BE*, May 09, 1885; "Gossip of the Town: The Trolley as Improver of the Streets," *BE*, December 18, 1892; "Evicting Squatters Is Not an Easy Task," *NYT*, November 20, 1910, X11.

30. Miller, Miller, and Karp, "The Fourth Largest City in America," 22–25; Schoenbaum, "Emerging Neighborhoods: The Development of Brooklyn's Fringe Areas, 1850–1930," 11–12, 55–58. For the development of a renter class in nineteenth-century New York, see Elizabeth Blackmar, *Manhattan for Rent, 1785–1850* (Ithaca: Cornell University Press, 1989).

31. "Rents Go Up in Brooklyn," *NYT*, February 25, 1881; "House Rents in Brooklyn," *NYT*, March 13, 1875. For the interchangeable use of *tenement* and *warehouse*, see "The Olden-Time in New York," *NYT*, November 4, 1852; Robert A. M. Stern, Thomas Mellins, and David Fishman, *New York 1880: Architecture and Urbanism in the Gilded Age* (New York: Monacelli Press, 1999), 389, 468, 501.

32. Stern, Mellins, and Fishman, *New York 1880*, 870–74, 880–82; "Coapartments Rising on Brooklyn Heights," *NYHS*, November 4, 1923; "$3,000 Cost for One Room Is Apartment Record," *SU*, May 6, 1924, "Complete Steel Frame for Big Heights Apartment," *BE*, January 27, 1924; "Valuable Heights Corner Is Sold for Apartment House," *BE*, April 4, 1923; "Brooklyn Market's Activity Continues," *NYT*, May 13, 1906, 17; "The Apartment House Situation—Three Unusually Active Areas," *NYT*, April 4, 1926, 1RE; "Brooklyn Prefers Apartment Houses," *NYT*, October 2, 1927, 11E; "French Flats and Apartment Houses in New York," *Carpentry and Building* 2 (January 1880); Michael Doucet and John Weaver, *Housing the North American City* (Montreal: McGill-Queen's University Press, 1991), 18; Plunz, *A History of Housing in New York City*, 88–93; "New York's Unchanging Scene," *New York Sunday News*, August 3, 1969, 24–27; "Developing. A Rapidly Growing Section of the City," *BE*, June 5, 1881, 2; "Improvements. Great Activity in Building," *BE*, June 19, 1881, 3; "The City's Gain. Building Improvements During the Past Season," *BE*, June 15, 1884.

33. "Modern Homes Are Being Built in Old Sections," *BE*, October 21, 1923; "Making over Old City Houses," *NYT*, March 30, 1919, 78; "Four Family Flats, New Law Permits Conversion of Four Story Dwellings," *NYT*, June 22, 1919, 104; "Rebuilding the 3-Family Home," *NYT*, May 25, 1919; David Ment, Anthony Robins, and David Framberger, *Building Blocks of Brooklyn, Brooklyn Rediscovery Brooklyn Educational and Cultural Alliance* (Brooklyn: Brooklyn Educational and Cultural Alliance, 1979), 80.

34. "The Decay of 'Brooklyn Heights,'" *NYT*, June 15, 1902.

35. *BHAB*, 1929, 2–3, Brooklyn Heights Association Folder 6, VFBHS. For similar activity in Manhattan, see "Ye Olde Settlers of the West Side Celebrate," *NYT*, March 24, 1912; Max Page, *The Creative Destruction of Manhattan, 1900–1940* (Chicago: University of Chicago, 1999).

36. Joshua Brown and David Ment, *Factories, Foundries, and Refineries: A History of Five Brooklyn Industries* (Brooklyn: Brooklyn Educational and Cultural Alliance, 1980), 5–6; Ralph Foster Weld, *Brooklyn Village 1816–1834* (New York: Columbia University Press, 1938), 11, 15–16.

37. New York State Department of Commerce, *New York State Commerce Review*, vol. 11, June 6, 1957, 5; John I. Griffin, *Industrial Location in the New York Area* (New York:

City College Press, 1956); "Department of City Planning Bulletin," December 1955, Box 14, Folder 233, RWPMA.

38. Martin B. Dworkis, ed., *The Port of New York and the Management of Its Waterfront* (New York: New York University Graduate School of Public Administration and Social Service, 1959), 25; "New York State Commerce Review," 1.

39. "Navy Yard Calls for Workers," *NYNYS*, April 3, 1945, 1; Joseph Palisi, "The Brooklyn Navy Yard," in *Brooklyn USA: The Fourth Largest City in America*, ed. Rita Seiden Miller (New York: Brooklyn College Press, 1979), 120–22; Dworkis, *The Port of New York*, 61; "Defense Oaks Grow from Little Acorns," *NB*, June 21, 1947; *Encyclopedia of New York*, s.v. "Bush Terminal," by John J. Gallagher.

40. Joshua B. Freeman, *Working Class New York: Life and Labor Since World War II* (New York: New Press, 2000), 13; "New York State Commerce Review," 3; "Defense Oaks Grow from Little Acorns," 21.

41. For a description of New York's "non-Fordist" economy and "flexible specialization," see Freeman, *Working Class New York*, 3–22; "New York State Commerce Review" listed a borough-wide increase of 212 firms or 4.2 percent with 1–19 employees from 1947 to 1954, 3–4.

42. Number of manufacturing jobs drawn from 1956 City Planning Conversion Districts 51-A3 and 64-A1 (map can be found in "Department of City Planning Bulletin"); Julius Mitzner, *Neighborhood Study of Park Slope Community in Brooklyn, Conducted Under the Auspices of the Brooklyn Council for Social Planning* (New York: New York School of Social Work, December, 1940), 85.

43. Lewis Mumford, "The Sky Line: From Blight to Beauty I," *NY*, April 25, 1953, 102–7; Lewis Mumford, "The Sky Line: From Blight to Beauty II," *NY*, May 9, 1953, 91–97; Brooklyn Chapter of the American Institute of Architects, "Civic Design Report," February 23, 1954, 12; Robert Stern, Thomas Mellins, and David Fishman, *New York 1960* (New York: Montacelli Press, 1995), 905–12; 1955 conversion district 64 A-2 listed 15,800 jobs in government, 17,500 in retail, 7,000 in public utilities, communication, and transportation, and 6,400 in FIRE industries.

44. "The Next Frontier," *AL*, April 1970; "Liberty Tower: A Residential Co-operative Gothic Skyscraper," advertisement brochure, Box 1, Folder 6, HDMBHS.

45. Pete Hamill, *A Drinking Life* (Boston: Little, Brown, 1994), 60.

46. The point about middle-class visitors to non-white neighborhoods is made by David Ley, *The Black Inner City as Frontier Outpost: Images and Behavior of a Philadelphia Neighborhood* (Washington: Association of American Geographers, 1974).

47. "Brooklyniana" was a name used by Walt Whitman for a series of articles on Brooklyn history he wrote for the *Brooklyn Standard*. I'm using it the same vein as "Victoriana" or "Americana" to describe a strand of Brooklyn nostalgia that developed in the 1970s. Walt Whitman, "Brooklyniana," in *The Uncollected Poetry and Prose of Walt Whitman*, ed. Emory Holloway (Garden City, NY: Doubleday, 1921), 222–321.

48. Lack of "neighborhood" sense is described by Suzanne Keller, "The Neighborhood," in *The Urban Neighborhood* (New York: Random House, 1968), 8–16; Herbert Gans, *The Urban Villagers: Group and Class in the Life of Italian-Americans* (New York: Collier Macmillan, 1962), 104–6; the concept of shifting and overlapping networks is also in Eliot Lebow, *Tally's Corner: A Study of Negro Streetcorner Men* (Boston: Little, Brown,

1967), 203; the "ordered segmentation" of urban space is described in Gerald Suttles, *The Social Order of the Slum: Ethnicity and Territory in the Inner City* (Chicago: University of Chicago Press, 1968), 13–38.

49. Christine McLaren Brown, "Social Contacts Within a Brooklyn City Block," M.A. thesis, Columbia University, 1938, 73, 77, 142, 156–58.

50. "Downtown Brooklyn," Protestant Council of the City of New York, 1955, 19; "Brooklyn Community Council Characteristics: Park Slope"; "Brooklyn Community Council Characteristics: South Brooklyn-Red Hook"; Paul Esposito, "The National Parish as a Factor in the Assimilation of Second and Third Generation Poles in South Brooklyn," MA thesis, St. John's University, 1968.

51. Ibid.

52. Robert Anthony Orsi, *The Madonna of 115th Street: Faith and Community in Italian Harlem, 1880–1950* (New Haven: Yale University Press, 1985), 34–35, 180; Donald Tricarico, *The Italians of Greenwich Village: The Social Structure and Transformation of an Ethnic Community* (Staten Island, NY: Center for Migration Studies, 1984), 4–10; Jerry Della Femina and Charles Sopkin, *An Italian Grows in Brooklyn* (Boston: Little, Brown, 1978), 38–39, 43; Hamill, *A Drinking Life*, 62.

53. For a description of Italian American neighborhoods as "domus centered societies" centered on family and home, see Orsi, *The Madonna of 115th Street*; "Dream Grows in Brooklyn," *NYT*, February 23, 1975; Sidney Smith, "Red Hook Section of Brooklyn," student project, New York School of Social Work, August 1942; Henry Claffin Wells, "Urban Political Development and the Power of Local Groups," Ph.D. diss., Columbia University, 1984, 150–66. For a discussion of ethnic routes and roots, see James Clifford, *Routes: Travel and Translation in the Late Twentieth Century* (Cambridge, MA: Harvard University Press, 1997).

54. Ramon Colon, *Carlos Tapia: A Puerto Rican Hero in New York* (New York: Vantage Press, 1976), 22, 35, 59; "Brooklyn Heights–Ft. Greene," chap. in *Brooklyn Communities: Population Characteristics and Neighborhood Social Resources*, vol. 1 (New York: Bureau of Community Statistical Services, September 1959); "South Brooklyn–Red Hook," in *Brooklyn Communities*; Virginia E. Sanchez Korrol, *From Colonia to Community: The History of Puerto Ricans in New York City* (Berkeley: University of California Press, 1983), 62. The South Brooklyn Youth Board estimated that approximately 25 percent of the borough's 40,299 Puerto Ricans lived in the area called South Brooklyn: "South Brooklyn Youth Board Area," New York City Youth Board Research Department, October 1955, Box 33, Folder 5.3.088, BCSP.

55. Colon, *Carlos Tapia*, 72–75; Korrol, *From Colonia to Community*, 57; Lawrence R. Chenault, *The Puerto Rican Migrant in New York City* (New York: Columbia University Press, 1938), 62–64, 103–6.

56. Connolly, *A Ghetto Grows in Brooklyn*, 3–67; Ernest Quimby, "Bedford Stuyvesant: A Brief Note," in *Brooklyn USA: The Fourth Largest City in America*, ed. Rita Seiden Miller (New York: Brooklyn College Press, 1979), 230–34.

57. Miller, Miller, and Karp, "The Fourth Largest City in America," 27; Connolly, *A Ghetto Grows in Brooklyn*, 129–34; Taylor, *The Black Churches of Brooklyn*, 102–3.

58. Connolly, *A Ghetto Grows in Brooklyn*, 130; Craig Wilder, *A Covenant with Color: Race and Social Power in Brooklyn* (New York: Columbia University Press, 2000), 183–211.

59. Hamill, *A Drinking Life*, 67.

60. For the social division between "corner boys" and "college boys" in Boston's North End, see William Foote Whyte, *Street Corner Society: The Social Structure of an Italian Slum* (Chicago: University of Chicago Press, 1943), 94–104; Gans, *The Urban Villagers*, 24–26. For a similar analysis of black streetcorner society, see Elliot Liebow, *Tally's Corner: A Study of Negro Streetcorner Men* (Boston: Little, Brown, 1967). In his study of Philadelphia, Elijah Anderson describes the community distinctions between "decent" and "street" families in inner-city Philadelphia; see Anderson, *Code of the Street: Decency, Violence and the Moral Life of the Inner City* (New York: W. W. Norton, 1999).

61. "GI and Young Wife 'Snagged' as Owners of Park Slope 'Trap,'" *BE*, November 24, 1952, 1, 11; *Life in One Room: A Study of the Rooming House Problem in the Borough of Manhattan* (New York: Committee on Housing of the Community Service Society, 1940); Brownstone Brooklyn was similar to other depressed inner-city areas; in a 1966 study of Newark's low-end neighborhoods, 42.8 percent of landlords possessed only one building. A majority of those landlords lived in the building or used to. Another 21.6 percent owned one or two more buildings. See George Sternlieb, *The Tenement Landlord* (New Brunswick, NJ: Rutgers University Press, 1966), 121–41.

62. "Park Slope," chap. in *Brooklyn Communities: Population Characteristics and Neighborhood Social Resources* (New York: Bureau of Community Statistical Research Department, September 1959), 2:28.

63. Ibid.; "Brooklyn Heights–Ft. Greene," in *Brooklyn Communities*, 1:73–74; "South Brooklyn-Red Hook," in *Brooklyn Communities*, 2:6; Charles Monaghan, interview by author, April 1, 2003, New York City.

64. Linda Dowling Almeida, *Irish Immigrants in New York City* (Bloomington: Indiana University Press, 2001), 5; Charles Monaghan, interview by author. For a discussion of parish boundaries and territoriality in postwar cities, see John T. McGreevy, *Parish Boundaries: The Catholic Encounter with Race in the Twentieth Century Urban North* (Chicago: University of Chicago Press, 1996); Gerald H. Gamm, *Urban Exodus: Why the Jews Left Boston and the Catholics Stayed* (Cambridge, MA: Harvard University Press, 1999); Eileen M. McMahon, *What Parish Are You From? A Chicago Irish Community and Race Relations* (Lexington: University of Kentucky Press, 1995).

65. "Brooklyn Heights–Ft. Greene," in *Brooklyn Communities*; Taylor, *Black Churches of Brooklyn*, 116; "Heights Sour on 'Kingdom Come,'" *NYDN*, March 9, 1969.

66. Jerome Krase and Charles LaCerra, *Ethnicity and Machine Politics* (New York: University Press of America, 1991), xii–xiv, 6–14, 65–66, 239; Charles McNickle, *To Be Mayor of New York: Ethnic Politics in the City* (New York: Columbia University Press, 1993), 51–53; "Reforming Tammany," *NYT*, June 28, 1946; "Democratic Units Agree," *NYT*, December 17, 1952; Charles Monaghan, interview by author. In other cities, an election district was called a "precinct" and an assembly district called a "ward"; Edward N. Costikyan, *Behind Closed Doors: Politics in the Public Interest* (New York: Harcourt, Brace and World, 1966), 4.

67. For a description of New York's diverse and overlapping spectrum of craft and industrial unions, see Freeman, *Working Class New York*, 40–47. For working-class identity of Brooklyn longshoremen, see William DiFazio, *Longshoremen, Community, and*

Resistance on the Brooklyn Waterfront (South Hadley, MA: Bergin and Garvey, 1985); Marc Levinson, *The Box: How the Shipping Container Made the World Smaller and the World Economy Bigger* (Princeton: Princeton University Press, 2006), 24–27.

68. Charles P. Larrowe, *Shape-Up and Hiring Hall: A Comparison of Hiring Methods and Labor Relations on the New York and Seattle Waterfronts* (Berkeley: University of California Press, 1955), 41–42; "Anastasia Gains in Union Mergers," *NYT*, April 30, 1956, 36.

69. Malcolm Johnson, *Crime on the Labor Front* (New York: McGraw-Hill, 1950), 97–98; Virgil W. Peterson, *The Mob: 200 Years of Organized Crime in New York* (Ottawa, IL: Green Hill, 1983), 277–80.

70. Vincent Riccio and Bill Slocum, *All the Way Down: The Violent Underworld of Street Gangs* (New York: Simon and Schuster, 1962); Salisbury, *The Shook-up Generation*; "3 Youth Gangs in Brooklyn Agree to Turn in Their Weapons to Police," *NYT*, November 27, 1950.

71. "Nodes" is from Lynch, *The Image of the City.*

72. Hamill, *A Drinking Life*, 61–62.

73. "Foes of Din Aghast at Court's Levity," *NYT*, November 24, 1937, 18; "Common Complaints," *BHP*, October 25, 1940; "Heights Lassie Nixes Advance of 2 'Wolves,'" *BHP*, June 28, 1944.

2 Concord Village

1. "Brooklyn Housing Ready," *NYT*, April 1, 1951, 223; "Brooklyn Development Aimed at Wall Streeters," *NYT*, March 10, 1957, R1.

2. "Concord Village on Brooklyn Heights," booklet by Concord Freeholders, February 1952, Downtown Brooklyn Folder, VFBHS; "Concord Village Brooklyn Heights," booklet by Punia and Marx Inc., Agents, estimated date early 1950s, Downtown Brooklyn Folder, VFBHS; "Apartment Building Has Music in Public Areas," *NYT*, December 27, 1959, R3.

3. "Brooklyn Center Now at Mid-point," *NYT*, November 5, 1955, 21; "Brooklyn Center Causes a Dispute," *NYT*, November 26, 1954, 50; "City Is Attacked on Cadman Plaza," *NYT*, September 20, 1961, 31; "Brooklyn Tenants March on Court and Win Delay in Mass Eviction," *NYT*, August 7, 1946, 26; "Evictions Are Stayed," *NYT*, August 19, 1947, 28.

4. The word "Manhattanization" is used here to described a shared concept, since the exact phrase was not widely used by Brooklynites in the 1950s. An early use of "Manhattanization" was by Londoners in the 1920s; "Londoners Lament Americanized City," *NYT*, July 23, 1927, E6. The contemporary use arose in gentrifying districts of San Francisco during the late 1960s; see "Bay Waterfront High-Rises Draw San Franciscan's Ire," *WP*, November 11, 1970, A3; "High Skyline Opposed on Coast," *NYT*, October 26, 1970, 39. See also "City Undergoing Vast Face Lifting," *NYT*, October 18, 1958, 23.

5. The historical literature on postwar urban redevelopment is extensive. For critical histories of Robert Moses and postwar redevelopment in New York City, see Robert Caro, *The Power Broker: Robert Moses and The Fall of New York* (New York: Knopf,

1974); Marshall Berman, *All That Is Solid Melts into Air: The Experience of Modernity* (New York: Penguin Books, 1983), 290–312. The most richly detailed account of the liberal growth coalition that supported Moses and postwar redevelopment is Joel Schwartz, *The New York Approach: Robert Moses, Urban Liberals and Redevelopment of the Inner City* (Columbia: Ohio State University Press, 1993). Recently scholars have begun to revaluate the legacy of Robert Moses and offer a balanced treatment of urban redevelopment; see Hilary Ballon and Kenneth T. Jackson, *Robert Moses and the Modern City: The Transformation of New York* (New York: W. W. Norton, 2007); Kenneth Jackson, "Robert Moses and the Planned Environment: A Reevaluation," chap. in *Robert Moses: Single-Minded Genius*, ed. Joann P. Krieg (Interlaken, NY: Heart of the Lakes Publishing, 1989), 21–30; Samuel Zipp, *Manhattan Projects: The Rise and Fall of Urban Renewal in Cold War New York* (New York: Oxford University Press, 2010).

6. "Master Plan of Brooklyn Civic Center and Downtown Area," City Planning Commission, May 9, 1945; "Brooklyn Center Now at Mid-Point."

7. "Brooklyn Progress: Annual Report of Borough President John Cashmore," 1960–61, 6; Orlindo Grossi, "Downtown Brooklyn Civic Center Report," report prepared for New York City Planning Commission and published by Pratt Institute, Brooklyn, December 1962; "The Civic Center—Crown Jewel of Brooklyn," *NYJA*, December 2, 1962, 2.

8. "Civic Center," *NYT*, November 9, 1955, 32; *Fort Greene: Slum Clearance Plan Under Title I of the Housing Act of 1949*, Box 43, Folder 513, VIPMA; Matthew Gordon Lasner, "Fort Greene Title I" and "Pratt Institute Title I," in *Robert Moses and the Modern City: The Transformation of New York*, ed. Hilary Ballon and Kenneth T. Jackson (New York: W. W. Norton, 2007); "Vacant Store Windows Stare at Once Bustling Flatbush Avenue," *NYT*, September 5, 1965; "Portfolio: An Information for Community Districts: Community District 2," City Planning Commission, December 1979; "Portfolio: An Information for Community Districts: Community District 6," City Planning Commission, December 1979.

9. "Our Changing City: Downtown Brooklyn Glistens," *NYT*, July 18, 1955; Marc Augé, *Non-Places: Introduction to an Anthropology of Supermodernity* (New York: Verso, 1995).

10. For a description of "pro-growth coalitions," see John Mollenkopf, *The Contested City* (Princeton: Princeton University Press, 1983). For a description of the "redevelopment machine," see Schwartz, *The New York Approach*, chap. 5. For a detailed description of the politics behind the Civic Center project, see Schwartz, *The New York Approach*, 239–47; "Area in Brooklyn Fights for Itself," *NYT*, October 8, 1961.

11. "Meany Backs Moses Plea for Union-Held Housing," *NYT*, December 19, 1955, 1; William Zeckendorf, *Zeckendorf: The Autobiography of William Zeckendorf* (New York: Holt, Rinehart and Winston, 1970), 227.

12. Edward Logue, "Urban Renewal—or Urban Ruin?" *NYT*, November 9, 1958, SM17; "Mr. Moses Dissects the 'Long-Haired Planners,'" *NYT*, June 25, 1944, 16; "Master Plan Ideas 'Silly' Says Moses," *NYT*, December 12, 1940, 56; "The Achievements of Robert Moses," *NYT*, December 13, 1953, SM 12. For a discussion of Le Corbusier's limited influence on American public housing and private development, see

Mardges Bacon, *Le Corbusier in America: Travels in the Land of the Timid* (Cambridge, MA: MIT Press, 2001), 168–73, 200–2; see also Nicholas Dagen Bloom, *Public Housing That Worked: New York in the Twentieth Century* (Philadelphia: University of Pennsylvania Press, 2008), 62.

13. "Brooklyn Progress: Annual Report of Hon. John Cashmore of Borough of Brooklyn, 1956–1957," 15–17.

14. Cleveland Rodgers, *New York Plans for the Future* (New York: Harper and Brothers, 1943), 152–53; "City Planning: Battle of the Approach," *Fortune*, November 1943, 226; "A Plea for Simple English, Moses Wonders: Is It Still Taught?" *NYWTS*, January 25, 1962. The connection between postwar liberalism and urban redevelopment has been told best by Schwartz, *The New York Approach*.

15. For similar definitions of urban modernism, see David Harvey, *The Condition of Postmodernity* (Cambridge, MA: Blackwell, 1990), 10–38; Ted Relph, *The Modern Urban Landscape* (Baltimore: Johns Hopkins University Press, 1987).

16. For pro-decentralization arguments, see Ralph L. Woods, *America Reborn: A Plan for Decentralization of Industry* (New York: Longmans, Green, 1939); Peter Hall, *Cities of Tomorrow: An Intellectual History of Urban Planning and Design in the Twentieth Century* (Oxford: Blackwell, 2002), 142–88. For a description of the "specter of decentralization," see Robert M. Fogelson, *Downtown: Its Rise and Fall, 1880–1959* (New Haven: Yale University Press, 2001), 218–48; Miles L. Colean, "Postwar Cities—with or Without Planning?" RERBG, February 6, 1943, 9; "City Planning: Battle of the Approach," *Fortune*, November 1943, 226.

17. Clarence S. Stein, "The Future of New York," *Postwar Planning News Digest*, July 10, 1943, 3.

18. "Downtown Enters a New Era," *NYT*, January 31, 1960, 14; Fogelson, *Downtown*, 346–52; "Shortage in Curbs. Cities Around the Nation Try Many Plans for Solving the Parking Problem," *NYT*, March 9, 1952, XX14.

19. Logue, "Urban Ruin—or Urban Renewal?" 17, 28, 30–33. For the varying and inconsistent definitions of "blight," see G. E. Breger, "The Concept and Causes of Urban Blight," *Land Economics* 43 (November 1967): 369–76; Mabel Walker, *Urban Blight and Slums: Economic and Legal Factors in Their Origin, Reclamation, and Restoration* (Cambridge, MA: Harvard University Press, 1938); Fogelson, *Downtown*, chap. 7.

20. "Summary of Report on Fort Greene Recreation Committee," March 29, 1949, Box 18, Folder 3.3.011, BCSP; Julius Samuels, "The Fort Green Recreation Project," New York School of Social Work, December 1946, Box 32, Folder 5.3.074, BCSP; "Downtown Brooklyn," report prepared by the Department of Church Planning and Research of the Protestant Council of the City of New York (Chicago: National Lutheran Council, 1955), 40–45; "The Fire at 1101 Bedford Avenue Brooklyn, the Remedies for Slums," Mayor's Special Committee, July 7, 1952, Series 1, Box 0064C6, Folder 3, NYCHA; Joseph Caccavajo, "Park Slope Survey Reveals It's Ripe for 'Blight Disease,'" *BE*, March 10, 1949.

21. "The DARE Area Renewal Survey," Downtown Area Renewal Effort, 1959, 4; Rodgers, *New York Plans for the Future*, 76.

22. Brooklyn Chapter of the American Institute of Architects, "Civic Design Committee Report," February 23, 1954, 1–5; "Fifth of State's Auto Accidents in Brooklyn," *BHP*,

March 15, 1940; "Today's Safe Driving Hint," *BHP* January 10, 1941, 4; see also *BHP*, December 12, 1940, December 6, 1940, December 27, 1940; *CN*, December 15, 1938, 9; *CN*, June 15, 1939, 6; *CN*, December 19, 1940, 12; Donald Cuming and Bernard Hayes, "The Parking Problem in Downtown Brooklyn: Its Control and the Design of Parking Facilities," bachelor's thesis, Polytechnic Institute of Brooklyn, June 1940; "Traffic Pictured as City Destroyer," *NYT*, September 29, 1949, 31; Robert A. M. Stern, Thomas Mellins, and David Fishman, *New York 1960* (New York: Monacelli Press, 1995), 24.

23. Martin B. Dworkis, ed., *The Port of New York and the Management of Its Waterfront* (New York: New York University Graduate School of Public Administration and Social Service, 1959), 78; John Griffin, *Industrial Location in the New York Area* (New York: City College Press, 1956), 63–64; City Club of New York, "The Wastelands of New York City: A Preliminary Inquiry into the Nature of Commercial Slum Areas, Their Potential for Housing and Business Development," October 1962, 10–11; "Loeser's Forced Closing Shocks Heights Residents," *BHP*, February 14, 1952, 1.

24. Nathan Glazer and Daniel Patrick Moynihan, *Beyond the Melting Pot: The Negroes, Puerto Ricans, Jews, Italians, and Irish of New York City* (Cambridge, MA: MIT Press, 1963), 25–29, 91–94.

25. *Brooklyn Communities Population Characteristics and Neighborhood Social Resources*, 1:xv–xx; "Brooklyn Could Become a Slum Rotarians Are Told," *BHP*, April 9, 1958; "Brooklyn Called Slum of the Future," *NYT*, April 3, 1958.

26. "Mile-Long Phalanx of Apartment Houses Being Built on Third Avenue," *NYT*, December 24, 1961, R1; Stern, Mellins, and Fishman, *New York 1960*, 174–75; "Apartment Boom Aids All Classes," *NYT*, June 12, 1966, 1; "Skyscraper Surge: New York Office Boom Grows as Firms Move from New to Newest," *WSJ*, January 7, 1966, 1; "New Construction Stirs Quiet Borders of Prospect Park," *NYT*, May 17, 1964, R1.

27. "Developers Mean Business as They Transform Traditionally Residential Park Ave.," *NYT*, October 7, 1956, 1; "Park Ave Home Life Gives Way to Business in New Construction," *NYT*, October 7, 1956, 1; "Many of the City's 'New' Buildings Are Just Old Ones Redressed," *NYT*, November 21, 1965, R1; "New Face for Old Landmark," *SM*, September 1963, 13.

28. "New Buildings Sprout Fast but Eager Tenants Still Stand in Line," *WSJ*, July 13, 1956; Edgar M. Hoover and Raymond Vernon, *Anatomy of a Metropolis: The Changing Distribution of People and Jobs Within the New York Metropolitan Region* (Cambridge, MA: Harvard University Press, 1959), 98–103; Robert Weaver, *The Urban Complex: Human Values in Urban Life* (New York: Doubleday, 1964), 8–14.

29. Daniel Bell, *The Coming of Post-Industrial Society: A Venture in Social Forecasting* (New York: Basic Books, 1973), 129–42; Leonard Silk, *The Research Revolution* (New York: McGraw-Hill, 1960), 108–11; Freeman, *Working-Class New York*, 167–68; Jean Gottmann, *Megalopolis: The Urbanized Northeastern Seaboard of the United States* (Cambridge, MA: MIT Press, 1961), 565–72; Mollenkopf, *The Contested City*, 146.

30. Gottmann, *Megalopolis*, 564; "command and control center" is from Saskia Sassen, *The Global City: New York, London, Tokyo* (Princeton, NJ: Princeton University Press, 1991).

31. Gottmann, *Megalopolis*, 584–92; Hoover and Vernon, *Anatomy of a Metropolis*, 102–3; Gerald Manners, "The Office in the Metropolis: An Opportunity for Shaping Metropolitan America," *Economic Geography* 50 (April 1974): 93–110.

32. Gottmann, *Megalopolis*, 577–90; Daniel Bell, "The Three Faces of New York," *Dissent*, Summer 1961, 222–29.

33. Robert M. Lichtenberg, *One Tenth of a Nation: National Forces in the Economic Growth of the New York Region* (Cambridge, MA: Harvard University Press, 1960), 154; James L. Baughman, "Take Me Away from Manhattan: New York City and American Mass Culture," in *Capital of the American Century: The National and International Influence of New York City*, ed. Martin Shefter (New York: Russell Sage, 1993), 118–31, 597–618.

34. "New York *Has* a Future," *NYT*, January 30, 1955, 22; "New York's Construction Surge Continues," *SM*, February 1963, 14.

35. "New York City Office-Tower Building Boom Fails to Satisfy Companies' Soaring Needs," *WSJ*, March 7, 1968, 32; "Beautification in Action," *SM*, October 1959, 20; "New Buildings Sprout Fast but Eager Tenants Still Stand in Line."

36. Raymond Vernon as quoted in Robert A. Futterman, *The Future of Our Cities* (Garden City, NY: Doubleday, 1961), 117.

37. For a critique of the modernist ideal of an "obsolescence-proof building," see Peter Blake, *Form Follows Fiasco* (Boston: Little, Brown, 1974), 25.

38. "Building Projects Altering Skyline," *NYT*, August 23, 1954, 19; "Fluorescent Glow Lights City Skyline," *NYT*, February 23, 1958, R1; "Vinyl Flooring Comes of Age," *SM*, March 1957, 14–15; *Office Buildings: An Architectural Record Book* (New York: Dodge Corp, McGraw-Hill, 1961), 222–26.

39. "Brooklyn Center Now at the Mid-Point," *NYT*; Lewis Mumford, "The Red-Brick Beehives," *NY*, May 6, 1950. For a description of Kazan's egalitarian belief in Modernist design, see Freeman, *Working Class New York*, 115–19. For the 1950s as a non-ideological bureaucratic society, see Daniel Bell, *The End of Ideology: On the Exhaustion of Political Ideas in the Fifties* (Glencoe, IL: Free Press, 1960). For the democratic and egalitarian aspirations of postwar mass culture and its failures, see Lizabeth Cohen, *A Consumers' Republic: The Politics of Mass Consumption in Postwar America* (New York: Knopf, 2003).

40. *Buildings for Industry* (New York: Dodge, 1957), 2–3; "Interior Planning Pays Off," *SM*, October 1957, 14–15; Joseph H. Abel and Fred N. Severud, *Apartment Houses* (New York: Reinhold, 1947), 160–63; Futterman, *The Future of Our Cities*, 117; "Flexible Layout Offered in Co-op," *NYT*, November 6, 1960; "Building to Offer Flexible Layouts," *NYT*, December 26, 1983; "Office Space Must Be Evaluated as a Business Instrument," *RERBG*, April 23, 1955. For a contemporary critique of planned obsolescence, see Vance Packard, *The Waste Makers* (New York: D. McKay, 1960). For a celebration of urban flexibility, see Eliel Saarinen, *The City: Its Growth, Its Decay, Its Future* (New York: Reinhold, 1943), 144–47.

41. Rodgers, *New York Plans for the Future*, 11–12; "Proposal for a Master Plan for a Regional Heliport System," address by Thomas M. Sullivan, April 24, 1956, Helicopters over Brooklyn Folder, Box 3, HCP; "Copter Service Offered," *Mirror*, July 20, 1961.

42. Mitchell Gordon, *Sick Cities* (New York: Macmillan, 1964), 6.

43. Cleveland Rodgers and Rebecca B. Rankin, *New York: The World's Capital City* (New York: Harper and Brothers, 1948), 231; "New York *Has* a Future"; "It's Not Smallness That's Wanted but Intelligent Bigness," *NYT*, January 25, 1959, BR5, 30.

44. "This Isn't Definitive, Just an Integration of Overall Operations," *WP*, September 19, 1943, B5. The entry for *integration* in the 1933 version of *The Oxford English Dictionary* has no reference to race. In the 1972 version, citations referring to race date only from the 1940s onward. In the South in the early twentieth century, "race integration" was sometimes juxtaposed to "miscegenation" to mean actually a reinforcement of racial difference. See "South Sounds Alarm," *WP*, December 16, 1914, 2. Some of the earliest *NYT* articles that use *integration* in a racial sense place the term in quotation marks, suggesting that the connotation is new. See "Pamphlet Urges New Plan of 'Integration,'" *NYT*, December 31, 1942, 6. For a history of integration in the corporate world, see Alfred D. Chandler, *The Visible Hand: The Managerial Revolution in American Business* (Cambridge, MA: Harvard University Press, 1977).

45. York Willbern, *The Withering Away of the City* (Tuscaloosa: University of Alabama Press, 1964); "Cities Urged to Reverse Deterioration," *Washington Post and Times Herald*, September 26, 1957, A19; Catherine Bauer Wurster as quoted in Gordon, *Sick Cities*, 274; "Population Shifts: Efforts Made to Find if They're Permanent," *WSJ*, September 22, 1942, 1; "Changes in Cities Due After the War," *NYT*, January 15, 1943, 31.

46. "This Balkanized City: The Five Boroughs of New York Are Jealous Rival States," *NYT*, April 23, 1939, 106; Futterman, *The Future of Our Cities*, 97; Gordon, *Sick Cities*, 272–79; Robert Wood, *1400 Governments: The Political Economy of the New York Metropolitan Region* (Cambridge, MA: Harvard University Press, 1961).

47. Rodgers, *New York Plans for the Future*, 3, 6; Jose Luis Sert, *Can Our Cities Survive?* (Cambridge, MA: Harvard University Press, 1947), 2.

48. For an analysis of the garden metaphor, see Robert Self, *American Babylon: Race and the Struggle for Oakland* (Princeton, Princeton University Press, 2003); Robert Weaver, *The Urban Complex: Human Values in Urban Life* (Garden City, NY: Doubleday, 1964); George Horne, "Kingless Jungle New York's Waterfront," *Nation*, February 21, 1953, 163; "City Is a 'Monster' to Paris Architect; A-Bomb Proposed to Erase Flaws," *NYT*, October 14, 1953; "Clergyman Finds a 'Jungle' Uptown," *NYT*, December 11, 1958, 6; Fogelson, 32–36, 349–52, 387–94; Edward Higbee, *The Squeeze: Cities Without Space* (New York: William Morrow, 1960), xi. For the influence of cybernetics on urban planning, see Hall, *Cities of Tomorrow*, 359–63.

49. "Modern City Rule Backed at Hearing," *NYT*, July 16, 1953; Futterman, *The Future of Our Cities*, 98; Rodgers, *New York Plans for the Future*, xiv, 143; "City Planners Ask Metropolitan Mergers to Speed Development of Dangerous Areas," *NYT*, April 29, 1947, 22.

50. Caro, 744–45; "The Emergence of Mayor Wagner," *NYT*, August 14, 1955, SM20; Mark Gelfand, *A Nation of Cities: The Federal Government and Urban America* (New York: Oxford University Press, 1975), 159; "Brooklyn to Open a Welfare Center," *NYT*, October 16, 1955; "Our Changing City: Downtown Brooklyn Glistens."

51. Caro, 621–28; Peter D. McClelland and Alan L. Magdovitz, *Crisis in the Making: The Political Economy of New York State Since 1945* (New York: Cambridge University Press, 1981), 214–15; Jameson Doig, *Empire on the Hudson: Entrepreneurial Vision and Political Power at the Port of New York Authority* (New York: Columbia University Press, 2001); Gerald Fetner, "Julius Henry Cohen and the Origins of the Public Authority," *American Journal of Legal History* 21 (January 1977): 20–21, 38.

52. "Brooklyn Progress: Annual Report of Hon. John Cashmore of Borough of Brooklyn," 1959; Freeman, *Working Class New York*, 162.

53. *Brooklyn Communities: Population Characteristics and Neighborhood Social Resources*, 1:xli; Arnold Harold Diamond, "The New York City Housing Authority: A Study in Public Corporations," Ph.D. diss., Columbia University, 1954, 47–90; Lewis Mumford, "The Sky Line: From Blight to Beauty," *NY*, April 25, 1953.

54. Rodgers, *New York Plans for the Future*, 297–302; Paul Windels to editor, *NYT*, March 29, 1943, 14; Edward Weinfeld to editor, *NYT*, April 2, 1943, 20; Schwartz, 84–107; "Big Apartment Colony Acquired in Brooklyn," *NYT*, June 24, 1960.

55. Jewel Bellush and Murray Hausknecht, "Urban Renewal: An Historical Overview," in *Urban Renewal: People, Politics, and Planning*, ed. Jewel Bellush and Murray Hausknecht (New York: Doubleday, 1967), 10–14.

56. Gelfand, *A Nation of Cities*, 283–84; "This Is ACTION," American Council to Improve Our Neighborhoods, 1961; Women's City Club of New York, "Housing Primer," February 1964, New York City Housing Authority Folder, VFMANYC.

57. "Housing Unit for Brooklyn," *NYT*, September 16, 1939; Wendell Pritchett, *Robert Clifton Weaver and the American City: The Life and Times of an Urban Reformer* (Chicago: University of Chicago Press, 2008), 250–52; Thomas Sugrue, *Sweet Land of Liberty: The Forgotten Struggle for Civil Rights in the North* (New York: Random House, 2008), 400–402; "Weaver Says Urban Renewal Depends on Mobility for Negroes," *NYT*, October 18, 1961; "Housing in North Sets Bias Picture," *NYT*, April 25, 1956.

58. For a nuanced take on the historic and architectural legacy of urban renewal, see Richard Longstreth, "The Difficult Legacy of Urban Renewal," *CRM: The Journal of Heritage Stewardship* 3, 1 (Winter 2006). For a balanced assessment of the legacy of urban renewal in New York City, see Ballon and Jackson, *Robert Moses and the Modern City*.

3   The Middle Cityscape of Brooklyn Heights

1. Truman Capote, "Brooklyn Heights: A Personal Memoir," *Holiday*, February 1959, 64; Capote had lived previously in the Heights in the 1940s, so his account was more a rediscovery of the area.

2. Ibid.

3. Capote, "A House on the Heights," in Andrew Wyatt Sexton, *The Brooklyn Reader: 30 Writers Celebrate America's Favorite Borough* (New York: Crown, 1994), 32.

4. Ibid.

5. Ibid., 28–29.

6. "Teen Problem? Depends on the Teenager," *BHP*, November 26, 1959; "'Community Life' Seen as Greatest Need Here: Annual Meeting Discusses Heights Problems and

Future," *BHP*, October 8, 1953, 1; "Special Survey—Do You Prefer Heights or Sub-urbs?" *BHP*, November 8, 1956, 1, 3.

7. Brooklyn Heights Association, *Brooklyn Heights: Yesterday—Today—Tomorrow* (Brooklyn Heights Association, 1937), 26; James Agee, "Southeast of the Island: Travel Notes," in *The Collected Short Prose of James Agee*, ed. Robert Fitzgerald (Boston: Houghton Mifflin Co., 1968), 181.

8. Capote, "Brooklyn Heights: A Personal Memoir," 66; "Experts Cite Heights Housing: Rooming Houses Disappearing?" *BHP*, September 5, 1957, 1; "Renaissance in Flower on Lower Hicks Street," *BHP*, January 22, 1959; "Newcomers Like Link with Past, Feel Area Is Symbol of Frontier," *NYWTS*, January 25, 1957.

9. Brooklyn Heights had a higher number of new residents than the rest of the borough. The averages for Brooklyn were 16 percent and 24 percent, respectively. U.S. Department of Commerce, Bureau of the Census, *Census of Population, 1960, Census Tract Statistics for New York City* (Washington, DC: U.S. Government Printing Office, 1962), Table H-2; Lee Adler, "A Statistical Portrait of Brooklyn Heights Prepared by Renewal Committee of the Brooklyn Heights Association," December 1965, Brooklyn Heights Folder, VFBCBPL.

10. "Increased Demand for Large Quarters Seen by J. Hanlin," *BHP*, March 21, 1941, 1.

11. "Brooklyn Heights Offers the 'Good Life,'" *HT*, November 11, 1957; "Magnetic Charm Is Friendliness and Romance," *NYWTS*, January 22, 1957; "Brooklyn Heights Village Boast a Heavy Concentration of the Arts," *NYWTS*, January 23, 1957; "Newcomers Like Link with the Past, Feel Area Is Symbol of Frontier, Artists, Writers Replace Age of Victorians," *NYWTS*, January 25, 1957.

12. "Who's Wild—and Where," *BHP*, July 19, 1956, 4; "Brooklyn Heights Village Boast a Heavy Concentration of the Arts."

13. Hoover and Vernon, *Anatomy of a Metropolis*, 171–72, 320; Joshua B. Freeman, *Working-Class New York* (New York: Free Press, 2000), 105.

14. Hoover and Vernon, *Anatomy of a Metropolis*, 171; "Remarks of Otis Pratt Pearsall at the Ceremonial Installation of Historic District Markers on Brooklyn Heights," in "The Origins of New York's Historic Districting, Compiled for the Brooklyn Heights Association's 30th Anniversary of the New York Landmark Preservation Law," BCBPL. See example of listings in *NYT*, January 22, 1955; January 9, 1955; March 9, 1958; January 19, 1958.

15. "Experts Cite Heights Housing: Rooming Houses Disappearing?" *BHP*, September 5, 1957, 1; "Renaissance in Flower on Lower Hicks Street," *BHP*, January 22, 1959.

16. "Beach, Bohemia, Barracks—Brooklyn," *NYT*, September 29, 1963.

17. "Brooklyn and Queens," *Fortune*, July 20, 1939, 145.

18. "New Resident Offers First Impressions," letter to the editor, *BHP*, October 15, 1953, 4; "BHP Writer Scores One for Good Old B'klyn," *BHP*, October 31, 1945, 1; "Brooklyn Heights Village Boast a Heavy Concentration of the Arts"; "Beach, Bohemia, Barracks—Brooklyn," *NYT*, 233.

19. Frank Lewis, "This Is Brooklyn?" *AM*, 161 (February, 1956), 38–39.

20. Lewis, "This Is Brooklyn?" 84; "BHP Writer Scores One for Good Old B'klyn."

21. "New Resident Offers First Impressions"; "You're Going to Live in Brooklyn?"; "Hoosier View of Heights," *BHP*, January 5, 1967, 8; "Artists Compares Heights to

Paris," *BHP*, April 11, 1957, 4; "Tony on Heights—'It's Like Chelsea,'" *BHP*, April 30, 1967, 1.

22. Bruce Greenfield, *Narrating Discovery: The Romantic Explorer in American Literature, 1790–1855* (New York: Columbia University Press, 1992), 165–67, 184–88.

23. Some Heights residents were unenthusiastic about the wave of urban discovery narratives. "Will it be worth it any longer to contemplate the splendor of that magic Esplanade if we have to fight our way past groups of young women in black stockings and dirty raincoats and young men in desert boots and slightly torn combat jackets—all arguing Existentialism in loud unpleasant tones?" implored one resident. "Let there be no more chatty pages in *Cue*, introspections in *Holiday*, commercials in the *World-Telegram and Sun*, or anything else anywhere." E. S. Seeley to editor, *BHP*, January 22, 1959; "Brooklyn Heights Offers the 'Good Life'"; "Magnetic Charm Is Friendliness and Romance"; "Charming Old Heights Clings to City Ways," *NYWTS*, January 22, 1957.

24. For a contemporary description of this new middle-class strain of anti-suburbanism in the 1950s and 1960s, see Herbert Gans, *The Levittowners: Ways of Life and Politics in a New Suburban Community* (New York: Columbia University Press, 1967), xxvii–xxiv. For a description of the "suburban ideal" see Kenneth Jackson, *Crabgrass Frontiers: The Suburbanization of the United States* (New York: Oxford University Press, 1985); Robert Fishman, *Bourgeois Utopias: The Rise and Fall of Suburbia* (New York: Basic Books, 1987); Lizabeth Cohen, *A Consumers' Republic: The Politics of Mass Consumption in Postwar America* (New York: Alfred A. Knopf, 2003), 194–97.

25. "The Heights as Suburbia," *BHP*, August 9, 1956, 4.

26. "Trouble in Paradise," *BHP*, May 23, 1957, 2.

27. "Suburbia and Other Sorrows," *BHP*, April 3, 1958, 2.

28. Harry Gantt to editor, *BHP*, January 31, 1957, 4. The celebration of the solitary, purposeless walker as an antidote to alienating mass commuting has been a trope of romantic urban writing since the beginnings of the separation of home from the workplace in the mid-nineteenth century; see Lawrence Buell, *Writing for an Endangered World: Literature, Culture, and Environment in the U.S. and Beyond* (Cambridge, MA: Harvard University Press, 2001), 94–103.

29. "Pastor Tells What Makes Suburbanites Run and Why," *BHP*, April 3, 1958, 1.

30. "Pastor Tells What Makes Suburbanites Run and Why"; "Janeways' Way: Back to the City," *BHP*, February 26, 1959, 6; "Art Reaches the Heights," *BHP*, October 2, 1958, 4.

31. "Civilization, the City and the Heights," *BHP*, May 14, 1959, 4; "For Those Who Can't Go Home Again . . . ," *BHP*, May 7, 1959, 4.

32. "Special Survey"; "One Last Valiant Effort," *BHP*, February 26, 1959, 4; "'Cult of mediocrity' in City and Suburb: Heights Depicted as 'Rare Island,'" *BHP*, March 20, 1958, 1; "Lower Hicks Is Melting Pot," *BHP*, October 8, 1959, 5; Edmund J. Pinto, "An Editor's First View of the Heights," *BHP*, January 2, 1954, 4.

33. "Brooklyn Is My Neighborhood," *Vogue*, 1941, reprinted in Alexander Klein, ed., *The Empire City: A Treasury of New York* (New York: Rinehart, 1955); "The Romance of the Other," chap. in Mary Corey, *The World Through a Monocle: The New Yorker at Midcentury* (Cambridge, MA: Harvard University Press), 102–3.

34. "A Professional Status Seeker Settles Down," *BHP*, June 18, 1959, 6.

35. Originally a 1949 article in *Harper's*, reprinted as "Highbrow, Middlebrow, Low-brow" in Russell Lynes, *The Tastemakers* (New York: Harper's, 1954); Corey, *The World Through a Monocle*, 11–12; Richard A. Peterson and Roger M. Kern, "Changing Highbrow Taste: From Snob to Omnivore," *American Sociological Review* 61, 5 (October 1996): 900–7; "Brooklyn Heights Village Boast a Heavy Concentration of Arts," *NYWTS*, January 23, 1957.

36. "Old vs. New: The Merchants Appraise Heights Customers," *BHP*, September 12, 1957, 1.

37. Gans as quoted in Robert Weaver, *Dilemmas of Urban America* (Cambridge, MA: Harvard University Press, 1965), 6; Lynes, *The Tastemakers*, 333; Corey, *The World Through a Monocle*, 113–14.

38. Charles Rolo, "The New Bohemia," *Flair*, February 1950, 27–28; for an example of this fusion of middle-class identities in Brooklyn Heights, see "Lewis Reed, Grace Ct. Resident Is Artist-Poet-Writer-Musician-Lawyer!" *BHP*, November 1953, 1.

39. Pinto, "An Editor's First View of the Heights."

40. "Whither Brooklyn Heights?" *BHP*, December 11, 1958.

41. "'Cult of Mediocrity' in City and Suburb: Mr. McKinney Hits 'Safe' Age," *BHP*, March 20, 1958; "Professor Blasts 'Status Seekers,'" *BHP*, July 30, 1959, 2.

42. Hoover and Vernon, 172.

43. Ibid., 171–72, 320.

44. "A False Assumption," *BHP*, April 18, 1957, 4; "A 'Village Far East' Visit," *NYWTS*, n.d. [est. early 1960s]; "Our Changing City: Downtown Brooklyn Glistens," 23.

45. "For Those Who Can't Go Home Again . . ."; "A House on the Heights," 27; "Brownstone Renaissance Puts Middle Class in Touch with Cultured Past," *Phoenix*, October 26, 1972, 8; Mitchell Schwarzer, "Myths of Permanence and Transience in the Discourse on Historic Preservation in the United States," *Journal of Architectural Education*, September 1994, 2–11.

46. Alfred Kazin, *A Walker in the City* (New York: Harcourt, Brace, 1951), 171–72. For a description of brownstone renovation and enthusiasm for the Victorian era in 1940s Greenwich Village, see Claude Lévi-Strauss, "New York in 1941," chap. in *View from Afar*, trans. Joachim Neugroschel and Phoebe Hoss (Chicago: University of Chicago Press, 1985), 263–64.

47. "Want Heaven on Earth? You'll Find It in the City," *BHP*, April 16, 1959, 7; Buell, *Writing for an Endangered World*, 84–89.

48. "Inspiration with Victuals? Beat It to 'Black Spring,'" *BHP*, January 9, 1959; "Touring Heights Leads to Rich Reminders of Literary History: Other Groups Here Outnumber Writers but Famous Scribes Shape Heights *Persona*," *BHP*, September 30, 1982.

49. Martin S. James, "Cadman Plaza in Brooklyn Heights: A Study of the Misuse of Public Power and Funds in Urban Renewal," June 13, 1961, Box 125, Folder 1799, RWPMA.

50. Elias Wilentz, "The Failure of Modern Architecture: Man Was Not Made for Dormitories," *VV*, November 10, 1960, 6.

51. "New Resident Offers First Impressions"; "'Town Drunk' Is Friend to Everyone on the Heights," *BHP*, October 8, 1953, 1.

52. Ibid.; "Magnetic Charm Is Friendliness and Romance"; Rod Phillips, *"Forest Beatniks" and "Urban Thoreaus": Gary Snyder, Jack Kerouac, Lew Welch and Michael McClure* (New York: Peter Lang, 2000), 2–25; Robert Fanuzzi, "Thoreau's Urban Imagination," *American Literature* 68, 2 (June 1996).

53. Neil Carson, *"A View from the Bridge* and the Expansion of Vision," in *Arthur Miller*, ed. Harold Bloom (New York: Chelsea House, 1987), 93–102; Leonard Moss, "The Perspective of a Playwright," in *Arthur Miller*, ed. Harold Bloom (New York: Chelsea House, 1987), 79–92.

54. Arthur Miller, "Death of a Salesman," in *Arthur Miller's Collected Plays* (New York: Viking Press, 1957), 134–35. In his 1968 play *The Price*, a soon-to-be demolished brownstone is a repository of memory for the protagonists.

55. Ibid., 180–81.

56. Albert Halper, *Atlantic Avenue* (New York: Dell, 1956); Irving Shulman, *The Amboy Dukes* (New York: Doubleday, 1947); Frank Paley, *Rumble on the Docks* (New York: Crown, 1953); Kenneth H. Brown, *The Narrows* (New York: Dial Press, 1970).

57. Hubert Selby Jr., *Last Exit to Brooklyn* (New York: Grove Press, 1957).

58. Norman Mailer, "The White Negro: Superficial Reflections on the Hipster," chap. in *Advertisements for Myself* (Cambridge, MA: Harvard University Press, 1959), 339.

59. Norman Mailer, *Barbary Shore* (New York: Random House, 1951); George Cotkin, "Norman Mailer's Existential Errand," chap. in *Existential America* (Baltimore: Johns Hopkins University Press, 2003), 184–209.

60. Mailer, "The Hip and the Square: The List," 424–25, and "The White Negro: Superficial Reflections on the Hipster," 339–40, in *Advertisements for Myself* (Cambridge, MA: Harvard University Press); "Inspiration with Victuals? Beat It to 'Black Spring'"; Ann Charters, ed., *Beat Down Your Soul* (London: Penguin, 2001); Lee Bartlett, ed., *The Beats: Essays in Criticism* (London: McFarland, 1981).

61. Bruce Davidson, *Brooklyn Gang* (New York: Twin Palm, 1998), 92, 95; see also Harrison Salisbury, *The Shook-Up Generation* (New York: Harper and Brothers, 1958), 211–12; Allen Ginsberg, *Howl and Other Poems* (San Francisco: City Lights, 1956); Ned Polsky, "The Village Beat Scene," *Dissent* 8 (Summer 1961): 348–53; Larry Sloman, *Reefer Madness: A History of Marijuana* (Indianapolis: Bobbs-Merrill, 1969), 174; Martin Booth, *Cannabis: A History* (New York: St. Martin's Press, 2003), 193–204; Marcus Boon, *The Road of Excess: A History of Writers on Drugs* (Cambridge, MA: Harvard University Press, 2002), 160–63.

62. Miller, *A View from the Bridge*.

63. Eleanor L. Brilliant, *The United Way: Dilemmas of Organized Charity* (New York: Columbia University Press, 1990), 28–46; Alice O'Connor, *Poverty Knowledge: Social Science, Social Policy and the Poor in Twentieth-Century U.S. History* (Princeton, NJ: Princeton University Press, 2001), chap. 4.

64. J. B. Maller, "Juvenile Delinquency in New York City: A Summary of a Comprehensive Report," November 1936, 14, 17–18, NYCMA; "Delinquency Rates by Health Districts and Location of Proposed Facility, 1954," Box 123, Folder 2141, RWPMA; "Report of First Year's Work of Brooklyn Street Clubs Project," *Youth Board News*, February-March 1953, 1.

65. "Teenage Gangs," New York City Youth Board, Box 123, Folder 2141, RWPMA.

66. Arthur Miller, "Memorandum on Juvenile Delinquency Film," July 21, 1955, Box 123, Folder 2141, RWPMA; Davidson, *Brooklyn Gang*; Salisbury, *The Shook-Up Generation*; Samuel Zipp, *Manhattan Projects: The Rise and Fall of Urban Renewal in Cold War New York* (New York: Oxford University Press, 2010), 157–61.
67. "H'ts Settlement to Mark 50th Year in November," *BHP*, June 17, 1954, 1; "The Very Image," *BHP*, September 25, 1958, 4.
68. For more on the historical connection between settlement work and romantic urbanism, see Buell, *Writing for an Endangered World*, 90–103.
69. Coldwell to editor, "Pleasure and Plain in Willowtown," *BHP*, July 12, 1956, 5.
70. George Chauncey, *Gay New York* (New York: Basic Books, 1994), 85; Eric C. Schneider, *Vampires, Dragons, and Egyptian Kings: Youth Gangs in Postwar New York* (Princeton, NJ: Princeton University Press, 1999), 133–36; Stephen O. Murray, "Machismo, Male Homosexuality, and Latino Culture," in *Latin American Homosexualities*, ed. Stephen O. Murray (Albuquerque: University of New Mexico Press, 1995), 49–70; Salisbury, *The Shook-Up Generation*, 34; "Growth of Overt Homosexuality in the City Provokes Widespread Concern," *NYT*, December 17, 1963; "Gay Bars as Private Places," *Landscape* 24, 1 (1980): 11–12.
71. Albert J. Reiss Jr., "The Social Integration of Queers and Peers," *Social Problems* 9, 2 (Autumn 1961); Schneider, *Vampires, Dragons, and Egyptian Kings*, 25, 134–35.
72. Vincent Riccio and Bill Slocum, *All the Way Down: The Violent World of Street Gangs* (New York: Simon and Schuster, 1962), 110–12.
73. Ibid.; Chauncey, *Gay New York*, 52–53; Maurice Leznoff and William A. Westley, "The Homosexual Community," *Social Problems* 3, 4 (April 1956): 260. In *Last Exit in Brooklyn*, Selby also captures the class differences between drag queens and working-class young men.
74. Chauncey, *Gay New York*, 151, 358; "Tenants at 2 Grace Court Face Up to a Serious Problem," *BHP*, September 25, 1966; "Homosexuality on the Heights," *BHP*, September 12, 1963; "Third Morals Arrest in Bar in 3 Weeks," *BHP*, September 5, 1963; name withheld upon request, "Homosexuality on the Heights," *BHP*, September 12, 1963; "Homosexuality Debate," *BHP*, September 19, 1963; "Editorial," *BHP*, July 21, 1966; "Heights Association Issues Statement on Homosexuals," *BHP*, May 26, 1966; "2 Regulars Speak," *BHP*, June 24, 1965; Mattachine Society to editor, *BHP*, June 9, 1966; see also letters June 24, 1965; June 9, 1966; July 15, 1965; July 29, 1965; "Areas Where Gays Gather and Suggested Number of Leaflets," Folder 1, Box 58, GABNYPL; "Perverts, Sots, Panhandlers Permeating Brooklyn Heights," *BHP*, March 17, 1949, 1; "Gay Alliance of Brooklyn Newsletter," April 25, 1972, GABNYPL, Folder 12; ibid., June 6, 1972.
75. Bennett Berger to editor, *Reporter*, January 5, 1961, 10.
76. Capote, "A House on the Heights," 39–41.

4   The Two Machines in the Garden

1. The distinction between old and new machines is made by Theodore J. Lowi, *The End of Liberalism: Ideology, Policy, and the Crisis of Public Authority* (New York: W. W. Norton, 1969), 200–6.

2. "The Heights Is Too Uniform," *BHP*, November 13, 1958, 5.

3. Sylvia Taylor to editor, "Four Suggestions," *BHP*, January 10, 1957, 4.

4. "Residents Name New Ways to Improve Life on the Heights," *BHP*, January 17, 1957, 1; Mrs. William R. Willets to editor, "Keep Village Out," *BHP*, January 24, 1957, 4; "Art Reaches the Heights," *BHP*, October 2, 1958, 4.

5. "Mendes Cites Youth Trend on Heights," *BHP*, March 28, 1957, 1; "New Program for the Changing Heights," editorial, *BHP*, April 4, 1957.

6. "The Pioneers: Renaissance in Flower on Lower Hicks Street," *BHP*, January 22, 1959, 5.

7. "The Rewards of Renovation Are Many," *BHP*, January 8, 1959, 1, 6.

8. Charles Lockwood, *Bricks and Brownstones: The New York Row House, 1783–1929* (New York: McGraw-Hill, 1972), xii–xiii.

9. "Levins Learn Renovating First Hand," *BHP*, January 15, 1959, 1.

10. "Is Rent Control for You?" *BHP*, July 30, 1959, 3.

11. "Progress and Poverty on the Heights," *BHP*, July 23, 1959, 2.

12. "State Street Is a Great Street These Days," *BHP*, February 12, 1959, 3.

13. For a discussion of "toxic discourses," see Lawrence Buell, *Writing for an Endangered World: Literature, Culture, and Environment in the U.S. and Beyond* (Cambridge, MA: Harvard University Press, 2001), 30–54.

14. "Art Reaches the Heights"; "Art Colony Is Flourishing on Hicks," *BHP*, November 13 1958.

15. "Willow Town Association," *BHP*, September 11, 1952, 3; "Willowtown Party to Be 'Carnival,'" *BHP*, May 23, 1957, 4.

16. "Brooklyn Brownstone Areas Boast Life Style and Architectural Diversity," *Phoenix*, February 8, 1973, 18; "Local Brownstoners Revive Skills and Arts of Craftsmanship," *Phoenix*, October 18, 1973, 8; Nan Ellin, *Postmodern Urbanism* (Princeton, NJ: Princeton University Press, 1996), 156–63; "Housing the Loft Generation," *NYT*, October 9, 1963.

17. "Willowtown Factory Has Growing Pains," *BHP*, October 25, 1956, 1.

18. "Heights Factory Wins Fight to Stay Here Neither Side Satisfied," *BHP*, November 15, 1956, 1; Malcolm Chesney Jr. to editor, *BHP*, November 15, 1956, 1.

19. "Heights Protests Garage Expansion," *BHP*, July 16, 1959, 1; "Garage Denied College Place Zone Variance," *BHP*, July 30 1959, 1.

20. "New Way to Be a Democrat," *BHP*, June 20, 1957, 1; "In the Future, a Fight," *BHP*, November 14, 1957, 2; "Reform Dems Hit 'One-Man' Rule, Name Candidates," *BHP*, March 13, 1958, 1; "Democracy Revisited," *BHP*, February 5, 1959, 4.

21. James Q. Wilson, *The Amateur Democrat: Club Politics in Three Cities* (Chicago: University of Chicago Press, 1962), 2–16, 41–43, 67–69; Daniel P. Moynihan, "'Bosses' and 'Reformers,'" *Commentary*, June 1961, 462–63.

22. "Heights GOP Edge Is More or Less (More or Less)," *BHP*, December 6, 1956; "Dorn Is in 3-Way Race to Keep 12th District in G.O.P. Column," *NYT*, October 23, 1958, 24.

23. "Republicans, Liberals Call Cronin Charge 'Ridiculous,'" *BHP*, October 30, 1958, 1; Roy Peel, "New Machines for Old: Decline of the Bosses," *Nation*, September 5, 1953, 89; Wilson, *The Amateur Democrat*, 36–40.

24. "Dr. Bowman Is a Modest Man," *BHP*, October 3, 1957, 1; "Best Man for the Job," *BHP*, October 17, 1957; "Candidates with a Difference," *BHP*, October 23, 1958.

25. "The Great Debates: 2 Candidates In Search of a Missing Councilman," *BHP*, October 31, 1957, 1; "Two Debates, One Winner," *BHP*, October 31, 1957, 2; "Best Man for the Job," October 17, 1957, 2.

26. Wilson, *The Amateur Democrat*, 52–56; "Images of Presidential Possibilities," Social Research, Inc., August 1956, Box 280, Folder 7, Series 4, Subseries 2, ASP; Thurston Macauley, "A Program to Break the Stevenson Egghead Myth, or the Old Shell Game," Box 287, Folder 4, Series 4, Subseries 2, ASP; Sam Polur, Students for Stevenson Fund, to Barry Bingham, February 27, 1956, Box 287, Folder 5, Series 4, Subseries 2, ASP; Pauli Murray to Arthur Schlesinger Jr., August 21, 1952, Box 238, Folder 3, Series 4, Subseries 1, ASP. For a famous criticism of American anti-intellectualism, see Brooklyn Heights resident Richard Hofstadter's *Anti-Intellectualism in American Life* (New York: Knopf, 1963).

27. "New Way to Be a Democrat"; "Reform Democrats Hit 'One-Man Rule'"; "Independent Dems to Fight Regulars," *BHP*, February 20, 1958, 1; "Where Do We Go from Here?" report by Stevenson campaign on November loss, Box 238 Folder 5, Series 4, Subseries 1, ASP. For similar events in Manhattan, see Moynihan, "'Bosses' and 'Reformers,'" 462, 465–66; Robert Lekachman, "How We Beat the Machine: Challenging Tammany at the District Level," *Commentary*, April 1958, 290–91; Dan Wakefield, "Greenwich Village Challenges Tammany," *Commentary*, October 1959, 309–10.

28. "In the Future, a Fight," *BHP*, November 14, 1957, 4; "Republicans, Liberals Call Cronin Charge 'Ridiculous'"; "Independent Democrats to Meet, Assess Primary," *BHP*, September 25, 1958, 2; "The Art of Losing," *BHP*, November 20, 1958, 4.

29. "Where We Stand," *BHP*, October 20, 1959, 4; "Candidates with a Difference"; Moynihan, "'Bosses' and 'Reformers,'" 462–63; Wakefield, "Greenwich Village Challenges Tammany," 308–9.

30. Norman M. Adler and Blanche Davis Blank, *Political Clubs in New York* (New York: Praeger, 1975), 174–75.

31. "Heroes and Heresies," *BHP* January 22, 1959, 2.

32. "West Brooklyn Independent Democrats," *NYWTS*, March 24, 1962; "Agenda," *The Independent Democrat*, February 1, 1962; "The Independent Dems Plan a New Service," *BHP*, January 8, 1959, 4; Monroe Singer to editor, *BHP*, January 15, 1959, 1; Costikyan, *Behind Closed Doors*, 35. For similar organizations in other cities, see James Ottenberg, *The Democratic Club Story* (New York: Lexington Democratic Club, 1960), 7–12, 45; Steven A. Mitchell, *Elm Street Politics* (New York: Oceana Publications, 1959), 40–41; Wilson, *The Amateur Democrat*, 226–57.

33. Wilson, *The Amateur Democrat*, 165–75; Mitchell, *Elm Street Politics*, 31.

34. Charles Monaghan, interview by author, April 1, 2003, New York City; Wilson, *The Amateur Democrat*, 258–88; Wakefield, "Greenwich Village Challenges Tammany," 308–9; Mitchell, *Elm Street Politics*, 46, 86–87.

35. James Q. Wilson, *Negro Politics: The Search for Leadership* (New York: Free Press, 1960), 44–76; Wilson, *The Amateur Democrat*, 280–82; Will Chasan, "Congressman Powell's Downhill Fight in Harlem," *Reporter*, July 10, 1958, 24–28; Meg Greenfield,

"Tammany in Search of a Boss," *Reporter*, April 13, 1961, 28–31; Adler and Blank, *Political Clubs in New York*, 187.

36. Wilson, *The Amateur Democrat*, 312–16.

37. Ibid., 258–88; "New York Committee Meeting," May 1, 1961, NYC Political Clubs Folder, VFMANYC; "Mendes Cites Youth Trend on Heights," *BHP*, March 28, 1957, 1.

38. Shirley Chisholm, *Unbought and Unbossed* (Boston: Houghton Mifflin, 1970), 34–36; Martha Biondi, *To Stand and Fight: The Struggle for Civil Rights in Postwar New York City* (Cambridge: MA: Harvard University Press, 2003), 216–17.

39. Chisholm, *Unbought and Unbossed*, 47–50; John C. Walter, *The Harlem Fox: J. Raymond Jones and Tammany, 1920–1970* (Albany: State University of New York Press, 1989), 124–37.

40. Chisholm, *Unbought and Unbossed*, 67–77; "Head of Operation Breadbasket Says He Opposes Mrs. Chisholm," *NYT*, November 27, 1972, 22; "Voice Articles Attacks Rep. Shirley Chisholm," *NYAM*, October 28, 1978, 1; Jim Sleeper, *The Closest of Strangers: Liberalism and the Politics of Race in New York* (New York: W. W. Norton, 1990), 56–67, 261–72.

41. "WBID Panel Cites Gains Made by Insurgent Dems," *BHP*, October 1, 1959, 1.

42. "Record Crowd Hears CCIC Housing Proposal," *BHP*, April 23, 1959, 1; "Mitchell Urges," *BHP*, April 28, 1959, 1; Otis Pratt Pearsall, "Reminiscences of the Nine Year Effort to Designate Brooklyn Heights as New York City's First Historic District and Its First Limited Height District," prepared on the occasion of the Historic District Council's 1993 Landmark Lion Award Presentation, Borough Hall, Brooklyn, March 8, 1993, BCBPL, 6; "Brooklynites Set Action on Heights," *NYT*, April 21, 1959, 37.

43. "Record Crowd Hears CCIC Housing Proposal," 1, 2. The "air conditioned nightmare" is from Henry Miller, *The Air-Conditioned Nightmare* (New York: New Directions, 1970 [1945]).

44. Samuel S. Spiegel, *The Forgotten Man in Housing* (New York: Author, 1959), 5.

45. For the similar role of urban renewal in creating a sense of "neighborhood" in Greenwich Village, see Peter J. Mesler, "Confrontation over Control of Neighborhood Renewal: The Relationship Between City Agencies and Local Residents in the Renewal of the West Village," Ph.D. diss., Columbia University, 1979, 77–85.

46. G. J. Bender to Robert Moses, August 3, 1956, Box 116, RMP.

47. Robert Moses to Otis Swann Carroll, July 18, 1956, Box 116, RMP; "Slum Clearance in the Heights—The Full Story," *BHP*, July 12, 1956, 1.

48. "A House to House Sampling," *BHP*, July 12, 1956, 1; Otis Swann Carroll to Robert Moses, July 15, 1956, Box 116, RMP.

49. "Slum Clearance in the Heights—The Full Story."

50. "Willowtown Drafts Petition for Survival," *BHP*, August 23, 1956, 1; "We Can Leave Heights Alone, Moses Writes," *BHP*, August 2, 1956, 1; "Willow Town Opposes Slum Study of Area," *BHP*, August 2, 1956, 1; Walter Bruchhausen to H. Haughton Bell, February 4, 1957, Box 116, RMP.

51. "A House-to-House Sampling"; "Willowtown Is Luke-Warm to New Housing Proposal," *BHP*, December 27, 1956, 1; "Willowtown Searches for New Housing

Solutions," *BHP*, January 24, 1957; "Willowtown Will Fix 'Soft Spots,'" *BHP*, April 25, 1957, 1.

52. "Willowtown Ready to Fight 'Master Builder,'" *BHP*, July 12, 1956, 1; "It's That Same Old Title," *BHP*, December 13, 1956, 2.

53. Robert Moses to Hugh Cole, April 15, 1957, Box 116, RMP; "Moses' Memory: Long on Peeves, Short on Names," *BHP*, November 22, 1956, 2; Bruchhausen to Bell; Robert Moses to G. J. Bender, August 8, 1956, Box 116, RMP.

54. Howard Swain to Robert Moses, April 9, 1957, Box 116, RMP; G. J. Bender to Robert Moses, December 5, 1959, Box 118, RMP.

55. "Cadman Plaza Survey in Progress: Co-op Sought," *BHP*, January 17, 1957, 1; "Skid-Row Gone, But . . . ," *BHP*, February 25, 1965, 1; "Century-Old Candy Plant in Brooklyn Will Be Converted into Artist Studios," *NYT*, March 3, 1968, R8; "Some Slum! Monroe Placers Retort," *BHP*, February 12, 1959, 1; Eric Meyer, "The Cadman Plaza Plan," *PPP*, July 1963, 1.

56. "Cadman Plaza Slum Survey in Progress," *BHP*, January 17, 1957, 1; "Tentative Sponsor Named for Cadman Development," *BHP*, December 18, 1958, 1.

57. "772-Unit Project Set for Brooklyn," *NYT*, April 20, 1959, 33. Robert Moses, "Press Release," April 20, 1959, Box 118, RMP.

58. Telegram from Algernon Black to Robert Wagner, June 25, 1956, Box 126, Folder 1799, RWPMA; point about low-income housing made by Freeman, *Working-Class New York*, 114.

59. Pearsall, "Reminiscences."

60. "New Group Charts Plan for Housing," *BHP*, December 24, 1958, 2; "CCIC Lists Housing Goals," *BHP*, January 1, 1958, 1.

61. "CCIC Lists Housing Goals."

62. Robert Moses to Harry J. Donnelly Jr., October 5, 1959, Box 118, RMP.

63. "Heights Architects Begin Local Survey," *BHP*, February 12, 1959, 1; "Brooklynites Set Action on the Heights, Residents Meet Tonight to Discuss How to Preserve Community's Charm," *NYT*, April 21, 1959, 37; "CCIC Gets Help from 60 Volunteers," *BHP*, May 21, 1959, 3.

64. Pearsall, "Reminiscences," 3; Clay Lancaster, *Old Brooklyn Heights: New York's First Suburb* (New York: Dover, 1979), x–xiii; "Felt Urges New Zone Law," *BHP*, April 9, 1959, 8.

65. Pearsall, "Reminiscences," 5–6; "Brooklyn Heights Association Pleads for Historic Zoning," *BHP*, April 16, 1959, 1.

66. "It Takes a Heap of Housing to Make the Heights a Home," *BHP*, April 2, 1959, 4; "Co-ops and the Populists," *BHP*, April 9, 1959, 2.

67. "City to Consider Brooklyn Co-ops," *NYT*, April 30, 1959, 33; "Vote on Co-op Delayed," *NYT*, February 24, 1960, 43.

68. "Five Boroughs Form New Plan Boards," *NYT*, July 5, 1963, 20; "Public Housing to Get New Look," *NYT*, May 5, 1957, 76; William Slayton, "The Operation and Achievements of the Urban Renewal Program," in *Urban Renewal: The Record and the Controversy*, ed. James Q. Wilson (Cambridge, MA: MIT Press, 1966), 191–95, 213–18; "City to Preserve Flavor of Area It Is Rebuilding," *NYT*, May 24, 1959, 1.

69. "Let's Support Urban Renewal," Richard Mendes to editor, *BHP*, October 24, 1957, 4.

70. "New Title I Plan Outlined for City by Housing Board," NYT, June 5, 1960, 1; New Agency Planned to Spur Relocation Task, *NYT*, July 8, 1962, 1.
71. "75 Picketing Mothers Demand Cashmore Back Cadman Co-ops," *NYT*, July 19, 1960, 31; "Pickets Denounce Unfair Relocation of Residents," *BHP*, November 21, 1963, 8.
72. "Compromise Adds Co-ops in Cadman," *NYT*, September 1, 1960, 29; "Relocation Data Given to Tenants," *NYT*, January 20, 1961, 33.
73. "City Plans Homes to Aid Relocation," *NYT*, January 20, 1961, 33; "Cadman Plaza Sponsor Chosen for Family Co-op Apartments," *NYT*, February 10, 1961, 31.
74. "Cadman Plaza Sponsor Chosen"; "Critic at Large: 'Human Scale' Is Urged in Gauging Need for Housing in Historic Brooklyn Heights," *NYT*, May 2, 1961, 34; Lancaster, *Old Brooklyn Heights*, xvii–xviii; James, "Cadman Plaza in Brooklyn Heights."
75. Lancaster, *Old Brooklyn Heights*, xix, xxiii; "'Old Brooklyn Heights' Groups Fighting to Preserve Buildings," *NYT*, December 9, 1961, 29; "Landmarks Group Proposed for City," *NYT*, December 3, 1961, 83; "City Acts to Save Historic Sites," *NYT*, April 22, 1962, 1.
76. "The Cadman Plaza Plan," *PPP*, July 1963, 5.
77. "Cadman Details Unveiled by City," *NYT*, March 6, 1962, 41; "Architects Back Cadman Project," *NYT*, April 10, 1962, 37.
78. "Urban Renewal Advances in City," *NYT*, November 19, 1962, 33.
79. "Statement of Housing and Redevelopment Board on Cadman Plaza," August 31, 1960, Box 126, Folder 1799, RWPMA.
80. Ibid.
81. Ibid.; Lawrence E. Gerosa, "Report to the Board of Estimate on Title I Slum Clearance Projects and Tax Exempt Housing Projects," May 9, 1956, Schedule III, 6, Box 116, RMP.
82. Jane Jacobs, *The Death and Life of Great American Cities* (New York: Vintage Books, 1961), 23, 189–90.
83. James, "Cadman Plaza in Brooklyn Heights," 16.
84. Roger Starr, *The Living End: The City and Its Critics* (New York: Coward-McCann, 1966), 55–56.
85. "Public Housing Project Dealt Knockout Blow," *BHP*, September 5, 1963, 1, 4; "The Independent Democrat," *West Brooklyn Independent Democrats Newsletter*, January 1963, 4.
86. "Fair Housing Committee Finds Minority Housing," *BHP*, April 2, 1964, 1; "Public Housing," *BHP*, July 2, 1964, 1; Brooklyn Heights Association to membership, April 1973, Brooklyn Heights Folder, VFBCBPL.
87. "Public Housing Project Dealt Knockout Blow"; "Heights Debates Shape of Future," February 7, 1965, 75; "Public Housing," *BHAB*, June 1963.
88. "Heights Debates Shape of Future"; "Where Is City Now?" *BHP*, February 27, 1964, 4; Elliot Willensky to editor, *BHP*, June 18, 1964, 4.
89. "Project Planned Adjoining Cadman," *NYT*, October 15, 1963, 41.
90. William B. Pennell to editor, *NYT*, August 26, 1964, 38; Paul Windels to editor, *NYT*, September 7, 1964, 18; J. Rullman to editor, *BHP*, August 27, 1964, 4.

91. Edwards F. Rullman, chairman, Brooklyn Heights Design Advisory Council, to Robert F. Wagner, April 7, 1963, Brooklyn Heights Association Folder, Box 1, HCP; "Residents Debate Cadman Proposal," *BHP*, June 11, 1967, 75.
92. "Where Is City Now?"; "New Cadman Plan Urged by Stark," *NYT*, August 12, 1964, 72.
93. "New Cadman Plan Urged by Stark"; "Integration in Brooklyn Heights," *NYT*, August 14, 1964, 26; Richard Mendes to editor, *BHP*, February 27, 1964.
94. "Heights Debate Shape of Future."
95. "Demolition Started on Cadman Renewal," *NYT*, February 27, 1964, 23.
96. "Remarks by Mayor Robert F. Wagner (Read by Council President Paul R. Screvane)," Box 126, Folder 1799, RWPMA.
97. "Cadman Plaza Co-op to Be Built After Eight Years of Disputes," *NYT*, April 12, 1964, R1; "Brooklyn Co-op Gains Approval," *NYT*, July 19, 1968, 20; "A Brooklyn Co-op Settling Down," *NYT*, August 5, 1973.
98. "Old Days Traced at Cadman Plaza Site; 'Archeologists' Find Early 19th Century Items in Brooklyn," *NYT*, June 30, 1965, 39; "8 Hunt Antiques in Doomed Homes; Items Saved from Wreckers by Brooklyn Heights Group," *NYT*, March 22, 1964, 61.
99. "The Middling Way," *BHP*, March 26, 1959, 4.

5   The Highway in the Garden and the Literature of Gentrification

1. Herbert J. Gans, "The Urban Village Revisited: The World of the West End Before Its Destruction," in *The Last Tenement: Confronting Community and Urban Renewal in Boston's West End*, ed. Sean M. Fisher and Carolyn Hughes (Boston: Bostonian Society, 1992), 17–18.
2. Martin S. James, "Cadman Plaza in Brooklyn Heights: A Study of the Misuse of Public Power and Funds in Urban Renewal," June 13, 1961, Box 125, Folder 1799, RWPMA.
3. Ibid., 1, 3–4.
4. Ibid., 3, 17–18; "Critic at Large: 'Human Scale' Is Urged in Gauging Need for Housing in Historic Brooklyn Heights," *NYT*, May 2, 1961, 34.
5. Robert Fishman, "Revolt of the Urbs," in *Robert Moses and the Modern City: The Transformation of New York*, ed. Hilary Ballon and Kenneth T. Jackson (New York: W. W. Norton, 2007); Hila Colman, *Peter's Brownstone House* (New York: Morrow, 1963); Richard Hedman and Fred Bair Jr., *And on the Eighth Day: Series of Essays and Tableaux on Planner and Planning* (New York: ASPO, 1967); Jane Jacobs and Eric Salzman to Hugh L. Carey, April 7, 1961, Brooklyn Heights Association Folder, Box 1, Hugh Carey Papers; Gans, "The Failure of Urban Renewal," in *Urban Renewal: The Record and the Controversy*, ed. James Q. Wilson (Cambridge, MA: MIT Press, 1966), 538. The middle-class character of the genre is also pointed to in George Sternlieb, *The Tenement Landlord* (New Brunswick, NJ: Rutgers University Press, 1966).
6. "Literary gentrification" is from Sharon Zukin, *Landscapes of Power: From Detroit to Disney World* (Berkeley: University of California Press, 1991), 35.
7. For the difference between place and locale, see John A. Agnew, *Place and Politics: The Geographical Mediation of State and Society* (Boston: Allen and Unwin, 1987).

8. The "highway in the garden" is of course indebted to Leo Marx, *The Machine in the Garden: Technology and the Pastoral Ideal in America* (New York: Oxford University Press, 1964).

9. Although my usage is slightly different, the distinction between complex and simple pastoralism is borrowed from Marx, *The Machine in the Garden*, 3–11. For a description of pastoral, anti-pastoral, and post-pastoral, see Lawrence Buell, *The Future of Environmental Criticism: Environmental Crisis and Literary Imagination* (Malden, MA: Blackwell, 2005), 144–45. For a discussion of the difference between dynamic and sedentarist concepts of place, see Karen Halttunen, "Groundwork: American Studies in Place—Presidential Address to the American Studies Association," *American Quarterly* 58 (March 2006): 1–17. For a caveat about forming too rigid a distinction between the two, see Lawrence Buell, "The Timeliness of Place: Response to the Presidential Address," *American Quarterly* 58 (March 2006): 17–22.

10. "A Reporter at Large: The Making of Boerum Hill," *NY*, November 17, 1977, 116.

11. Robert F. Pecorella, *Community Reform in a Postreform City* (Armonk, NY: M. E. Sharpe, 1994); Ricard Edward DeLeon, *Progressive Politics in San Francisco, 1975–1991* (Lawrence: University Press of Kansas, 1992); Hugh Wilford, *The New York Intellectuals: From Vanguard to Institution* (Manchester, UK: Manchester University Press, 1995), 10–12.

12. Irving Howe, "New York in the Thirties: Some Fragments of Memory," *Dissent* 8 (Summer 1961): 241–50; Lionel Abel, "New York City: A Remembrance," *Dissent* 8 (Summer 1961): 251; Daniel M. Friedenberg, "Real Estate Confidential," *Dissent* 8 (Summer 1961): 260.

13. Mike Miller and Carl Werthman, "Public Housing: Tenants and Troubles," *Dissent* 8 (Summer 1961): 282; Harrison Salisbury, *The Shook-Up Generation* (New York: Harper and Brothers, 1958), 75–76. For a description of "gothification," see Lawrence Buell, *Writing for an Endangered World: Literature, Culture, and Environment in the U.S. and Beyond* (Cambridge, MA: Harvard University Press, 2001), 135–42.

14. Ernest van den Haag, "Notes on New York Housing," *Dissent* 8 (Summer 1961): 277.

15. Alfred Kazin, *A Walker in the City* (New York: Harcourt, Brace, 1951), 12–14.

16. Ibid., 141.

17. Ibid., 169–70.

18. Michael Harrington, "Slums, Old and New," *Commentary*, August 1960, 118–19; Michael Harrington, *The Other America: Poverty in the United States* (New York: Simon and Schuster, 1962), 147.

19. Harrington, *The Other America*, 142.

20. Jane Jacobs, *The Death and Life of Great American Cities* (New York: Vintage Books, 1961), 4–25. De Certeau also famously makes a similar descent from the bird's-eye perch, see Michel De Certeau, "Walking in the City," in *The Practice of Everyday Life*, trans. Steven Rendall (Berkeley: University of California Press, 1988).

21. Jacobs, *Death and Life*, 13.

22. Ibid., 50–51. Claude Lévi-Strauss offers a similar celebration of the messiness of Greenwich Village in "New York in 1941." In his 1951 description of Calcutta, the "street ballet" is less appealing; see Lévi-Strauss, *Tristes Tropiques*, trans. John and Doreen Weightman (New York: Atheneum, 1974), 134–35.

23. Jacobs, *Death and Life*, 146.

24. Ibid., 193.

25. Ibid., 138. For a description of the importance of privacy, see ibid., 58.

26. Ibid., 114–17. For a description of "Whitmanian modernism," see Buell, *Writing for an Endangered World*, 90–103, 109.

27. Jacobs, *Death and Life*, 138, 193.

28. Ibid., 236–37.

29. Ibid., 244.

30. Gans, *The Urban Villagers*, 9–15.

31. Gans, *The Levittowners; Gans, Popular Culture and High Culture: An Analysis and Evaluation of Taste* (New York: Basic Books, 1974); Gans, "The Failure of Urban Renewal."

32. Gans, *Urban Villagers*, 3–4.

33. Ibid., 11–12.

34. Ibid., 16.

35. Ibid., 150. For more on the romantic urbanist themes of settlement writing, see Buell, *Writing for an Endangered World*, 9–18.

36. Gans, *Urban Villagers*, 105.

37. Ibid., 3–4.

38. Ibid., 304.

39. Ibid., xi.

40. Robert Caro, *The Power Broker: Robert Moses and the Fall of New York* (New York: Vintage Books, 1974), 521.

41. Ibid.

42. Ibid., 522–23.

43. Ibid., 524.

44. Ibid., 850–94.

45. Marshall Berman, *All That Is Solid Melts into Air* (New York: Penguin Books, 1982), 291.

46. Ibid., 292–96.

47. Ibid., 291, 326–27.

48. Ibid., 337.

49. Ibid., 341–44.

6   Inventing Brownstone Brooklyn

1. "Brownstoner's Fair Attended by 2000," *NYT*, October 28, 1973, 120.

2. "Settlement Survey Points Out Four Problem Areas," *BHP*, February 4, 1965; Manuel S. Emanuel, *South Brooklyn Vest Pocket Study*, Department of City Planning, May 1969, 8–9.

3. Irene Wilson to Captain Harold I. Venokur, August 24, 1963, PSCC.

4. "Blockbusters Turn to Park Slope for Home Speculations," *NYWTS*, August 9, 1962, B1; "Downhill Walk on St. Johns Pl.," *NYWTS*, July 30, 1962, B1.

5. "Teen Gangs War with Subways a Battle a Battleground," *HT*, October 24, 1964, 1; "Students Clash in Two Boroughs," *NYT*, October 24, 1964, 1; "Park Slope Fears

Summer Gang Wars," *NYJA*, February 19, 1962, 1; "Negroes in Park Slope Attacked by Whites," *NYAN*, March 12, 1966.

6. *Plan for New York City 1969: A Proposal*, vol. 1: *Critical Issues* (New York: Department of City Planning, 1969), 142; Shirley Bradway Laska and Daphne Spain, eds., *Back to the City: Issues in Neighborhood Renovation* (New York: Pergamon Press, 1980).

7. L. J. Davis, "Boom at Boerum Hill," *NYM*, July 14, 1969, 40.

8. "Reporter at Large: The Making of Boerum Hill," *NY*, November 14, 1977, 116; Philip Kasinitz, "The Gentrification of 'Boerum Hill': Neighborhood Change and Conflicts over Definitions," *Qualitative Sociology* 11 (Fall 1988): 169.

9. For the demographic similarities of the back-to-the-city movement and the back-to-the-land movement, see Larry Long, "Back to the Countryside and Back to the City in the Same Decade," in *Back to the City: Issues in Neighborhood Renovation*, eds. Shirley Bradway Laska and Daphne Spain (New York: Pergamon Press, 1980), 61–77. For a cultural and social analysis of the ties between the two movements, see Daphne Spain, "Been-Heres Versus Come-Heres," *Journal of the American Planning Association* 59, 2 (Spring 1993).

10. Marshall Berman, *All That Is Solid Melts into Air* (New York: Penguin Books, 1982), 31; "Neighborhood Power—A Term Representing a New Constituency Entering National Political Life," *NYT*, August 19, 1979, E23; Robert Goodman, *After the Planners* (New York: Touchstone, 1971), 190–91. For a description of the "community revolution" and "neighborhood revolt" in San Francisco and Boston, see John H. Mollenkopf, *The Contested City* (Princeton, NJ: Princeton University Press, 1983), 180–81. The "neighborhood movement" is also described in Jon C. Teaford, *The Rough Road to Renaissance: Urban Revitalization in America, 1940–1985* (Baltimore: Johns Hopkins University Press, 1990), 240–52; David Morris and Karl Hess, *Neighborhood Power: The New Localism* (Boston: Beacon Press, 1975). "High modernism" is from David Harvey, *The Condition of Postmodernity: An Enquiry into the Origins of Cultural Change* (Malden, MA: Blackwell Press, 1990), 35–36. For a description of the links between the counterculture, the neighborhood movement, and gentrification in six Canadian cities, see Ley, *The New Middle Class*.

11. "Cobble Hill: Land of Meat Pies . . . ," *BHP*, July 23, 1959.

12. "City Weighs Cobble Hill Low-Rent Housing Veto," *BHP*, March 26, 1959; "Cobble Hill: Land of Meat Pies . . ."

13. "Cobble Hill—An Area of Sharp Contrasts," *BHP*, February 4, 1965, 8; "City Plans Low Rent Units on Atlantic," *BHP*, March 12, 1959, 1; "Cobble Hill Meets to Eliminate Threat of Destruction of Homes," *BHP*, November 20, 1958, 3; "The Restoration of Cobble Hill: Pride Plus Action Barred Slum," *NYT*, February 28, 1960; "City Weighs Cobble Hill Low-Rent Housing Veto," 1, 6; "City Acts on Park for Cobble Hill," *NYT*, October 4, 1962, 41.

14. "Rescue Operation on 'Boerum Hill,'" *NYWTS*, March 24, 1964; Kasinitz, "The Gentrification of 'Boerum Hill,'" 166; "Reporter at Large: The Making of Boerum Hill," 96; Emanuel, *South Brooklyn Vest Pocket Study*, 8–9; Downtown Area Renewal Effort, "Dare Area Renewal Study: A Pratt Institute Planning Project," 1959.

15. "Rescue Operation on 'Boerum Hill.'"

16. Classified ads in *NYT*, May 5, 1962; May 4, 1962; Federal Writers' Project of the Works Progress Administration in New York City, *The WPA Guide to New York City: The Federal Writers' Project Guide to 1930's New York* (New York: Pantheon Books, 1982), 450–54, 478; "Clinton Hill," *NYT*, January 29, 1942, 18; "Fulton Street Elevated Removal Spurs Brooklyn Hill Improvements Homes Remodeled on Brooklyn Hill," *NYT*, August 10, 1941, RE1; "Brooklyn Losing Mansions on Housing Site; Old Pratt Home and Others in 'Hill' Neighborhood to Be Demolished," *NYT*, February 1, 1942, RE1.

17. For a contrast of the name Boerum Hill with the flat topography of the area, see Kasinitz, "The Gentrification of 'Boerum Hill,'" 166.

18. Kasinitz, "The Gentrification of 'Boerum Hill,'" 168; L. J. Davis, *History of Boerum Hill* (New York: Boerum Hill Association, 1967), Boerum Hill Folder, BCBPL; Jeanette Jeanes, "A History of Carroll Gardens," 1970, Carroll Gardens Folder, VFBHS; Clay Lancaster, "Carroll Gardens: An Architectural Evaluation," VFBHS; "Clinton Hill: Spring and House and Garden Tour," pamphlet, May 4, 1975, Clinton Hill Folder, VFBHS.

19. "The Making of Boerum Hill," 113–14; "A Revival of the Fittest," *Newsday*, September 8, 1966; Kasinitz, "The Gentrification of 'Boerum Hill,'" 175; L. J. Davis, "Block Associations: Power to the Neighborhoods," *NYM*, June 29, 1970, 20.

20. Davis, "Block Associations."

21. Salvatore "Buddy" Scotto, interview by author, October 6, 2003; "2 Rival Groups Vying for Role in Governing South Brooklyn," *NYT*, May 21, 1971; "Neighborhoods: The Mood Is Changing Along Gowanus Canal," *NYT*, September 20, 1969, 17; "Neighborhoods: Gowanus vs. Organized Crime," *NYT*, February 5, 1970, 41; Susan Jacoby, "A Dream Grows in Brooklyn," *NYT*, February 23, 1975, SM11.

22. Ibid.

23. Ibid.; William B. Winship, Executive Committee, Cadman Plaza Cooperative Association, to Hugh Carey, November 17, 1961; Brooklyn Heights Association Folder, Box 1, HCP.

24. Even in the 1970s in the midst of widespread abandonment and poverty, Bedford-Stuyvesant retained a significant number of African American homeowners. In 1974, according to the Bedford-Stuyvesant Restoration Corporation, half of the one- and two-family structures were owner occupied. On some blocks the homeownership rate was over 50 percent. See *BSRCN*, January-February 1974; United Homeowners Association, Minutes of Meeting, August 7, 1971, Bedford-Stuyvesant Folder, VFBHS; *GN* 1, 2; "Prospect-Lefferts Gardens Neighborhood Association Spreading the 'Good News,'" *City Limits Community Housing News*, Association of Neighborhood Housing Developers, Inc., May 1976. Mrs. Jones is quoted by Jerome Krase, "Stigmatized Places, Stigmatized People: Crown Heights and Prospect-Lefferts Gardens," in *Brooklyn USA: The Fourth Largest City in America*, ed. Rita Seiden Miller (New York: Brooklyn College Press, 1979), 258.

25. Joseph Ferris, interview by author, May 3, 2003; Charles Monaghan, interview by author, April 1, 2003; "Park Slope Betterment Committee," *CN*, November 1966, 17–18; "Park Slope Group Presses Renewal," *NYT*, July 10, 1966, 241; "P.S. Betterment Committee Meets in Future Art Gallery," *HRSN*, March 17, 1967, 16; "Open

House in Park Slope," *NYP*, May 16, 1968, 26. For a joint study of Park Slope neighborhood change by two activists and participant observers, see Timothy O'Hanlon, "Neighborhood Change in New York City: A Case Study of Park Slope, 1850–1980," Ph.D. diss., City University of New York, 1982; Francine Cyvia Justa, "Effects of Housing Abandonment, Resettlement Processes, and Displacement on the Evolution of Voluntary Community Organizations in Park Slope, Brooklyn, New York," Ph.D. diss., City University of New York, 1984.

26. Ibid.

27. "Breukelen Open House. The Patton Residence: Former Glory Restored in Garfield Pl. Brownstone," *HRSN*, September 19, 1969, 12; "Boerum Hill Association Plans First House Tour," *BHP*, May 12, 1966, 1; Boerum Hill Association, "The First Annual House Tour of Boerum Hill," 1966, Boerum Hill Folder, VFBCBPL. For a similar analysis of house tours in Boerum Hill, see Kasinitz, "The Gentrification of 'Boerum Hill,'" 171–74.

28. "More on Mortgages," *CN*, March 1963, 14; "Brooklyn Renewal Is an Uphill Fight; Mortgages Are the Main Hurdle in Historic Brooklyn Area," *NYT*, March 20, 1966, 300; "Making of Boerum Hill," 117; "Bankers Wary of Brownstones; Buyers Must 'Shop' for Loans," *NYT*, April 12, 1964, R1.

29. "Basic Training for the Financing Fight," *TB*, November 1968, 7; Joy and Paul Wilkes, *You Don't Have to Be Rich to Own a Brownstone* (New York: Quadrangle, 1973), 29–38; "Sickening 70s: BRC Mortgage Survey," *TB*, February 1, 1977, 1.

30. Elish, "Brownstone Revival in New York City," 13–14.

31. "Group Offers Preservation Guide," *NYT*, July 17, 1966, 223; "New Directory of Old-House Products," *CN*, February 1976, 10; "Brownstoners' Bibliography," *TB*, November 1968, 4; Wilkes, *You Don't Have to Be Rich to Own a Brownstone*; Brownstone Revival Committee, *Home-Buyers Guide to New York City Brownstone Neighborhoods* (New York: Brownstone Revival Committee, 1969); John Berenyi, *Up Against New York: A Handbook for Survival in the City* (New York: William Morrow, 1971).

32. *TB*, November 1969; *GG*, September 22, 1971; "Local Papers Slug It Out," *Newsday*, November 4, 1986.

33. Seymour Krim, "Who's Afraid of the New Yorker Now?" *VV*, November 8, 1962; "Brooklyn: The Sane Alternative," *NYM*, July 14, 1969; Peter Hellman, "The Urban Strategist: Condominiums vs. Co-ops," *NYM*, January 5, 1970; "The Best French Pastry Shops in Town," *NYM*, August 17, 1970; Julie Baumgold, "A Guide to the Hidden Meanings of New York Parties," *NYM*, April 28, 1969; Dan Greenburg, "Facing Up to the Hamptons," *NYM*, July 2, 1973; Ellen Stock, "You Mean You Pay More than $50 a Month Rent? We Don't," *NYM*, January 26, 1970; Peter Hellman, "Now's the Time to Buy a Brownstone," *NYM*, January 11, 1971; Nicholas Pileggi, "The Great Apartment Grope," *NYM*, September 30, 1968.

34. "Berkeley Place," *CN*, February 1966, 24; "Garfield Place," *CN*, February 1966, 2; "The Block Association, Boon to City Activists," *NYT*, October 19, 1969, R1.

35. "Gay Nineties Again in Park Slope," *CN*, September 1971, 4; "Lincoln Place Block Association," *CN*, July 1971, 15; "President Street," *CN*, July 1969, 7, 12–13; "House Tour," *GN*, August 1972, 1; "Meet Clinton Hill: A Community Sampler," poster for house tour, Clinton Hill Vertical Files, VFBHS.

36. Interview with Joseph Ferris, 2009; "Tree Committee Plans," *CN*, October 1964, 4; "Progress and Challenge," *CN*, February 1962, 8; "Cobble Hill Sinks Its Roots," *BHP*, December 10, 1959, 6; "A Half-Million Street Trees and More on the Way," *NYT*, August 15, 1971, R1. For a description of urban tree planting drives in the early twentieth century, see Max Page, *The Creative Destruction of Manhattan, 1900–1940* (Chicago: University of Chicago, 1999), 194–215.

37. "A Half-Million Street Trees."

38. "Rising out of the Rubble, Green Things Are Growing Among the City's Canyons," *NYT*, June 20, 1976, 95.

39. "Restoration of Fort Greene Park to Begin," *NYT*, June 10, 1973, 119; "Ft. Greene Park to Be Restored to Original Plan," *Phoenix*, October 19, 1972, 2.

40. "A Real Farmyard in Prospect Park Delights Children," *NYT*, January 26, 1965, 31; "Wollman Memorial Rink to Open in Brooklyn," *NYT*, December 20, 1961, 30. For a description of the early twentieth-century shift from the Romantic park movement to the Progressive playground movement, see Peter Schmitt, *Back to Nature: The Arcadian Myth in Urban America* (New York: Oxford University Press, 1969), 66–76.

41. "Boathouse Saved at Prospect Park," *NYT*, December 11, 1964; Clay Lancaster, "Carroll Gardens: An Architectural Evaluation," Carroll Gardens Folder, VFBHS.

42. "Prospect Park's Future Is Pondered: A Place to Play or a Place to Find Tranquility?" *NYT*, February 28, 1971, BQ84; "Boathouse Saved at Prospect Park," *NYT*, December 11, 1964, 57; "Restoration of Fort Greene Park to Begin," *NYT*, June 10, 1973, 119; "Carnival in the Parks," *CN*, June 1968.

43. "A Pier Is Planned in Prospect Park," *NYT*, November 14, 1964, 30; "Future Is Unsure for Prospect Park's Old Boathouse," *NYT*, September 19, 1964, 29; "Children's Farm in Park Opposed," *NYT*, February 23, 1966, 80; "Ft. Greene Park to Be Restored to Original Plan," *Phoenix*, October 19, 1972, 2; Clay Lancaster, *Prospect Park Handbook* (New York: W. H. Rawls, 1967). For a description of park politics in the 1960s, see August Heckscher, *Alive in the City: Memoirs of an Ex-Commissioner* (New York: Charles Scribner's Sons, 1974); Roy Rosenzweig and Elizabeth Blackmar, *The Park and the People: A History of Central Park* (Ithaca, NY: Cornell University Press, 1992), 489–98.

44. "Farmers Battle Bureaucracy," *NYM*, July 23, 1979, 5; "Outdoor Markets Here Offer Bargains for Buyers with Keen Eye for Quality," *NYT*, March 19, 1955; "The City's Greenmarkets: Fresh Produce and Controversy," *NYT*, May 26, 1979, 9.

45. For a detailed list and analysis of Park Slope's improvement associations in the 1970s and 1980s, see Justa, "Effects of Housing Abandonment," 203–48; "Brooklyn's 7th Heaven," *NYT*, May 12, 1978, C18.

46. "Seventh Avenue Vicinity," *DB*, April 1975, 4; "Knell for Irish Bars Echoes in Brooklyn," *NYT*, July 18, 1971; "Park Slope Night Life Scene Emerges on Seventh Avenue," *Phoenix*, February 8, 1973, 5.

47. "The Nineteenth Century: A Growth Industry for Brooklyn," *CN*, October 1975, 4; "Bronze Plaques," *CN*, August 1971, 18; "Other Block Associations," *CN*, February 1968, 14; "Local Hearth Specialist Is Doing Blazing Business in Brownstone Brooklyn," *Phoenix*, February 24, 1977, 13. The term "heritage industry" is borrowed from Ellin,

Postmodern Urbanism, 81–85. See also "Private Reinvestment and Neighborhood Change, New York Department of City Planning," March 1984, 116, Box 2, Folder 11, HDMBHS.

48. Merle Goldberg, "Cabash in Brooklyn," *NYM*, July 14, 1969, 62; Herb Goro and Ellen Stock, "Atlantic Avenue: Boulevard of Dreams," *NYM*, July 16, 1973, 45–49; "Atlantic Avenue Study," Box 1, Folder 3, HDMBHS; "Atlantic Ave. Zoning Plan Backed at Public Hearing," *NYT*, June 16, 1974, 94; "2 Camels Help Brooklyn Mark Atlantic Antic Day," *NYT*, September 28, 1975, 59; "Diversity of Atlantic Ave. Fair Draws Throngs to Brooklyn," *NYT*, September 19, 1977, 39; "Statement of Community District Needs," New York City Department of Planning, January 1982.

49. "Brownstoners' Hold Revival Meeting," *NYT*, February 25, 1968, R1; D. Kenneth Patton, "First, Pick a Good Name for the Product," in *Back to the City: Proceedings of the Back to the City Conference in New York City, September 13–16, 1974*, by the Brownstone Revival Committee of New York, 10.

50. "'Back to City' Conference Set," *NYT*, August 25, 1974, 453; Brownstone Revival Committee, *Back to the City: Proceedings of the Back to the City Conference*.

51. "Banks Relaxing Brownstone Ban," *NYT*, June 6, 1971, BQ82; "Park Slope Betterment Committee."

52. "New Brownstone Insurance Program," *CN*, May 1974; "Brownstoners Here Try New Insurance: Premium Rates Drop and Coverage Grows," *BHP*, April 17, 1975, 1.

53. "A Happening on Berkeley," *CN*, March 1968, 16–17; "'Urban Revival Movement' Given Boost by Private Industry," *BHP*, January 11, 1968; "Brooklyn Brownstone Center Open," *NYT*, October 26, 1975, 125; "Lindsay Praises Start of 'Operation Better Block,'" *NYT*, June 16, 1968.

54. Interview with Charles Monaghan; interview with Salvatore "Buddy" Scotto.

55. Another useful term to describe this in-between stage is Guian McKee's "local liberalism"; see McKee, *The Problem of Jobs: Race and Deindustrialization in Philadelphia* (Chicago: University of Chicago Press, 2008).

56. "Lindsay Names 21 Top Officials of New Housing Superagency," *NYP*, November 28, 1967, 14; "Lindsay Creates Agency to Direct Fight on Slums," *NYT*, November 23, 1966; "Three Little City Halls Helping Thousands Fight City Hall as Opposition Mounts in the Council," *NYT*, June 9, 1967; Mary Perot Nichols, "The Two Mayor Lindsays—But That's Not Enough," *VV*, June 11, 1970; Mayor's Urban Task Force, "Summer in the City, 1967 and 1968, Report to Mayor John V. Lindsay," New York, 1968; Charles R. Morris, *The Cost of Good Intentions: New York City and the Liberal Experiment, 1960–1975* (New York: W. W. Norton, 1980), 37–38, 46–55. For the conflicting agenda of the Great Society, see Sidney M. Milkis, "Lyndon Johnson, the Great Society, and the 'Twilight' of the Modern Presidency," in *The Great Society and the High Tide of Liberalism*, ed. Sidney M. Milkis and Jerome M. Mileur (Amherst: University of Massachusetts Press, 2005), 1–37.

57. "Urban Renewal—Approach and Practice," *CN*, September 1965, 4.

58. "New Housing and Industry Suggested on 18 City Sites," *NYT*, May 1, 1961, 1; "Planners Hailed on New Approach," *NYT*, May 25, 1961, 37; Downtown Area Renewal Effort, "Dare Area Renewal Study: A Pratt Institute Planning Project."

59. "Park Slope Neighborhood Conservation Committee Minutes of First Meeting," July 15, 1965, PSCC; "Park Slope Conservation Committee Is Organized," *HRSN*, July 30, 1965; "The Rehabilitation of St. John's Place—An Experiment in Philanthropy," *BWT*, March 29, 1966, 1; "Rehabilitation Proceeds," *CN*, December 1966, 18; "Urban Design Project Wins Federal Honors," *NYT*, November 10, 1968; see also O'Hanlon, "Neighborhood Change in New York City," 165–66, 183–84.

60. "First Edition," *BSRCN*, October 1, 1969, 4; "First Superblock Dedication," *BSRCN*, December 2, 1969, 2, 7; "Rehabilitation in Bedford-Stuyvesant," *BSRCN*, January 1, 1972, 1; "Weeksville," *BSRCN*, September-October 1973, 2–3.

61. "Brooklyn Renewal Slowly Advances," *NYT*, June 17, 1973; "Renewal Raises Brooklyn Hopes," *NYT*, June 24, 1968;

62. "First Steps Taken Toward Creation of 'Linear City,'" *NYT*, November 13, 1967; Rogers, Taliaferro, Kostritsky, and Lamb, Architects, *Linear City and Cross Brooklyn Expressway, "Plan for Planning" Report* (Baltimore, 1967).

63. "More than 500 City Officials, Businessmen Civic and Community Leaders Gathered to Celebrate Downtown Brooklyn's 'Being' at DBDA's First Annual Luncheon," *DB*, June 1972, 1.

64. "Small Merchants Hail Brooklyn Mall," *NYT*, October 30, 1973, 47; "Planners Approve 3 Landmark Sites," *NYT*, January 5, 1975, 181; "A Brooklyn Mall Planned by the City," *NYT*, October 29, 1973, 76; "Fulton Mall Plan Lauded by Mayor," *NYT*, November 2, 1973, 45; Edward T. Rogowsky et al., "New York City's Outer Borough Strategy: Case Studies in Revitalization," in *Urban Revitalization Policies and Programs*, ed. Fritz Wagner, Timothy E. Joder, and Anthony J. Mumphrey Jr. (Thousand Oaks, CA: Sage Publications, 1995), 80–87.

65. Donald Elliott to Edward J. Logue, December 17, 1971, #959, Series VIII, Box 317, Folder 1041, ELP; "Waterfront Housing Between Two Bridges Planned in Brooklyn," *NYT*, October 1, 1969; "The Fight Goes On," *BHAB*, December 1968; "A Touch of Frisco in Brooklyn Is Proposed," *NYT*, December 19, 1971, 12; "The Young Relish Haven by the River," *NYT*, September 9, 1972, R1; "'Brooklyn Acting to Set Up a Fulton St. Artists' Colony," *NYT*, November 25, 1972, 33; "Fulton Ferry Shaping Up as a Landmark," *NYT*, July 29, 1973, 90; "Fulton Ferry Historic District, Potential Northern Extension of Heights, Reborn in 70s," *BHP*, January 31, 1980. For a similar trajectory in Manhattan's SoHo, see Sharon Zukin, *Loft Living: Culture and Capital in Urban Change* (Baltimore: Johns Hopkins University Press, 1982).

66. George M. Raymond and Ronald Shiffman, "The Pratt Center for Community Improvement: A University Urban Action Program," *PPP*, June 1, 1964, 27.

67. "The Fact Sheet *Corrected!*" Boro Hall Community Association, Cobble Hill Folder, VFBCBPL; "The Bitter Battle of Cobble Hill," *BWT*, May 7, 1962; Daniel Kelly to Park Slope Civic Council, September 11, 1965, PSCC; Irene Wilson to Daniel Kelly, June 24, 1965, PSCC.

68. "To All Members of the Brooklyn Heights Association," flyer, Cobble Hill Folder, VFBCBPL; William Jesinkey to Irene Wilson, August 12, 1965, PSCC.

69. "Urban Renewal Plan for Cobble Hill Area May Be Cut by 35%," *BWT*, June 18, 1962, 1. For budgetary reasons, the city replaced the original conservation district proposal with a plan for a smaller federally funded code enforcement program;

"Code Enforcement Program," *CN*, September 1969, 4, PSCC; also quoted in O'Hanlon, "Neighborhood Change in New York City," 167–70; "The Pratt Center for Community Improvement," 28.

70. "Meat Market Approved by City," *NYT*, December 5, 1969; "New York, Life's Loser, Does It Again," March 9, 1969; "Bill Suggested to Create a Sports Authority," *NYT*, February 9, 1973; "Arena Plan Is Pressed by Brooklyn," *NYT*, July 24, 1974.

71. "X-Way Protest Rally Planned," *FL*, October 19, 1968; Ada Louise Huxtable, "How to Build a City, If You Can," *NYT*, March 12, 1967; "First Steps Taken Toward Creation of 'Linear City,'" *NYT*, November 13, 1967; Rogers, Taliaferro, Kostritsky, and Lamb, Architects, *Linear City and Cross Brooklyn Expressway.*

72. Timothy Berg, "Reshaping Gotham: The City Livable Movement and the Redevelopment of New York City," Ph.D. diss.. Purdue University, 1999; "Housing Protest in Boerum Hill," *NYT*, February 6, 1972, 59; "Urban Redevelopment Plan Near Downtown," *NYT*, November 24, 1976, 67; "Brooklyn Acting to Set up a Fulton St. Artists Colony."

73. "Public Sector Failing to Close Housing Gap," *NYT*, March 14, 1971, 1; "City Must Reduce Its Housing Plans," *NYT*, December 14, 1970, 1; "Public and Publicly-Aided Housing, 1927–1973," New York City Planning Commission, September 1974; Norman I. Fainstein and Susan S. Fainstein, "Governing Regimes and the Political Economy of Development in New York City, 1946–1984," in *Power, Culture, and Place: Essays on New York City*, ed. John Mollenkopf (New York: Russell Sage Foundation, 1988), 178–84.

74. "Homesteaders Combating Urban Blight," *NYT*, September 16, 1973, 1; "City Selling Houses for $10 Each for People Willing to Fix Them," *NYT*, May 6, 1976; "Self Help Housing: Within Limits It Works," *NYT*, July 11, 1976, 188; "Planning Unit Introduces Neighborhood 'Miniplans,'" *NYT*, June 26, 1974, 89; "Zuccotti, Planning Unit Head, Ranks High with Beame," *NYT*, November 29, 1974, 41; "Plazas for People: Streetscape and Residential Plazas," New York City Department of City Planning, September 1976; "Why City Is Switching from Master Plan to 'Miniplan,'" *NYT*, June 27, 1974; Fainstein and Fainstein, "Governing Regimes and the Political Economy of Development in New York City, 1946–1984," 183–84; David P. Varady, *Neighborhood Upgrading: A Realistic Assessment* (Albany: State University of New York Press, 1986), 37–50; Robert F. Pecorella, *Community Power in a Postreform City* (Armonk, NY: M. E. Sharpe, 1994), 126–29, 138–40.

75. J. Thomas Black, Allan Borut, and Robert Dubinsky, *Private-Market Housing Renovation in Older Urban Areas* (Washington, DC: Urban Land Institute, 1977), 1; Teaford, *Rough Road to Renaissance*, 251–52; "Local Landmarks Get Federal Tax Break," *TB*, April 2, 1978, 1.

76. Vance Packard, *A Nation of Strangers* (New York: David McKay, 1972); quoted in Joy and Paul Wilkes, *You Don't Have to Be Rich to Own a Brownstone* (New York: Quadrangle Books, 1973), vii–xii.

77. Ibid.

7   The Neighborhood Movement

1. "Slate-making, Building Coalitions and Other Views of Local Politics," *BHP*, June 20, 1972, 7.

2. L. J. Davis, "The Day They Almost Stole Brooklyn," *NYM*, May 4, 1970; "Brooklyn's Six-Day War," *TB*, June 3, 1970, 1–2; "Hospital Expansion Controversy Erupts in Cobble Hill," *TB*, April 5, 1973; "Hospitals Say Expansion—Communities Say Encroachment," *TB*, April 6, 1972, 1–2; "South Brooklyn Containerport: Community Claims Victory," *BT*, April 11, 1972, 5.

3. "Union-5th Area Still Simmers," *Phoenix*, July 12, 1973, 3; "7 Seized in June Riots After Appeals in Park Slope," *NYT*, November 1, 1973, 47; "Five Youths Shot in Brooklyn Riot," *NYT*, June 28, 1973, 1.

4. "Residents up on Slope Take Little Notice of Turmoil Only Blocks Away," *Phoenix*, July 12, 1973, 3.

5. "Park Slope Talks Yield Agreement," *NYT*, June 30, 1973, 34; Jim Sleeper, *Closest of Strangers: Liberalism and the Politics of Race in New York* (New York: W. W. Norton, 1990), 116–19.

6. "'New Group' at Election Night; Feels They're on Way Up," *HRSN*, December 8, 1967, 2; "Urban Settlers; With Sweat and Money, Affluent Young Families 'Unslum' a Community," *WSJ*, November 29, 1971, 1.

7. "Conference to Explore Neighborhoods," *BHP*, April 15, 1976, 1.

8. "Hospitals and Neighbors Clash in Slope, Hill," *Phoenix*, December 21, 1972; "Park Slope Residents vs. Hospital on Housing," *NYT*, October 31, 1971, 17; "Methodist Hospital Modifies Its Plans," *NYT*, December 15, 1974, 130; interview with Joseph Ferris, 2009.

9. "Hanging Out the Windows at 60–66 Clark Street," *Township*, November 11, 1970; "An Aye on Rent Control," *Independent Democrats*, March 16, 1961, 3; "'Tenant Power' Is a Spreading Slogan; Grievances Include Rents and Security," *NYT*, March 19, 1973, 27; Peter Hellman, "The Revolt of the $800-a-Month Tenants," February 2, 1970, 25.

10. "Officials Are Cautious on Co-ops for Poor," *NYT*, March 21, 1971, R1; "New York's Squatters: Vanguard of Community Control?" *City*, Fall 1971, 35–38; "The Squatters of New York," *NYP*, August 8, 1970; "Chelsea Brownstone Occupied as Squatter Movement Gains," *NYDN*, July 20, 1970; "Houses in Columbia Area 200 Squatters Occupy 2," *NYDN*, July 27, 1970. For an example of brownstoner support, see "Operation Move-in," *TB*, December 5, 1970, 3, 7. For more on "guerilla architecture," see Goodman, *After the Planners*, 187–89.

11. "Citibank Is Planning to Commit $10 Million to Mortgage Program," *NYT*, November 22, 1977; "A Detailed Study Charges 'Redlining' by Major Savings Bank in Brooklyn," *NYT*, December 6, 1976, 37; "The Long Redline in Brooklyn," *NYP*, October 5, 1977, 31; "Redline Fever: How People Are Beating the Banks," *VV*, March 13, 1978, 1; "Redlining: A Clash of Capitalists and Populists," *Phoenix*, August 25, 1977, 12–13. For a critical take on AID as a pro-gentrification organization by former members, see Timothy O'Hanlon, "Neighborhood Change in New York City: A Case Study of Park Slope, 1850–1980," Ph.D. diss., City University of New York, 1982; Francine Cyvia Justa, "Effects of Housing Abandonment, Resettlement Processes, and Displacement on the Evolution of Voluntary Community Organizations in Park Slope, Brooklyn, New York," Ph.D. diss., City University of New York, 1984.

12. "Church Recruits Court Watchers," *NYT*, May 21, 1972, 54; interview with Charles Monaghan, April 1, 2003.

13. "City Schools Found Wanting," *TB*, October 4, 1970, 1; "PS 321 Lands a Home Site," *BWT*, February 5, 1964, 1; Jennifer Monaghan, diary entry, n.d. [ca. 1969], BCCC.

14. John Louis Flateau, "Black Brooklyn: The Politics of Ethnicity, Class, and Gender," Ph.D. diss., City University of New York, 2005, 47–55; John Hull Mollenkopf, *A Phoenix in the Ashes: The Rise and Fall of the Koch Coalition in New York City Politics* (Princeton, NJ: Princeton University Press, 1992), 89–92; Craig Steven Wilder, *A Covenant with Color: Race and Social Power in Brooklyn* (New York: Columbia University Press, 2000), 235–39; "Minutes of the Steering Committee of the National Action Council Meeting," April 11, 1964, Reel 1, Section 1, CORE; "Black Churches Struggle Within," *NYT*, July 21, 1969.

15. Interview with Charles Monaghan; Monaghan, "New View on Community Control," *CN*, June 14, 1969; "Minutes of PTA Meeting," January 1969, BCCC. For more on the ties between middle-class whites and African American activists in the school decentralization fight, see Jerald E. Podair, *The Strike That Changed New York: Blacks, Whites, and the Ocean Hill–Brownsville Crisis* (New Haven: Yale University Press, 2002).

16. Jennifer Monaghan, "Address to Park Slope Civil Council," September 30, 1969, BCCC; "Minutes of PTA Meeting," June 19, 1969, BCCC; "Minutes of PTA Meeting," March 1969, BCCC; "Minutes of PTA Meeting," February 5, 1969, BCCC.

17. Tom Wolfe, *Radical Chic and Mau-Mauing the Flak Catchers* (New York: Farrar, Straus and Giroux, 1970); "'Black Panthers' Tell It on the Heights," *BHP*, August 15, 1968, 8.

18. "Is There 'Far Left' Strength in Brooklyn Heights?" *BHP*, January 17, 1974, 1.

19. "Grassroots in Park Slope," *CN*, October 1968; "Martin Luther King Coalition," *CN*, October 1968.

20. Charles Green and Basil Wilson, *The Struggle for Black Empowerment in New York City: Beyond the Politics of Pigmentation* (New York: Praeger, 1989), 104–8; Wendell Pritchett, *Brownsville, Brooklyn: Blacks, Jews and the Changing Face of the Ghetto* (Chicago: University of Chicago Press, 2002), 193–94, 215–16, 255; Joe Klein, "The Power Next Time?" *NYM*, October 10, 1983.

21. Interview with Joseph Ferris; "Trend Is Seen in Mall Rejection," *NYT*, December 2, 1973; "Neighborhoods: Nostalgia in Park Slope," *NYT*, August 6, 1969. For the use of ethnic identity as bulwark against urban renewal projects, see Teaford, *Rough Road to Renaissance*, 192–99. For the use of pastoral imagery in white ethnic backlash, see Jonathan Reider, *Canarsie: The Jews and Italians of Brooklyn Against Liberalism* (Cambridge, MA: Harvard University Press, 1985). For descriptions of opposition to busing as a form of "reactionary populism," see Ronald P. Formisano, *Boston Against Busing: Race, Class and Ethnicity in the 1960's and 1970's* (Chapel Hill: University of North Carolina Press, 1991), 172–73, and Matthew D. Lassiter, *The Silent Majority: Suburban Politics in the Sunbelt South* (Princeton: Princeton University Press, 2006), 148–74.

22. Pete Hamill, "The Revolt of the White Lower Middle Class," *NYM*, April 14, 1969; Craig Karpel, "Not Much Cream in Their Coffee," *NYT*, August 24, 1969, D1.

23. Teaford, *Rough Road to Renaissance*, 203–13; William Julius Wilson, *The Truly Disad-vantaged: The Inner City, the Underclass, and Public Policy* (Chicago: University of Chicago Press, 1987), 22–26; "Murder Wave of the 1970's Appears to Ebb in Cities," *NYT*, January 11, 1976, 1; "Crime Fear Levels Off, Polls Find," *NYT*, December 18, 1977, 45.

24. "Overflow Brooklyn Heights Meeting Protests Rising Crime and Asks Aid," *NYT*, February 1, 1971, 33; "Crime Wave Hits Heights: Youth Stabbed, Saved," *Phoenix*, June 22, 1972, 3; "Everyone's Triple Locking," *Phoenix*, June 22, 1972, 2; "TA Police Custody Unclear as Subway Criminals Molest Hts. Straphangers," *BHP*, August 8, 1974; "Burglaries Jump 37% Police Urge 'Prevention,'" *BHP*, August 7, 1975. Town-house renovators elsewhere in the country turned to similar historically themed window bars and gates; see Daphne Spain, "Been-Heres Versus Come-Heres," *Journal of the American Planning Association* 59, 2 (Spring 1993).

25. "The Civil Right," *BHP*, August 29, 1968.

26. "Heights Association Pushes Block Watching," *BHP*, October 25, 1973; "Police," *BHAB*, April 69, 1969, 4; "the importance of participatory democracy in crime pre-vention," quoted in *Brooklyn Heights Association Newsletter*, July 1974.

27. L. J. Davis, "The Happy Awakening of Clinton Hill," *NYM*, February 2, 1970, 41; "Union-5th Area Still Simmers."

28. "Lindsay and Aides Looking to Smooth over Police-Hippie Clash," *NYT*, June 1, 1967, 45; "The Police," *BHP*, September 17, 1959, 4.

29. "Lindsay Urges Computers to Raise Police Efficiency," *NYT*, June 18, 1965, 1; "Lindsay Adding 710 Patrolmen to Police Force," *NYT*, January 28, 1968, 1; "Dial 911 for the Police in City Starting Monday," *NYT*, June 27, 1968, 45; "Police Computer Will Speed Help," *NYT*, August 30, 1966, 43; "'Gestapo' or 'Elite'?—The Tactical Patrol Force," *NYT*, July 21, 1968, 6.

30. Vincent J. Cannato, *The Ungovernable City: John Lindsay and His Struggle to Save New York* (New York: Basic Books, 2001), 155; Michael Flamm, *Law and Order: Street Crime, Civil Unrest, and the Crisis of Liberalism in the 1960s* (New York: Columbia University Press, 2005), 76–80; "City's Bar Urges Civilian Control of Police Review," *NYT*, August 6, 1965, 1; "And Now, the Issues; With 3 Weeks to Go, the Candidates for Mayor Are Taking Up Positions," *NYT*, August 21, 1965.

31. "3rd AD Liberals Petition for Police Board," *BHP*, October 1, 1964, 4; "Residents Raise Funds for Ad Favoring Civilian Review Board," *BHP*, November 3, 1966, 5; "Hts. Leaders Support Review Bd.," *BHP*, November 3, 1966, 4.

32. "Review Board Debate Stirs Hot Reaction in Park Slope," *HRSN*, October 7, 1966, 1.

33. "Azadian to Conservatives: 'Truce on Name Calling,'" *HRSN*, October 14, 1966, 13.

34. "Heights Vote Approves Neighborhood Assembly," *Township*, April 5, 1972; "Edito-rial," *Township*, December 15, 1971, 2; "Busing or Community Control? Make Your Choice," *Township*, November 20, 1971, 2; "The Township: Our Policy," *Township*, November 20, 1971, 5.

35. "Norman Mailer—The Candidate," *BHP*, May 1, 1969.

36. Robert Side, "Summing Up the 1970's: A Political Columnist's View," *BHP*, January 31, 1980, 22; Joseph Ferris, interview by author; "Brooklynite's Campaign Attracts Students: Eikenberry Would 'Take War from Asia and Fight Slums at Home,'" *Christian Science Monitor*, June 2, 1970; "Peace Coalition Will Lead Mass March to Rooney's

Office," *HRSN*, April 2, 1971; "How a Super Hawk Turned Dove," *NYP*, May 26, 1970; O'Hanlon, "Neighborhood Change in Park Slope," 185–86; Justa, "Effects of Housing Abandonment," 158.

37. "Hugh Carey Battles for Re-Election in 15 C.D.," *HRSN* November 3, 1972.

38. "Here Is How John Lindsay Conquered Park Slope," *HRSN*, February 4, 1966, 22; Cannato, *The Ungovernable City*, 469–70, 437–38.

39. "Reform Democrats' Clubhouse in Brooklyn Damaged by Bomb," *NYT*, May 31, 1977, 17; "Cobble Hill Democrats Undeterred by Blast," *NYT*, June 1, 1971, 80.

40. "Redistricting the Reformers," *NYT*, May 2, 1972. For an excellent treatment of Brownstone Brooklyn reform politics in the 1970s from the perspective of a young, idealistic Italian American reformer, see Michael L. Pesce, "Notes Toward a Blue Collar Reform Movement," in *Pieces of a Dream: The Ethnic Worker's Crisis with America*, ed. Michael Wenk, S. M. Tomasi, and Geno Baroni (New York: Center for Migration Studies, 1972), 162. See also Andrew Cooper and Wayne Barrett, "Chisholm's Compromise: Politics and the Art of Self Interest," *VV*, October 30, 1978.

41. "'New Group' at Election Night; Feels They're on Way Up"; Bernard Strassberg, "'New' and 'Old' Groups Should Have Same Goal," *HRSN*, December 22, 1967; "Writer Says 78th Pct. Elections Were 'Miscarriage of Democracy,'" *HRSN*, December 8, 1967; Dorothy Evans, "Impressions," *HRSN*, November 24, 1967, 32. Demographics eventually turned the tide; see Justa, "Effects of Housing Abandonment," 257–65.

42. Richard Cummings, *The Pied Piper: Allard K. Lowenstein and the Liberal Dream* (New York: Grove Press, 1985), 435–52; William H. Chafe, *Never Stop Running: Allard Lowenstein and the Struggle to Save American Liberalism* (New York: Basic Books, 1993), 368–83.

43. Cummings, *Pied Piper*; Chafe, *Never Stop Running*; "Lowenstein: Winner at Thickheadedness," *VV*, September 28, 1972.

44. Susan Jacoby, "A Dream Grows in Brooklyn," *NYT*, February 23, 1975.

45. Pesce, "Notes Toward a Blue Collar Reform Movement," 154.

46. "A Magnolia Tree Grows in Brooklyn," *VV*, September 17, 1970; "Pesce Talks About Ideas and Action," *BHP*, December 14, 1972, 2; Joseph Ferris, interview; "How the Reformers Sold Out," *VV*, January 27, 1975.

47. O'Hanlon, "Neighborhood Change in New York City," 171–72.

48. "Berkeley Place," *CN*, July 12, 1969.

49. Carroll Gardens Brownstoners, "Historic Preservation for Carroll Gardens," Statement of Ira S. Levine to Landmarks Preservation Committee, May 26, 1970, Carroll Gardens Folder, VFBHS; "Neighborhood Revival Brings Landmark Status to Clinton Hill," *Phoenix*, February 25, 1982.

50. "2 Zoning Plans in Brooklyn Provoke Community Debates," *NYT*, April 7, 1974, 108; "Pathmark Mall Wins Final 'OK' from City Board," *BHP*, June 30, 1977, 1; Barbara Habenstreit, *Fort Greene U.S.A.* (New York: Bobbs-Merrill, 1974), 8–9; Justa, "Effects of Housing Abandonment," 242–45; Joseph Ferris interview.

51. Pamphlet by James Weir Inc., Brooklyn Heights Folder, VFBHS; "Having It Their Way: Burger King Takes over Old Bank Building on Montague Street," *BHP*, July 18,

1974, 1; "Anti-Burger King Meeting Kicks Off Local Fight," *BHP*, August 8, 1974, 4; "Anti-Whopper Rally Slated to Harass Pillsbury," *BHP*, August 22, 1974, 5; "Neighborhood Decline," *BHP*, August 22, 1974, 5; "Economics and Aesthetics," *BHP*, September 12, 1974, 6.

52. "A Matter of Taste," *BHP*, February 5, 1975, 7; "Burger King and the Reform Dems," *BHP*, September 12, 1974, 8.

53. "Busing or Community Control? Make Your Choice," *Township*, November 20, 1971, 2.

54. "Heights Association Position," *BHP*, March 19, 1964; "St. Ann School Defends Against Charge of Hurting Pairing," *BHP*, October 28, 1965; "P.S. 8," *BHP*, April 27, 1978, 21; "My Neighborhood . . . Boerum Hill," *Phoenix*, October 2, 1975;

55. Walter Bursten to the editor, *BHP*, April 2, 1964; "Equal and Swinging," *NYAM*, January 16, 1971, 25; "Brooklyners Seeking an L-Shaped Rhodesia," *VV*, February 25, 1971, 31.

56. Rita Leah Brown, "South Brooklyn Containerport: Community Claims Victory," *BT*, April 11, 1972, 5; "Environmentalists Stage Pier 6 Bazaar in Brooklyn," *NYT*, May 30, 1972, 74.

57. "Park Slope Presses Renewal," *NYT*, July 10, 1966, 241; "A Brownstone Pitfall: Evicting Tenants," *NYT*, May 26, 1974, 300; "Single-Room Tenants Are Losing Out," *NYT*, November 17, 1968, 1; "Tensions Rising in Brownstone-Eviction Disputes," *NYT*, January 31, 1970.

58. "Nobody Wins in the Tenant-Landlord Game," *TB*, April 4, 1974, 1.

59. Diana Foster, "Protecting the Perimeter," *BHP*, March 9, 1967, 5, and March 16, 1967, 5.

60. David Preiss, "Perfecting the Perimeter," *BHP*, March 23, 1967, 5; Daniel Icolari to editor, *BHP*, April 6, 1967, 4.

61. Paula Fox, *Desperate Characters* (New York: W. W. Norton, 1970); L. J. Davis, *A Meaningful Life* (New York: Viking Press, 1971); Hal Ashby, *The Landlord*, produced by Norman Jewison, 106 min., Mirisch Production Company, 1971. For a similar sentiment in a gentrifying district of London, see V. S. Naipaul, "What's Wrong with Being a Snob," *Saturday Evening Post*, June 3, 1967, 12.

62. For a description of the "anti-regime" in 1970s San Francisco, see Richard Edward Deleon, *Left Coast City: Progressive Politics in San Francisco, 1975–1991* (University of Kansas, 1992).

Conclusion: Brownstone Brooklyn Invented

1. Erik Lewis, *Where Can I Live? A Story of Gentrification*, New York: Cinema Guild, 1983.

2. "The New Elite and Urban Renaissance," *NYT*, January 14, 1979; "Measuring Change in the Cities," *WP*, February 22, 1979; "How Whites Are Taking Back Black Neighborhoods," *Ebony*, September 1978.

3. "Attack from a New Quarter: Urban 'Gentrification,'" *TB*, February 1, 1978, 1; William H. Whyte, *City: Rediscovering the Center* (New York: Doubleday, 1987), 327.

4. "The Urban Crisis Leaves Town," *Harper's*, December 1978; Joshua B. Freeman, *Working Class New York: Life and Labor Since World War II* (New York: New Press,

2000), 293; Matthew P. Drennan, "The Decline and Rise of the New York Economy," in *Dual City: Restructuring New York*, ed. John Hull Mollenkopf and Manuel Castells (New York: Russell Sage Foundation, 1991).

5. "Private Reinvestment and Neighborhood Change," New York Department of City Planning, March 1984; "Downtown Brooklyn: A Report by the Regional Plan Association," *RPN*, No. 114, June 1983; Lewis, *Where Can I Live?*

6. Chester Hartman, Dennis Keating, and Richard LeGates, *Displacement: How to Fight It* (Berkeley, CA: National Housing Law Project 1982). Starting in 1983, converting a Class B dwelling (SROs and rooming houses) required a "certificate of no harassment" from the Department of Housing Preservation and Development. To earn a certification, owners had to demonstrate that no harassment of tenants was used to empty the building for three years. Conversion of SROs after July 1982 was no longer were eligible for J-51 benefits. In 1983, the city amended the J-51 law to be available only for units with post-rehabilitation assessed value of less than $38,000. Another new provision required all projects to file affidavits with the city attesting that no property owners involved had harassed or unlawfully evicted any tenant. In 1980, the city established a new J-51 category for moderate rehabilitation that hoped to spark reinvestment without displacement of tenants by increasing tax benefits if at least 60 percent of units remained occupied during construction. The Participation Loan Program and SRO loan program required that rents remain affordable for low-income people; see "Private Reinvestment and Neighborhood Change," New York Department of City Planning, March 1984.

7. "Park Slope Action Democrats," pamphlet, n.d., Park Slope Folder, VFBHS; Jim Sleeper, "Neighborhood Gentrification: More Inequity than Meets the Eye," *Dissent*, April 1982, 170–71. For a description of the emerging battles between civic groups in Park Slope in late 1970s, see Francine Cyvia Justa, "Effects of Housing Abandonment, Resettlement Processes, and Displacement on the Evolution of Voluntary Community Organizations in Park Slope, Brooklyn, New York," Ph.D. diss., City University of New York, 1984.

8. "The Biggest Ripoff Since Yankee Stadium," *Soho Weekly News*, November 18, 1976, 8; "Plan Stirs a Battle of Boerum Hill," *NYDN*, May 17, 1978; "Brownstoners Fight Low-Income Housing," *NYDN*, May 15, 1978; Eileen Powis, "Boerum-Gowanus Low-Moderate Income Housing Proposal Threatens Boerum Hill Stability," *Phoenix*, May 4, 1978.

9. John Hull Mollenkopf, *A Phoenix in the Ashes: The Rise and Fall of the Koch Coalition in New York City Politics* (Princeton, NJ: Princeton University Press, 1992), 100–28.

10. That the name Boerum Hill was used by anti-gentrification activists is noted in Philip Kasinitz, "The Gentrification of 'Boerum Hill': Neighborhood Change and Conflicts over Definitions," *Qualitative Sociology* 11 (Fall 1988).

11. For similar rates of loss of SROs in Park Slope from both gentrification and abandonment in the 1970s, see "Private Reinvestment and Neighborhood Change," New York Department of City Planning, March 1984. For a similar study of Clinton Hill and Harlem in a later period, see Lance Freeman, *There Goes the 'Hood: Views of Gentrification from the Ground Up* (Philadelphia: Temple University Press, 2006).

12. David Rogers, "Community Control and Decentralization," in *Urban Politics: New York Style*, eds. Jewel Bellush and Dick Netzer (Armonk, NY: M. E. Sharpe, 1990); Alan Altshuler and David Luberoff, *Mega-Projects: The Changing Politics of Urban Public Investment* (Washington, DC: Brookings Institution Press, 2003), 27–42.

13. Wolf Von Ekhardt, "The Future Is Behind Us: Make Way for the Past," *WP*, December 30, 1978; Nan Ellin, *Postmodern Urbanism* (Princeton, NJ: Princeton Architectural Press, 1999); Christine M. Boyer, "Manhattan Montage," chap. in *The City of Collective Memory: Its Historical Imagery and Architectural Entertainments* (Cambridge, MA: MIT Press, 1996).

14. Dennis Holt, "Counting Downtown Brooklyn Neighborhoods: 1980 Census Show a Resurgence of Buying Power in Brownstone Brooklyn Areas," *Phoenix*, October 20, 1983; "Looking How Things Changed in One Set of Neighborhoods," *Phoenix*, October 20, 1983; "Statement of Community District Needs: Fiscal Year 1983," Department of City Planning, January 1982; "Private Reinvestment and Neighborhood Change," Department of City Planning, March 1984.

15. Delmos J. Jones, "Not in My Community: The Neighborhood Movement and Institutionalized Racism," *Social Policy*, September-October 1979; Ada Louise Huxtable, "Stumbling Toward Tomorrow: The Decline and Fall of New York Vision," in *In Search of New York*, ed. Jim Sleeper (New Brunswick, NJ: Transaction, 1989), 53–55; Susan S. Fainstein, *The City Builders: Property, Politics and Planning in London and New York* (New York: Blackwell, 1994), 101–2, 225–29; Michael Sorkin, ed., *Variations on a Theme Park: The New American City and the End of Public Space* (New York: Hill and Wang, 1992).

16. Robert Berkhofer Jr., "Reclaiming the City: A Historical Perspective," *TB*, April 2, 1976, 5, 11.

17. Ian Rosenberg, "Park Slope: Notes on a Middle-Class 'Utopia,'" in *In Search of New York*, ed. Jim Sleeper (New Brunswick, NJ: Transaction, 1989), 159. For a further analysis of the 1980s yuppie, see Bruce Schulman, *The Seventies: The Great Shift in American Culture, Society, and Politics* (New York: Free Press, 2001), 241–46.

Index

Note: Page numbers in *italics* refer to illustrations.

CPSIA information can be obtained
at www.ICGtesting.com
Printed in the USA
BVOW04s1201270517

485126BV00003B/10/P